Complexity and Knowledge Management

Understanding the Role of Knowledge in the Management of Social Networks

Andrew Tait

Idea Sciences

Kurt A. Richardson

Institute for the Study of Coherence and Emergence

INFORMATION AGE PUBLISHING, INC.
Charlotte, NC • www.infoagepub.com

Library of Congress Cataloging-in-Publication Data

Complexity and knowledge management : understanding the role of knowledge in the management of social networks / [edited by] Andrew Tait, Kurt A. Richardson.
    p. cm. – (Managing organizational complexity)
  Includes bibliographical references.
  ISBN 978-1-60752-355-0 (pbk.) – ISBN 978-1-60752-356-7 (hardcover) – ISBN 978-1-60752-357-4 (e-book)
1. Knowledge management. 2. Social networks. 3. Complex organizations–Management. I. Tait, Andrew. II. Richardson, Kurt A. (Kurt Antony)
  HD30.2.C639 2010
  658.4'038–dc22

2009043802

Complexity and Knowledge Management

Understanding the Role of Knowledge in the Management of Social Networks

A volume in
Managing Organizational Complexity
Kurt A. Richardson and Michael R. Lissack, *Series Editors*

Managing Organizational Complexity

Kurt A. Richardson and Michael R. Lissack, *Series Editors*

To Dominic . . . always one step ahead of me.
—AT

*For Alexander, Albert and William . . . whose nonsense
makes more sense than not!*
—KAR

CONTENTS

SECTION 3

TOOLS FOR CREATING, MAINTAINING, AND USING KNOWLEDGE

INTRODUCTION

Are we crazy?! Seemingly not content to grapple with the amorphous science that is complexity, we've decided to edit a book that throws the equally nebulous concept of knowledge into the mix! Shouldn't we try and deal with them separately before getting them all tangled up?

Well...as complexity researchers[1] we have no choice but to tackle everything at once. This is the cross we bear for being right, isn't it? More than once we've been importuned by our partners to "Focus!" only to plead, "But it's complex!"

There would seem to be a strong case for studying knowledge as a socially constructed phenomenon—to put it mildly (Surowiecki, 2004; Sanger, 2007). In this case, knowledge is clearly inseparable from the complex social systems that spawn it (and their management)—which leads us to this ambitious volume.

Writing an introduction to an edited collection is something that we take very seriously. Many talented researchers have taken the time to write thoughtful and insightful articles. We are responsible for preparing the reader to embark on his journey through the intellectual landscape created by the assembled authors.

Writing about complexity is challenging. It is a constant battle to maintain any kind of consistency. The very nature of a traditional article—a linear presentation of ideas—tugs at the foundation of most complexity research. This is exacerbated when writing about a complex collection of complexity articles. A golden opportunity was missed in the third volume of this series—Making Healthcare Care (Letiche, Lissack and Richardson, 2007)—to study the correlation between seeing the world in complexity terms and the use of Prozac®.

Complexity and Knowledge Management, pages xi–xiv
Copyright © 2010 by Information Age Publishing
All rights of reproduction in any form reserved.

So, what is the role of an introduction to this kind of collection? Is it to provide a short description of each article, allowing the reader to selectively delve into the volume? No. We believe that the best summaries of the articles are provided by the authors' own titles and introductions. Our clumsy attempts to distil the contents of an article into a sentence could only do violence to the carefully crafted ideas.

Should an introduction attempt to classify the collection—e.g., to make it more manageable? In a sense, we've done this by splitting the volume into three sections.[2] However, if we're honest, this classification is no more that a loose indication of the general thrust of an article. We felt guilty even as we included it in the call for papers. Any further classification would be intellectual fraud.

What about using the introduction to present our own vision of the role knowledge plays in the management of social networks? This would seem to be a little arrogant. We have no special insight into this issue—just our own views to add to the rest. If we have something to say, we should say it in one of the collected papers like everyone else.

No, we don't believe that these "traditional" forms of introduction serve us or, more importantly, the collected authors, well. Instead, we'd like to use the introduction to elaborate on the problems and questions that led us to instigate this project. It is these that provide the context for what is to follow.

Oh, and we'll try and keep it short—so you might actually read it. We know from our own experiences as readers that we rarely peruse introductions that are as long as the articles themselves. If we're going to invest that time it'll be in the main feature—not the commentary.

As we write this introduction, it seems as if attempts to use knowledge to understand and manage social networks are everywhere. Millions, if not billions, of dollars are being spent in an attempt to derail terrorist networks (Harris, 2006), with much of it being invested in making sense of massive data streams (DeYoung, 2007). There is growing concern that much of this money is being squandered on approaches that will never deliver on their promises (Schneier, 2007).

Our armed forces are being prepared to combat terrorist threats by the introduction of "network centric approaches" and "digital battlefields"—basically attempts to provide warfighters with a complete picture of the battlespace. However, the experience of practitioners suggests that the "data smog" this creates is actually counterproductive.[3]

From the arena of politics, the recent invigorating battle between senators Clinton and Obama has thrown the spotlight on the deficiencies in political polling (Economist, 2008b). Changes in the structure of the situation (e.g. high turnouts) have thrown the whole industry into chaos. Complexity is being discounted and the results are stark. The conclusion formed in the media was that the situation was wildly unpredictable (so anyone's to win), and ended up having real consequences for the Democratic challenger in November 2008 (Baldwin, 2008).

Turning to business, we find that Société Générale recently lost $7.2bn as the result of a single rogue trader making a series of bogus transactions amid turbulent markets in 2007 and 2008 (Viscusi & Chassany, 2008). There has been much speculation on what was known, when it was known, and who knew it (Economist, 2008a). In other words, we have speculation that this is an example of the role of knowledge in the *mis*management of social networks—with spectacular effect.

And last, but by *no* means least, we have the issue of man-made global warming. For those considering the role of knowledge in the management of (social) networks, this is surely a doozy.

At a glance, the problems highlighted above seem positively overwhelming. Where do you start? But start we must. Simple "cause and effect" thinking doesn't seem to be able to cut the mustard. There is broad agreement that even if the Kyoto targets were fully met, on schedule, by 2100 it would only delay the warming of the planet by six years (Parry *et al.,* 1998). We need to utilize knowledge in new ways... or maybe uncover insights from old ways.

It is tempting to see the need to understand the role of knowledge in managing social networks as a relatively recent requirement. Certainly the rapid growth in the use of Information and Communications Technologies in the latter decades of the twentieth century is an obvious catalyst—as is the globalization it has spurred. Of course, the challenge has been with us since the dawn of life. Ecological systems have been utilizing knowledge (at varying degrees of consciousness) to adapt to their environments for millions of years. In fact, a recent collection of papers attempts to show us how the study of natural systems can help us design effective security in the post 9/11 era (Sagarin & Taylor, 2008).

We find it hard to think of something more worthy of attention than the role of knowledge in the management of complex systems.

In addition to grasping the issues, we need, as a research community, to put tools in the hands of decision and policy makers. The research paradigm we share advocates engagement with the environment, yet, paradoxically, we don't seem to have managed to make mainstream tools available to those outside of the community. This is a major failing. If we can't provide these tools, we will continue to punch below our intellectual weight. In editing this volume, and others, we are regularly struck by how little of the great ideas we are privileged to see make it all the way to being adopted by the "great unwashed."

As we press forward, in all areas of complexity research, we must be cognizant of the need to help our ideas make a difference. Unless we can take them all the way, we will be little more than a reading group.

So, let us now take a step back and let greater minds than ours enthrall you with such heady topics as the definition of knowledge, the role knowledge plays in creating and managing complex system, and the application of these ideas to enhancing the world in which we live.

NOTES

1. We use the term "complexity researchers" to refer to all those working in the complexity field (e.g. academic researchers, practitioners). After all, all those utilizing complexity concepts are liable to find themselves at the bleeding edge.
2. "What is knowledge?", "The role of knowledge in social networks" and "Tools for creating, maintaining and using knowledge."
3. Expressed in a private communication between one of the authors and a senior military officer.

REFERENCES

Baldwin, T. (2008). *Democrats fear that civil war may draw crowds but end in bloodshed.* The Times, 10 March 2008.

DeYoung, K. (2007). *Terror Database Has Quadrupled In Four Years.* Washington Post, 25 March 2007.

Economist (2008a). *Looking for answers.* The Economist, 29 January 2008.

Economist (2008b). *Obama by one. No, ten. No, five.* The Economist, 01 March 2008.

Harris, S. (2006). *Terrorist Profiling, Version 2.0.* National Journal, 20 October 2006.

Letiche, H., Lissack M.R. and Richardson K.A. (2008). *Managing the Complex: Making Healthcare Care.* Information Age Publishing Inc., Charlotte, NC.

Parry, M. *et al.* (1998). *Adapting to the inevitable.* Nature, 365 (1998).

Sagarin, R.D., and Taylor, T. [eds.] (2008). *Natural security: a Darwinian approach to a dangerous world.* University of California Press, CA.

Sanger, L. (2007). *Who Says We Know: On The New Politics of Knowledge.* Edge, Edge Foundation, Inc.

Schneier, B. (2007). *How To Not Catch Terrorists,* Forbes, 26 March 2007.

Surowiecki, J. (2004). *The Wisdom of Crowds: Why the Many Are Smarter Than the Few and How Collective Wisdom Shapes Business, Economies, Societies and Nations.* Doubleday.

Viscusi, G. and Chassany, A. (2008). *Societe Generale Reports EU4.9 Billion Trading Loss.* Bloomberg.com, 24 January 2008.

SECTION 1

WHAT IS KNOWLEDGE?

CHAPTER 1

WHAT IS THE SCIENCE OF COMPLEXITY?

Knowledge of the Limits to Knowledge

P. M. Allen

INTRODUCTION

In a recent article (Allen, 2001), the underlying assumptions involved in the modeling of situations were systematically presented. In essence we attempt to trade "complexity" of the real world for the "simplicity" of some reduced representation. The reduction occurs through assumptions concerning:

1. The relevant "system" boundary (exclude the less relevant)
2. The reduction of full heterogeneity to a typology of elements (agents that might be molecules, individuals, groups, etc.)
3. Individuals of average type
4. Processes that run at their average rate

If all four assumptions can be made then our situation can be described by a set of deterministic differential equations (system dynamics) that allow clear predictions to be made, and "optimizations" to be carried out. If the first 3 assumptions can be made, then we have stochastic differential equa-

Complexity and Knowledge Management, pages 3–22
Copyright © 2010 by Information Age Publishing
All rights of reproduction in any form reserved.

tions that can self-organize as the system may jump between different basins of attraction that reflect distinct patterns of dynamical behavior. With only assumptions 1 and 2, our picture becomes one of adaptive evolutionary change, in which the pattern of possible attractor basins changes and a system can spontaneously evolve new types of agent, new behaviors and new problems. In this case, naturally we cannot predict the creative response of the system to any particular action we may take, and the evaluation of the future "performance" of a new design, or action is extremely uncertain (Allen, 1988, 1990, 1994a, 1994b). In summary, previous articles showed how the science of complex systems could lead to a table concerning our limits to knowledge. If we now take the different kinds of knowledge that we may be interested in concerning a situation, then we can number them according to:

1. What type of situation or object we are studying (classification—"prediction" by similarity)
2. What it is made of and how it works
3. Its history and why it is as it is
4. How it may behave (prediction)
5. How and in what way its behavior might be changed (intervention and prediction)

Then we can establish Table 1.1 which therefore in some ways provides us with a very compressed view of the Science of Complexity.

TABLE 1.1   Systematic Knowledge Concerning the Limits to Systematic Knowledge

Assumptions	2	3	4	5
Type of Model	Evolutionary	Self-Organising	Non-Linear Dynamics (including chaos)	Equilibrium
Type of system	Can change structurally	Can change its configuration and connectivity	Fixed	Fixed
Composition	Can change qualitatively	Can lead to new, emergent properties	Yes	Yes
History	Important in all levels of description	Is important at the system level	Irrelevant	Irrelevant
Prediction	Very limited inherent uncertainty	Probabilistic	Yes	Yes
Intervention and Prediction	Very limited inherent uncertainty	Probabilistic	Yes	Yes

The idea behind the modeling approach is not that it should create true representations of reality. Instead it is seen as one method that leads to the provision of causal conjectures that can be compared with and tested against reality. When they appear to fit that reality, then we may feel temporarily satisfied, and when they disagree with reality, we can set about examining why the discrepancy occurred. This model is our "interpretive framework" for sense-making and knowledge building. It will almost certainly change over time as a result of our experiences. It is developed in order to answer questions that are of interest to the developer, or the potential user, and both the model and the questions will change over time. The questions that are addressed influence the variables that are chosen for study, the mechanisms that are supposed to link them, the boundary of the system considered, and the type of scenarios and events that are explored. The model is not reality, but merely a creation of the modeler that is intended to help reflect on the questions that are of interest. The process involved is not telling us whether our current model is true or false, but rather whether it appears to work or not. If it does then it will be useful in answering the questions asked of it. If it doesn't, then it is telling us that we need to re-think our interpretive framework, and that some new conjecture is needed.

The usefulness may well come down to a question of the spatio-temporal scales of interest to the modeler or user. For example, if we compare an evolutionary situation to one that is so fluid and nebulous that there are no discernible forms and no stability for even short times, then we see that what makes an evolutionary model possible is the existence of quasi-stable forms for some time at least. If we are only interested in events over very short times compared to those usually involved in structural change, then it may be perfectly legitimate and useful to consider the structural forms fixed. This doesn't mean that they are, but it just means that we can proceed to do some calculations about what can happen over the short term without having to struggle with how forms may evolve and change. Of course, we need to remain conscious that over a longer period forms and mechanisms will change and that our actions may well be accelerating this process, but nevertheless it can still mean that some self-organizing dynamic is useful.

Equally, if we can reasonably assume not only that system structure is stable but in addition fluctuations around the average are small, then we may find that a prediction using a set of dynamic equations provides useful knowledge. If fluctuations are weak, then it means that large fluctuations capable of kicking the system into a new regime/attractor basin are very rare and infrequent. This gives us some knowledge as to the probability that this will occur over a given period, so our model can allow us to make predictions about the behavior of a system as well as the associated probabilities and risk of an unusual fluctuation occurring and changing the regime. An example of this might be the idea of a 10-year event, and a 100-year event in weather forecasting where we use the statistics of past history to suggest how frequent critical fluctuations are. Of course, this assumes an overall "stationarity" of the system, supposing that processes like climate change, for example, are not happening. Clearly, when 100-year events start to occur more often, we are tempted to suppose that the system is not stationary, and that climate change is occurring. But this would be after the facts, not before.

These are examples of the usefulness of different models, and the knowledge that they provide us with, all of which are imperfect and not strictly true in an absolute sense, but some of which are useful. Systematic knowledge therefore should not be seen in absolute terms, but should be seen as being possible for some times and some situations, providing we apply our "complexity reduction" assumptions honestly. Instead of simply saying that "all is flux, all is mystery," we may admit that this is so over the very long term (who wants to guess what the universe is for?). But, for some times of interest and for some situations, we can obtain useful knowledge about their probable behavior, and this can be updated by continually applying the learning process of trying to model the situation.

INTERACTIVE SUBJECTIVITY

The essence of complex systems is that they represent the joining of multiple subjectivities—multiple dimensions interacting with overlapping but not identical multiple dimensions. In a traditional "system dynamics" view, a flow diagram represents a series of reservoirs that are connected by pipes and a unidimensional flow takes place between them (see Figure 1.1). Typically some simple laws express the rate of flow between the reservoirs, possibly as a function of the height of water. Instead of this, in the system (b) we find that the real world consists of connected entities that have their own perceptions, inner worlds, and possibilities of action. We may contrast

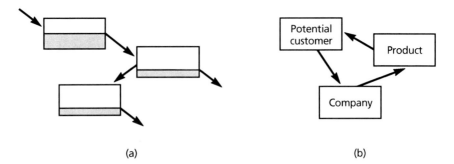

(a)   (b)

Figure 1.1   Comparison between a simple and a complex system.

a flow diagram of money or water with an "influence" diagram that notes that one component affects another.

The water flowing through (a) is totally different and subject to accountability rules compared to the system (b), which shows how a company, its products, and its potential customers interact. Let us consider *briefly* the three "simple" arrows of our system (b).

1. Potential customers influence the company to design a product that they think will be successful. But this requires the company to seek information about potential customers and therefore to think of ways to do this. It requires the generation of knowledge or belief about what kind of customers exist, and what they may be looking for, and this essentially must be based on a series of conjectures that the company must make about the nature of the different subjectivities that are in the environment. In essence the company must make a gamble that its conjectures about possible customers and their desires are sufficiently correct to make enough of them buy the product.

2. The company produces a particular product. This results from the beliefs that the company has arrived at concerning the kind of customers who are "out there" and the qualities they are looking for at the price they are willing to pay. The arrow therefore encompasses the way in which the marketing people in the company have been able to affect the designer and the new product development process to try to produce the "right thing at the right price," and secondly that the designer knows how to put components together in such a way that the product or service delivers what was hoped for.

3. The product then attracts or fails to attract potential customers. But this requires the potential customers to look at the product and to see what it might do for them, and at what cost. Customers must be able to translate the attributes of the product or service has into the fulfilment of some need or desire that they have. The interaction between the product and the customer must be engineered by the company so that there will be some encounter with potential customers. The locations and timings must therefore be suited to the movements and attention of the potential target customers.

4. The arrow from the customer to the company finally consists of a flow of money that occurs when a potential customer becomes an actual customer. This part is physical and real and can be stored easily on a database. However, it is the result of a whole lot of less palpable processes, of conjecture, of characterization, and of information analysis, most of which do not correspond to flows of anything accountable.

What is important is that inside each box there are multiple possible behaviors. Ultimately this comes down to the existence of internal microdiversity that gives each box a range of possible responses. These are tried out and the results used either to reinforce or to challenge their use. Each box is therefore trying to make sense of its environment, which includes the other boxes and their behaviours.

The real issue is that the boxes marked "company" and "potential customer" actually enclose different worlds. The dimensions, goals, aims, and experiences in these boxes are quite different. Most importantly, each box contains a whole range of possible behaviors and beliefs, and the agents inside may have mechanisms that enable them to find out which ones work in the environment. What this means is dealt with in the next section. When the boxes interact, therefore, as reflected in some simple "arrows" of influence, what we really have is the communication of two different worlds that inhabit different sets of dimensions. But to successfully connect two different boxes so as to achieve some joint task requiring co-operation requires some human intervention to translate the meaning that exists in one space into the language and meaning of the other.

The simple arrow of connection therefore will not be a simple connection, but instead may require a person who is capable of speaking across the boxes and who possibly has experience of both worlds. It is also the core reason that explains the need for interdisciplinary studies. Each discipline takes a partial and particular view of a situation, and in so doing promotes analysis and expertise at the expense of the ability to have integration, synthesis, and a holistic view. Management is really the domain in which the multidisciplinary, integrative approach is required if we are to get real results in dealing with a real-world problem. The science of complex systems is really extremely important for management and for policy since only with an integrated, multidimensional approach will advice be related successfully to the real-world situation. And this may indeed spell the limits to knowledge and turn us from the attractive but misleading mirage of prediction.

STRUCTURAL ATTRACTORS

If we consider the use of the word "attractor" in non-linear dynamics, then its meaning is associated with the long-term destination of system trajectories. These can either end at a steady final value—a point attractor—or in stationary cyclic or chaotic motion. The attractor that it ends up in will depend on the "richness" of the possible behaviors generated by the particular non-linear equations, and the point from which the system starts. So we may have a situation as shown in Figure 1.2 where there are several

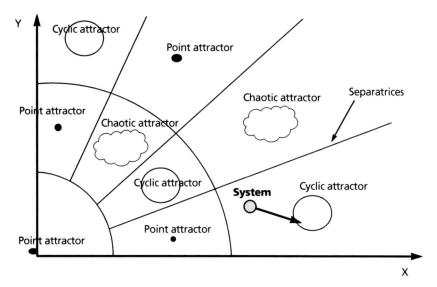

Figure 1.2 An imaginary view of the possible attractors of a particular set of non-linear equations. All the attractors correspond to stationary, cyclic or chaotic values of x and y. These are not "structural attractors."

attractors of different types, and the equations drive the system towards the long term stationary attractor of whichever "basin of attraction" it starts in.

But these attractors correspond really to the end states of a *given* dynamic. The variables in play are fixed and do not change. Only their values change, and so the dimensionality of the system remains constant. But in Table 1.1 we see that this corresponds only to systems that can legitimately be described by a set of dynamical equations describing the changes over time in the values of a given set of variables. Even if we consider self-organizing systems that have probabilistic rates of interactions, the noise can simply push the system over the boundaries separating attractor basins, leading to changes in the configuration and behavioral regime of the given set of variables. Even then the only dimensional changes that can occur are those associated with the emergent properties of the whole system. The internal dimensions of the interacting variables are not changed.

But what happens if we consider the evolution of a system that has different types of individual interacting—different subjectivities—with different dimensions and attributes. We may say that if all the possible types were present simultaneously then we would have an enormously diverse system with a vast range of attributes and dimensions present. However, evolution results in a selection process that reduces the types of individual or agent that can inhabit the system to those that can co-exist with or have synergy with the other types present.

For this simple model we consider the interaction of populations of agents with different attributes and behaviors that may affect, positively or negatively, the populations with which they co-habit. This leads to a model in which the pay-offs that are found for the behavior exhibited by a particular population type depend on the other behaviors present in the system. Instead of the problem being one in which the evolutionary task is to explore and climb a fixed landscape of fitness or pay-off, the landscape itself is changed by the presence of the different players in the game.

In order to examine how populations may evolve over time, let us consider 20 possible populations, agent types or behaviors. In the space of possibilities, numbered 1 to 20, closely similar behaviors are considered to be most in competition with each other, since they occupy a similar niche in the system. Any two particular populations i and j may have an effect on each other. This could be positive, in that side-effects of the activity of j might in fact provide conditions or effects that help i. Of course, the effect might equally well be antagonistic, or neutral. Similarly, i may have a positive, negative, or neutral effect on j (see Figure 1.3) For our simple model, therefore, we shall choose values randomly for all the possible interactions between all i and j; fr describes the average strength of these, and $2*(rnd - .5)$ is a random number between -1 and $+1$.

$$Interaction(i,j) = fr*2*(rnd - .5)$$

The effect of behavior i on j will be proportional to the size of the population i. If i is absent then there will be no effect. Similarly, if j is absent, then it cannot feel the effect of i. For each of 20 possible types we choose the possible effect i on j and j on i randomly, where $random(j,i)$ is a random number between 0 and 1, and fr is the strength of the interaction. Clearly, on average we shall have equal numbers of positive and negative interactions.

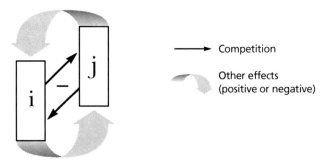

Figure 1.3   For each pair of possible behaviors, types i and j, have several possible effects on each other. First they compete for resources. But secondly each one may have effects that are either antagonistic, neutral, or synergetic on the other.

Each population that is present will experience the net effect that results from all of the other populations that are also present. Similarly, it will affect those populations by its presence.

$$\text{Net Effect on } i = \sum_j x(j).\text{Interaction}(j,i)$$

The sum is over j including i, and so we are looking at behaviors that in addition to interacting with each other also feed back on themselves. There will also always be a competition for underlying resources, which we shall represent by:

$$\text{Crowding}(i) = \sum_j \frac{x(j)}{\left(1 + \rho\text{Distance}(i, j)\right)}$$

At any time, then, we can draw the landscape of synergy and antagonism that is generated and experienced by the populations present in the system. We can therefore write down the equation for the change in population of each of the x_i. It will contain the positive and negative effects of the influence of the other populations present, as well as the competition for resources that will always be a factor, and also the error making diffusion through which populations from i create small numbers of off-spring in $i{+}1$ and $i-1$.

$$\frac{dx(i)}{dt} = b(fx(i) + .5(1 - f)x(i-1) + .5(1 - f)x(i+1))$$

$$(1 + .04\text{Neteff}(i))(1 - \text{Crowding}(i) / N) - mx(i)$$

where f is the fidelity of reproduction. The first group of terms corresponds to growth of $x(i)$, due to natural growth, and as inward diffusion from the populations of type $x - 1$ and $x + 1$. The growth rate reflects the "net effects" (synergy and antagonism) on $x(i)$ of the presence of populations other than $x(i)$. There are limited resources (N) available for any given behavior, so it cannot grow infinitely. The final term merely reflects the natural lifetime of any active x.

Let us consider a typical simulation that this model produces. If we start initially with a single population present—for example, $x(11) = 5$ and all other populations are 0. If we plot the net effect of this population on the other 19 possible populations it will provide a simple one-dimensional "landscape" showing the potential synergy/antagonism that would affect each population if it were to appear. The only population initially present is $x(11)$ and therefore the evolutionary landscape in which it sits is in fact that which it creates itself. No other populations are present yet to contribute to the overall landscape of mutual interaction.

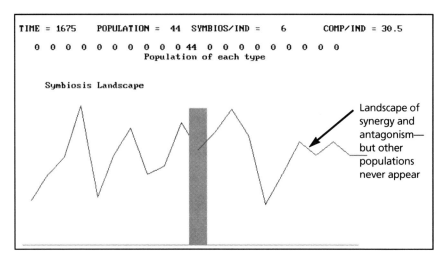

Figure 1.4   With no exploration in character space, fidelity $f = 1$, the system remains homogeneous, but its performance will only support a population of 44.

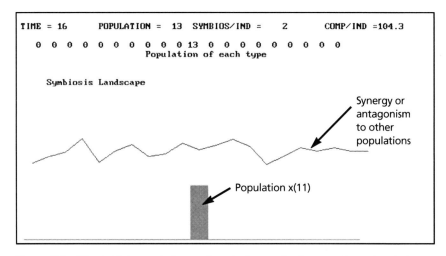

Figure 1.5   The initial population and evolutionary landscape of our simulation. (Time 16).

The system rapidly reaches a steady state with the low population of 44. The competition per individual is over 30 units and symbiosis per individual is only 6.

If the same simulation is repeated with the same hidden pair interactions and the same initial conditions but this time there is a 2% "exploration" from any population into the adjacent character cells, then the result is shown in the series of Figure 1.5 and 1.6. We see that the performance of the

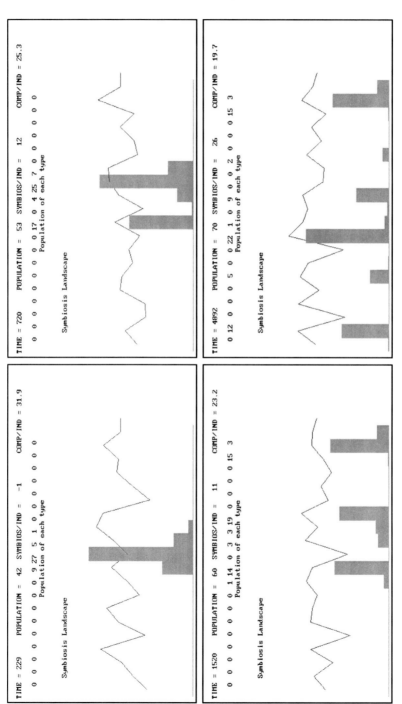

Figure 1.6 The sequence of events (times 229, 720, 1520 and 4892) that lead to a structural attractor involving populations 2, 6, 9, 12, 15, 19, 20.

system increases to support a population of 72, the competition experienced per individual falls to 19 and the symbiosis per individual rises to 26.

What matters then, is how the population 11 affects itself. This may have positive or negative effects depending on the random selection made at the start of the simulation. However, in general the population 11 will grow and begin to "diffuse" into the types 10 and 12. Gradually, the landscape will reflect the effects that 10, 11, and 12 have on each other, and the diffusion will continue into the other possible populations. Hills in the landscape will be climbed by the populations, but as they climb, they change their behavior and therefore change the landscape for themselves and the others. Figures 1.4 and 1.5 show this process taking place over time.

However, we can ask whether this "structural attractor," involving the reduced dimensions and attributes associated with the populations that coexist in the attractor, is the only one possible for a given set of potential interaction between the i and j. The answer is no. There are several attractors possible, and they involve different populations, and different dimensions and attributes. They are qualitatively different from the first attractor. For example, in Figure 1.7 we see a stable structure that results when the same system as before is started from $x(1)$ instead of $x(11)$.

Clearly, this shows us that the dynamics is path dependent and so even with the same potential interactions, qualitatively different situations can emerge. Obviously, if we choose a different set of pair interactions to "explore" with our model, we shall find different attractors.

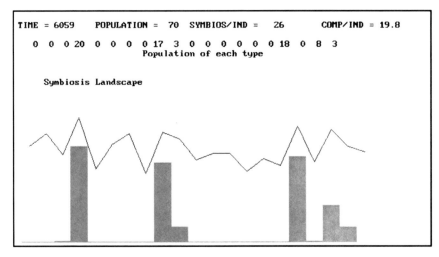

Figure 1.7 An alternative outcome for identical pair interactions, but for an initial seed placed at population 1 instead of 11. This involves 4, 9, 10, 17, 19 and 20.

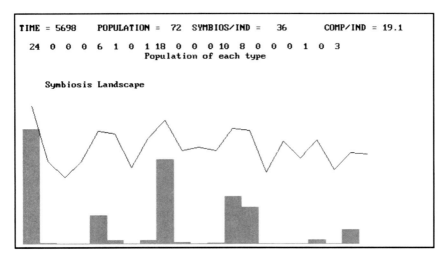

```
TIME = 5698     POPULATION =  72  SYMBIOS/IND =    36        COMP/IND = 19.1

 24  0  0  0  6  1  0  1 18  0  0  0 10  8  0  0  0  1  0  3
                    Population of each type


    Symbiosis Landscape
```

Figure 1.8   If there are different pair interactions between potential populations, then the model generates a different set of attractors.

IMPLICATIONS—WHAT IS A COMPLEX SYSTEM?

There are several important points about these results. The first is that it they are very generic and the results apply very generally. If we cannot make the assumptions 3 and 4 mentioned in the introduction (average behavior, smooth processes) that take out the microdiversity and idiosyncrasy of real-life agents, actors, and objects, then we *automatically obtain the emergence of a structural attractor*. This is a complex system of interdependent behaviors whose attributes are on the whole synergetic. These have better performance than their homogeneous ancestors, but are less diverse than if all possible behaviors were present. They correspond to the emergence of hypercycles in the work of Eigen and Schuster (1979). Those present result from the particular history of search undertaken, and on their synergy. In other words, a structural attractor is the emergence of a set of interacting factors that have mutually supportive, complementary attributes.

What are the implications of these structural attractors:

- Search carried out by the "error-making" diffusion in character space leads to vastly increased performance of the final object. Instead of a homogeneous system, characterized by intense internal competition and low symbiosis, the development of the system leads to a much higher performance—one that decreases internal competition and increases synergy.

- The whole process leads to the evolution of a complex, a community of agents whose activities, whatever they are, have effects that feed back positively on themselves and the others present. It is an emergent team or community in which positive interactions are greater than the negative ones.
- The diversity, dimensionality, and attribute space occupied by the final complex is much greater than the initial homogeneous starting structure of a single population. However, it is much less than the diversity, dimensionality, and attribute spaces that all possible populations would have brought to the system. The structural attractor therefore represents a reduced set of activities from all those possible in principle. It reflects the discovery of a subset of agents whose attributes and dimensions have properties that provide positive feedback. This is different from a classical dynamic attractor that refers to the long-term trajectory traced by the given set of variables. Here, our structural attractor concerns the *emergence* of variables, dimensions, and attribute sets that not only coexist but actually are synergetic.
- A successful and sustainable evolutionary system will clearly be one in which there is freedom and encouragement for the exploratory search process in behavior space. The system can generate a fairly stable community of agents or actors by having the freedom to explore. Also, the self-organization of our system leads to a highly cooperative system, where the competition per individual is low, but where loops of positive feedback and synergy are high. In other words, the free evolution of the different populations, each seeking its own growth, leads to a system that is more co-operative than competitive. The vision of a modern, free market economy leading to and requiring a cut-throat society where selfish competitiveness dominates is shown to be false, at least in this simple case.

The most important point really is generality of the model presented above. The model concerns the exploration of possible behaviors by agents, each with their own characteristics and dimensions, and a selection process that retains the successful experiments and suppresses the unsuccessful. Clearly, this situation characterizes almost any group of humans: families, companies, communities, and so on, but only if the exploratory learning is permitted will the evolutionary emergence of structural attractors be possible. If we think of an artifact, some product resulting from a design process, then there is also a parallel with the emergent structural attractor. A product is created by bringing together different components in such a way as to generate some overall performance. But there are several dimensions to this performance, concerning different attributes. These, however, are correlated so that a change that is made in the design of one component will have consequences for the performance in different attribute spaces. Some may be made better and some worse. Our emergent structural attractor is therefore relevant to understanding what successful products are and how they are obtained. Clearly, a successful product is one that has attributes that are in synergy, and which lead to a high average performance. From all the possible designs and modifications we seek a structural attractor that has dimensions and attributes that work well together. This is arrived at by R&D that must imitate the exploratory search of possible modifications and concepts that is schematically represented by our simple model above. A successful design for an automobile, aircraft, or even a simple wine glass, will be a structural attractor within the space of possible designs, techniques, and choices that have emerged through a search process.

This shows us that although a wine glass is not itself a complex system, it is produced by a complex system. The complex system searches and discovers what combinations of shape, thickness, glass composition, and so on, lead to attributes that are mutually compatible and that are desired. Part of the complex system that produces the wine glass is about the technology and production processes that led to the attributes of the emergent objects. This is why the organizational forms, the technologies, and the skill bases

Attributes	Thickness	Clarity	% lead	Strength	Temp Resistance	Good for bouquet	Stability	Weight
Thickness		−2	−1	1	−2	0	0	2
Clarity	−2		2	−1	0	0	0	−1
% lead	−1	2		−1	−1	0	0	2
Strength	1	−1	−1		−1	−1	1	1
Temp resistance	−2	0	−1	−1		0	0	1
Good for bouquet	0	0	0	0	0		0	0
Stability	0	0	0	1	0	0		1
Weight	2	−1	2	1	1	0	1	

Figure 1.9 Imaginary pair-wise attribute interaction table for a wine glass. This would replace our random assignment in the general model above.

that underlie wine glasses over time will in fact evolve through successive stages, just like our simple model above.

However, although our model shows us how the presence of exploration in character space will lead to emergent objects and systems with improved performance, it is still true that we cannot predict what they will be. Mathematically we could solve our equations to find the values of the variables for an optimal performance. But we do not know *which* variables will be present, and therefore we do not know *which* equations to solve or optimize. In our model we used random numbers to choose pair-wise interactions in an unbiased way, but in fact in a real problem these are not random but reflect the underlying physical, psychological, and behavioral reality of the processes and components in question. By considering the underlying reality, we could estimate these values for each pair and then see what kind of structural attractors our simulation might produce. This would lead to a "cladistic diagram" (a diagram showing evolutionary history) suggesting how a system had changed and evolved structurally over time. It would generate an evolutionary history of both artifacts and the organizational forms that underlie their production (McKelvey, 1982, 1994; McCarthy, 1995; McCarthy, Leseure, Ridgeway, & Fieller, 1997).

Another important point, particularly for scientists, is that it would be extremely difficult to discern the "correct" model equations even for our simple 20 population problem, from observing the population dynamics of the system. Because any single behavior could be playing a positive, or negative role in a self, or pair or triplet etc. interaction, it would be impossible to untangle its interactions and write down its the equations simply by noting the population's growth or decline. Despite the difficulty of an "observing scientist" predicting the structural attractor, the system itself can generate one quite easily. All it needs is to have the micro-diversity of its error-making search process running, and it will find stable arrangements of multiple actors. It will discover a balance between the agents in play and the interactions that they bring with them. But although the system can do this automatically, it does not mean that we can know what the web of interactions really is. This certainly poses problems for the rational analysis of situations, since this must rely on an understanding of the consequences of the different interactions that are believed to be present. We cannot really know from the de-contextualized data of growth and decline how the circles of influence really operate. Our only choice might be to ask the actors involved, in the case of a human system. And this in turn would raise the question of whether people really understand the foundations that sustain their own situation, and the influences of the functional, emotional, and historical links that build, maintain, and cast down organizations and institutions. The loops of positive feedback that build structure introduce a truly collective aspect to any profound understanding of their nature, and this will be beyond any simple rational analysis, used in a goal-seeking local context.

CONCLUSION

The Science of Complex Systems is about systems whose internal structure is not reducible to a mechanical system. In particular it is about connected complex systems, for which the assumptions of average types and of average interactions are not appropriate and are not made. Such systems co-evolve with their environment being "open" to flows of energy, matter and information across whatever boundaries we have chosen to define. These flows do not obey simple, fixed laws but instead result from the internal "sense-making" going on inside them, as experience, conjectures and experiments are used to modify the interpretive frameworks within. Because of this, the behaviour of the systems with which each system is co-evolving are necessarily uncertain and creative, and is not best represented by some predictable, fixed trajectory. This takes some steps towards the "post-modern" point of view. But as Cilliers (1998) indicates, the original definition of post modernism (Lyotard, 1984) does not take us to the situation of total subjectivity where no assumptions can be made, but rather to the domain of evolutionary complex systems discussed in this paper.

Instead of a fixed landscape of attractors, and of a system operating in one of them, we have a changing system, moving in a changing landscape of potential attractors. Providing that there is an underlying potential of diversity, then creativity and noise (supposing that they are different) provide a constant exploration of other possibilities. Our simple model only supposed 20 possible underlying behaviors, but obviously in any realistic human situation the number would be very large. In dealing with a changing environment, therefore, we find a "law of excess diversity" in which system survival long-term requires more underlying diversity than would be considered requisite at any time. Some of these possible behaviors mark the system and alter the dimensions of its attributes, leading to new attractors, and new behaviors, towards which the system may begin to move, but at which it may never arrive, as new changes may occur on the way.

The real revolution is not therefore about a neo-classical, equilibrium view as opposed to non-linear dynamics having cyclic and chaotic attractors, but instead is about the representation of the world as a non-stationary situation of permanent adaptation and change. The picture we have arrived at here is one that Stacey, Griffin and Shaw (2000) refer to as a "transformational teleology," in which potential futures (patterns of attractors and of pathways) are being transformed in the present. The landscape of attractors we may calculate now is not in fact where we shall go, because it is itself being transformed by our present experiences.

The macro-structures that emerge spontaneously in complex systems constrain the choices of individuals and fashion their experience. Behaviors are being affected by knowledge, and this is driven by the learning experience of individuals. Each actor is co-evolving with the structures resulting from the behavior and knowledge/ignorance of all the others, and surprise and uncertainty are part of the result. The selection process results from the success or failure of different behaviors and strategies in the competitive and co-operative dynamical game that is running.

But there is no single optimal strategy. What emerge are structural attractors, *ecologies* of behaviors, beliefs and strategies, clustered in a mutually consistent way, and characterised by a mixture of competition and symbiosis. This nested hierarchy of structure is the result of evolution, and is not necessarily optimal in any way, because there are a multiplicity of subjectivities and intentions, fed by a web of imperfect information and diverse interpretive frameworks. In human systems, at the microscopic level, behavior reflects the different beliefs of individuals based on past experience, and it is the interaction of these behaviors that actually creates the future. In so doing, it will often fail to fulfill the expectations of many of the actors, leading them either to modify their (mis)understanding of the world, or alternatively simply leave them perplexed. Evolution in human systems is therefore a continual, imperfect learning process, spurred by the difference between expectation and experience, but rarely providing enough information for a complete understanding.

Although this sounds tragic, it is in fact our salvation. It is this very "ignorance" or multiple misunderstandings that generates micro-diversity and leads therefore to exploration and (imperfect) learning. In turn the changes in behavior that are the external sign of that learning induce fresh uncertainties in the behavior of the system, and therefore new ignorance (Allen, 1993). Knowledge, once acted upon, begins to lose its value. This offers a much more realistic picture of the complex game that is being played in the world, and one that our models can begin to quantify and explore.

In a world of change, which is the reality of existence, what we need is knowledge about the process of learning. From evolutionary complex systems thinking, we find models that can help reveal the mechanisms of adaptation and learning, and that can also help imagine and explore possible avenues of adaptation and response. These models have a different aim from those used operationally in many domains. Instead of being detailed descriptions of existing systems, they are more concerned with exploring possible futures, and the qualitative nature of these. They are also more concerned with the mechanisms that provide such systems with the capacity to explore, to evaluate, and to transform themselves over time. They address the "what might be," rather than the "what is" or "what will be." It is the entry into the social sciences of the philosophical revolution that Prigogine wrote about in physics some 25 years ago. It is the transition in our thinking from "being" to "becoming." It is about moving from the study of existing physical objects using repeatable objective experiments, to methods with which to imagine possible futures and with which to understand how possible futures can be imagined. It is about system transformation through multiple subjective experiences, and their accompanying diversity of interpretive, meaning-giving frameworks. Reality changes, and with it experiences change, too. In addition, however, the interpretive frameworks or models people use also change, and what people learn from their changed experiences are also transformed. Recognizing these new limits to knowledge, therefore, should not depress us. Instead we should understand that this is what makes life interesting, and what life is, has always been, and will always be about.

ACKNOWLEDGEMENTS

This work was partially carried out under the EPSRC Nexsus Network program. The idea of "structural attractors" occurred during a discussion with J. McGlade and M. Strathern.

REFERENCES

Allen, P. M. (1988). Evolution: Why the whole is greater than the sum of its parts. In W. F. Wolff & C. J. Soeder (Eds.), *Ecodynamics* (pp. 2–31). Berlin: Springer Verlag.

Allen, P. M. (1990). Why the future is not what it was. *Futures, 22*(6), 555–569.

Allen, P. M. (1993). Evolution: Persistant ignorance from continual learning. In R.H. Day & P. Chen (Eds.), *Nonlinear dynamics & evolutionary economics* (pp. 101–112). Oxford: Oxford University Press.

Allen, P. M. (1994a). Evolutionary complex systems: Models of technology change. In L. Leydesdorff & P. van den Besselaar (Eds.), *Chaos and economic theory* (pp. 1–19). London: Pinter.

Allen, P. M. (1994b). Coherence, chaos and evolution in the social context. *Futures, 26*(6), 583–597.

Allen, P. M. (2001). Knowledge, learning and ignorance. *Emergence, 2*(4), 78–103.

Allen, P. M. & McGlade, J. M. (1987). Evolutionary drive: The effect of microscopic diversity, error making and noise. *Foundations of Physics, 17*(7), 723–728.

Cilliers, P. (1998). *Complexity and post-modernism*. London: Routledge.

Eigen, M. & Schuster, P. (1979). *The Hypercycle*. Berlin: Springer Verlag.

Lyotard, J.-F. (1984). *The post-modern condition: A report on knowledge*. Manchester: Manchester University Press.

McCarthy, I. (1995). Manufacturing classifications: Lessons from organisational systematics and biological taxonomy. *Journal of Manufacturing and Technology Management- Integrated Manufacturing Systems, 6,*(6), 37–49.

McCarthy, I., Leseure, M., Ridgeway, K. & Fieller, N. (1997). Building a manufacturing cladogram. *International Journal of Technology Management, 13*(3), 2269–2296.

McKelvey, B. (1982). *Organizational systematics.* Berkeley: University of California Press.

McKelvey B. (1994). Evolution and organizational science. In J. Baum & J. Singh (Eds.), *Evolutionary Dynamics of Organizations* (pp. 314–326). Oxford: Oxford University Press.

Stacey, R., Griffin, D., & Shaw, P. (2000). Complexity and Management. London: Routledge.

CHAPTER 2

THE DEATH OF THE EXPERT?

Kurt A. Richardson
Institute for the Study of Coherence and Emergence

Andrew Tait
Idea Sciences

INTRODUCTION: TRADITIONAL EXPERTISE

The concept of expertise and the associated experts themselves play a central role in modern organizations. Whenever a problem arises, an almost automatic response triggers us to seek out the relevant expert who, given their superior credentials, will solve the problem at hand. The entire consultancy industry relies on this unquestioned institutionalism. Billions of dollars are paid to those we see as experts. But what exactly do we mean by the term? The Oxford English Dictionary (Expert, 2009) offers the following:

1. One who is expert or has gained skill from experience.
2. One whose special knowledge or skill causes him to be regarded as an authority.

The terms used here such as "experience," "knowledge," and "authority" are used so often these days that their meanings are rarely, if ever, questioned. We assume that "experience" is a legitimate way to develop under-

Complexity and Knowledge Management, pages 23–39
Copyright © 2010 by Information Age Publishing
All rights of reproduction in any form reserved.

standing; we assume that "knowledge" is something tangible that can be shifted from context to context without loss; we assume that "authority" resides with those who are "in the know." Beneath these assumptions are rather simplistic notions of how the world operates, and how we may learn of these operations.

THE AIMS OF THIS CHAPTER

In this chapter we argue that our contemporary notions of "experience," "knowledge," "authority," and therefore "expertise" and "expert" are outdated and inappropriate for the complex globalized (i.e., connected) times we find ourselves experiencing. They represent artifacts of the reductionist view of reality that regards the universe as the ultimate well-oiled, exquisitely complicated, machine.

The aim of this chapter is to review these basic notions from a complexity science perspective. Our focus will be on the concept of knowledge and the inescapable limits that are placed upon us as a direct result of the universe's inherent complexity. We will argue that a commodity-based view of knowledge is inadequate and often wholly inappropriate given the requirements of today's organizations. From this revision of the concept of knowledge an extended notion of the "expert" will be developed.

THE COMMODITIZATION OF KNOWLEDGE

Contemporary philosophers regard the perspective that there is an absolute reality that might be absolutely understood through method (such as the "scientific method") as "modern." "Modernists," those who espouse the "modern" view of knowledge, believe that science, or for that matter any sense making, is simply a matter of map making (Wilbur, 2007). We look at the world as it appears to our perceptions (which are presumed to be largely unbiased), map it, and within that map find. It's a seductive promise: Map the world and understanding shall be yours.

As this understanding is taken to be absolute and perfect, then control is possible. If we know how something works then we can predict how it will evolve. Therefore, we can change it (because we can predict how our actions will affect the behavior of it) so that it behaves in a predictable way which meets our needs and desires. With knowledge comes the power to control. And with control comes reward. This is the promise that a modernist view of knowledge offers.

In a world dominated by (linear) mathematics, quantification is of prime importance. If something can be counted, then one can measure the success of an action designed to change the amount of that something. As the song writer Roger Waters sings, "It all makes perfect sense expressed in dollars and cents, pounds, shillings and pence." And, because the effect of my actions is apparently predictable then I can design specific actions to effect specific quantities in a specific way. But this is not the only benefit of "reductionist" knowledge. Scientific understandings are generalizations. This means that such knowledge is applicable in a wide range of circumstances or contexts. So if I have experience of a wide range of situations then I have the knowledge to deal with many future situations I've yet to experience. This is essentially how we go about our lives (Kelly, 1955/1992). Scientific knowledge is transferable from one context to another. It doesn't matter that the new context might be slightly different from previous contexts that we have experience of—that would just mean that our knowledge would have to be slightly adjusted to match up with the new context. Let's look at a specific example.

Most readers will be familiar with Newton's famous second law: "The acceleration of an object is directly proportional to the resultant force acting on it and inversely proportional to its mass. The direction of the acceleration is in the direction of the resultant force." Or, in mathematical terms: F (vector force acting on the object) = m (mass of the object) × a (acceleration of the object, or the rate of change of the rate of change of distance with time). This equation (up until Einstein's discovery of relativity anyway) was assumed to be true in every context regarding an object with a force acting upon it. For example, let us consider a 20 kg rock being pushed along by a child who is applying a force of 10 Newtons.[1] Neglecting friction, it is a simple matter to calculate the acceleration of the rock resulting from the child's 10 N effort. Using $F = m \times a$ we find that $a = 0.5 \ ms^{-2}$ which means that after 10 seconds the rock would be moving at 5 meters per second, or 2.2 miles per hour. Clever stuff!

Now let's consider a coin falling from a sixth story window. What would be the force due to gravity acting on the coin? This would appear to be a very different situation, or context, from the previous example. But according to Newton's second law it is much the same as the first. All we need to know is the mass of the coin, 2 grams say, and the acceleration due to gravity, which on Earth has been found to be about 9.8 ms^{-2}. With this data in hand it is a trivial matter to calculate the force acting on the coin by the Earth, 0.02 kg × 9.8 ms^{-2} = 0.2 Newtons. So we not only have numeric accuracy, but we have knowledge transferability as well.

Despite the obvious differences between these two contexts, the same law of motion applied, and it was a trivial matter to adjust the law to the features of each context. Newton's second law is plainly valid for a wide range of contexts. This is the case for all scientific knowledge. All the laws of science are generalizations extracted from observations made of a wide range of different (but apparently similar at a deeper level) contexts. They are statistical truths—averages—that are taken to be absolute for many different occasions. They are true not only in space (i.e., where events happen), but also in time (i.e., when they happen). So Newton's laws of motion will be as valid tomorrow as they are today as they were yesterday, whether the event is taking place in your hometown, on the other side of the world, or even on the other side of the universe (we tend to assume).

If (scientific) knowledge were not transferable, then life would be very much more complicated and difficult than it is. What would happen if I went to the doctor's and found that my physiology was so unique and different from others' that the doctor had to start from scratch in developing knowledge of how I functioned? What if we all functioned completely differently? Every time the doctor met a new patient he would be unable to use any of his prior knowledge based on other patients to help attend to his new patient's ailments. He would have to develop a unique knowledge base for every patient. Of course, we are all unique in some ways (which is why drugs tend to have a range of effectiveness in treating any particular individual's ailments), but generally we all function in more or less the same way; blood is pumped around our body by our heart, we develop a sore throat and fever when we catch the cold virus, we all suffer brain damage when our brains are starved of oxygen for a sufficiently long duration, and so on. There is a vast body of knowledge concerning the human body that is essentially true for everybody. Medical knowledge is indeed transferable across a wide range of contexts—contexts that are different, but somehow similar.

What about organizations? What about management? Though some might argue as to whether or not management is a science, management science is still taught at business schools, and the knowledge acquired is treated very much in the same way as scientific knowledge is—that is, it is absolute and transferable. What value would there be in calling in a management consultant if all his knowledge was incongruent with your needs? There would be no value at all. The fact that the knowledge the consultant has accumulated throughout his or her career does have (apparently) some value to your company means that similarities do exist between different business contexts. We won't dwell upon management knowledge any longer, as it is our contention that much of it is in fact not "scientific" and therefore not easily transferable. Nonetheless, many organizational boards still rely on outside management consultants, or business experts, in the belief that their knowledge is relevant to them—that is, it is transferable.

How would a mechanic fix your car? How could you drive a variety of different vehicles? How would an electrician repair your TV? How could you make food? How could you find your way to the pub? How could you make sense of the words on this page, unless knowledge were transferable between contexts? Cars are mostly based on combustion engine technology, and they don't evolve into apples when you're not looking! They mostly operate using either a manual or automatic gearbox with an accelerator and a brake. Most (modern) TVs are based on LCD technology. Most recipes will give the same results whether it is a Monday or a Tuesday. The way to the pub does not depend upon whether there is a full moon or not. And though interpretations of words do vary, we can at least make sense of reasonably well constructed sentences.

With specialist scientific knowledge, the limits of what we humans can achieve seems unlimited. The latest and possibly greatest technological achievement is that of computers. We can construct unimaginably complicated devices that operate in predictable ways to perform mind-boggling calculations, render intricate and (almost) believably realistic graphics, model the circulation of blood through the heart, and so on.

In the modern world everything is seen as analyzable and in some way amenable to science. Scientific knowledge can be obtained about anything we choose to consider. And, scientific knowledge is the *only* knowledge worth having. There is no other substitute for the certainty and absolute power of science. At least that's what we're supposed to believe.

The fact that many different contexts seem to share common features has led many scientists to believe that there do in fact exist a set of features that are common to *all* possible contexts. The set of features, or laws, is referred to as the "Theory of Everything." Everything in the entire universe is apparently reducible to a small collection of fundamental rules. From these fundamental rules we obtain the vast diversity apparent in the observable universe. This is the ultimate reductionist dream—a theory, some scientific knowledge, that can account for it all. Such a theory would truly be the thought in the Creator's mind. Some believe that such a discovery would be the end of science itself. Others believe that science will continue, but it will simply be a case of filling in the details left by the Theory of Everything. Still others believe that science has already reached the point at which it now continues only to fill in the details left by the Standard Model (Horgan, 1997)—easily the most successful model in the history of humankind.

But, if scientific knowledge is so wonderful, why on earth are we witnessing more human suffering than ever before? It has been suggested that our knowledge has resulted in technology that if used might even (however inadvertently) destroy the environment we rely on for our ongoing survival as a species (e.g., CFCs and lead in fuel, the use of which has been reduced radically once their dire environmental effects were realized). If knowledge allows us to control and construct whatever world we might desire, why have we, frankly, done such a shit job of it?

To understand the limitations of scientific knowledge, we need to understand the assumptions that the scientific worldview is built upon.

The common feature between the various scientific knowledge domains is that the objects of interest are pretty much stable over time (or at least they are presumed to be). When stability dominates, then the reductionist approach to knowledge generation appears to be a wholly appropriate approximation to make. It works—there's no point in denying its power. But what about unstable, or at least non-stable, systems? The human mind, for example—the way we view the world continually evolves and changes. Anything vaguely human-like seems to slip through the scientific net. The sciences that have been regarded as successful are the natural sciences—physics and chemistry mainly, but also some branches of biology. Why haven't the social, or human, sciences such as psychology, sociology, linguistics, etc. achieved the respected status of the natural sciences? The presumption—for example, by proponents of rational choice theory (Allingham, 2002)—has always been that the two branches would equally benefit from the application of the scientific method. This would imply that the objects of interest are at their heart the same, but evidence is increasingly being offered that the two areas of interest are quite different (Shneiderman, 2008).

The scientific method has repeatedly demonstrated it inefficacy when it comes to addressing social issues. Transport models fail to predict future road usage. Traditional economics models—well, they just don't seem to predict anything much (Economist, 2002)![2] Social models fail to predict episodes of rioting (Economist, 2003). Scientific knowledge of social systems seems to be utterly useless and worthless and creates more trouble than it's worth. Our principle assertion of this chapter is that science has thus far developed to deal very well indeed with complicated systems, whereas many of the problems that seem intractable to reductionist scientific methods are in fact better described as "complex." We also suggest that the prevalent notion of expertise today is again associated with knowledge of complicated systems rather than complex ones. It is to this complicated/complex distinction that we will now consider.

A BRIEF INTRODUCTION TO COMPLEXITY THINKING

What if human organizations were really just *complicated* rather than *complex*? The simple answer to this question is that the possibility of an all-embracing "Theory of Management" would almost certainly exist. This would make management very easy indeed, as there would be a book of theory (*The Management Bible*—it would probably challenge the current all-time bestseller in sales!) that would tell the practicing manager what to do in any given context. The means of achieving effective and efficient organizational management would no longer be a mystery. But what is it about the concept of "complicated" that makes this scenario plausible? Why has the possibility of a final (scientific) management theory not been realized yet, given the millions of man-hours and published pages devoted to the search? Why does approaching organizations as "complex" rather than "complicated" deny us of this possibility?

A very common (but incomplete) description of a complex system is that such systems are made up of a large number of nonlinearly[3] interacting parts. By this definition, the modern computer would be a complex system. A modern computer is crammed full of transistors that all respond nonlinearly to their input(s). Despite this "complexity," the average PC does not show signs of emergence or self-organization; it simply processes (in a linear fashion) the instruction list (i.e., a program) given to it by its programmer. Even the language in which it is programmed is rather uninteresting. Although there are many programming languages, they are *commensurable* with each other. A line of code in C# can be translated into Visual Basic .NET (VB.NET) relatively easily—the one line of C# code may require more lines of VB.NET code to achieve the same functionality, but it can be done in the vast majority of cases (and when it can't one of the languages is often extended to fill such a "commensurability gap"). The universal language into which all such languages can be translated without loss is called "logic" (more accurately, Boolean, or even binary, logic). More often, though, if a programmer wants to use a language very close to the universal language of computing, *assembly* is used, as this at least contains concepts that are more easily read by mere mortal programmers (although the domain knowledge—microelectronics—needed to program in assembly is a major requirement). This is then translated (without loss) into machine code (which is based on Boolean logic)—writing sophisticated programs directly in the language of the 0s and 1s of Boolean logic is nigh on impossible. The computer cannot choose the way it interprets the program, it cannot rewrite the program (unless it is programmed to in a prescribed manner), and it cannot get fed up with running programs and pop to the pub for a swift pint! So, what is it about the modern computer that prevents it from being labeled a *complex* system, but rather a *complicated* system?

The critical element is *feedback*. It is the existence of nonlinear feedback in complex systems that allows for *emergence, self-organization, adaptation, learning* and many other key concepts that have become synonymous with complexity thinking—and all the things that make management such a challenge. It is not just the existence of feedback loops *per se* that leads to complex behavior. These loops must themselves interact with each other. Once we have three or more *interacting* feedback loops (which may be made up from the interactions of many parts), accurately predicting the resulting behavior via standard analytical methods becomes problematic (at best) for most intents and purposes. In a relatively simple complex system containing, say, fifteen parts/components, there can be hundreds of interacting feedback loops even if there are only a few interconnections between neighboring parts. In such instances the only way to get a feel for the resulting dynamics is through simulation, which is why the computer (despite its rather uninteresting dynamics) has become so important in the development of complexity thinking. We say that the prediction of overall system behavior from knowledge of its parts is *intractable*. Basically, *absolute knowledge about the parts that make up a system and their interactions provides us with very little understanding indeed regarding how that system will behave overall.* Often the only recourse we have is to sit back and watch. In a sense the term "complex systems" refers to systems that, although we may have a deep appreciation of how they are put together (at the *microscopic* level), we may be completely ignorant of how the resulting *macroscopic* behavior comes about—that is, complexity is about limits to knowledge, or our inevitable ignorance. Without this understanding of causality, planning for particular outcomes is very difficult indeed. In the computer (which we will now class as a complicated system), causality is simple (i.e., low dimensional)—few (interacting) feedback loops (although there are many millions of connections). In complex systems, causality is networked, making it very difficult indeed, if not impossible, to untangle the contribution each causal path makes. It is hard enough to grasp the possibilities that flow from a small group of people, let alone the mind-boggling possibilities that might be generated from a large multi-department organization. Maybe this is why a major part of management tends to be suppressing all these possibilities so that one individual might begin to comprehend what remains—departmentalization is an obvious example of a complexity reduction strategy.

Another unexpected property of complex systems is that there exist stable abstractions (it is these stable abstraction that science is so adept at formalizing into laws), not expressible in terms of the constituent parts, that themselves bring about properties different from those displayed by the parts. This sentence is a bit of a mouthful, but we have here succinctly described the process of emergence, although in a rather awkward way. This is deliberate. More often than not, emergence is portrayed as a process from which macroscopic properties "emerge" from microscopic properties—that is, the properties of the whole emerge from the properties of its parts. But this in an overly simplistic view of emergence.

When recognizing the products of emergence, we are abstracting away from the description in terms of parts and interactions and proposing a new description in terms of entities or concepts quite different from those parts and interactions. We ignore certain features in favor of paying attention to other features that comprise a recognizable pattern, while retaining our awareness that the "lower"-level parts and interactions somehow naturally result in the "higher"-level parts and interactions. Regarding an organization as a collection of interacting departments rather than a collection of individual people is a common application of this idea.

"Emergent" entities have novel properties in relation to the properties of the constituent parts—for example, whole departments do not act like individual people, and "team-ness" is not the same as "person-ness." What is even more interesting is that these supposed abstractions can interact with the parts from which they emerged—a process known as *downward causation* (Emmeche, Köppe, & Stjernfelt, 2000). I won't go into the problematic nature of the concept of emergence any further here—please refer to Richardson (2004)—suffice to say that the view that the process of emergence is captured by the expression "the whole is greater than the sum of its parts" is far too simplistic.

In specially idealized complex systems such as in cellular automata (Wikipedia, Cellular Automata) the parts are very simple indeed, and yet they still display a great deal of emergent phenomena and dynamical diversity. Complex systems that contain more intricate parts are often referred to as *complex adaptive systems* (CASs), in which the parts themselves are described as complex systems. The parts of CASs contain local memories and have a series of detailed responses to the same, as well as different, contexts/scenarios. They often have the ability to learn from their mistakes and generate new responses to familiar and novel contexts. Because of this localized decision-making/learning ability, such parts are often referred to as (autonomous) agents. There is a profound relationship between simple complex systems (SCSs) (i.e., complex systems comprised of simple parts) and CASs (i.e., complex systems comprised of intricate agents). The Game-of-Life (Wikipedia, Game-of-Life), a particularly well-known SCS, shows how a CAS can be abstracted, or emerge, from a SCS! Intuition would tell us that a CAS is simply a more intricate SCS. The Game-of-Life[4] demonstrates that our intuition is, as is often the case in complexity thinking, too simplistic.

Complexity and Incompressibility

Cilliers (2005) introduces the idea of incompressibility: "We have seen that there is no accurate (or rather, perfect) representation of the system which is simpler than the system itself. In building representations of open systems, we are forced to leave things out, and since the effects of these omissions are nonlinear, we cannot predict their magnitude" (p. 13).[5]

It is this concept of incompressibility that leads us away from a managerial monism—a definitive theory of management—to a managerial pluralism (assuming organizations are complex rather than merely complicated) in which many theories co-exist, each with their own unique strengths and weaknesses. Restating Cilliers, the best representation of a complex system is the system itself, and any representation of the system will be incomplete and, therefore, can lead to incomplete (or even just plain wrong) understanding. One must be careful in interpreting the importance of incompressibility. Just because a complex system is incompressible it does not follow that there are (incomplete) representations of the system that cannot be useful—otherwise how could we have knowledge of anything, however limited? Incompressibility is not an excuse for not bothering. This is rather fortunate, otherwise the only option available, once we accept the impossibility of an ultimate theory, is to have no theory at all—not a very satisfactory outcome (and contrary to what experience would tell us). We think it is better to know something that is wrong rather than nothing at all. Knowing something and knowing *how* it is wrong is even better! Equally useful is knowing something that is wrong, but knowing *why* it is wrong.

Building on the work of Bilke and Sjunnesson (2001), Richardson (2005) recently showed how Boolean networks (which are a type of SCS) could be reduced/compressed in such a way as to not change the qualitative character of the uncompressed system's phase space—that is, the compressed system had the same functionality as the uncompressed system. If nothing was lost in the compression process, then Cilliers's claim of incompressibility would be incorrect. However, what was lost was a great deal of detail of how the different attractor basins (regions that describe qualitatively different system's behavior) are reached. Furthermore, the reduced systems are not as tolerant to external perturbations as their unreduced parents. This evidence would suggest that stable and accurate—although imperfect—representations of complex systems do indeed exist (and hence explains why and how science can work at all). However, in reducing/compressing/abstracting a complex system, certain significant details are lost. Different representations capture different aspects of the original system's behavior. We might say that, in the absence of a complete representation, the overall behavior of a system is *at least* the sum of the behaviors of all our simplified models of that system. Richardson (2005) concludes that:

> Complex systems may well be incompressible in an absolute sense, but many of them are at least quasi-reducible in a variety of ways. This fact indicates that the many commentators suggesting that reductionist methods are in some way anti-complexity—some even go so far as to suggest that traditional scientific methods have no role in facilitating the understanding complexity—are overstating their position. Often linear methods are assessed in much the same way. The more modest middle ground is that though complex systems may indeed be incompressible, most, if not all, methods are capable of shedding some light on certain aspects of their behavior. It is not that the incompressibility of complex systems prevents understanding, and that all methods that do not capture complexity to a complete extent are useless, but that we

need to develop an awareness of how our methods limit our potential understanding of such systems. (p. 380)

In short, all this is saying is that we can indeed have knowledge of complex organizations, but that this knowledge is approximate and provisional.
This may seem like common sense, but it is surprising how much organizational knowledge is acted upon *as if* it were perfectly correct.

The suggestion that there are multiple valid representations of the same
complex system is not new. The complementary law (e.g., Weinberg, 1975)
from general systems theory suggests that any two different perspectives
(or models) about a system will reveal truths regarding that system that are
neither entirely independent nor entirely compatible. More recently, this
has been stated as: a complex system is a system that has two or more non-
overlapping descriptions (Cohen, 2002). We would go as far as to include
"potentially contradictory," suggesting that for complex systems (by which
we really mean any part of reality we care to examine) *there exists an infini-
tude of equally valid, non-overlapping, potentially contradictory descriptions.* Maxwell (2000), in his analysis of a new conception of science, asserts that: "Any
scientific theory, however well it has been verified empirically, will always
have infinitely many rival theories that fit the available evidence just as well
but that make different predictions, in an arbitrary way, for yet unobserved
phenomena" (p. 17–18).

The result of these observations is that to have any chance of even beginning to understand complex systems we must approach them from many directions—we must take a pluralistic stance. This pluralist position provides
a theoretical foundation for the many techniques that have been developed
for group decision making, bottom-up problem solving, and distributed
management (Richardson, Tait, Roos, & Lissack, 2005)—any method that
stresses the need for synthesizing a wide variety of perspectives in an effort
to better understand the problem at hand and how we might collectively
act to solve it.

Now that we have explored the essential differences between what we
mean by complicated and complex, we can now explore the implications
for the nature of knowledge and the notion of expertise.

THE PROBLEMATIZATION OF KNOWLEDGE

The "modern," some might say "linear," concept of knowledge assumes that
the systems of which we claim to have knowledge about are "complicated."
As such, models/representations of such systems can be built (maps can be
constructed), that, although maybe not complete, do not lead to radically
incorrect understanding. This is because small differences between what

actually exists and what we think exists are assumed to be irrelevant; that is, small mistakes in the map making process lead to small mistakes in our understanding and so can be easily corrected for when the time comes. It also follows that the objects of our representations map neatly to the objects of reality, albeit with some small discrepancies. This is also related to the assertion that knowledge in one context is valid in another similar context. Although two similar contexts are not identical, it is assumed that the differences are irrelevant; that an abstraction exists in which the two contexts are exactly the same as in the rock being pushed and the coin being dropped examples earlier. In this way knowledge of one context can be extended to many contexts, which leads to the notion of domain expertise. Such an expert is able to transfer his or her knowledge to many different contexts because of the assumption that there exists an abstraction that makes them all equivalent to each other in a way that allows the application of the same knowledge.

Modernist knowledge also assumes that causality is simple—that is, if a change in object A results in a change in object B, we have a tendency to assume that such a correlation points to a causal mechanism—"A caused B to. . . ." So not only do the objects A and B exist as such—because our model says so—they also affect each other directly.

Perhaps a more important implication of modernist knowledge is that because there is such a close relationship between reality and our models of reality, we can, through the application of rigorous methods, determine unambiguously which model best describes any circumstance. This results in the claims for "objective" knowledge, that is, the right, absolutely true way to understand some feature of reality. If truth can be argued to be absolute, then any knowledge an "expert" has is unquestionable. This is at the heart of the modernist notion of expertise: An expert is someone who has spent considerable time and effort in learning/discovering unquestionable (and universal) truths about a particular domain of interest. As such, if you have a problem that falls into the domain of a particular expert then you simply give that person a call, and after some time during which the expert has determined the appropriate abstraction for your particular problem, he simply regurgitates his knowledge of that particular abstraction. You then use that knowledge to design an action (or simply choose from a set of predesigned actions that worked in similar scenarios). Then, after successfully performing that action, you move on to worry about the next problem . . . that always seems to follow so closely behind the first! It is as easy as that.

So 'modernist' knowledge is fixed, absolute, and transferable, and modernist expertise is the ability to map contexts to such knowledge. This particular paradigm for knowledge and expertise is far from ineffective. There are many contexts that one can assume to be well described as linear and complicated, for which such knowledge is an invaluable tool supporting our ability to shape and effect such contexts such that they lead to desired outcomes.

But what if a context is best described as complex, or the manifestation of nonlinear causal processes?

NEO-EXPERTISE

As already indicated above in the discussion of incompressibility, if it is assumed that the system of interest, or the context of interest, is complex, or is the emergent result of underlying complex (nonlinearly fed-back) processes, then there is no one abstraction or description capable of capturing all the details required to make perfect predictions about how the affair of interest will unfold, or how our interventions might effect that unfolding. Furthermore, even a nearly perfect description may result in completely imperfect understanding, or at least understanding that is only useful for a certain length of time. This is the result of small differences growing to dominate—small changes cannot simply be averaged out like they can for complicated systems. Our best understanding can be no more than approximate and time-limited. As already proposed, approaching a "complex affair of interest" from more than one direction, a strategy known as "perspective-based pluralism," can be used in conjunction with critical reflection to synthesize a problem-specific time-limited map, rather than overlaying an existing map and force-fitting the complex affair of interest to that map.

If we reduce the notion of reductionist expertise to mean no more than overlaying a limited number of pre-existing maps known to the "expert" on to a particular context, then we can begin to see what neo-expertise might be in the light of complexity. A "neo-expert" is an expert in *custom* map-making (rather than just map-mapping), who recognizes that potentially useful maps are not only those that he or she is aware of. The word "making" in the previous sentence is most significant. The term highlights that a neo-expert is really a process expert—the process being the mechanism by which multiple perspectives are gathered, critiqued, and synthesized to inform decision-making. This process also includes the mechanisms in place that recognize that the understanding informing any decision-making is limited, and that implementation of any decision-taking must be monitored in order to facilitate recognition of when the decision taken might be wrong, or when the "synthetic" map is no longer useful. So neo-experts are not only concerned with the process of producing context-specific understanding, but also with the care that must be taken in applying such understanding in the real world. This still means that the neo-expert has a central role to play in complex problem solving. But rather than being the source of the relevant domain-specific knowledge, he or she is there to bring the expertise of the many organizational stake-holders together in a coherent fashion to facilitate the definition of the problem space, and the development of strategies to guide an organization, department, or individual in a particular direction—a rather harder proposition than just supplying textbook knowledge. Modernist experts do our thinking for us, whereas neo-experts help us think for ourselves.

Some readers may think that our neo-expert is the type of consultant who "borrows your watch to tell you the time." This could not be further from the truth. As conceived, our neo-experts would bring a range of skills to a client organization, including:

- An ability to identify discontinuities in an organization's life-cycle;
- An understanding of the dynamics of organizational politics;
- The ability to exploit the "wisdom of crowds"; and
- Knowledge of tools to study complex processes.

Whereas modernist experts attempt to replicate successful patterns, neo-experts attempt to create *new* successful patterns (or behaviors) for each intervention. The neo-expert may employ modernist expertise in the course of an intervention, but only in isolated pockets. These new patterns will be determined through close engagement with the client organization, and neo-experts will need to focus on the transfer of skills to their clients. As the organizational context is in continual flux, the "solution" must be continually monitored in case environmental changes render it impotent—or even dangerous. If the consultant fails to provide the organization with these monitoring skills, the client will become dependent on him.

This concept of "neo-expertise" brings to light one of the major weaknesses of management consulting. Many interventions are conceived as "one-shot" projects. The consultancy organization comes in and suggests some changes that are adopted, and the client presses on. However, the recommendations are invariably made within the context of a given business climate. Rarely are the assumptions underlying a corporate strategy regularly and formally tested. However, the neo-expert, with his focus on the context, is constantly butting up against these assumptions—questioning the efficacy of a strategy as soon as it is put into practice. While this may be seen as creating continuous instability, it is, in fact, recognizing the realities of doing business in the 21st century. Good neo-experts will attempt to minimize the adverse impact of change while accepting that businesses must evolve to survive.

It is be tempting to propose a methodology that would systematically determine how the neo-expert should go about this process of multi-perspective synthesis. However, there are an enormous number of ways to exploit pluralism, each with its own idiosyncrasies, so we prefer to point out that many good frameworks and methodologies already exist that can support the work of the budding neo-expert. Suggesting just one would leave us open to the charge of masquerading as "experts" in the process of knowledge production! It is really quite remarkable that these existing frameworks and methodologies have been largely ignored by the complexity community (see, for example, Jackson & Keys, 1984; Flood, 1995; or Midgley, 2000). Complexity thinking and soft systems thinking, for instance, have a great deal in common.

FINAL REMARKS

So does an increasingly connected world signal the death of the expert? Certainly not. There is still a major role for reductionist knowledge in the development of strategies for the management of complexity. However, exploring complex problem spaces requires a different kind of expertise than that that has traditionally been given priority. This neo-expertise is built on the skills to allow a group of stakeholders to "emergently" arrive at a context-specific—limited but useful—understanding of their circumstances to enable them to act in order to achieve certain preferred outcomes more often than not. This facilitative role is very challenging as anyone familiar with the process of facilitation will tell you—one article compares this process to midwifery (McMorland & Piggot-Irvine, 2000). It is an approach to the development of understanding, and decision-making that also has profound implications for how any organization may operate; we have barely scratched the surface of these implications in this chapter. Traditional experts can still be major contributors in this critical and pluralist process. The main change to their role is that their special type of knowledge is no longer regarded without question as the most important source of understanding in an evolving landscape of interactions and variations.

NOTES

1. The Newton is the standard measure for force and 1 N is defined as the force that, when acting on a 1 kg mass, produces an acceleration of 1 ms^2.
2. As economists are fond of saying, "Prediction is difficult—especially when it's about the future."
3. 'Nonlinearly' simply means that the parts are constructed in a way such that the output from one particular part is not necessarily proportionate to its input. The weather system is an oft cited example in which small additions of energy don't necessarily lead to small changes in the system's behavior.

4. The Game-of-Life offers an entertaining way to learn a great deal about complex systems dynamics, and to begin to develop a deep appreciation for the systems view of the world.
5. This statement risks conflating the concept of incompressibility with the problem of identifying a bounded description of a complex system. These two concerns are not equivalent; just because a particular system cannot be bounded easily is not what incompressibility is all about. Incompressibility derives from the interacting nonlinear feedback loops that exist even in well bounded complex systems, i.e., a bounded complex system is still incompressible.

REFERENCES

Allingham, M. (2002). *Choice theory: A very short introduction*. Oxford: Oxford University Press.

Bilke, S. & Sjunnesson, F. (2002). Stability of the Kauffman model. *Physical Review E*, *65*(2:1), 016129.1–016129.5.

Cilliers, P. (2005). Knowing complex systems. In K.A. Richardson (Ed.), *Managing organizational complexity: Philosophy, theory, and application* (pp. 7–19). Greenwich, CT: Information Age Publishing.

Cellular Automata. (2009). Wikipedia: Celluar Automata. Retrieved October 24, 2009 from http://en.wikipedia.org/wiki/Cellular_automaton

Cohen, J. (2002). Posting to the Complex-M listserv, 2nd September.

Crystal balls-up. (2003, August 7th). *Economist*, Retrieved November 11, 2009 from http://www.economist.com/.

Emmeche, C., Köppe, S. & Stjernfelt, F. (2000). Levels, emergence, and three versions of downward causation. In P.B. Andersen, C. Emmeche, N.O. Finnemann, & P.V. Christiansen (Eds.), *Downward Causation*. Aarhus, Netherlands: Aarhus University Press.

Expert, *n.* (2009). *Oxford English Dictionary* (online edition), Retrieved November 11, 2009 from http://www.oed.com/.

Flood, R. L. (1995). Total systems intervention (TSI): A reconstitution. *Journal of the Operational Research Society, 46,* 174–191.

Game-of-Life. (2009).Wikipedia: Game-of-Life. Retrieved October 24, 2009 from http://en.wikipedia.org/wiki/Conway%27s_Game_of_Life.

Horgan, J. (1997). Why I think science is ending. Retrieved October 24, 2009 from http://www.edge.org/documents/archive/edge16.html.

Jackson, M. C. & Keys, P. (1984). Towards a system of systems methodologies. *Journal of Operational Research Society, 35,* 473–486.

Kelly, G. (1992). *The psychology of personal constructs*. New York: Routledge. (Original work published 1955)

Maxwell, N. (2000). A new conception of science, *Physics World*, August, 17–18.

McMorland J., & Piggot-Irvine E. (2000). Facilitation as midwifery: Facilitation and praxis in group learning. *Systemic Practice and Action Research, 13*(2), 121–138.

Midgley, G. (2000). *Systemic intervention: Philosophy, methodology, and practice*. New York: Kluwer Academic / Plenum Publishers.

Reckoning trouble. (2003, August 7th). *Economist*, Retrieved November 11, 2009 from http://www.economist.com/.

Richardson, K.A. (2004, January). *On the relativity of recognizing the products of emergence and the nature of physical hierarchy*. Paper presented at the Second Biennial International Seminar on the Philosophical, Epistemological and Methodological Implications of Complexity Theory, Havana, Cuba.

Richardson, K.A. (2005). Simplifying Boolean networks. *Advances in Complex Systems*, *8*(4), 365–381.

Richardson, K.A., Tait, A., Roos, J., & Lissack, M.R. (2005). The coherent management of complex projects and the potential role of group decision support systems. In K.A. Richardson (Ed.), *Managing organizational complexity: Philosophy, theory, and application* (pp. 433–458). Greenwich, CT: Information Age Publishing.

Shneiderman, B. (2008). Science 2.0, *Science*, *319*(5868), 1349–1350.

Waters, R. (1992). Perfect Sense, Part I. On *Amused to Death*. UK: Sony.

Weinberg, G. (1975). *An introduction to general systems thinking*. New York: John Wiley.

Wikipedia (2009). "Newton's laws of motion," Retrieved November 11, 2009 from http://en.wikipedia.org/wiki/Newton's_laws_of_motion.

Wilbur, K. (2000). *A theory of everything: An integral vision for business, politics, science, and spirituality*. Boston, MA: Shambhala.

CHAPTER 3

THE EMERGENCE OF KNOWLEDGE IN ORGANIZATIONS[1]

Ralph Stacey

This chapter argues for a particular way of interpreting analogies from the complexity sciences as the basis for a perspective on knowledge creation in organizations called complex responsive processes of relating (Stacey, 2000; Stacey, Griffin, & Shaw, 2001; Stacey, 2001). From this perspective, knowledge is continuously reproduced and potentially transformed in processes of interaction between people. It follows that people cannot "share" knowledge, because one cannot share the actions of relating to others, only perform them. It also follows that knowledge as such is not stored anywhere. All that can be stored is reifications in the form of artifacts, or tools, which can only become knowledge when used in communicative interaction between people.

It becomes impossible to talk about measuring knowledge as "intellectual capital," because knowledge itself does not exist in measurable or any other reified form. Indeed, putting the words "intellectual" and "capital" together makes little sense. The notion put forward by some (for example, Roos, Roos, Dragonetti, & Edvinsson, 1997; Sveiby, 1997) that an organiza-

Complexity and Knowledge Management, pages 41–56
Copyright © 2010 by Information Age Publishing
All rights of reproduction in any form reserved.

tion can own "intellectual capital," that is, can own the attitudes, competence, and intellectual agility of individuals, becomes highly dubious, since
no one can own relationships. The conclusion is that while it is possible to
nurture knowledge, it is impossible to "manage" it, when "manage" is understood in its conventional sense.

The chapter first highlights the central concepts of mainstream thinking about knowledge creation and management in organizations, and then
outlines the perspective of complex responsive processes of relating.

MAINSTREAM THINKING ABOUT KNOWLEDGE CREATION IN ORGANIZATIONS

"Mainstream thinking" is a term used in this chapter to indicate the key
concepts to be found in the most quoted writings on organizational learning and knowledge creation (Senge, 1990; Nonaka & Takeuchi, 1995).
These writings in turn locate their theoretical frameworks in systems dynamics (Forrester, 1961, 1969, 1971; Meadows, 1982), sender–receiver
models of knowledge transmission from information theory (Shannon &
Weaver, 1949), distinctions between tacit and explicit knowledge (Polanyi,
1958, 1960), notions of individual mental models, single- and double-loop
learning (Bateson, 1973; Argyris & Schon, 1978; Argyris, 1990), and dialog
as a special form of communication (Bohm, 1965, 1983). These concepts
are to be found in most of the literature on knowledge management (for
example, Burton-Jones, 1999; Davenport & Prusak, 1998; Kleiner & Roth,
1997; Leonard & Strauss, 1997; Sveiby, 1997; Quinn, Anderson, & Finkelstein, 1996; Garvin, 1993; Brown, 1991).

Throughout the above body of work, the individual and the collective—
such as the group, the organization, and society—are always treated as two
distinct phenomenal levels requiring different explanations of how learning and knowledge creation take place. The connection between the two
levels is usually understood to lie in the interaction of individuals to create
the level of group/organization, which then constitutes the context influencing how individuals interact. It is usually explicitly stated that it is individuals who learn and create knowledge, although this is almost always
coupled with an emphasis on the importance of the teams within which this
takes place. A key question then becomes whether a team, group, or organization can be said to learn, or whether it is just their individual members
who do so. In mainstream thinking, in the end, it is usually individuals who
learn and create knowledge, and the principal concern from an organizational perspective is how that individual learning and knowledge might be
shared across an organization, and how it might be captured, stored, and
retained by the organization. Sometimes, the group/social level is treated

as a kind of transcendental group mind, common pool of meaning, or flow of a larger intelligence, for example in Bohm's notion of dialog.

Mainstream thinking assumes that individuals communicate by transmitting signals to each other, and a distinction is usually drawn between transmissions of data, information, knowledge, insight, and wisdom, all as the basis of action (for example, see Davenport & Prusak, 1998). As regards the transmission of knowledge, the distinction between explicit and tacit knowledge (Nonaka& Takeuchi, 1995) is thought to be particularly important. Explicit knowledge is systematic and easily transmitted from one person to another in the form of language. Tacit knowledge takes the form of mental models below the level of awareness and is displayed as skill or "know-how." Mental models are representations of the world and the individual in that world, which are historically determined by the experience of the individual. New knowledge is said to come from tapping the tacit knowledge located in individual heads, and this process of tapping is understood as one of translating the tacit knowledge in individual heads into explicit forms available to the organization. However, the process of translation does not explain how completely new tacit knowledge comes to arise in individual heads; for an approach claiming to explain the creation of knowledge, this is a major limitation. As knowledge is dispersed through an organization by the movement between tacit and explicit, it must be tested, which requires discussion, dialog, and disagreement.

This is where it becomes important to work and learn in teams. The knowledge, information, and data that individuals transmit to each other become shared routines; that is, they are stored in the form of culture, social structure, organizational procedures, traditions, habits, and group norms. This constitutes a level above that of the individual, which forms the social context within which individuals live, act, and relate to each other. In mainstream thinking, then, there is a circular, systemic interaction between individuals at one level and the group/organization/society at a higher level. The nature of this circular interaction is considered to be of central importance to the possibility of learning and knowledge creation. It is widely held that effective learning and knowledge creation require widespread sharing of values having to do with openness, trust, affirmation, dialog, and empowerment. The effectiveness of these processes is also said to require particular forms of leadership that establish values of this kind and provide a central vision to guide the learning and knowledge creation process.

Mainstream thinking is, therefore, firmly based in systems thinking and an understanding of mind drawn from cognitivist psychology, which holds mind to be a computing function of the brain (McCullough & Pitts, 1943; Gardner, 1885).

Over the past few years, developments in the natural complexity sciences (particularly Kauffman, 1995; Gell-Mann, 1994; Holland, 1998) have attracted the attention of some writers concerned with organizational knowledge. The tendency, however, is to regard the complexity sciences as an extension of systems thinking (for example, Nonaka & Takeuchi, 1995; Boisot, 1998). It can be argued that this interpretation of the complexity sciences does not lead to any significant change in the underlying frame of reference described above (see Stacey, Griffin, & Shaw, 2001). Consider now an alternative way of drawing on insights from the complexity sciences.

ANALOGIES FROM THE COMPLEXITY SCIENCES

Most systems theories envisage the systemic unfolding of that which is already enfolded, usually by a designer, in the definition or identification of the system itself. In other words, the system unfolds mature forms of an identity that is already there in some embryonic sense. This offers the prospect of control from outside the system, by a designer, and any transformation of the system's identity must also be determined from outside by a designer. However, at least some of those modeling complex adaptive systems (for example, Kauffman, 1995) are trying to simulate evolution as an internal dynamic that expresses identity and difference at the same time. When this process of evolution is modeled as a "system" of interacting entities, that "system" has a life of its own, rendering it much less susceptible to control from outside, if at all.

However, extreme care needs to be taken in using such modeling as a source domain for analogies with human action. The very act of modeling requires an external modeler, and the specification of the model requires the initial design of a system, even though what is being modeled is an evolutionary process that is supposed not to depend on any outside design. When one turns to this work as a source domain for human action, therefore, it is important to realize that there is no analogy in human action for the external designer, programmer, or model builder.

Furthermore, if one takes the "model" or the "system" as the analogy for human interaction, one reifies human interaction and implies that one can stand outside of it and observe it. However, as a human, one can never stand outside of human interaction, since the very act of observing others interacting is itself an interaction. Systems thinkers have tried to deal with this problem by widening the boundary of the system to include the observer, but in doing so they always locate some kind of agency outside the boundary. For example, an observer including himself in the system is then observing himself observing. The argument leads to infinite regress (see Stacey, Griffin, & Shaw, 2001). When one focuses attention on the "system," one tends to lose sight of centrality of the process of interaction, which perpetually constructs itself as continuity and transformation.

It follows, therefore, that there is no analogy in human action for the "system." Instead, it is the process of interaction in the simulation that provides an analogy for human action (Stacey, 2001). Although scientists who work with the concept of complex adaptive systems are clearly doing so within a systems framework, they are modeling processes that display the internal capacity to produce coherence spontaneously, as continuity and transformation, solely through local interaction in the absence of any blueprint or external designer. This work demonstrates the possibility that processes of interaction in local situations have the intrinsic capacity for patterning themselves as continuity and transformation at the same time. It is this insight that holds out the prospect of a different way of thinking about knowledge creation in organizations.

Nevertheless, the modeling of abstract interactive processes cannot directly say anything about human acting and knowing. It requires imagination to avoid thinking about the abstract model from an external perspective as a system and to think, instead, about what the modeling of interaction might be saying from a perspective within that interaction. It is for this reason that complexity theories cannot simply be applied to human action; they can only serve as a source domain for analogies with it. Furthermore, the models of complex adaptive systems are nothing more than abstract sets of relationships demonstrating possible properties of those relationships. The abstract relationships are completely devoid of the attributes of any real processes and, therefore, their use as analogies requires imaginative acts of translation if they are to say anything about real processes.

This chapter suggests that human interaction is analogous to the abstract interaction modeled by complex adaptive systems. The suggestion is that human relating intrinsically patterns living human experience as the coherence of continuity and transformation. This coherence is meaning, that is, knowledge emerging in the living present in local interactions without any global blueprint, plan, or vision.

MODELING INTERACTION IN THE MEDIUM OF DIGITAL SYMBOLS

The action of complex adaptive systems is explored using computer simulations in which each agent is a computer program, that is, a set of interaction rules expressed as computer instructions. Since each instruction is a bit string, a sequence of symbols taking the form of 0s and 1s, it follows that an agent is a sequence of symbols, arranged in a particular pattern specifying a number of algorithms. These algorithms determine how the agent will interact with other agents, which are also arrangements of symbols. In other words, the model is simply a large number of symbol patterns arranged so that they interact with each other. It is this local interaction between symbol patterns that organizes the pattern of interaction itself, since there is no set of instructions organizing the global pattern of interaction. The programmer specifies the initial symbol patterns; then the computer program is run and the patterns of interaction are observed. Simulations of this kind demonstrate the possibility of symbolic interaction, in the medium of digital symbols arranged to algorithmic rules, patterning itself.

For example, in his Tierra simulation, Ray (1992) designed one bit string, one symbol pattern, consisting of 80 instructions specifying how the bit string was to copy itself. He introduced random mutation into the replication and limited the computer time available for replicating as a selection criterion. In this way, he introduced chance, or instability, into the replicating process and imposed conditions that both enabled and constrained that process. This instability within constraints made it possible for the interaction to generate novel attractors. The first attractor was that of exponentially increasing numbers of individual symbol patterns, which eventually imposed a constraint on further replication. The global pattern was a move from sparse occupation of the computer memory to overcrowding. However, during this process, the individual symbol patterns were gradually changing through random bit flipping, thus coming to differ from each other. Eventually, distinctively different kinds of symbol patterns emerged, namely, long ones and short ones. The constraints on computer time favored smaller ones, so that the global pattern shifted from one of exponential increase, to one of stable numbers of long bit strings, to one of decline in long strings accompanied by an increase in short ones. The model spontaneously produced a new attractor, one that had not been programmed in.

In other words, new forms of individual symbol patterns and new overall global patterns emerged at the same time, since there can be no global pattern of increase and decline without simultaneous change in the length of individual bit strings, and there can be no sustained change in individual bit string lengths without the overall pattern of increase and decline. Individual symbol patterns, and the global pattern, are forming and being formed by each other, at the same time. To repeat, the new attractor is evident both at the level of the whole population and at the level of the individual bit strings themselves at the same time.

Furthermore, the new attractors are not designed but emerge as self-organization, where it is not individual agents that are organizing themselves but, rather, the pattern of interaction, and it is doing so simultaneously at the level of the individuals and the population as a whole. It is problematic to separate them out as levels, since they are emerging simultaneously. No individual bit string can change in a coherent fashion on its own, since random mutation in an isolated bit string would eventually lead to a completely random one. In interaction with other bit strings, however, advantageous mutations are selected and the others are weeded out. What is organizing itself, through interaction between symbol patterns, is then changes in the symbol patterns themselves. Patterns of interacting are turning back on themselves, imperfectly replicating themselves, to yield changes in those patterns of interaction.

Ray, the objective observer external to this system, then interpreted the changes in symbol patterns in his simulation in terms of biology, and in particular, the evolution of life. Using the model as an analogy, he argued that life has evolved in a similar self-organizing and emergent manner. Other simulations have been used to suggest that this kind of emerging new attractor occurs only at the edge of chaos where there is a paradoxical pattern of both stability and instability at the same time.

The computer simulations thus demonstrate the possibility of digital symbols self-organizing, that is, interacting locally in the absence of a global blueprint, in the dynamics at the edge of chaos to produce emergent attractors of a novel kind, provided that the symbol patterns are richly connected and diverse enough. Natural scientists at the Santa Fe Institute and elsewhere then use this demonstration of possibility in the medium of digital symbols as a source of analogy to provide explanations of phenomena in particular areas of interest such as biology. The interaction between patterns of digital symbols can also provide an abstract analogy for human interaction, if that interaction is understood from the perspective of Mead's thought on mind, self, and society.

MEAD'S THEORY OF THE EVOLUTION OF MIND, SELF, AND SOCIETY

For Mead (1934), human societies are not possible without human minds, and human minds are not possible in the absence of human societies.

Humans must cooperate to survive, and they also have an intense, intrinsic need for relationship and attachment to others. Indeed, the human brain seems to be importantly shaped by the experience of attachment (Schore, 1994, 1997). Mead therefore sought an explanation of how mind and society, that is, cooperative interaction, evolved together.

He adopted a phenomenological, action-based account of how mind and society might have evolved from the interactive behavior of the higher mammals. He pointed to how dogs relate to each other in a responsive manner, with the act of one fitting into the act of the other, in aggressive or submissive interactions. One dog might make the gesture of a snarl and this might call forth a counter snarl on the part of the other, which means a fight, or it might call forth a crouching movement, which means submission. In other words, the gesture of one animal calls forth a response from another, and together gesture and response constitute a social act, which is meaning. This immediately focuses on interaction, that is, a rudimentary form of social behavior, and on knowing and knowledge as properties of interaction, or relationship. Meaning does not first arise in an individual and is then expressed in action, nor is it transmitted from one individual to another. Rather, meaning emerges in the interaction between them. Meaning is not attached to an object, or stored, but repeatedly created in the interaction.

Mead described the gesture as a symbol in the sense that it is an action that points to a meaning. However, the meaning could not be located in the symbol taken on its own. The meaning only becomes apparent in the response to the gesture and therefore lies in the whole social act of gesture–response. The gesture, as symbol, points to how the meaning might emerge in the response. Here, meaning is emerging in the action of the living present, in which the immediate future (response) acts back on the past (gesture) to change its meaning. Meaning is not simply located in the past (gesture) or the future (response), but in the circular interaction between the two in the living present. In this way the present is not simply a point but has a time structure. Every gesture is a response to some previous gesture, which is a response to an even earlier one, thereby constructing history.

This process of gesture and response between biological entities in a physical context constitutes simple cooperative social activity of a mindless, reflex kind. The "conversation of gestures" is both enabling and constraining at the same time, and it constitutes meaning, although animals acting in this meaningful way are not aware of the meaning. At this stage, meaning is implicit in the social act itself, and those acting are unaware of that implicit meaning.

Mead argued that humans must have evolved from mammals with similar rudimentary social structures to those found in present-day mammals. The mammal ancestors of humans evolved central nervous systems that enabled them to gesture to others in a manner that was capable of calling forth in themselves a range of responses similar to those called forth in those to whom they were gesturing. This would happen if, for example, the snarl of one called forth in itself the fleeting feelings associated with counter snarl and crouching posture, just as they did in the one to whom the gesture of snarl was being made. The gesture, as symbol, now has a substantially different role, namely, that of a significant symbol, which is one that calls forth a similar response in the gesturer as in the one to whom it is directed. Significant symbols, therefore, make it possible for the gesturer to "know" what he is doing.

This simple idea is a profound insight. If, when one makes a gesture to another, one is able to experience in one's own body a similar response to that which the gesture provokes in another body, then one can "know" what one is doing. It becomes possible to intuit something about the range of likely responses from the other. This ability to experience in the body something similar to that which another body experiences in response to a gesture becomes the basis of knowing and of consciousness. Mead suggested that the central nervous system, or better still the biologically evolved whole body, has the capacity to call forth in itself feelings that are similar to those experienced by other bodies. The body, with its nervous system, becomes central to understanding how animals "know" anything.

The neuroscientist Damasio (1994, 1999) argues that the human brain continuously monitors and integrates the rhythmical activity of the heart, lungs, gut, muscles, and other organs, as well as the immune, visceral, and other systems in the body. At each moment the brain is registering the internal state of the body, and Damasio argues that these body states constitute feelings. This continuous monitoring activity, that is, registration of feeling states, is taking place as a person selectively perceives external objects, such as a face or an aroma, and experience then forms an association between the two. Every perception of an object outside the body is associated, through acting into the world, with particular body states, that is, patterns of feeling. When a person encounters situations similar to previous ones, he or she experiences similar feeling states, or body rhythms, which orient the way that person acts in the situation. In this way, human worlds become affect-laden, and the feeling states unconsciously narrow down the options to be considered in a situation. In other words, feelings unconsciously guide choice, and when the capacity to feel is damaged, so is the capacity to select sensible action options rapidly. Damasio suggests that, from a neurological standpoint, the body's monitoring of its own rhythmic patterns is both the ground for its construction of the world into which it acts and its unique sense of subjectivity.

Possessing this capacity, the maker of a gesture can intuit, perhaps even predict, the consequences of that gesture. In other words, they can know what they are doing, just before the other responds. The whole social act, that is, meaning, can be experienced in advance of carrying out the whole act, opening up the possibility of reflection and choice in making a gesture. Furthermore, the one responding has the same opportunity for reflecting on, and so choosing from, the range of responses. The first part of a gesture can be taken by the other as an indication of how further parts of the gesture will unfold from the response. In this way, the two can indicate to each other how they might respond to each other in the continuous circle in which a gesture by one calls forth a response from the other, which is itself a gesture back to the first. Obviously, this capacity makes more sophisticated forms of cooperation possible.

The capacity to call forth the same response in oneself as in the other is thus a rudimentary form of awareness, or consciousness, and together with meaning, emerges in the social conversation of gestures. At the same time as the emergence of conscious meaning, there also emerges the potential for more sophisticated cooperation. Human social forms and human consciousness thus both emerge at the same time, each forming and being formed by the other at the same time, and there cannot be one without the other. As individuals interact with each other in this way, the possibility arises of a pause before making a gesture. In a kind of private role-play, emerging in the repeated experience of public interaction, one individual learns to take the attitude of the other, enabling a kind of trial run in advance of actually completing or even starting the gesture.

In this way, rudimentary forms of thinking develop, taking the form of private role-playing, that is, gestures made by a body to itself, calling forth responses in itself. Mead said that humans are fundamentally role-playing animals. He then argued that the gesture that is particularly useful in calling forth the same attitude in oneself as in the other is the vocal gesture. This is because we can hear the sounds we make in much the same way as others hear them, while we cannot see the facial gestures we make as others see them, for example. The development of more sophisticated patterns of vocal gesturing, that is, of the language form of significant symbols, is thus of major importance in the development of consciousness and of sophisticated forms of society. Mind and society emerge together in the medium of language.

However, since speaking and listening are actions of bodies, and since bodies are never without feelings, the medium of language is also always the medium of feelings. Furthermore, the public and private role-plays, or conversations, which constitute the experience of the interacting individuals, actually shape the patterns of connections in the plastic brains of each (Freeman, 1995). Both public and private conversations are shaping, while being shaped by, the spatio-temporal patterns of brain and body. This simultaneous public and private conversation of gestures takes place in the medium of significant symbols, particularly those of language, and it is this capacity for symbolic mediation of cooperative activity that is one of the key features distinguishing humans from other animals.

As soon as one can take the attitude of the other, that is, as soon as one can communicate in significant symbols, there is at least a rudimentary form of consciousness. In other words, one can "know" the potential consequences of one's actions. The nature of the social has thus shifted from mindless cooperation to mindful, role-playing interaction, made more and more sophisticated by the use of language. Meaning is now particularly constituted in gesturing and responding in the medium of vocal symbols, that is, conversation. Mind, or consciousness, is the gesturing and responding action of a body directed toward itself as private role-play and silent conversation, and society is the gesturing and responding actions of bodies directed toward each other. Conversational relating between people is the process in which meaning, that is, knowledge, perpetually emerges.

As more and more interactions are experienced with others, so, increasingly, more roles and wider ranges of possible responses enter into the role-playing activity that is continuously intertwined with public gesturing and responding. In this way, the capacity to take the attitude of many others evolves, and this becomes generalized. Each engaged in the conversation of gestures can now take the attitude of what Mead calls the generalized other. Eventually, individuals develop the capacity to take the attitude of the whole group, that is, the social attitude, as they gesture and respond. The result is much more sophisticated processes of cooperative interaction.

The next step in this evolutionary process is the linking of the attitude of specific and generalized others, even of the whole group, with a "me." In other words, there evolves a capacity to take the attitude of others not just toward one's gestures but also toward oneself. The "me" is the configuration of the gestures/responses of the others/society to one as a subject, or an "I." What has evolved here is the capacity to be an object to oneself, a "me," and this is the capacity to take the attitude of the group, not simply to one's gestures, but to oneself. A self, as the relationship between "me" and "I," has therefore emerged, as well as an awareness of that self, that is, self-consciousness. Mead argued that this "I" response to the "me" is not a given but is always potentially unpredictable, in that there is no predetermined way in which the "I" might respond to the "me." In other words, each of us may respond in many different ways to our perception of the views that others have of us.

Here, Mead is pointing to the importance of difference, or diversity, in the emergence of the new, that is, in the potential for transformation. In addition to Mead's argument, one could understand the response as simultaneously called forth by the gesture of the other and selected or enacted by the responder. In other words, the response of the "I" is both being called forth by the other and being enacted, or selected by the history—biological, individual, and social—of the responder. Your gesture calls forth a response in me, but only a response that I am capable of making, and that depends on my history. This adds a constructivist dimension to Mead's argument, suggesting a paradoxical movement in the response of selection/enactment and evocation/provocation at the same time. In this way, the reproduction and potential transformation of historical responses in the living present are held in tension with the reproduction and potential transformation of evocation.

The social, in human terms, is a highly sophisticated process of cooperative interaction between people in the medium of symbols in order to undertake joint action. Such sophisticated interaction could not take place without self-conscious minds, but neither could those self-conscious minds exist without that sophisticated form of cooperation. In other words, there could be no private role-play, including silent conversation, by a body with itself, if there were no public interaction of the same form. Mind/self and society are all logically equivalent processes of a conversational kind.

However, the symbolic processes of mind/self are always actions, experienced within a body as rhythmic variations, that is, feeling states. Mind is the action of the brain, rather like walking is the action of the body. One would not talk about walking emerging from the body, and it is no more appropriate to talk about mind emerging from the brain. Note how the private role-play, including the silent conversation of mind/self, is not stored as representations of a pre-given reality. It is, rather, continuous spontaneous action, in which patterns of action are continuously reproduced in repetitive forms as continuity, sameness, and identity, and simultaneously as potential transformation of that identity. In other words, as with interaction between bodies (the social), so with interaction of a body with itself (the mind); there is the experience of both familiar repetition of habit and the potential of spontaneous change. The process is not representing or storing, but continuously reproducing and creating new meaningful experience. In this way, the fundamental importance of the individual self and identity is retained, along with the fundamental importance of the social. In this way, too, both continuity and potential transformation are always simultaneously present. Furthermore, there is no question of individuals at one level and the social at another. They are both at the same ontological level.

THE CONNECTION WITH THE COMPLEXITY SCIENCES

The process of interaction between people is a continuous circular one that takes place in the medium of embodied symbols—for example, in sounds called words. However, as one imagines such interaction between larger and larger numbers of individuals, one wonders how any kind of global coherence could arise in such huge numbers of local interactions. This is not an issue with which Mead dealt, but it is one where the complexity sciences offer important insights.

Some of the work in the complexity sciences explores the properties of abstract models of continuous circular processes of interaction between computer programs in the medium of digital symbols. It is possible that certain properties of interaction demonstrated in the abstract models might, therefore, offer analogies for human interaction, interpreted through Mead's thought. The modeling of complex interactions demonstrates the possibility that interactions between large numbers of entities, each entity responding to others on the basis of its own local organizing principles, can produce coherent patterns with the potential for novelty in certain conditions, namely, the paradoxical dynamics at the edge of chaos.

In other words, the very process of self-organizing interaction, when sufficiently richly connected, has the inherent capacity to spontaneously produce coherent pattern in itself, without any blueprint or program. Furthermore, when the interacting entities are different enough from each other, that capacity is one of spontaneously producing novel patterns in itself. In other words, abstract interactions can pattern themselves where those patterns have the paradoxical feature of continuity and novelty, identity and difference, at the same time.

By analogy, the circular process of gesturing and responding between people who are different to one another can be thought of as self-organizing relating in the medium of symbols having intrinsic patterning capacity. In other words, patterns of relating in local situations in the living present can produce emergent global patterns in the absence of any global blueprint. And emergent patterns can constitute both continuity and novelty, both identity and difference, at the same time. This is what is meant by a complex responsive process of relating and it amounts to a particular causal framework, where the process is one of perpetual construction of the future as both continuity and potential transformation at the same time. Individual mind and social relating are patterning processes in bodily communicative interaction, forming and being formed by themselves.

The complex responsive process of relating perspective, then, is one in which the individual, the group, the organization, and the society are all the same kinds of phenomena, at the same ontological level. The individual mind/self is an interactive role-playing process conducted privately and silently in the medium of symbols by a body with itself, and the group, organization, and society are all also interactive processes in the medium of the same symbols, this time publicly and often vocally between different bodies. The individual and the social, in this scheme, simply refer to the degree of detail in which the whole process is being examined. They are fractal processes.

Culture and social structure are usually thought of as repetitive and enduring values, beliefs, traditions, habits, routines, and procedures. From the complex responsive process perspective, these are all social acts of a particular kind. They are couplings of gesture and response of a predictable, highly repetitive kind. They do not exist in any meaningful way in a store anywhere, but, rather, they are continually reproduced in the interaction between people. However, even habits are rarely exactly the same. They may often vary as those with whom one interacts change and as the context of that interaction changes. In other words, there will usually be some spontaneous variation in the repetitive reproduction of patterns called habits.

These habits and routines, values, and beliefs are not at some higher onto-logical level. They are part of the pattern of interaction between people.

Furthermore, there is no requirement here for any sharing of mental contents, or any requirement that people should be engaging in the same private role-plays. The only requirement for the social, understood as hab-its, routines, and so on, is that people should be acting them out.

Systems, databases, recorded and written artifacts are usually thought of as stores of knowledge. From the complex responsive process perspective, they are simply records that can only become knowledge when people use them as tools in their processes of gesturing and responding to each other. What is captured in these artifacts is inevitably something about the mean-ings of social acts already performed. Since a social act is ephemeral and since knowledge is social acts, it can never be stored or captured. Habits here are understood not as shared mental contents but as history-based, repetitive actions, both private and public, reproduced in the living present with relatively little variation.

CONCLUSION

There are profound implications of this way of thinking for how one under-stands learning and knowledge creation in organizations. From mainstream perspectives, knowledge is thought to be stored in individual heads, largely in tacit form, and it can only become the asset of an organization when it is extracted from those individual heads and stored in some artifact as explicit knowledge. From a complex responsive process perspective, knowledge is always a process of responsive relating, which cannot be located simply in an individual head, then to be extracted and shared as an organizational as-set. Knowledge is the act of conversing, and new knowledge is created when ways of talking, and therefore patterns of relationship, change.

Knowledge, in this sense, cannot be stored, and attempts to store it in artifacts of some kind will capture only its more trivial aspects. The knowl-edge assets of an organization then lie in the pattern of relationships be-tween its members and are destroyed when those relational patterns are destroyed. Knowledge is, therefore, the thematic patterns organizing the experience of being together. It is meaningless to ask how tacit knowledge is transformed into explicit knowledge, since unconscious and conscious themes organizing experience are inseparable aspects of the same process. Organizational change, learning, and knowledge creation are the same as change in communicative interaction, whether people are conscious of it or not. This perspective suggests that the conversational life of people in an organization is of primary importance in the creation of knowledge.

NOTE

1. This chapter is based on Stacey (2001).

REFERENCES

Argyris, C. (1990). *Overcoming Organizational Defenses: Facilitating Organizational Learning.* Needham Heights, MA: Allyn and Bacon.

Argyris, C. & Schon, D. (1978). *Organizational learning: A theory of action perspective.* Reading, MA: Addison Wesley.

Bateson, G. (1973). *Steps to an ecology of mind.* St Albans, UK: Paladin.

Bohm, D. (1965). *The special theory of relativity.* New York: W. A. Benjamin.

Bohm, D. (1983). *Wholeness and the implicate order.* New York: Harper and Row.

Boisot, M. (1998). *Knowledge assets: Securing competitive advantage in the knowledge economy.* Oxford, UK: Oxford University Press.

Brown, J. S. (1991). Research that reinvents the corporation. *Harvard Business Review,* Jan–Feb., 97–107.

Burton-Jones, A. (1999). *Knowledge capitalism: Business, work and learning in the new economy.* Oxford, UK: Oxford University Press.

Damasio, A. (1994). *Descartes' error: Emotion, reason and the human brain.* New York: Picador.

Damasio, A. (1999). *The feeling of what happens: Body and emotion in the making of consciousness.* London: Heinemann.

Davenport, T. H. & Prusak, L. (1998). *Working knowledge: How organizations manage what they know.* Cambridge, MA: Harvard University Press.

Forrester, J. (1961). *Industrial Dynamics.* Cambridge, MA: MIT Press.

Forrester, J. (1969). *Urban Dynamics.* Cambridge, MA: MIT Press.

Forrester, J. (1971). The counter intuitive behavior of social systems. *Technology Review,* Jan., 52–68.

Freeman, W. J. (1995). *Societies of brains: A study in the neuroscience of love and hate.* Hillsdale, NJ: Lawrence Erlbaum Associates.

Gardner, H. (1985). *The mind's new science: A history of the cognitive revolution.* New York: Basic Books.

Garvin, D. A. (1993). Building a learning organization. *Harvard Business Review,* July–Aug., 80–96.

Gell-Mann, M. (1994). *The quark and the jaguar.* New York: Freeman & Co.

Holland, J. H. (1998). *Emergence from chaos to order.* New York: Oxford University Press.

Kauffman, S. A. (1995). *At home in the universe.* New York: Oxford University Press.

Kleiner, A. & Roth, G. (1997). How to make experience your best teacher. *Harvard Business Review,* Sept–Oct., 172–177.

Leonard, D. & Strauss, S. (1997). Putting your company's whole brain to work. *Harvard Business Review,* July–Aug., 77–84.

McCulloch, W. S., & Pitts, W. (1943), A logical calculus of ideas imminent in nervous activity. *Bulletin of Mathematical Biophysics, 5,* 115–33.

Mead, G. H. (1934). *Mind, self and society*. Chicago: Chicago University Press.

Meadows, D. H. (1982). Whole earth models and system co-evolution. *Co-evolution Quarterly*, Summer, 98–108.

Nonaka, I. & Takeuchi, H. (1995). *The knowledge creating company: How Japanese companies create the dynamics of innovation*. New York: Oxford University Press.

Polanyi, M. (1958). *Personal knowledge*. Chicago: Chicago University Press.

Polanyi, M. (1960). *The tacit dimension*. London: Routledge and Kegan Paul.

Quinn, J. B., Anderson, P., & Finkelstein, S. (1996). Managing professional intellect: Making the most of the best. *Harvard Business Review*, March–April, 102–112.

Ray, T. S. (1992), An approach to the synthesis of life. In G. C. Langton, C. Taylor, J. Doyne Farmer, & S. Rasmussen (eds.), *Artificial Life II*, Santa Fé Institute, Studies in the Sciences of Complexity, vol. 10, Reading, MA: Addison-Wesley.

Roos, J., Roos, G., Dragonetti, N. C., & Edvinsson, L. (1997). *Intellectual capital: Navigating the new business landscape*. London: Macmillan.

Schore, A. N. (1994). *Affect regulation and the origin of the self: The neurobiology of emotional development*. Hillsdale, NJ: Lawrence Erlbaum Associates, Inc.

Schore, A. N. (1997). Early organization of the nonlinear right brain and development of a predisposition to psychotic disorder. *Development and Psychopathology*, *9*, 595–631.

Senge, P. (1990). *The fifth discipline: The art and practice of the learning organization*. New York: Doubleday.

Shannon, C. & Weaver, W. (1949). *The mathematical theory of communication*. Urbana, IL: University of Illinois Press.

Stacey, R. (2000). *Strategic management and organisational dynamics: The challenge of complexity*. London: Pearson Education.

Stacey, R. (2001). *Complex responsive processes in organizations: Learning and knowledge creation*. London: Routledge.

Stacey, R., Griffin, D., & Shaw, P. (2001). *Complexity and management: Fad or radical challenge to systems thinking?* London: Routledge.

Sveiby, K. E. (1997). *The new organizational wealth: Managing and measuring knowledge-based assets*. San Francisco: Berrett-Koehler.

SECTION 2

THE ROLE OF KNOWLEDGE IN SOCIAL NETWORKS

CHAPTER 4

STORIED SPACES

The Human Equivalent
of Complex Adaptive Systems

Ken Baskin

INTRODUCTION

On a flight to El Paso in 2006, two voices behind me, belonging to women in their early 40s, sounded like a couple of executives doing a corporate marketing exercise. They might have been asking, "So, if we increase gasoline prices three cents a gallon, how will that impact demand?" But no, they were talking about *The Book of Revelation*—the Apocalypse, the Rapture, and . . . how the war in Iraq fit in.

At first, I experienced an all-too-brief flush of superiority. After all, they were mixing two utterly different worlds—nearly 2,000-year-old Christian myth and a very real event, taking place as they spoke. Unlike me, I thought, they were living in a mythic world. But then I remembered a conversation I had with evolutionary biologist Jack Cohen in 2003. We don't experience life, he told me. We experience the stories we tell to explain what happens to us. Suddenly, my feeling of superiority melted away, and I realized that I was much more like those two women than I wanted to believe. All of us,

Complexity and Knowledge Management, pages 59–75
Copyright © 2010 by Information Age Publishing
All rights of reproduction in any form reserved.

including you, dear reader, experience life as a space defined by the stories we've accepted to explain the events that have happened, and continue to happen, around us.

In this chapter, I want to examine the nature of such "storied space." From my point of view, we human animals experience the world in terms of the stories that we believe tell us what "reality" is, stories that we ourselves co-create as we interact with others in our various social environments— families, organizations, professions, and so on—each of which functions as its own storied space. My purpose, then, is to explore the possibility that these storied spaces function as the human equivalent of complexity's complex adaptive systems. To do so, I shall analyze four issues:

- The function of storytelling in the world described in complexity thinking
- Storied space as the social ecosystem by which we humans have adapted to our world, whose dynamics are driven by the interaction between two types of stories—narrative, by which people describe the past, and antenarrative, by which they try to describe the present
- Two organizational examples of the dance that arises in that interaction and how our knowledge emerges from that dance
- Some of the implications of this conception of social environments as storied spaces, especially for organizational managers and consultants

The one perception I hope the reader will come away with is that every story we humans create to explain our world, even the most accurate and helpful in our lives, is *partial. No* story can be the *whole* story, The Truth. As a result, I'm acutely aware of a self-referential irony—that I am creating my own story about our use of stories to co-create our social worlds, a story which, in my own words, must be partial. So I offer this essay to you not as The Truth, but, rather, as my partial, not-quite-humble contribution to the ongoing discussion of social systems as complex entities.

COMPLEXITY AND INTERNAL STORYTELLING

When I was 25, I was furious with my mother and father for "parenting" me so badly. At the time, it was a very satisfying explanation for many of my life problems, but, eventually, I realized how oversimplified this linear explanation was. After all, if my parents were responsible for *my* difficulties in dealing with life, then *their* parents were responsible for those of my parents; my grandparents' parents were responsible for their difficulties; and the buck passed on, until I would have to blame about a tenth of the Jewish population of Central Europe. My parents' behaviors had also been shaped by any number of other factors—from their parents' being immigrants to the Great Depression and World War II; from the ideas of Newton and, then, those of Einstein to American Capitalism in the 20th century and the polio epidemic of the 1950s. I could go on and on. What had been a satisfying, simple story of my parents ruining my life was becoming a bewilderingly complex tapestry involving millions of people. Add to all this the multiple self-reinforcing feedback loops, blurring the distinction between cause and effect, and I was left with the world of complexity studies, where any event can be enmeshed with almost any other event *and* where new, unexpected things are continually emerging, much more like Chinese philosophy's world of "inherent causality" than that the cause-and-effect world of traditional Western science. (For a fuller examination of the similarities between Chinese philosophy and complexity thinking, see Baskin, 2007a).

Given such a world, dominated by interconnection, multiple causality, positive feedback loops, and emergence, the key challenge *any* complex system faces is "knowing" what to do to adapt to any situation. In living systems, as Plotkin (1993: 20–21) puts it, knowledge is "the relationship between the organization of *any* part of a living creature's body and particular aspects of order in the world outside that creature" (author's italics). He adds that living things adapt through their knowledge, thereby surviving. In the course of evolution, such adaptive structures have become increasingly varied. Bacteria have proteins that catch passing food molecules and drag them inside. Some flowers mimic the sexual parts of bees so those bees will fertilize them. Multi-cellular organisms eventually developed nervous systems, spinal chords, and the brain, from which mind emerged.

Mind and conscious learning distinguish human life and seem to make human social systems different from the complex adaptive systems of complexity studies, as Stacey (2001) notes. For me, the critical difference is the ability of human beings to tell stories, to imagine new futures, act on those stories, and change the world so that they can realize such futures. How critical is this ability? Fisher (1987) suggests that human beings are essentially story tellers, *Homo narrans*. Stewart and Cohen argue that the ability to tell the stories was so central to *Homo sapiens'* evolution that we should be called *Pan narrans,* the storytelling ape (Pratchett, Stewart, & Cohen, 2002: 325). I agree that this ability to tell stories is mankind's key survival strategy, but for an additional reason. Stories, it seems to me, enable us to reduce, internally, the complexity of the world around us in order to understand it enough to choose appropriate actions in response to what we are experiencing. This reduction of complexity, however, occurs only at the level of individuals. As Bahktin (1981) notes, we often incorporate misunderstandings of what others say and do in our storying of events. So, in our interaction with others, our storying of events, whose purpose is to reduce complexity for us, often ends up increasing complexity in our social environment. Boje's (1995) conception of the organization as Tamara, a house where people in different "rooms" story their common experiences differently and must then negotiate a shared reality, is an excellent example of human complexity.

What, then, do I mean by a story? In creating a story, the teller chooses and orders events for inclusion or exclusion, putting them in sequence and indicating cause-and-effect relationships. (Such stories can be fictional or constructed from life as we experience it. For the purposes of this chapter, I am ignoring fictional stories.) Each of us does this *unconsciously* hundreds, maybe thousands of times every day, as we interpret our world in order to respond. While storytelling may be highly self-conscious when performed for others, internal storying appears to be *pre-conscious*. Through the choices any of us make, the story becomes, as Bateson (1979: 14) put it, a "little knot" of relevance, providing the context with which we create meaning. Similarly, for Kaufmann (2000: 135), stories are "how we tell ourselves what happened and its significance." Thus, stories enable us to reduce the bewildering complexity of the external world to comprehensibility. Feyerabend (1993: 21) even defines scientific knowledge as "an ever increasing *ocean of mutually incompatible alternatives*, each single theory, each fairy-tale, each myth that is part of the collection forcing the other into greater articulation..." (author's italics). But stories are *always* reductions, and we can construct apparently incompatible stories from the same events. For Cohen (2003), this ability to create apparently contradictory meanings from the same reality is a central quality of all complex systems. Meaning emerges from the storyteller's particular choosing and sequencing of events. (See also Weick, 1995 or Boje, 2001.)

In this sort of personal, internal storytelling, we seem to be creating the human equivalent of the "schemas" that Gell-Mann (1994: 23–25) discusses in explaining how complex adaptive systems learn. Such schemas summarize previous data in order that the systems understand present data, determine appropriate behavior, and predict what the results of that behavior might be. These "real world" results act as feedback, or "selection pressures," on competing schemas, until one or more become dominant. Similarly, stories simplify the swirl of events in our environment (Gell-Mann refers to this task as "compression"), enabling us to choose behavior and predict how others will respond. These stories, by which we capture events around us, much like Boje's "antenarrative" (see below), are open to revision when their predictions are inaccurate. The stories that survive this human equivalent of Gell-Mann's "selection pressures" become the dominant narratives by which we live.

Much of the literature on the subject of storytelling—White and Epston (1990) in therapy, for example, or Weick (1995) in organizations—discusses it in terms of narrative "sensemaking," structuring events in order to make them sensible with a view toward past events that already make sense. While this may sound like my conception, the personal, internal storying I am talking about seems to be more fundamental. Human beings, I am convinced, transform events around them into stories unconsciously, *before* the attempt to make sense of them. Such storying is, for us, a biological imperative in a confusingly complex world. In Stewart and Cohen's words, "Our minds are too limited to grasp the world for what it is" (Pratchett et al., 2002: 326). Moreover, we tell stories not just to make sense of the world, but more importantly to help us *discover the actions we must take in order to survive.* Human beings are born knowing how to suck milk from their mothers' breasts. However, we have to learn how to gather, grow, or hunt our food; how to bring up our children; how to build our shelters. Stories enable people to perform all these activities essential for survival by distinguishing noise from information and then transforming information into the knowledge they need to survive in a continually changing world. This is the power of storytelling.

STORIED SPACES

Actually, it is only one of the powers of storytelling. Once we humans begin telling stories to others, something fascinating happens: By negotiating our stories at various levels of group experience—the family/small group, organization, market/profession, nation, religion, and civilization—we shape the world that we experience, creating a self-reinforcing feedback loop that enables us to define our stories as the whole story, The Truth. At all times and places, people in the thrall of such stories are able to justify almost any act. What the Crusaders of the 12th and 13th centuries, Torquemada's Inquisition, and today's Islamists have done to fulfill the stories of their "true" religions, the Germans and Japanese could do to fulfill their "true" national stories in World War II. People could commit these atrocities because, as human beings, they did not experience the world and events around them *except as interpreted through the storied space they co-created* to explain their lives.

The human ability to kill others, against whom we have no personal animosity, and do so on a terrifyingly large scale, *because we have accepted a story as The Truth,* may be the most dramatic example of how what we know—that is, what we accept as true beyond doubt—often depends on the stories negotiated in our social environments. Others, however, are so mundane that we never think about this relationship. For instance, the information that the sun appears most mornings on one side of the sky and disappears on the other has generated a variety of knowledge. At various times people have known that Apollo drives his chariot across the sky, that the sun rotates around the Earth, or that the Earth rotates around the sun. What determines their knowledge about this fact is whether they accepted the stories of Greek mythology, the Bible, or the Big Bang, respectively. For the most part, what anyone "knows" about any information appears to depend largely on the narrative, socially negotiated stories through which he or she processes that information. In the terms of this essay, our knowledge and experience of life depends largely on the storied spaces that we have co-created.

This "greater" storied space appears to be an intensely complex nested network of less inclusive storied spaces that function as the human equivalent of complexity study's complex adaptive systems. Such storied spaces form an intricate network of stories, knowing, and meaning, as powerful a constraint on our behavior, individually and collectively, as our physical environment, perhaps more so. This nested network of storied spaces includes the categories in Table 4.1.

All of these storied spaces are swirling, dynamic environments, much as Dervin's process of sense-making (Dervin, Foreman-Wernet, & Lauterback, 2003) or Boje's (1995) Tamara described them—the interactions grounded in different people telling different stories about the same events—a process whose products are forged in the inevitable conflict that occurs when people, with their varied functions, desires, and experiences, live and work together. Moreover, this network is powerfully complex because we can belong to so many different storied spaces—a family of origin and one's own family, a work group or two, a religious congregation, a political party, sports teams, the list goes on and on. Often, elements of some of these storied spaces can contradict those of others, as when I moved, about 30 years ago, from being a liberal member of academia to writing corporate public relations for an oil company.

The dynamics of such storied spaces arise is the interaction of two very different types of stories, which reflect Gell-Mann's theory (1994: 23–25) of how complex adaptive systems learn—that is, come to *know* about their environments. Gell-Mann suggested that complex adaptive systems learn through the way they process information. That is, they condense experi-

TABLE 4.1

Storied space	Adaptive behavior	Narrative
Small group/family	Dynamics	How we act together
Organization/community	Culture	How we "do things around here"
Market/profession	*Discourse*	How we perform specific tasks
Nation	Culture	How we behave together to survive
Religion/philosophy/science	*Episteme*	How we know

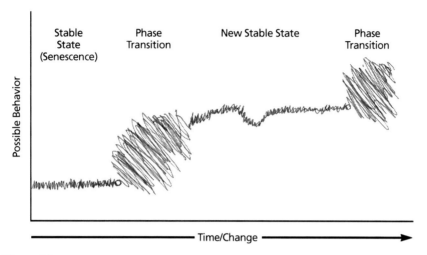

Figure 4.1

ence into "schemas," respond to new information by predicting from those schemas, observe the results, and either select effective schemas or generate new ones (learn). The first type of story is the narrative—the fixed accounts of past events, the historically grounded, control-oriented retellings, whose function in storied spaces is to keep our behavior congruent with ways that have always worked, much like complexity's attractors. I've depicted the life cycle of attractors in this Figure 4.1.

The stable state of any entity—from a pot of water to a rain forest ecosystem—is formed in the phase transition, where the entity's components explore their environment to discover which behaviors enable them to survive. When they find those behaviors, their interaction determines the attractor of their entity's stable state—that is, the limited number of all possible behaviors that become characteristic of it. Thus, water can be gas, liquid or solid, depending on its environment, but only one at a time. The stable state will adapt to changes in its environment until the point where its components become so interdependent that the system becomes unable to adapt—Salthe (1993) calls this "senescence"—and the system subsumes changes in the environment. Eventually, changes in the environment become so great that the system can no longer survive—its "bifurcation point"—and the system must either dissipate or go into another phase transition. This is essentially the pattern described by Gould (2002) as "punctuated equilibrium."

In any storied space, the dominant narrative resembles Gell-Mann's schemas, the models of the world that people accept as "true" and that drive the equivalent of attractors in human social systems. I have elsewhere examined (Baskin, 2007b) narrative in these terms as illustrated in Foucault's theory of the evolution of Western *episteme* and *discourse*. In a more personal example, my parents accepted, as part of their dominant narrative, that to succeed I would have to graduate college, and made significant sacrifices to help me do so. When, before the beginning of my sophomore year, I suggested taking a semester off, they objected and convinced me to continue college uninterrupted. On the other hand, by the time my son went to college, I had accepted the narrative that college would be a waste of time if he wasn't committed to it. (It helped that, unlike my parents, I knew about Bill Gates, Harvard dropout.) And when my son dropped out for lack of interest after his freshman year, I applauded, even though I wasn't sure why he had chosen to drop out. My mother, on the other hand, was appalled.

The tentative stories I told myself about my son's problems with college exemplify the second type of story, what Boje (2001) calls "antenarrative." (Boje uses this term because this type of story both comes before, Latin *ante*, narrative forms and because it is a bet, like an ante in poker, that it's possible to create meaning from an event.) Antenarrative is the flexible, ongoing attempt to explain what is currently happening, resembling the feedback of Gell-Mann's model, with which complex adaptive systems must compare their models so that they can learn as their environments change. In storied space, antenarrative provides flexible feedback to people about recent happenings that may call for behaviors quite different from those driven by their storied space's narratives. As Boje (2001) notes, traditional analysis of storytelling, starting with Aristotle, has focused on narrative. However, it is only through considering the interplay between the narratives and antenarratives in any storied space that we can come to understand its dynamics and, especially, its evolution.

What makes human social systems so complex are the dynamics that emerge as people behave as agents in an intricate nested network of storied spaces. For contrast, consider the dynamics of evolution in a natural ecosystem—the African savannah, for example. DNA is the biological equivalent of a dominant narrative, driving any animal's historically based attractor. Mutations on the molecular level in the DNA of, say, a tiger then act much like a biological antenarrative, enabling the tiger to adapt. If such a mutation increases the speed of the tiger and allows the tiger to hunt more successfully, that mutation is likely to be selected and, in time, all the tigers in the ecosystem are likely to become faster. That change will drive mutations in the species the tigers prey on. Those species that don't adapt may be hunted to extinction. Changes in those other species may also drive other adaptations across the ecosystem. In this way, the biological antenarrative of mutation in one species can drive changes in the DNA of many species and even shift the attractor of the ecosystem as a whole. This kind of co-evolution enables species throughout the ecosystem to survive until the ecosystem reaches a bifurcation point, the attractor for the ecosystem falls apart, and species across the ecosystem enter phase transition.

Humans, on the other hand, live in many small groups— families, work groups, sports teams, and club groups—which also exist in many organizations—businesses, religious congregations, political parties. Each of these organizations, in turn, must adapt to the market *discourses* in which they exist. And all of this is part of a national culture. Every one of these human systems has a dominant narrative that shapes the behaviors of all the people within them. As a result, each person must internalize a variety of small group dynamics and organizational cultures. Moreover, each person is continually creating antenarratives so that he or she can interpret events as they happen. Sometimes, these antenarratives fit neatly into existing dominant narratives. This is what Weick (1995) means by sensemaking. However, in other situations, events demand that people behave in ways that are not defined in their dominant narratives. If the dominant narratives do not offer ways for people to test antenarrative perceptions—as shaped, for instance, by their work group storied spaces—that do not fit with those narratives, then behavior is likely to become what is called "dysfunctional." Here I agree with family therapist Lynn Hoffman (2002). The word "dysfunctional," with its implication of illness, is misleading, because such behavior is not sickness, but *maladaptation.*

As long as the storied space in which a small group or organization exists remains in its stable-state attractor, such maladaptation is generally not dangerous. However, once a government or business, for instance, moves into phase transition, a dominant narrative that offers no way for people to enact their antenarratives can become dysfunctional and face extinction, as much as the tiger prey that cannot adapt to the tiger's increased speed.

To develop a deeper understanding of the dynamics of storied space and its relationship to how humans develop knowledge, I want to turn now to the example of organizations as storied spaces. In particular, I want to illustrate these dynamics in two organizations, both of which evolved recognizing the importance of technological antenarratives—Xerox and 3M.

THE DYNAMICS OF STORIED SPACE
IN TWO ORGANIZATIONS

If one views organizations as evolving storied spaces, they should be largely formed by dominant narratives (Gell-Mann's schema as organizational cultures), developed in its organization's phase transition (see Figure 4.1). Organizational culture should largely shape the behavior of its individuals, and it also reflects several levels of storied space—work groups, departments, divisions, and so on. In addition, organizations should function within the dominant narratives of their markets—such as oil, auto makers, and healthcare—and a variety of professions—accounting, marketing, and quality control, for instance. Because individuals in their work groups are continually providing antenarrative input, such organizations should be able to evolve through the dynamic interaction of their dominant narratives and antenarrative feedback, as their environments shift, *depending on their ability to listen to those antenarratives and enable their people to enact them so that they will learn what new products and services will succeed—that is, develop new organizational knowledge.*

To test this conception of organization, I would like to contrast two organizations—AT&T and 3M. Both companies are so well known that most Americans identify them by their initials, rather than their full names, American Telephone and Telegraph and Minnesota Mining and Manufacturing. The success of both depended on technological innovation. Over their histories, these two companies boasted a history of highly successful inventions—from transistors to solar voltaic cells and the Unix operating system at AT&T; from water-proof sandpaper to Scotchgard fabric protector and Post-it Notes at 3M. Yet, while the inventions from AT&T have been more technologically important and created the potential for far more value than those of 3M, it is 3M that has continued to evolve and adapt over the last 30 years, while AT&T repeatedly stumbled, eventually being acquired by SBC in 2005.

If the theory of organizations as one example of storied spaces presented in this essay is valid, it should offer a compelling explanation of why these two companies have performed as they did and why 3M was so much more effective in transforming its technological innovations into organizational knowledge. Such a consideration must examine: how the phase transition in which each company formed implied its dominant narrative/culture; how that narrative drove an attitude toward innovation as enacted technological antenarrative; and how changes in international markets, which became evident in the 1970s, drove 3M's continuing evolution and AT&T's ultimate failure.

AT&T

In 1878, two years after he'd demonstrated the first telephone, Alexander Graham Bell and his financiers tried to sell rights to his new invention to Western Union for $100,000. When Western Union refused, they created a company, initially National Bell Telephone Company, to market telephone service. In 1880, it became American Bell Telephone Company, and in 1885, it created a new company, American Telephone and Telegraph Company to provide long-distance service across the country. On the next to last day of 1899, AT&T bought American Bell for legal reasons just in time for the beginning of 1900.

For our purposes, and following the pattern depicted in Figure 4.1, the phase transition in which AT&T was formed lasted from 1878 to 1907, when company President Theodore Vail articulated his vision as "One Policy, One System, Universal Service." While this organizational narrative emphasized the vision of the persons at the top of the organization (Bell and Vail), it also recognized the critical importance of technological innovation, as one would expect. As early as 1881, the company had purchased a controlling share of Western Electric Co. in order to manufacture its own equipment. Then, in 1913, AT&T bought Lee DeForest's patents for the vacuum tube. By 1918, the company's annual report boasted that it "owned, controlled or was licensed under" 4,424 U.S. patents, issued or pending (Fagen, 1975: 46).

By the early 1920s, "within the Bell System, there was a visionary group of technical executives who foresaw the growth of a highly complex system and the need for a . . . theoretical approach based on analysis and measurement" (Fagen, 1975: 44). This recognition would lead to the forming of Bell Labs in 1925, where a remarkable collection scientists and engineers were free to work on the basic research that resulted in a difficult-to-believe list of potential products, including the first working facsimile machine (1925), an electronic speech synthesizer (1937), the transistor (1947), solar voltaic cells (1954), a functioning laser (1964), the LED (1962), the Unix operating system (1967), and digital cellphone technology (1980). Almost as remarkable as this list of products is the inability of AT&T to profit from many of them. AT&T sold the license for making transistors to Sony in 1955 for only $50,000 (Riordan & Hoddeson, 1998). An estimate of how much Sony has profited from this investment over the last 50 years would probably run in the order of magnitude of $100 billion.

Why was AT&T unable to profit from some of the most important inventions of the 20th century? The theory of storied spaces developed here offers a convincing explanation. AT&T's dominant narrative emerged from its beginnings from Bell's technological vision and Vail's business vision. This narrative recognized the critical importance of technological innovation and developed Bell Labs to provide it. What the narrative did not recognize was that technological innovation could act as a research equivalent of antenarrative; it could introduce "stories" that would enable the company to develop new types of knowledge that would enable it to adapt to the changes in its markets. Rather, because the dominant narrative insisted that senior management could pick and choose the technologies that the company needed, AT&T provided no way for its researchers and engineers to enact their antenarratives as viable products that the company could incorporate. Moreover, with nearly half a century as one of the nation's most successful companies, AT&T had little reason to do so. As a result, the corporate dominant narrative and its antenarratives could exist side by side without anyone testing whether these antenarratives could be incorporated as new knowledge to make the dominant narrative more powerful, and no one had to.

The stories one hears about working at AT&T reflect this dominant narrative. When I was working at Bell Atlantic, one of the "Baby Bells" resulting from AT&T's 1984 divestiture, in the early 1990s, I spoke with many veterans of the old Bell System. They all talked fondly of their experience. Mama Bell, they all agreed, took care of its own. You did what was asked of you and you were taken care of. The idea of taking risks was entirely alien.

Starting in the 1970s, however, technological innovation began to accelerate, and the land line telephones of AT&T were no longer the only communications game in town. Starting with the introduction of microwave communications (MCI), AT&T could no longer maintain its monopoly. In an agreement with the government, AT&T divested its local service in 1984, retaining its long-distance service. Faced with increasing competition, its senior management made a series of catastrophic mistakes, such as the purchase of NCR in 1991 to enter the market for personal computers, even though the Bell Labs had invented UNIX operating system nearly 20 years earlier. By 2005, what was left of this once great company was purchased by SBC, the victim of a storied space that kept company employees from integrating some of the most valuable technological antenarrative of the 20th century.

3M

Unlike AT&T, Minnesota Mining and Manufacturing began as a business that wasn't quite sure what its market should be. Founded in 1902 to take advantage of the discovery of corundum, a strong abrasive, the company "kept stumbling along," as the official history puts it (*Our Story So Far*, 1977), for about 20 years, until its president, Richard McKnight, got a letter from Francis Okie in Philadelphia, asking for samples of all of 3M's abrasives. Fascinated, McKnight contacted Okie and discovered that he was trying to invent a waterproof sandpaper. In 1922, Okie came out to St. Paul to work on his invention with the employees at 3M. The resulting product, "Wetordry" sandpaper, proved ideal for finishing auto paint jobs, right at the time when the American auto industry was taking off. By 1926, it had become 3M's first major success. (For a fuller discussion of this story, see Baskin, 1998.)

This period (1902–1926) was the phase transition in which the dominant narrative of 3M's storied space emerged. Like AT&T, 3M's success was technology based; McKnight had started up its first laboratory around 1914. But unlike AT&T, 3M's first success came to it from the outside. Okie's idea for waterproof sandpaper was a technological antenarrative that 3M encouraged him to enact, and, not surprisingly, McKnight recognized that it was the individual inventor, enabled in pursuing his ideas, who could help the company develop new organizational knowledge with which to meet emerging customer needs. As a result, McKnight created the company's 15 Percent Rule, which still encourages technical employees to spend as much as 15% of their time pursuing their own ideas. Other company programs gave these employees institutionalized ways of getting access to the resources they need in these efforts, and the company's communication network helps them connect with other employees whose assistance they need. Once they create their products, employees can take advantage of a management review system that enables the company to manufacture and market them. Such inventors are often promoted. Among the most successful of the products developed through the 15 Percent Rule are masking tape in the 1930s, Scotchgard fabric protector in the 1950s, and Post-it Notes in the 1970s (Baskin, 1998).

Not surprisingly, 3M's dominant narrative is also reflected in a variety of stories its employees tell. Only, unlike those at AT&T, 3M's stories are about people taking risks, sometimes risks that seem foolish, and succeeding because of them. One of former CEO Lew Lehr's favorites concerns an employee who *knew* he had a winner for the company. After several warnings from his manager, the employee continued working on his idea and was fired. However, he was so devoted to the idea that he continued working on it, without pay, in an unused office. Eventually, he began to succeed, was rehired, and, after the product became a big winner for the company, was promoted to vice-president. Such a story would be unimaginable in the storied space of AT&T.

In effect, 3M's dominant narrative of innovation enables the company to create a series of minor phase transitions in its 15 Percent Rule technological antenarratives. The projects that emerge from this rule introduce perceptions of changes in the market environment, which, in turn, allow the company to adapt in an ongoing manner. Doing so is undoubtedly costly. According to Art Fry, who invented Post-it Notes, it can take "5,000 to 6,000 raw ideas to find one successful business" (Hindo, 2007). Moreover, the exploratory behavior that characterizes any phase transition makes it impossible to innovate in a highly efficient way. Extensive trial and error is essential. On the other hand, the institutionalized expectations that people will enact their technological antenarratives so that they can be guided to the market have kept 3M from experiencing the invent-and-overlook syndrome that Bell Labs demonstrated.

With its storied space continually driving employees to test new ideas to meet customer needs, 3M was much better positioned than AT&T to prosper in the post-1970s period of technological acceleration. From 1985–1995, 3M was consistently on *Forbes Magazine*'s Most Admired Company list. This isn't to say that the company had a free ride. The growth of international competition in the 1970s and 1980s forced the company to become more financially careful, and several of the old-timers I've spoken with sounded very disappointed. Then, in the late 1990s, 3M made some management mistakes, so much so that its stock missed the boom of that period. At the end of 2000, the company hired James McNerney, a manager in the GE tradition, as CEO. He introduced some much-needed cost-cutting and instituted Six Sigma. As a result, McNerney helped the company's operating margins to jump from 17% in 2001 to 23% in 2005. At the same time, innovation slowed so that the percentage of sales from new products, less than five years old, dropped from one-third to one-quarter. McNerney left in 2004 and was followed as CEO by 3M veteran George Buckley, who has made a variety of changes to spur innovation again (Hindo, 2007).

In the end, both AT&T and 3M were deeply affected by the market shifts of the last 30-some years. However, having a dominant narrative that *invited* technological antenarratives and then provided systems for enacting them and creating new organizational knowledge gave 3M an enormous advantage. An organizational storied space thus open to antenarrative provides a powerful explanation of the difference in the profitability that these two organizations were able to derive from their significant programs of technological development, and, perhaps, the way 3M remains a viable corporation while AT&T has become little more than the name for another organization.

IMPLICATIONS FOR FURTHER STUDY

Of course, not all antenarrative is technological. As I've show elsewhere (Baskin, 2005a, 2005b), organizational storytelling offers a window to issues ranging from identifying conflicts to opportunities for motivating employees to make further contributions. These antenarratives can also point toward issues in finance, marketing, the success of all sorts of corporate programs, but only *if management makes a commitment to listen.* Moreover, if this theory of storied spaces as the human equivalent of CASs is valid, then many of the implications of this analysis should be applicable to other human groupings and, therefore, worth serious examination. Among those implications, three seem central:

- *Dynamics.* All storied spaces generate behavior that reflects the interplay between their historically grounded dominant narratives and antenarratives by which individuals express emerging events in the environment. No storied space can exist without both. The identity of any group, organization, profession, or nation is expressed in its dominant narrative, the story of what people in it must do, as they have in the past, for it to survive. Dominant narratives drive the human equivalent of complexity's attractors. Antenarratives, on the other hand, enable people to perceive and act on emerging events, as those perceptions are shaped by the circumstances of the storied spaces to which they belong. The multiplicity of viewpoint in storied spaces such as organizations or nations offers the possibility of a complexity of perception equal to the complexity of current environments. When possible, people will fit their antenarratives into the existing dominant narrative. The test of any storied space's ability to adapt is its members' ability to recognize antenarratives that do *not* fit in with the dominant narrative and then make appropriate shifts in their dominant narrative.

- *Knowledge generation.* In such heteroglot (Bakhtin, 1981: 291) storytelling environments, knowledge evolves, as stories are enacted and create the expected results, from guesses at the meaning of events in antenarrative, through the higher degree of sureness in narrative and, finally, to the relative certainty of dominant narrative, which I earlier (Baskin, 2005b) referred to as "myth." The ability of any storied space to take advantage of such knowledge in order to adapt successfully to changes in the environment depends to a high degree on that space's openness to relatively new knowledge. Such new knowledge can become more readily available in storied spaces where the dominant narrative encourages people throughout it to spread and enact their antenarratives. In this way, AT&T could be highly successful during a period of relative stability, when its relatively "closed" dominant narrative encouraged people at the top of the organization to judge which technical antenarratives were needed to respond to markets; yet the company faltered in the last quarter of the 20th century when markets became more chaotic. In such chaotic environments, 3M could be more successful because its more "open" dominant narrative encouraged employees to enact their technical narratives. Similarly, Western nations with relatively free elections and press have been able to respond more successfully to emerging dangers, such as industrial pollution, than nations such as China and Russia, where both the political system and media are more stringently controlled.
- *Leadership.* One reason open dominant narratives are essential in more chaotic environments is the universal temptation to believe that highly successful dominant narratives are *the whole story.* As noted elsewhere (Baskin, 2005a), the human desire for certainty in an uncertain world consistently drives people to mistake their dominant narratives for The Truth. The temptation to make this equation is strongest among those who lead any storied space. Surround-

ed by their peers in a cabinet or office of the CEO, such leaders receive enormous rewards, hold significant amounts of power, and are often praised beyond their accomplishments. As I noted in the three hospitals in my study (Baskin 2005a, 2005b), senior executives have the least reason to doubt either their narratives or antenarratives. In addition, the vast majority of literature on storytelling in organizations focuses on *telling* stories. Yet the richness of information and knowledge available in the antenarrative polyphony of any storied space is extremely valuable, especially in a chaotic period like our own. As a result, this theory of storied spaces suggests that leadership in our current environment should include a significant component of listening. After all, when leaders *don't* listen, as Pres. George W. Bush didn't listen to his generals' advice to go into Iraq with overwhelming force, the results can be catastrophic.

If this theory is valid, the three issues listed above are only a beginning. Examining organizations and professions, families and nations, markets and religions, as storied spaces is an enormous task. In a time, however, when our world appears to be changing to a state that is already significantly different fro what many of us grew up with, it is an effort well worth the effort, even if only to demonstrate where it goes wrong.

REFERENCES

Bakhtin, M.M. (1981). Discourse in the novel. In M. Holquist (Ed.); C. Emerson & M. Holquist (trans.), *The dialogic imagination: Four essays by M.M. Bakhtin.* Austin, TX: University of Texas Press.

Baskin, K. (1998). *Corporate DNA: Learning from life.* Boston: Butterworth-Heinemann.

Baskin, K. (2005a). Story telling and the complex epistemology of organizations. In. K. Richardson (Ed.), *Managing the complex: Philosophy, theory and applications* (pp. 331–344). Greenwich, CT: Information Age.

Baskin, K. (2005b). Complexity, stories and knowing. *Emergence: Complexity & Organization, 7*(2), 32–40.

Baskin, K. (2007a). Ever the 'twain shall meet. *Chinese Management Studies 1*(1), 57–68.

Baskin, K. (2007b). Foucault, complexity, and myth: Toward a complexity-based approach to social evolution (a.k.a. history). In K.A. Richardson & P. Cilliers (Eds.), *Explorations in complexity thinking: Pre-proceedings of the 3rd International Workshop on complexity and philosophy* (pp. 1–13). Mansfield, MA: ISCE Publishing.

Bateson, G. (1979). *Mind and nature: A necessary unity.* New York: E.P. Dutton.

Boje, D.M. (1995). Stories of the storytelling organization: A postmodern analysis of Disney as "Tamara-land." *Academy of Management Journal, 38*(4), 997–1035. (Or see http://cbae.nmsu.edu/~dboje/papers/DisneyTamaraland.html.)

Boje, D. M. (2001). *Narrative methods for organizational and communication research.* London: SAGE Publications.

Cohen, J. (2003, February). *Why is negentropy, like Phlogiston, a privative?* Paper presented at the International Nonlinear Sciences Conference, Vienna, Austria.

Dervin, B., Foreman-Wernet, L. & Lauterback, E. (Eds.). (2003). *Sense-making methodology reader: Selected writings of Brenda Dervin.* Cresskill, NJ: Hampton Press.

Fagen, M.D.(Ed.). (1975). *A history of engineering and science in the Bell System* (Vol. 1). New York: Bell Telephone Labs.

Feyerabend, P. (1993). *Against method* (3rd ed.). New York: Verso.

Fisher, W. R. (1987). *Human communication as narration: Toward a philosophy of reason, value, and action.* Columbia, SC: The University of South Carolina Press.

Gell-Mann, M. (1994). *The quark and the jaguar: Adventures in the simple and complex.* New York: W.H. Freeman and Co.

Gould, S.J. (2002). *The structure of evolutionary theory.* Cambridge, MA: The Belknapp Press.

Hindo, B. (2007, June 11). At 3M, a struggle between efficiency and creativity. *BusinessWeek* [online]. Retrieved November 20, 2007 from http://www.businessweek.com/print/magaine/content/07_24/b4038406.htm?chan=gl.

Hoffman, L. (2002). *Family therapy: An intimate history.* New York: W.W. Norton.

Kaufmann, S. (2000). *Investigations.* New York: Oxford University Press.

Our story so far: Notes from the first 75 years of 3M Company. (1977). St. Paul, MN: Minnesota Mining and Manufacturing Co.

Plotkin, H. (1993). *Darwin machines and the nature of knowledge.* Cambridge, MA: Harvard University Press.

Pratchett, T., Stewart, I., & Cohen, J. (2002), *The science of Discworld II: The Globe.* London: Edbury Press.

Riordan, M. & Hoddeson, L. (1998). *Crystal fire: The birth of the information age.* New York: W.W. Norton.

Salthe, S. W. (1993). *Development and evolution: Complexity and change in biology,* Cambridge, MA: MIT Press.

Stacey, R.D. (2001). *Complex responsive processes in organizations: Learning and knowledge creation.* New York: Routledge.

Weick, K. E. (1995). *Sensemaking in organizations.* London: Sage Publications.

White, M. and Epston, D. (1990). *Narrative means to therapeutic ends.* New York: W.W. Norton.

CHAPTER 5

COMPLEX INFORMATION ENVIRONMENTS

Issues in Knowledge Management and Organizational Learning

Duska Rosenberg

INTRODUCTION

Making the best use of knowledge as one of the most important organizational resources is a major aim of sound management practice, striving to achieve reduction of risk, duplication of effort, and uncertainty in the day-to-day work of an organization (Galbraith, 1994; Sanchez & Heene, 1997). A survey of literature on organizational requirements for knowledge management indicates that the matter is also of some theoretical importance, having brought to light several reasons for the attention that knowledge management is currently receiving.

Knowledge sharing, learning from experience, and open access to information about the ways an organization works are made possible by advanced information and communications technologies (ICT). ICTs have increased access to and decentralization of informational resources and thus

Complexity and Knowledge Management, pages 77–91
Copyright © 2010 by Information Age Publishing
77

stimulated organizational learning (Walsh & Ungson, 1991). Furthermore, the emergence of the global business community through ecommerce and ebusiness has brought to light considerable benefits that enhanced conditions for partnership and trust can bring to distributed organizations. In particular, their access to global markets is considered to be the key to their success, as it enables timely and effective response to changing customer demands (Nonaka, 1991).

The concepts of knowledge management and organizational learning have also been related to the particular, situated aspects of day-to-day working practices of a distributed organization. They are applied to the study of teamwork in physical, media, and virtual environments, where cognitive and social aspects of organizational processes determine the requirements for technological platforms and applications (Davenport, De Long, & Beers, 1998). Studies of individual workers' circumstances, in the workplace, at home, and on the move, emphasize their need to access an organization's knowledge networks, through both formal and informal channels (Stuckey & Smith, 2004).

In this context, there is a clear distinction between "hard" and "soft" knowledge. Hard knowledge is treated as some kind of commodity that can be exchanged, transferred, and coded into documents, records, charts, and other similar informational artifacts (Teece, 1998). Increasingly, however, we consider the importance of "soft" knowledge, the implicit communication and tacit understanding of the particular situations in which knowledge is put to use. Tacit knowledge can be transmitted through concrete examples, experience, and practice through personal interactions (Boisot, Griffiths, & Moles, 1997).

The work presented in this chapter is based on the study of tacit knowledge that is communicated within and between teams of knowledge workers "on the move." Their experiential knowledge is shared through personal interactions in real-life tasks, carried out by agile teams in construction who work together on a joint project while being employed by different subcontracted firms. Construction teams are agile in the sense that they have flexible, *ad hoc* organizational structures, which increase their mobility and their responsiveness to continuously changing circumstances on the construction site. Although they have strict formal channels of communication and established procedures and protocols, most of their day-to-day working life is oriented toward informal social networks created through experience. It is those informal networks that help individuals cope with the continual change that characterizes their work environment, and enables them to work as part of distributed teams, across physical, cultural, and organizational divides. For these reasons, agile teams in construction are taken as an example of a distributed organization held together by informal social networks that support shared tacit knowledge of the ways the teams can work together effectively.

The study builds on recent research within the academic community concerned with the study of distributed organizations, but focuses on a practical knowledge management project, CICC.[1] The main aim of the project was to improve relationships between people, technology, and information content in the real-world environment of a large construction project. CICC technologies were designed and implemented bearing in mind that introducing them into a real-life working environment requires sensitivity, awareness, and understanding of the human dimensions of construction teams' work.

As teamwork is essentially social in nature, the CICC technologies predominantly address the need for increased connectivity between people in order to improve knowledge sharing within and between construction teams. Knowledge management applications developed within CICC include intranets, organizational memories, and general knowledge management tools. Intranets enable networked access to people and the informational networks to which they belong (Rosenberg, 2000). Knowledge repositories and organizational memories provide access to the pool of knowledge that an organization has about its past projects (Perry, Fruchter, & Rosenberg, 1999). Management tools are focused on knowledge networking practices (Rosenberg & Holden, 2000), recognizing not only the strategic importance of data resources that underpin the creation of knowledge assets, but also the need to support exploratory learning of individuals in organizations that "will enhance their personal effectiveness and their overall capacity to interpret and make sense of experiences" (Boisot, 1999, p. 266).

COORDINATING AGILE TEAMS

Agile teams working on a shared problem face challenges at two levels. First, the usual composition of such teams requires that participants have diverse expertise and thus their distinct contributions to the shared task have to be coordinated. Second, agile teams are created to work together on a specific project and are dissolved when the project is finished. Thus, the team members rarely know each other well prior to starting work on a joint task, and consequently their individual perspectives on the collaborative situation must be coordinated "on the fly."

In the study of coordination of work within agile teams, the focus was on the effect that these two factors—diverse expertise and team agility—have on the coordination of joint activities. The main aim was to find out how various informational resources available in the work environment aid (or obstruct, as the case may be) the coordination of both task-oriented and communication-oriented aspects of collaboration. Particular attention was paid to the role of advanced communications technology in facilitating such coordination when the teams are not only agile, but also geographically dispersed. New technologies such as multimedia, mobile telephones, wearable computers, and video have the potential for supporting working environments characterized by professional and cultural diversity. It is important that this technology fits in unobtrusively with the working practices of particular communities, supporting the interactions and activities that have naturally evolved as part of social life in the workplace (Winograd & Flores, 1986).

Coordination of distributed work activities is crucial for the success of a collaborative task. Such coordination is also central to the study of collaboration within CSCW (computer-supported cooperative work), where the focus is on "how co-ordination emerges, how it is maintained and what happens when it breaks down" (Rogers, 1993, p. 295). In particular, the entire working environment is examined to find the features that facilitate coordination of distributed activities. The most important of these are the shared artifacts—also referred to as common artifacts (Robinson, 1993), boundary objects, communicative artifacts, collective cognitive artifacts, or common objects—that are used by teams to create and maintain mutual understanding of the work process.

Shared artifacts provide the resources for people to focus their collaborative activities and to obtain facilitative feedback from each other about the current state of the activity. They can be regarded as loci, or physical manifestations of what is essentially purposeful social action. For example, a simple common object such as a set of pigeonholes in a university department has a structure consisting of slots for holding mail, documents, and messages for individual staff. It also has an informative function, since it makes it easy to see if an individual has any mail. A pigeonhole that is full may mean that the owner is not back from a vacation or conference, or perhaps that there is substantial marking to be done. The set of pigeonholes also shows at a glance the size of the department, thus providing some information about both individuals and their organization.

The starting assumptions behind the work presented in this chapter are that shared artifacts are the key to investigating the coordination of distributed activities, and that this coordination takes place at two levels simultaneously. At the task level, participants coordinate their perspectives on the job in hand in order to establish the common ground for joint problem solving. At the communicative level, participants negotiate in order to reach agreements on how what is said and done should be interpreted. The distributed activities are thus coordinated by participants monitoring the progress, noting the changes, and providing feedback about their own actions and reactions, relying on the shared artifacts for this purpose.

Personal interactions follow a general pattern: The participants establish contact, make their situation visible to others, and then together build a shared environment where they cooperate to solve the current problem (see Gumpertz & Hymes, 1972). Participants focus on shared artifacts in the process of negotiating the meanings of words or images presented there (Robinson, 1993). They thus create the common ground: "a sine qua non for everything we do with others... the sum of [the participants'] mutual, common or joint knowledge, beliefs, and suppositions" (Clark, 1996, p. 92).

Within the boundaries of the common ground, the participants can identify the objects referred to, come to understand each other's goals and purposes, cooperate, and coordinate their actions. Indeed, common ground is regarded as fundamental to all coordination activities and to collaboration (Clark & Brennan, 1991). One of the key research questions for the CICC project was how people create the common ground in situations where the contact between them is influenced or mediated by technology (Rogers, 1993; Fulk & Collins-Jarvis, 2001; Dourish & Bellotti, 1992).

Assuming that common ground is fundamental, it is important for the designers of technology to understand what representations should be employed in order to design usable interactive technology. In her analysis of technology-based shared artifacts, Rogers distinguishes between two main kinds of mediating mechanisms: "explicit representations which are intended to provide specific information about the status and properties of actions and artifacts that constitute the work, and implicit representations where an action or some form of communication signifies a change in status of an object or process" (1993, p. 296).

Some of the mediating mechanisms have universally accepted meaning, while the meaning of others is negotiated and interpreted anew in each particular context. A further dimension to the mediating mechanisms is added in the practice theories of culture that emphasize the importance of language use in "cultural meaning making." Placing language at the center of the creation of social meaning and the consequent building of communities, practice approaches also take into account the resources available in the community's environment. The resources that enable participants to create distinct communities include various designed artifacts—such as documents, instruments, computer applications, and others—that are at the center of personal interactions among team members. In such situations, the technology provides the shared artifact needed for the coordination of distributed activities, and the nature of computerized representations, both explicit and implicit, becomes a critical issue. Such technology is expected to facilitate not only access to the data that an organization has, but also to facilitate the processes that shape human cognition and communication in the significant social and cultural contexts, thus fitting in with normal human activities in the workplace.

THE PEOPLE AND THE INFORMATION FINDER

The working assumption behind the design of usable interactive technology within the CICC project was that it forms an integral part of the entire information environment created by the interaction of people, organizations, and artifacts, where information is generated, exchanged, stored, processed, internalized, and externalized. An interactive multimedia technology prototype, People and Information Finder (PIF)[2] was designed to provide explicit representations of people, their organizations, and teams, as well as the projects on which they were working. Multimedia facilities were used to increase the richness of the information about the PIF people and their workplace. These included visual channels with both abstracted and image-based data. Such increased media richness was expected to enhance the creation of common ground among the PIF users, thus enabling tacit knowledge sharing in communication mediated by the PIF. The main research questions concerned the content of multimedia displays and explicit representations, as well as their informativeness and implicit representations.

As the main aim was to improve communications and to offer a richer information environment for the PIF people, a key research issue was to find out how the explicit and implicit representations in the PIF could help them to initiate and maintain contact with one another. Such a facility is particularly useful in situations where a stable organizational form is absent, as a team is created for the purposes of a particular project or a task and is dissolved once this is completed. The work on the task itself represents a period during which cooperation is vital. Problems of lack of shared culture have to be addressed, and this is usually done with a series of induction meetings and seminars at the start of the project. This is a vital yet time-consuming team-building stage and is undermined by individuals joining projects at later stages with consequent integration problems (Rosenberg, Perry, Leevers, & Farrow, 1997). Poor communication causes serious problems in day-to-day activities that require continuous cooperation and coordination (Fruchter, 1998).

One of the key roles intended for the PIF was to become an important shared artifact and a vehicle for soft knowledge management practices, designed to help those who need to learn about a given project and its organization. Such learning would take place in "communication at arm's length" mediated by the PIF, which would enable people to assimilate the project culture without disturbing the established flow of activities on the site. The social relevance of the PIF as the shared artifact could then be analyzed as a matter of system-in-use that systematically interacts with the organization that uses it.

As a technological artifact, the PIF is a web page populated with information about its owners, using standard web technology and programming in html underpinned by JavaScript. It comprises a technological platform— more precisely, a configuration of communications technologies such as telephone; network technology such as the web; and advanced interactive technology, such as virtual and augmented reality. It thus provides an integrated service that helps the user to choose between various channels of communication, from voice link to videoconferencing, and to browse through a collection of similar pages created by different owners according to a predesigned template.

It also provides a richer experience of people and their work environment in a particular organization; in other words, it supports the creation of common ground between the PIF people. They obtain information from people, from informational resources such as documents or databases, or from the real world where PIF owners live and work, and the structure of the PIF page reflects this. It is divided into three main components. The first contains information that helps visitors to locate the owners in their physical space, giving name, address, phone number, and email address, as well as photographs and video images showing their offices, desks, and terminals. This makes it possible for the visitor to choose how to contact them, via telephone, ordinary mail, email, or videoconferencing. The second, "nearest neighbors," provides information about the organizational space that a team occupies, giving similar information about accessing other PIF owners who are engaged in comparable or related work. The third component describes the owners' projects and activities, both present and past, comprising the part of the real world in which the owner's work is done.

As a knowledge management tool, the PIF provides a facility for accessing information about an organization or a team in the construction industry, the people who work for it, and the activities in which they engage. The status of information ranges from personally owned (or private), which is accessible only to the owner, to information that is distributed (or shared) between members of a group. Alternatively, information may be public (or visible), which the owner is willing to show to the general public or to a selected group of collaborators. This nonproprietary information forms part of the informational resources used by the organization or the group as a whole.[3]

The PIF thus has the potential for enabling innovation in cooperative work within agile teams. In order to understand more about this potential, a preliminary study of communication mediated by the PIF prototype was carried out in interviews with a small group of informants. Their responses were elicited in open and in structured interviews, as well as focus groups. The data analysis was oriented toward explicating the informational links between what visitors could observe in the communicative situations displayed on the pages and how they interpreted the information presented there.

The main aim was to find out what general interactive strategies people use when learning about a team, its people, and their work. In particular, the focus was on discovering what knowledge, presuppositions, and beliefs people bring with them to joint activities, and how the external representations designed in the PIF could influence the creation of common ground.

ANALYZING SOCIAL KNOWLEDGE

In the analytical framework developed for studying the use of the PIF in a real-life setting, the Common Ground Framework was extended and adapted for the study of representations in the PIF pages in order to identify the features that would facilitate the communication it mediated.

The original framework views communication as joint activity between two or more participants engaged in a shared task (Clark & Brennan, 1991; Grosz & Sidner, 1986; Clark & Schaefer, 1989) who, in the process of carrying out this task, have to establish the common ground for mutual understanding and trust. Clark (1996, p. 43) divides the common ground into three parts:

1. *Initial common ground.* This is the set of background facts, assumptions, and beliefs the participants presupposed when they entered the joint activity.
2. *Current state of the joint activity.* This is what the participants presuppose to be the state of the activity at the moment.
3. *Public events so far.* These are the events the participants presuppose have occurred in public leading up to the current state.

In the modified framework, the presuppositions determining the initial common ground were classified into those related to the background knowledge characterizing participants' expertise and the more personal, experiential knowledge of teamwork on construction projects. The former includes, for example, individual expertise in architecture, construction management, structural engineering, or any other relevant profession that determines the nature of their contribution to the process and task activities. The latter is based on the experience of working on construction projects, with particular partners, and the trust that such an experience generates. These form the starting context for joint activities and influence the manner in which participants recognize standard procedures, identify their own roles and responsibilities as well as those of others, and decide how to organize joint activities. Special attention was given to the social knowledge that forms part of the initial common ground and, more specifically, how the explicit representations of the PIF interact with the creation of the tacit knowledge about its owners.

The visitors to the PIF pages were observed in a "conversation at arm's length" with the owners, where the main goal was to learn about the "project people." Observations of visitors navigating through the sample were focused on ease of use and on the extent of the support for learning that it offered. Two main research questions guided both the data collection and the interpretation of the informants' responses. The first was concerned with the informativeness of various pages in terms of content. The second question was whether or not the principles that govern social action and face-to-face interaction in the real world would be equally valid in the mediated interaction in the media space and the virtual world.

REPRESENTATIONS OF THE PHYSICAL AND SOCIAL SPACES

The information that the visitors picked up from the web pages was considerably richer than that explicitly expressed. Much of this richness was related to the social and organizational characteristics of the owners' physical environment. For example, the "god's eye view" of the office layout helped them to infer the social structure of the group inhabiting the space. The assumptions normally made about the social significance of physical spaces in the real world were also made about the virtual world.

Knowledge of the ways in which real organizations structure their working space helped visitors to interpret the social aspects of the situation presented on the screen. For example, they understood that people who have their own offices are higher up in the organizational hierarchy, and that those who are physically collocated usually belong to the same working group. The external representation of the office space thus plays an important part in identifying the owners' status and relationships.

REPRESENTATIONS OF PERSONAL SPACES

Interpretations of individual web pages confirmed the importance of links between the images of the physical environment and the socially relevant information inferred from it. Different views of the physical location reflect the personal image of the owners as if they were wearing "electronically augmented clothes." For example, the scene of papers scattered all over the desk makes the owner appear as an untidy but creative person, someone who works with paper and computers, which indicates a high level of education and might be seen as serious, reliable, and responsible.

A detailed view of the workspace also contributes to familiarization with the owner. The owner of a particular space may be assumed to be creative and clever, as he or she works with computers and has lots of paper scattered around, working on knowledge-intensive tasks, spending much of his or her time at the terminal if there is a comfortable chair in front of the computer.

THE INFORMATION ENVIRONMENT

Originally, the design intention was for the personal page to provide information about the owners' availability by making their situation at work more visible to potential visitors. The possibility of intrusion into the owner's space at an inopportune time would thus be reduced. A camera placed in the owner's office was the main source of this kind of information, enabling visitors to make informed decisions about whether the owners should be approached via an intrusive medium such as telephone or videoconferencing, or whether an email message would be more appropriate.

Messages left on the screen when there is no activity are a very important guide to availability. For example, Post-it® notes saying "Back this afternoon/tomorrow/next week" give immediate guidance on when the owner can be contacted. A collection of such messages creates the context for interpreting similar situations when there is no action on the screen. Thus, the view of an empty office without a message would mean that the owner is momentarily absent, perhaps talking to a colleague in the corridor or having lunch, while a message saying "Goodbye" would mean that a longer, or maybe indefinite, period of absence was intended.

People who share the working environment with the owner can provide an alternative point of contact if the owner is not available. Particularly useful features are the links with closest collaborators within the intellectual space they share, indicating to the visitor that close collaboration is no longer restricted to people inhabiting the same physical working space. The PIF is therefore an informational resource that can transcend the limitations of the real world; this is where the visitors saw possible new uses of this technology in their own lives. The general image was of an impressive technological achievement providing a novel service.

The overriding principle in visitors deciding whom to contact was the awareness that they may be intruding into other people's working spaces and they were therefore looking for signs of invitation. In general, they expected a virtual host to help them orient themselves in the organizational environment and to act as a focal point to which they would return when they get lost in the virtual space they were navigating. The host was also expected to sanction the appropriate forms of contact and determine the acceptable degree of intrusion in any given circumstances.

Particularly important was the realization that the owners had full control over the cameras in their offices, so when they did not wish to be watched they could turn the camera off. This meant that if the camera was on, the visitors were invited to enter, but they were still aware of different degrees of intrusion possible in the circumstances. For example, accessing a database or clicking on a document was equivalent to a permission to "enter without knocking," and sending an email message was comparable to leaving a message on the door, but videoglance helped with the choice whether to knock or not. Videoconferencing, being the most intrusive call for contact, required the most explicit permission.

The scenes offered by the camera were interpreted in the light of such social considerations. The "degree of closeness" between owners and visitors was often determined by interpretation of symbols: for example, a highlighted name in the "nearest neighbors" section was seen to be an invitation to contact that person rather than somebody else. Rules that are observed in face-to-face interaction also played a part in decisions to establish contact, so that people whose faces were turned toward the camera were generally considered to be more friendly and approachable.

Most visitors saw the intranet page as providing much more than a home page on the web. They used it as a traveling map, helping them to locate the owners within the wider context of their organization. The context was referred to simultaneously as the physical and informational space the owners occupied. The global function of the page from the visitors' point of view was that of an augmented map enabling a view of individuals in relation to their neighbors and to other sources of information available in the real and virtual worlds.

CONVERSATIONS IN PERSONAL SPACES

Conversations among construction workers are normally centered on the object being designed or under construction and the actions required to get the design or construction process going. In this context, people suggest new tasks, justify their actions, and check that the tasks have been done. At the same time, they negotiate their responsibilities, evaluate contributions, and establish individual authority.

The content of their conversations also refers to actions on design or media objects, such as showing a file or drawing, creating the design objects or media objects, such as PowerPoint slides that represent the design objects. In the course of a team session, design decisions have to be made, both choosing among the alternative solutions to design problems and about the responsibilities and contributions of individual team members. In the traditionally organized physical workspace, these conversations have naturally evolved. The powerful new technology promises that such naturalness can be maintained in conversations where people are not physically present together, but are in contact through telephones, videoconferencing, email, virtual reality, and other similar technology applications.

The findings of this study suggest that more work needs to be done before this promise is fully realized in practice. They also suggest that a significant aspect of future work should be devoted to theoretical issues of interdisciplinary research. A main problem that needs to be addressed at the start involves the study of interactions in physical, media, and virtual spaces—in particular, the linguistic approaches to conversation analysis. These are traditionally focused on the study of face-to-face conversations where two participants jointly create the "frame" of the conversation. The findings of this study show that the initial common ground is much more varied and comprises considerably more social knowledge and assumptions than the traditional studies within the common ground framework have so far acknowledged.

Furthermore, in a real-life workplace there is a greater number and a greater variety of conversations than face-to-face encounters. It is often impossible for people to participate actively in a conversation, so they may overhear, monitor, or ignore it, while still being aware that a conversation has taken place. The understanding of the overhearers is different from the understanding of the active participants (Clark, 1996), and this should be taken into account, both in scientific coverage of interactions in the workplace and in the design of technology that supports them.

Many joint activities of teams are carried out "at arm's length," instead of face to face, where the possibilities of misunderstanding are greater and the facilities for repair reduced. It is therefore important for communications technologies to observe the established representations of information in terms of rules, regulations, and etiquette that is easily accepted by team members. It is even more important for the technologies to enhance the representations of information to include more personal and less structured requirements, such as helping people to build the common ground that ultimately leads to trust.

CONCLUSIONS

Several principles governing social interaction in establishing face-to-face contact also apply to the situation of virtually visiting an organization and its people using the intranet example described in this study. The prototype makes a person's environment visible to others at remote locations and helps in creating a common ground to underpin joint activities. An important social (and design) principle is related to intrusion into another person's space, be it physical, organizational, or informational. Invitations into such spaces can be communicated indirectly, and visitors will look for them in the objects presented on the page, such as the videoglance, shrunken screen, and highlighted names. This will happen even if the designers of the page have not explicitly intended for these objects to have such a communicative function.

Another important principle concerns the construction of initial common ground. Visitors' interpretations of the information presented on a personal page will be considerably richer and with more social detail than the literal meaning of the text, pictures, or graphics presented. This is where the metaphor of "electronically augmented clothes" is particularly apt. Decisions are made not only about the appropriate means to obtain information by accessing the sources that it makes available, but also about personalities and possible relationships between them, the nature of the organization, and maybe even the quality of work that can be expected of them.

The information displayed on the intranet pages is therefore interpreted within a rich context of natural human communication, where the accepted social norms that determine appropriate behavior apply. The extended common ground framework developed here provides the conceptual basis, as well as methods and techniques for discovering and formulating the social constraints that regulate joint activities and communication at arm's length. It is the framework for the design of technology that brings together people, their social relationships, and the resources they need in order to carry out the joint activities in the workplace, which are the stated aims of knowledge management in practice.

NOTES

1. EU AC017, CICC (Collaborative Integrated Communications for Construction). A detailed report is available on the author's website, http://ww.rhbnc.ac.uk/~uhtm059/index.html.
2. The People and Information Finder is a multimedia prototype developed as part of the CICC project.
3. The team involved in the development of the PIF prototype consisted of Nicholas Farrow, David Leevers, Mark Perry, and Duska Rosenberg (cf. Rosenberg et al., 1997).

REFERENCES

Boisot, M. (1999). *Knowledge assets*. Oxford, UK: Oxford University Press.

Boisot, M., Griffiths, D., & Moles, V. (1997). The dilemma of competence: Differentiation versus integration in the pursuit of learning. In R. Sanchez & A. Heene (Eds.), *Strategic Learning and Knowledge Management* (pp. 65–82). New York: John Wiley.

Clark, H. (1996). *Using language*. Cambridge, UK: Cambridge University Press.

Clark, H. & Brennan, S. (1991). Grounding in communication. In L. B. Resnick, J. M. Levine, & S. D. Teasley (Eds.), *Perspectives on socially shared cognition* (pp. 127–149). Washington, DC: American Psychological Association.

Clark, H. & Schaefer, E. (1989). Contributing to discourse. *Cognitive Science, 13*, 259–292.

Davenport, T. H., De Long, D. W., & Beers, M. C. (1998). Successful knowledge management projects. *Sloan Management Review, 39*(2), 43–57.

Dourish, P., & Bellotti, V. (1992). Awareness and coordination in shared workspaces: Proceedings of the 1992 ACM conference on Computer-supported cooperative work. pp 107–114. Toronto, Ontario, Canada.

Fruchter, R. (1998). Roles of computing in P5BL: Problem-, project-, product-, process-, and people-based learning. *Artificial Intelligence for Engineering Design and Manufacturing, 12*, 65–67.

Fulk, J., & Collins-Jarvis, L. (2001). Wired meetings: Technological mediation of organizational gatherings. In F. Jablin & L. Putnam (Eds.), *New handbook of organizational communication* (2nd ed., pp. 624–703). Newbury Park, CA: Sage.

Galbraith, J. (1994). Competing with flexible lateral organizations (2nd ed.). Boston: Addison-Wesley.

Grosz, B. & Sidner, C. (1986). Attentions, intentions and the structure of discourse. *Computational Linguistics, 12*, 175–204.

Gumpertz, J. & Hymes, D. (1972). *Directions in sociolinguistics: The ethnography of communication*. New York: Holt, Rinehart and Winston.

Hindmarsh, J., Fraser, M., Heath, C., Benford, S., & Greenhalgh, C. (1998, November). Fragmented interaction: Establishing mutual orientation in virtual environments. *ACM98 Proceedings of CSCW98* (pp. 217–226). Seattle, Washington.

Nonaka, I. (1991). The knowledge-creating company. *Harvard Business Review, 69*(6), 96–104.

Perry, M., Fruchter, R., & Rosenberg, D. (1999). Co-ordinating distributed knowledge: A study into the use of an organisational memory. *Cognition, Technology and Work, 1*, 142–152.

Robinson, M. (1993, September). Design for unanticipated use. In De Michaelis, Simone, & Schmidt (Eds.), *Proceedings of the Third European Conference on Computer-Supported Cooperative Work* (pp. 187–202). Milan, Italy, Amsterdam: Kluwer.

Rogers, Y. (1993). Coordinating computer-mediated work. *Computer Supported Cooperative Work, 1*, 295–315.

Rosenberg, D. (2000). 3 steps to ethnography: A discussion of inter-disciplinary contributions. *Artificial Intelligence and Society*, special issue ed. L. Pemberton, "Communications in Design," 15(1).

Rosenberg, D. & Holden, T. (2000). Interactions, technology, and organizational change. *Emergence, 2*(2).

Rosenberg, D., Perry, M., Leevers, D., & Farrow, N. (1997). People and information finder: Informational perspectives. In R. Williams (Ed.), *The Social Shaping of Multimedia: Proceedings of International Conference COST-4.* Luxembourg: European Commission DGXIII.

Sanchez, R. & Heene, A. (Eds.). (1997). *Strategic learning and knowledge management.* New York: Wiley.

Stuckey, B., & Smith, J. D. (2004). Building sustainable communities of practice. In P. M. Hildreth & C. Kimble (Eds.), *Knowledge networks: Innovation through communities of practice* (pp. 150–164). London: Idea Group Publishing.

Teece, D. J. (1998). Capturing value from knowledge assets: The new economy, markets for know-how and intangible assets. *California Management Review, 40*(3), 55–79.

Walsh, J. P. & Ungson, G. R. (1991). Organizational memory. *Academy of Management Review, 16*(1), 57–91.

Winograd, T. & Flores, F. (1986). *Understanding computers and cognition: A new foundation for design.* Norwood, NJ: Ablex.

CHAPTER 6

KNOWLEDGE GENERATION AS A COMPLEX RELATIONAL PROCESS

Absorbing, Combining, Transfer and Stickiness in the Organizational Context

Jane Galloway Seiling

Organizations are comprised of a large number of diverse agents who interact locally and dynamically as social systems, often orchestrating small changes that can lead to large effects, especially around knowledge processing and knowledge management. Also, according to Maguire and McKelvey (1999), organizations are human organizations that represent *complex adaptive systems.* As such, organizations are functional and dysfunctional, healthy and diseased (Richardson, 2005). The people in them make them so. The most functional organizations are those who are purposely adaptive, using behaviors that occur as an outcome of individual and interactive activities that generate and process useful understandings (Kawai, 2005). Because humans naturally exchange information, the combination of current and known information

Complexity and Knowledge Management, pages 93–108
Copyright © 2010 by Information Age Publishing
All rights of reproduction in any form reserved.

with new information in insightful ways occurs in organizations on a regular basis, not just when it is a unique or orchestrated occasion.

This chapter looks at knowledge through a complexity lens, suggesting that knowledge is in a continual state of emergence and is always incomplete; information is elusive and language formation and understanding is limited; and cooperation and collaboration are usually insufficient to reach understanding. Yet, despite these limitations, there are extensive opportunities for cooperative and collaborative practice that orchestrate emergence, and there are many new methods of inquiry and explanation that call for new approaches to the acquisition and formation of knowledge and understanding. Within these various approaches, listening to multiple voices, whether directly or indirectly offered, is essential to the design of new approaches and understandings.

Organizations "struggle to grapple with the dynamic nature of organizational processes" (Simpson, 2005, p. 94), including the dynamic nature of relationships within life in general and especially in organizations (Stavros & Torres, 2005). In organizations, the complexity of knowledge creation, transfer, and replication is complicated by this dynamism while being vital to effective capacity building in complex groups and communities that exist as adaptive systems (McGrath & Argote, 2001) and the interchange between their members for the purpose of knowledge generation. Thus, the following discusses the issue of "knowledge-ability" of groups and organizations that are concerned with knowledge generation.

KNOWLEDGE GENERATION

According to McElroy (2003), learning includes first-generation approaches to expanding the ability to create sustainable advantage in business, creating "*the ability to learn faster than your competitors*" (p. 19; italics in original). Regarding second-generation approaches to knowledge management (KM), McElroy also states:

- "*Knowledge processing* is a set of social processes through which people in organizations create and integrate their knowledge.
- *Knowledge management* is a management activity that seeks to enhance *knowledge processing*" (p. 34).

Morgan (1986) emphasizes the need to design organizations with a capacity "not just to process information but also to learn so as to

- Encourage openness and reflectivity that accepts error and uncertainty in a complex environment

- Encourage exploration of different viewpoints
- Avoid limiting inquiry by the overuse of goals and objectives
- Create structures that encourage the preceding" (Morgan, 1986 as cited in Price, 1999, p. 172).

Adaptive and responsive behavior, which includes the above, is essential to the location and design of knowledge as it is a "highly situational, relational, interactive, and contestable process" (Patriotta, 2003, p. vii). According to Murray (2005), "Social systems evolve by exploring their space of possibilities…" (p. 229). In complex adaptive systems, environmental interdependence with no absolute boundaries leads to both more complexity and to the potential experience of more effectiveness when occurring during favorable conditions (Lawrimore, 2005; Gilpin, 2005). Accordingly, complex adaptive systems, states Richardson (2005), "often have the ability to learn from their mistakes and generate new responses to familiar and novel contexts" (pp. 110–111), expanding opportunities to contribute to organizational achievement. Schulz (2004) defines *organizational knowledge* as "knowledge and information held by an organization that all, part or parts of the organization share" (p. 662; Huber, 1991).

Fundamentally, knowledge creation and integration is a social process (Stacey, 1996) that is evolutionary (Spender, 1996) at the individual and group learning level. McElroy (2003) suggests there are three levels of learning or *knowledge domains* in an organization: the top-level organization or enterprise, subgroups within the organization, and individuals who may or may not be members of groups. This writing will focus on the subgroups and the participation of the people who enhance learning and knowledge production in organizations at this level—where the knowledge is designed and used.

Researchers have offered the terms *absorptive capacity* (AC) and *combination capability* (CC) as language to focus on ongoing knowledge creation and production in organizations (Cohen & Levinthal, 1990; Zehra & George, 2002; Jansen, Van den Bosch, & Volberda, 2005). Although they overlap, in this chapter AC and CC will be examined separately. It should be noted that, although not directly discussed, exploration and exploitation of knowledge are also key elements of knowledge processes and knowledge management (Zehra & George, 2002), existing within the practice and production of both AC and CC.

Absorptive Capacity

Absorptive capacity (AC) is defined by Zehra and George (2002) as "a set of organizational routines and processes by which firms acquire, assimilate, transform, and exploit knowledge to produce a dynamic organizational capability" (p. 186). They also suggest that absorptive capacity, at the organizational level, is reflected in the organization's "knowledge creation and utilization that enhances a firm's ability to gain and sustain a competitive advantage" (p. 185). AC is the ability to take new and potentially useful information and to transfer that information into corporate routines and processes that are an advantage to the firm's future.

Differing contexts impact the transfer of knowledge based on the receiving person or team's ability to adequately absorb information that is identified as being potentially usable knowledge (Dixon, 2000). Introduced by Cohen and Levinthal (1990), AC assumes that there is (1) prior related knowledge that includes basic knowledge regarding the noted topic or skill that allows the identification of usefulness, (2) shared language (those words or terms related to the topic or skill) and, if needed, (3) technical knowledge (how to do what is suggested) (Dixon, 2000). This allows the perception that the new information can be transferred into the current context.

It may be that the needed information is readily available but attention has not been given to absorbing the information into the collective thinking patterns of the group or organization. The challenge is to support, strengthen, and amplify organizational members' ability to tap into these basic learning patterns for individual and group knowledge creation. Szulanski (1996), in a study of 122 "best practice" transfers in eight companies, found that the inability to absorb new information was a major barrier to knowledge transfer within organizations. The same is true regarding transfer of knowledge between organizations.

Combination Capability

Combination capability (CC) involves "new combinations—incrementally or radically—either by combining elements previously unconnected or by developing novel ways of combining elements previously associated" (Nahapiet & Ghoshal, 1998, p. 248). Zahra and George (2002) included combination capability in their dimension of "transformation," saying, "Transformation denotes a firm's capability to develop and refine the routines that facilitate combining existing knowledge and the newly acquired and assimilated knowledge" (p. 190). New and combined knowledge can trigger transformation and has the ability to sustain competitive advantage while expanding resources and adjusting capabilities.

The ability of an organization to learn, process information, and then manage information is crucial in today's complex environments, occurring in formal and informal venues. Multiunit organizations often share information across units and levels in the form of hunches, hints, ideas, and informal conversations, including customer knowledge, how to use equipment effectively, what can be done to avoid certain situations, and so on, ultimately benefiting the collective organization (Tsai, 2001). The sufficiency of organizational knowledge is impacted by the ability to identify potential barriers to knowledge acquisition, combination, and transfer within the organizational context. The ability to absorb new information and the ability to create and apply learned knowledge inside routines is significant to creating opportunities for organizations to expand, profit, and remain viable.

KNOWLEDGE LOCATION

Adding emphasis to the essentialness of relationships within social processes in complex adaptive systems, knowledge generation is influenced by the purposeful design of what Nebus (2006) notes as *advice networks*—the location of particular people who are seen as potentially instrumental in achieving a desired outcome (Stokman & Doreian, 1997). Ho, Rousseau, and Levesque (2006) suggest the importance of *friendship networks*—"relationships that are social in nature and are characterized by positive interactions" (p. 465) that offer participants trust and social support, and include frequent, strong interactions that are affective in nature.

An additional resource for locating knowledge are those people who inhabit *structural holes*—"individuals who broker a link between otherwise unconnected groups or individuals" (Ho et al., 2006, p. 463; Burt, 1992). The ability to access knowledge and talents from outside normal availability, such as other departments and organizations—as well as the willingness to reciprocate—enhances opportunities for locating, absorbing, and combining information effectively. The people in these locations can simplify complexity and activate relationships.

Nebus' *network generation theory* utilizes individual choice models in linking an individual's actions to network formation and continuance. According to Nebus (2006, p. 217), "In the context of advice networks, selection [of participants] entails choosing persons to contact for information." This is no less true in friendship networks and the people who inhabit structural holes. Convenient and cooperative pools of advice and information offer both opportunity and restraint in the amount and validity of information found inside a network. Restraint occurs through (1) biases that develop within the network, (2) the exercise of choices regarding person(s) to tap for advice, (3) the relevance of the experience and expertise provided, (4) the availability of the preferred advice providers, and (5) knowledge that is always in the process of formation, changing as it is offered and taken in (Nebus, 2006).

Maintaining the availability of advice providers for future contact involves the nurturance of relationships with those perceived as providing the most benefit as future advice consultants. It must be emphasized that *the formation and nurturance of networks is imperative to fostering creativity* (Nebus, 2006). Within one's networks are "doubters" (those who challenge and question what is offered) and "believers" (those who look for the strengths, not weaknesses, of what is offered) (Belenky & Stanton, 2000); both are important to the expansion and validity of useful knowledge. The tendency of the knowledge seeker to move toward network participants who share his or her stance (belief) is counter to locating the best knowledge-producing outcome.

Social Capital

Nahapiet and Ghoshal (1998) verify the importance of access to others. They argue that organizations facilitate the creation of knowledge through the generation of social capital "by affecting the conditions necessary for exchange and combination to occur" (p. 250). They also propose that a precondition for the creation of new intellectual capital is combination capability—the ability to combine information/knowledge into a new creation. From their view, social capital consists of three dimensions: *structural* (network ties, network configuration, and appropriable organization), *cognitive* (shared language and shared narratives), and *relational* (trust, norms, obligation, and identification). Bapuji and Crossan (2005) suggest that Nahapiet and Ghoshal's approach to knowledge combination and exchange (access to others for combination/exchange, anticipation of value, and motivation to combine/exchange knowledge) does not fully take into account the complex social processes involved in the co-evolution of knowledge.

KNOWLEDGE CREATION

Most organizations of today are still immersed in efficiency and linear causality in which managers intervene as needed to control the dynamics of the system (Gilpin, 2001), while pretending the system is not dynamic and complex. In this environment, valued and valuable information moves downward through the organization; it does not move upward or across, forming new messages of merged knowledge. Yet managers are only part of the larger system (Salthe, 2005) and not the location of all knowing. Since they are only part of what Chia (1998) notes as *dynamic complexity*, organizations must address the issues around the expansion of knowledge within the group and across the larger system through encouraging a free flow of information. Inside information free flow are questions and explanations that otherwise may not be heard.

Fortunately, the turbulence of organizing has brought a focus in recent years on knowledge as a dominant source of competitive advantage (Spender, 1996; Jansen, Van den Bosch, & Volberda, 2005). Two assumptions are clear relating to knowledge creation in organizations. First, knowledge is dynamically embedded in networks and processes, and second, there is of necessity a reliance on learning anew and the self- and group-organization of new knowledge in order to adapt to changing environments (Thatkenkery, 2004). Knowledge is embedded in the minds of people, and it is difficult to get it out. If opportunities arise, people must be motivated to share and combine knowledge with others (Davenport & Prusak, 1998). Thus, it is appropriate to add a third assumption: Knowledge is socially constructed (Bapuji & Crossan, 2005), requiring relational learning and exchange. It occurs through mutual experiences, casual sharing, observation of the activities of others, or purposeful efforts to design knowledge through activities of interaction and transaction (Thatkenkery, 2005).

Relational Learning

Hall and Kahn (2002) define relational learning as "*the enlargement of an individual's capacities to approach new situations, integrate and interpret new information, to learn about the self, and act effectively in those situations through relationships with other individuals or groups at work*" (p. 53, italics in original). Thus, knowledge creation occurs through activities of co-construction. The construction of knowledge includes consideration of observations, experiences, historical understandings, and offerings of others (Gergen & Gergen, 2003). It also includes the possibility of these exchanges becoming transformation-producing opportunities. The social construction of mutually relevant and combined knowledge is vital to personal and organizational growth and achievement.

A Non-Linear Activity

Knowledge creation is an ongoing, non-linear, complexity-producing process. It can be confusion-producing, conflictive, and innovative in nature. It can be achieved through observation, conversations, and reflection (Weick, 1995). Every day people learn from, create and share knowledge with others, and take action based on old and new learning that is seen as relevant to a situation or circumstance. "Learning aimed at increasing our fund of knowledge, at increasing our repertoire of skills, at extending already established cognitive capacities into new terrain," notes Kegan (2000, p. 48); "serves the absolutely crucial purpose of deepening the resources available to an existing frame of reference."

Human Memory

Complexity theory suggests that most knowledge is the result of numerous events, observations, experiences, learnings, and reactions occurring over extended periods of time, rather than being a result of a critical event (Dooley, 2002). The minds of organizational members hold "collective memory" (Probst, Raub, & Romhardt, 2000), "transactive memories" (Wegner, 1987) and/or "collective beliefs" (Gilbert, 2000) that enable or constrain the emergence of knowledge, allowing an organization to adjust or adapt to situations. According to Probst et al. (2000, p. 231) "Collective memory is not just so much historical baggage; it can also be extremely productive." Fineman, Sims and Gabriel (2005) tell a story of one of the authors overhearing pilots in a restaurant in the Denver, Colorado, airport when delayed because of bad weather:

> As he sat at a café, waiting for his flight to be announced, he overheard the conversation of four pilots sitting at a table near his. The conversation made uncomfortable hearing, as the pilots recounted some of the most terrifying experiences of their careers—near collisions, failure of equipment, freak weather phenomena, dangerous passengers and so forth. What the author gradually realized was that the pilots were not just trying to impress each other with ever more scary stories, but rather were passing very useful information of the sort that may not be found in their flight manuals to their colleagues— they were *sharing knowledge*, in other words, giving tips, comparing experiences, making judgments, drawing very fine distinctions and so forth. They were, in effect, acting as a knowledge network or members of a "community of practice." (p. 33)

Memories and beliefs are useless if homeostatic responses to new approaches and learning occur. This occurs when (1) people do not ask for input or support (it is not part of the culture of the organization); (2) the common we-tried-it-before-and-it-didn't-work is received; (3) the common not-invented-here-syndrome viewpoint is held (Dixon, 2000); or (4) time and opportunity are not available to share knowledge. These attitudes and situations are both evident and located in the metaconversations (background, unnoticed, culture-evident) of organizations, putting up barriers to the transfer of knowledge.

Because human memory is fleeting and dynamic (Probst et al., 2000), combination capability must reside in ongoing intra- and interpersonal activities of seeking opportunities for combining current and new knowledge. Social capital (relationships, obligations and connections) (Bourdieu, 1986) and human capital (knowledge, skills and experiences) (Lin, 2001; McElroy, 2003) are altered through mutual efforts to create. Information for combination may be located inside the organization or require effort to locate it beyond the boundaries of the organization, even within other organizations.

Relational learning networks provide opportunities for learning. Information, guesses, suppositions, and data are offered, exchanged, considered, and distributed, utilizing a sensemaking process that is expansive and influential. The people who have information offer it to others, are willing to hear what others have to offer in return, expand and combine, and then take that information to others to be part of new sensemaking, making it a complex, dynamic process.

KNOWLEDGE TRANSFER

The best way an organization can transfer knowledge, according to Davenport and Prusak (1998), is to "hire smart people and let them talk to one another" (p. 88). Letting them talk and act in ways that create knowledge is difficult to purposely orchestrate. In a complex adaptive system, healthy networks can exist for transfer of knowledge from the originating location (Dixon, 2000). Working directly with the originator allows the recipient(s) to see into the knowledge situation and compare/contrast what is possible in their own situation. This allows for a *perceptual rehearsal*, a mental run-through or simulation, that is highly valuable to the transfer and transformation of information. Energy and thought are expended toward addressing transfer issues with the originators of the considered knowledge. The possibility of adaptation is enhanced, creating the possibility of bidirectional learning. In this process, the cooperative evolution of thought and the synergy created by bringing together people with like or different issues and situations creates opportunities for insightful reflection and sensemaking (Hinrichs, Stavros, & Seiling, 2005). Achieving this "cooperative evolution" and the synergy necessary to encourage transfer is far from easy (Szulanski, 1996, 2003).

Of significance to social constructionist thinking is the idea that knowledge cannot be "given to" another person. That is, according to Harlene Anderson (personal communication, October 10, 2006), "We can share our knowledge with another but the other brings his or her pre-understandings and meanings to the interactive process, creating something unique and meaningful to him or her around that information." Of course, it is a challenge to know what the other person(s) is thinking and reflecting around the offered knowledge.

Keeping the conversation going, keeping the space for pauses, reflection and exchange, helps to identify what has been considered about the information in the responders thinking. Sheila McNamee (personal communication, October 10, 2006) adds to this approach, "From the standpoint of communication, knowledge generation is always active, whether in the pauses of conversation or during active interaction. There is a flow that cannot be stopped even when we do not fully understand what each is offering the other."

From this perspective, Anderson and McNamee agree with Davenport and Pusak (1998) that there is a transfer of knowledge in organizations whether it is paid attention to or not. In everyday work, the transfer of knowledge is located in applying old knowledge to a new situation or taking available resources and "making do" to apply in other ways (Weick, 1995); it is transferred tacitly through mimicry of someone who is seen as a professional, expert, mentor, or teacher; or it is offered as a legacy by a retiring member to a "staying" member. Under certain circumstances, the acquirer observes, copies, and practices the knowledge-action and internalizes it for future use. The new holder of knowledge may transfer it to others through communication, or others may also learn by practicing mimicry (Stacey, 2001).

Dixon (2000) identified four levels of transfer of knowledge to others as: serial transfer, near transfer, far transfer and strategic transfer. These levels of transfer identify knowledge sharing as reflecting the resource-based view, identifying the transfer of knowledge as vital to competitive advantage for organizations.

Serial Transfer

Serial transfer is the transfer of knowledge from performing in one setting to doing the same task in a different setting. Examination is made of an activity immediately after performance so learning can occur prior to the next performance. The U.S. Army uses this approach in order to bring the unique knowledge of each person into the group for consideration and possible sensemaking and integration by the whole team. British Petroleum borrowed the "after action review" approach used by the U. S. Army, calling it "learning during," tying it to "learning before" and "learning after." BP designed a set of knowledge management practices for performing serial transfer in a systemic way (Dixon, 2000).

Near Transfer

Near transfer applies when information is transferred between a similar source team and a receiving team *on a routine basis*. Although geographic location is not a significant issue for near transfer, "a learning experience resembles the place and situation where the knowledge will be used on the job" (Dixon, 2000, p. 54). Organizations that intentionally bring people together regularly to demonstrate/discuss new thinking, processes, and procedures, or locate useful knowledge on a localized database that is retrievable by others, are examples of practicing near transfer. Failed ideas or processes are also examined in order to identify changes that can be made or to locate other uses for a failed product that has not met its purpose. The goal is to improve effectiveness whether it is a simple change, a more complex procedure or a series of steps that bring improvement (Dixon, 2000).

Far Transfer

Far transfer occurs when one group has learned something that can assist other parts of the organization and would like to make it available to those interested who are doing similar work. It is different from near transfer in that it is *non-routine*, as needed. It often includes tacit information, not explicit information. It also involves work that is unique to a situation and receiver use is likely to be very different from those who originated the information and experience. In far transfer, reciprocity is built into the activity of exchange; participants from groups learn from each other during the activity of transfer. This does not suggest that the receiving team will use the knowledge in the same way as originally offered. It is customized for use in the new context (Dixon, 2000).

Strategic Transfer

Strategic transfer takes place when a *one-time or infrequent* project takes place and there is a need for information from others in other parts of the organization who have experience in similar work. It is located in the mind of the organization and is tapped to gain knowledge that could be of great value. Strategic transfer can save time and money in that it avoids having to reinvent the wheel. Strategic transfer "impacts large parts of the organization" (Dixon, 2000, p. 102) and involves both tacit and explicit knowledge needed to accomplish a task that may have a strategic influence on the organization.

Strategic transfer is now being approached through virtual connections. The transfer of knowledge through face-to-face conversations is being threatened by the burgeoning growth of virtual teams and offices. Although the collection of various talents, skills, and viewpoints is highly important to effectiveness, the focus on cost and time savings through relating in a totally virtual environment requires attention to the relational aspects of knowledge and innovation producing groups. "Groupness" must emerge from the dynamics of virtual communication (Wallace, 1999); the lack or lessening of face-to-face connection can make it difficult to establish trust in groups. Water cooler talk, talk rooms, face-to-face casual encounters in the hall, meeting in the lunch room, and other spontaneous activities *are opportunities for productive work* that are difficult to duplicate virtually, creating added complexity to orchestrating successful virtual networks for knowledge creation.

INFORMATION "STICKINESS"

Organizations have long been concerned about how to pull in, adapt, and hold new and existing knowledge, products, and processes—in other words, how to make it "stick." For the purposes of this writing, "stickiness" is defined as the *need and desire* for continued utilization of knowledge. In order for knowledge to be seen as worthy of continued utilization, it must be *used*.

Within organizations, different groups and departments differ in their ability to internalize and retain information and capabilities (Tsai, 2001; White, 1999). The ability to absorb new information and the ability to create and apply learned knowledge inside routines is significant to creating opportunities for organizations to expand, profit, and remain viable. To lose valuable information because of lack of use or a perception of lack of value can result in unfortunate results. Networks of shared knowledge can expand the likelihood of stickiness. If one person or group is not currently using a resource of knowledge, another area of use can keep it alive and available, perhaps adding to the storehouse of information and use. As noted, retaining knowledge for future use is a factor in effective utilization of accessible knowledge. To think back where certain information can be found or retrieved can be a vital nugget of information at a given moment (who mentioned that, where did I see that, in what computer file did I put something about this?), making it possible to re-assemble what was done and what can be done at this moment.

From an attention perspective (Jones, 1976) or an information bias viewpoint (Geen, Beatty & Arkine, 1984), the listener may be diverted from hearing what is offered by conceptual, motivational, or situational issues. Taylor and Fiske (1978) note that people often respond with relatively little thought or top-of-the-head responses (Geen et al., 1984). There is little hope, it is thought, for innovative knowledge creation or stickiness to occur when people do not reflect on the possibilities of the offered information.

Parks-Daloz (2000, p. 110) notes the importance of "constructive engagement with otherness." An encounter must cause purposeful consideration and reflection. Yet top-of-the-head responses can trigger thoughts in others that can bring forward productive thoughts and responses. From the sensemaking view, giving attention to or being responsive to different or out-of-the-norm information is significant to the person's ability to successfully notice and move toward opportunities to learn and act on new sense.

Szulanski (1996) noted four sets of influencing factors that make it difficult to transfer knowledge—characteristics of the knowledge transferred, the source, the recipient, and the context in which the transfer takes place—thus adding to the level of the task and relational complexity and potentially interfering with possibilities of stickiness.

FINAL THOUGHTS

More and more, organizations are depending on the creation of knowledge that is pooled, often created with others. Unique interpretations of combined knowledge, experience, and observations are designed into new sense (Weick, 1969, 1995). As such, all knowledge starts with local knowledge that is co-constructed with others (Gergen, 1999). Intentional behavior and action toward knowledge creation and transfer must be learned, even required, in order for an organization to be a healthy, adaptive system that combines, adapts, reforms, and reframes knowledge into new, different, emerging information. Salthe (2005, p. 103) states, "The primary assertion of complexity theory is that variations arising out of the interactions between entities, whether human or nonhuman, are the source of new, self-organized order in complex systems." This statement is especially pertinent to efforts toward the identification of new, contradictory, or complementary information and the acceptance of intellectual diversity.

REFERENCES

Bapuji, H., & Crossan, M. (2005). *Co-evolution of social capital and knowledge: An extension of the Nahapiet and Ghoshal (1998) framework.* Academy of Management Best Conference Paper, annual conference, Honolulu, Hawii.

Belenky, M. Field, & Stanton, A. V. (2000). Inequality, development, and connected knowing. In J. Mezirow & Associates (Eds.), *Learning as transformation: Critical perspectives on a theory in progress* (pp. 71–102). San Francisco: Jossey-Bass.

Bourdieu, P. (1986). The forms of capital. In J. G. Richardson (Ed.), *Handbook of theory and research for the sociology of education* (pp. 241–258). Westport, CT: Greenwood.

Burt, R. S. (1992). *Structural holes: The social structure of competition.* Cambridge, MA: Harvard University Press.

Chia, R. (1998). From complexity science to complex thinking: Organization as simple location. *Organization, 5,* 341–369.

Cohen, W. M., & Levinthal, D. (1990). Asset stock accumulation and sustainability of competitive advantage. *Management Science, 35,* 128–152.

Davenport, T. H., & Prusak, L. (1998). *Working knowledge: How organizations manage what they know.* Boston: Harvard Business School Press.

Dixon, N. M. (2000). *Common knowledge: How companies thrive on sharing what they know.* Boston: Harvard Business School Press.

Dooley, K. (2002). Organizational complexity. In M. Warner (Ed.), *International encyclopedia of business and management* (pp. 5013–5022). London: Thompson Learning.

Fineman, S., Sims, D., & Gabriel, Y. (2005). *Organizing and organizations, 3rd edition.* Thousand Oaks, CA: Sage.

Geen, R.G., Beatty, W.W., & Arkine, R. (1984). *Human motivation: Psychological, behavioral, and social approaches.* Boston: Allyn & Bacon.

Gergen, Kenneth J. (1999). *An invitation to social construction.* Thousand Oaks, CA: Sage.

Gergen, K. J. & Gergen, M. (2003). Knowledge as socially constructed. In M. Gergen & K. J. Gergen (Eds.), *Social construction: A reader* (pp. 15–17). Thousand Oaks, CA: Sage.

Gilbert, M. (2000). *Sociality and responsibility: New essays in plural subject theory.* New York: Rowman & Littlefield.

Gilpin, D. R. (2005). A complexity-based scrutiny of learning from organizational crisis. In K. A. Richardson (Ed.), *Managing organizational complexity: Philosophy, theory, application* (pp. 373–388). Greenwich, CT: Information Age Publishing.

Hall, D. T., & Kahn, W. A. (2002). Developmental relationships at work: A learning perspective. In C. L. Cooper & R. J. Burke (Eds.), *The New World of Work* (pp. 49–74). Malden, MA: Blackwell.

Hinrichs, G., Stavros, J.M. & Seiling, J.G. (2005, March/April). *Sensemanaging as the soul of improvisation.* Presentation at the Midwest Academy of Management 48th Annual Conference, Chicago, IL.

Ho, V. T., Rousseau, D. M., & Levesque, L. L. (2006). Social networks and the psychological contract: Structural holes, cohesive ties, and beliefs regarding employer obligations. *Human Relations, 59*(4), 459–481.

Huber, G. P. (1991). Organizational learning: The contributing processes and the literatures. *Organizational Science, 2,* 88–115.

Jansen, J.J.P., Van den Bosch, F. A. J., & Volberda, H. W. (2005). Managing potential and realized absorptive capacity: How do organizational antecedents matter? *Academy of Management Journal, 48,* 999–1015.

Jones, E. E. (1976). How do people perceive the causes of behavior? *American Scientists, 64,* 300–305.

Kawai, T. (2005). The improvised-orchestration model of organizational evolution. In K. A. Richardson (Ed.), *Managing organizational complexity: Philosophy, theory, application* (pp. 313–329). Greenwich, CT: Information Age Publishing.

Kegan, R. (2000). What "form" transforms? A constructive-developmental approach to transformative learning. In J. Mezirow & Associates (Eds.), *Learning as transformation: Critical perspectives on a theory in progress* (pp. 35–69). San Francisco: Jossey-Bass.

Lawrimore, B. (2005). From excellence to emergence: The evolution of management thinking and the influence of complexity. In K. A. Richardson (Ed.), *Managing organizational complexity: Philosophy, Theory, Application* (pp. 115–132). Greenwich, CT: Information Age Publishing.

Lin, N. (2001). *Social capital: a theory of social structure and action.* Cambridge, UK: Cambridge University Press.

Maguire, S. & McKelvey, B. (1999). Complexity and management: Moving from fad to firm foundations. *Emergence, 1,* 3–13.

McElroy, M. W. (2003). *The new knowledge management: Complexity, learning, and sustainable innovation.* Boston: Butterworth-Heinemann.

McGrath, J. E., & Argote, L. (2001). Group processes in organizational contexts. In M. A. Hogg & S. Tindale (Eds.), *Handbook of social psychology: Group processes* (pp. 602–627). Malden, MA: Blackwell.

Morgan, G. (1986). *Images of organization.* San Francisco: Sage.

Murray, R. C. (2005). Theory of integral complex organization. In K. A. Richardson (Ed.), *Managing organizational complexity: Philosophy, theory, application* (pp. 217–235). Greenwich, CT: Information Age Publishing.

Nahapiet, J., & Ghoshal, S. (1998). Social capital, intellectual capital, and the organizational advantage. *Academy of Management Review, 23,* 242–266.

Nebus, J. (2006). Building collegial information networks: A theory of advice network generation. *Academy of Management Review, 31,* 615–637.

Parks-Daloz, L. A. (2000). Transformative learning for the common good. In Mezirow & Associates (Eds.), *Learning as transformation: Critical perspectives on a theory in progress* (pp. 103–123). San Francisco: Jossey-Bass.

Patriotta, G. (2003). *Organizational knowledge in the making: How firms create, use, and institutionalize knowledge.* New York: Oxford University Press.

Price, I. (1999). Images or reality? Metaphors, memes, and management. In M. R. Lissack & H. P. Gunz (Eds.), *Managing complexity in organizations* (pp. 165–179). Greenwich, CT: Information Age Publications.

Probst, G., Raub, S. & Romhardt, K. (2000). *Managing knowledge: Building blocks for success.* New York: John Wiley & Sons.

Richardson, K. A. (2005). Section introduction: Pluralism in management science. In K. A. Richardson (Ed.), *Managing organizational complexity: Philosophy, theory, application* (pp. 109–114). Greenwich, CT: Information Age Publishing.

Salthe, S. E. (2005). Causality in organized complexity: The role of management. In K. A. Richardson (Ed.), *Managing organizational complexity: Philosophy, theory, application* (pp. 79–92). Greenwich, CT: Information Age Publishing.

Schulz, M. (2004). The uncertain relevance of newness: Organizational learning and knowledge flows. *Academy of Management Journal, 44,* 661–681.

Simpson, B. (2005). Advancing complexity theory into the human domain. In K. A. Richardson (Ed.), *Managing organizational complexity: Philosophy, theory, application* (pp. 93–114). Greenwich, CT: Information Age Publishing.

Spender, J. C. (1996). Making knowledge the basis of a dynamic theory of the firm. *Strategic Management Journal, 17* (Winter Special Issue), 45–62.

Stacey, R. D. (1996). *Complexity and creativity in organizations.* San Francisco: Berrett-Koehler.

Stacey, R. D. (2001). *Complex responsive processes in organizations: Learning and knowledge creation.* New York: Routledge.

Stavros, J.M. & Torres, C.B. (2005). *Dynamic relationships: Unleashing the power of appreciative inquiry in daily living.* Chagrin Falls, OH: Taos Institute Publishing.

Stokman, F., & Doreian, P. (1997). Evolution of social networks: Processes and principles. In P. Doreian & F. Stokman (Eds.), *Evolution of social networks* (pp. 233–250). Amsterdam: Gordon and Breach.

Szulanski, G. (1996). Exploring internal stickiness: Impediments to the transfer of best practice within the firm. *Strategic Management Journal, 17*(Winter Special Issue), 27–43.

Szulanski, G. (2003). *Sticky knowledge: Barriers to knowing in the firm.* Thousand Oaks, CA: Sage.

Taylor, S. E., & Fiske, S. T. (1978). Salience, attention, and attribution: Top of the head phenomenon. In L. Berkowitz (Ed.), *Advances in experimental social psychology* (Vol. II) (pp. 250–288). New York: Academic Press.

Thatkenkery, T. J. (2004). *Appreciative sharing of knowledge: Leveraging knowledge management for strategic change.* Chagrin Falls, OH: Taos Institute Publishing.

Tsai, W. (2001). Knowledge transfer in intraorganizational networks: Effects of network position and absorptive capacity on business unit innovation and performance. *Academy of Management Journal, 44,* 996–1004.

Wallace, P. (1999). *The psychology of the internet.* New York: Cambridge University Press.

Wegner, D. M. (1987). Transactive memory: A contemporary analysis of the group mind. In B. Mullen and G. R. Goethals (Eds.), *Theories of group behavior* (pp. 185–205). New York: Springer-Verlag.

Weick, K. E. (1969). *The social psychology of organizing.* Reading, MA: Addison-Wesley.

Weick, K. E. (1995). *Sensemaking in organizations.* Thousand Oaks, CA: Sage.

White, M. (1999). Adaptive corporations. In M. R. Lissack & H. P. Gunz (Eds.), *Managing complexity in organizations* (pp. 281–191). Greenwich, CT: Information Age Publications.

Zehra, S. A., & George, G. (2002). Absorptive capacity: A review, reconceptualization, and extension. *Academy of Management Review, 27,* 185–203.

CHAPTER 7

SHIFTING LANDSCAPE

Differences that Spawn New Knowledge

Ann C. Baker

> Complex network organizations are continually emerging . . .
> *innovative organizations . . . are always in the process of becoming*
> *rather than ever reaching equilibrium.*
> —Rycroft & Kash, 1999, pp. 66–67

Organizational life has become too complex for a single individual, profession, or discipline to grasp and understand (Rycroft & Kash, 1999), and traditional models of management and communication are inadequate in the face of such complexity. These models reflect worldviews and frames of reference that limit imagination, constrain perceptions, and hinder problem-solving. Alternatively, complexity theories offer conceptual frameworks for articulating organizational and societal complexities with more fluidity and imagination.

Historically most products, services, and the processes that created them were simple enough for capable individuals to grasp and learn. That simplicity evaporated in recent decades in many parts of the world. There was "more information produced in the last 30 years than in the previous 5,000, and the information supply available to us doubles every five years" (Pritchett as cited

Complexity and Knowledge Management, pages 109–122
Copyright © 2010 by Information Age Publishing
109

in Tymon & Stumpf, 2003, p. 12). The changing faces of economics, trade, education, government, and diplomacy involve unprecedented complexity.

The purpose of this chapter is to explore innovative ways to meet the challenges of organizational and societal complexity. At the core of innovation is the never-ending creation of new knowledge, and the vast differences among people are invaluable resources for spawning knowledge creation. Yet accessing these differences in ways that foster innovation and creativity is an obstacle. Working at the edge of chaos offers a conceptual framework for the kind of organizational context within which to access differences creatively. The landscape of organizations must shift, though, away from traditional emphases on structure and predictability toward more fluid supportive contexts for social networks to thrive. Rather than focus on "the role of knowledge in social networks," I draw attention to the role of social networks in knowledge creation.

KNOWLEDGE MANAGEMENT
AND KNOWLEDGE CREATION

Though the term *knowledge management* is in this book's title, the emphasis in this chapter is more specifically on *knowledge creation* because of relevance to the message. It is important to differentiate whether the primary purpose of work is the linear *transmitting* of existing information, the *sharing* of existing knowledge, or the *creating* of new knowledge. While organizations benefit from information exchange, the exchange can have multiple kinds of purposes. When the sole purpose is to transmit information, it is often in the form of one-way communication, much like a one-direction monologue, memo, or email rather than an interactive give and take. In one-way communications, questions are discouraged or impossible. If the routine modes tend to be one-directional, the challenge is to step back and ask if the approach serves or stymies the current purpose. One-directional communication is highly functional for some purposes, though in complex environments, it often leads to incomplete information, misunderstanding, and information hoarding. It thwarts learning and creativity.

If organizational purpose includes innovation and knowledge creation, the organization needs a "building process of shared information [that] works like the coral reef, built in a fractal formation... as opposed to a linear mode" (Davis & Brewer, 1997, p. 137). Building "coral reefs" requires interactive media to facilitate texture and depth, nuance, and opportunities for growth. Applying the coral reef analogy to organizational settings supports more fluid, open *sharing* of information and *creating* new knowledge and new ways of knowing among people.

Rigid structures, competitive conduct, and excessive rationality impede sharing and creating behaviors. Sharing and creating behaviors grow out of social, relational dynamics. "Knowledge is not just embedded in the invisible cognitive worlds of individuals, but exists within the multiple relationships and evolving memberships of individuals and groups in society" (Richter, 1998, p. 312). This chapter explores how to facilitate multiple relationships and evolving memberships of individuals and groups in society that encourage cognitive learning and knowledge creation. Conversations among diverse people and groups can increase creativity and minimize polarization as people share.

COMPLEXITY AS DISTINCT FROM LINEARITY

Rarely do people in contemporary society work alone, yet education and training for most experts, such as engineers or economists, are increasingly specialized and narrow. Incentive structures in the West tend to reward individual accomplishment and the development of more specific and deeper, rather than wider, expertise. As the range of proficiency narrows, experts see smaller and smaller slices of the complexities of organizational and societal life, thus distorting perceptions. Given the intricate webs of human behavior, it is more important than ever for organizations to support dynamic social networks of people engaged in emergent interactions.

Also, human behavior often is not rational and can be wildly erratic. As collections of widely diverse people interact, the complexity increases exponentially. There are almost as many different interpretations of what is going on in a given setting as there are participants. For these challenges, this chapter proposes two areas of focus. One is to expand the worldviews that frame people's perceptions. The other is to tap people's wisdom and knowledge through their interpersonal interactions in a process called conversational learning, a topic explored later.

Let's think first about constraining worldviews. In complex organizational settings, linear thinking and cause-and-effect problem-solving can blind people to critical parts of the picture. Given the multitude of conflicting interests at play inside organizations, across them, and with external environments, linear thinking that seeks to find one or a few causes of problems is profoundly inadequate. Moreover, because this approach gives the illusion of predictability and control, it can actually exacerbate problems.

Traditional management theories and linear thinking encourage managers to avoid disequilibrium, even though shaking stability is a fundamental element of innovation. Shaking stability is at the core of George Cowan's message, "The moment you depart from the *linear approximation*, you're navigating on a very broad ocean" (as quoted in Waldrop, 1992, p. 66; emphasis added). Relinquishing the "linear approximation" is tantamount to letting go of assumptions about how to navigate change and assumptions about how the world works—that is, worldviews. Nonetheless, innovation and substantial organizational change that can have long-term impact involve reconsidering each unexamined assumption. They involve engaging with unfamiliar and surprising ideas. Expanding one's worldview depends upon learning how to navigate that "broad ocean" and the opposing forces of energy bouncing off of each other.

Stuart Kauffman describes complexity as "a natural expression of a universe that is not in equilibrium...differences, potentials, drive the formation of complexity" (1995, p. 19). Waldrop uses simple and direct language to describe his meaning of *complexity* by saying that it is where a "great many independent agents are interacting with each other in a great many ways" (1992, p. 11). Disequilibrium is an inherent part of complex environments, meaning that ambiguity and lack of predictability are givens.

In the biological world, molecules that are thriving in rich and nourishing environments are continually combining to form more complex molecules. Likewise, in the organizational world, people in innovative organizations are interacting in constantly changing ways, developing more complexity. Their differing perspectives and expertise can stimulate new ideas that can lead to increasing innovation as they self-organize into various ad-hoc groupings and communities-of-practice (Wenger, 1998)—that is, highly creative, dynamic environments that serve people, organizations, and society. A fundamental dimension of innovative contexts is the churning of diverse kinds of knowledge among people. When people are working together in these churning contexts, they are maneuvering in spaces similar to a transitional space at the edge of chaos.

As Kaufman (1995) suggests, complexity is an unavoidable expression of natural interactions, and these dynamics can be illustrated along a continuum from rigid order to utter chaos as in Figure 7.1.

In complex systems, there are strong attractions in dialectically opposing directions (Capra, 1991, 1982). *Order* at the far left end of the continuum represents the mindset bent on the perpetuation of the *status quo, modus operandi,* and an *all-is-well* mindset. Chaotic unpredictability is at the opposite extreme. The *tensions* between the two extremes of order and chaos come together in a fragile transitional area at the *edge of chaos.* Whenever there is not enough tension between the two extremes, order takes over, and organizations become routinized, rigid, stagnant, and dull. On the other hand, if the tension becomes too strong, chaos and anarchy reign.

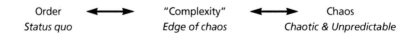

Figure 7.1

Not only are some groups or organizations more likely to fit on one part of this continuum than another, but there also are internal variations. For example, within an organization there may be groups that tend to be quite orderly in their deliberations and others that tend to be more chaotic. Or the pace of the work demands within a group may vary erratically day by day or from one time of the year to another because of seasonal demands—such as a certified public accountant in the months before taxes are due.

Figure 7.2 provides a more graphic illustration of this delicate middle zone at the edge of chaos.

At its extreme, order is inflexible, immovable, and solid as ice. In organizations, we see this extreme when people try to maintain predictability through rigid adherence to elaborate rules and procedures such as in bureaucracy, traditional top-down management, and other inflexible hierarchies.

At the opposite end of the continuum far away from order, there is *chaos*, where there is no rhyme or reason to what is happening. Everything is erratic and discontinuous. An analogy in the physical world is the rapid melting of ice that becomes water and evaporates at high temperature into gaseous turbulence. In chaotic organizations, people have no sense of how their roles fit into broader organizational goals or purposes. They feel like their positions

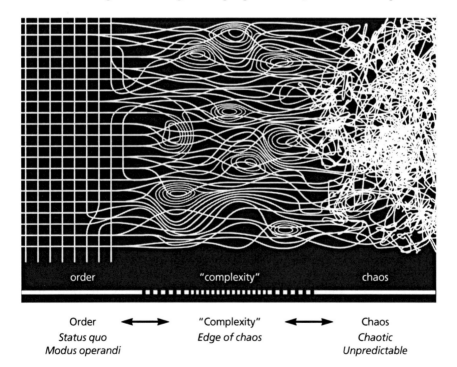

Order		"Complexity"		Chaos
Status quo	⬅➡	*Edge of chaos*	⬅➡	*Chaotic*
Modus operandi				*Unpredictable*

Figure 7.2

are extremely precarious. Their work lives are constantly changing in ways over which they have no control and which they perceive as irrational.

Chaotic systems are overtaken by "weirdly unpredictable gyrations" that "dissolve into turbulence" (Waldrop, 1992, p. 12). Waldrop's example of an organizational context that is chaotic is one in which people do not know what they are supposed to do; they work at cross-purposes. According to chaos theory, very small changes are amplified into unpredictable, widespread effects in the system (Kaufman, 1995; Waldrop, 1992).

When people try new ideas, are open to unexpected opportunities, and are responsive to customers' needs, they move away from the maintenance of order toward chaos as they try to work closer to the transitional region often referred to as "complexity." To continue the water metaphor, imagine a pot of barely boiling water. At the surface, there is a thin edge of turbulence—an edge of chaos—as the water evaporates and changes into a vapor-like steam (Waldrop, 1992).

The most fundamental challenge for people working in transitional zones at the edge of chaos is not to be overtaken by either extreme. The advantage, though, is that often the most promising opportunities for generative alternatives to emerge and for knowledge creation are in this fragile zone. Life there is ambiguous and unpredictable because it involves living in the tension between the strong attractions toward each pole. Slater describes it as "hovering delicately in the spaces between things" (as quoted in Wikstrom, Mitroff, & Normann, 1994, p. xvii) because the space that nourishes new possibilities is not stable.

At the edge of chaos,

> the components of a system never quite lock into place, and yet never quite dissolve into turbulence...[it is] where life has enough stability...and enough creativity...where new ideas and innovative genotypes are forever nibbling away at the edges of the status quo. (Waldrop, 1992, p. 12)

The edge of chaos is where a shift in the *status quo* is more possible. According to Waldrop (1992), examples of society operating in this transitional region are major social movements, such as the end of slavery and the civil rights movement in the United States. At an organizational level, embarking on a substantial cultural change moving away from rigid hierarchy toward a flatter organization is an example of operating in this fragile zone. Adopting and successfully implementing a broadly inclusive hiring and promotion system to create a truly diverse organization is another example. Applying these kinds of new knowledge to organizational practice alters the status quo.

Creativity and innovation are stifled when organizations lock people and ideas tightly into place and rigidly maintain the status quo. Likewise, when organizations try to transform the status quo overnight, the workplace can dissolve into turbulence. Support for the most creative behaviors in the middle ground between the two extremes increases the potential to "nibble away" successfully at the status quo and smoothes the progress for substantive, long-term change.

Work at the edge of chaos is tenuous and challenging. To avoid slipping into chaos or retreating into the familiarity of order and stability, organizations must be highly *intentional.* To take advantage of the potential of this fragile zone, people must get support for risk-taking, learn from unfamiliar voices, and have opportunities for reflection. It is important not to pull away all forms of structure because that can push people into bewildering places of too much ambiguity and risk where, for example, they do not know how decisions will get made, who will make them, or how budgets will be met. In fact, people need extra preparation and support during transitions in complex settings. Underestimating the interdependencies of the complex dynamics in these spaces can unintentionally drive groups over the edge into chaos or drive them backward where they seek order so desperately that they accept rigidly controlling behavior.

CONVERSATIONAL LEARNING AT THE EDGE OF CHAOS

To work most effectively in the fragile transitional region at the edge of chaos, many kinds of support are needed. This chapter specifically addresses how people interact with each other—that is, how they talk to each other. Conversations are pervasive in organizations and are a primary medium for work. I propose here a particular kind of conversation, conversational learning, to increase the capacity for innovation and knowledge creation in complex settings.

Each person's perspectives, values, and experiences are part of an organizational milieu. Whether they verbalize them or are silent, they collectively give shape to the environments. Therefore, who is in the conversation and how it develops is critical. How differences emerge can have a negative impact, or the differences can become positive resources for organizations prompting learning, adaptation, improved quality, flexibility, and innovation.

Even when people strongly disagree, if they are intentional about how they talk with each other and stay engaged in conversation, they can learn more about how and why they see things differently. They can spark new ideas, ways of thinking, and imagination. Conversations that incorporate differences generate learning and broader understandings that are fundamental to thriving organizations as documented now in a wealth of research (Argyris, 1997; Baker, Jensen, & Kolb, 2002; Brown & Duguid, 2000; Eisenhardt, Kahwajy, & Bourgeois, 1997; Isaacs, 1999; Rycroft & Kash, 1999).

Conversational learning is a self-organizing phenomenon in which people create knowledge out of their collective experiences. "From a theoretical and practical perspective, the holistic complexity of [*conversational learning*]…draws upon the most fundamental simplicity of attending to how we talk to each other" (Baker, Jensen, & Kolb, 2005, p. 426). In conversational learning, people explore their common goals and their differences (e.g., of opinion, values, experience, points of view), looking at them from a variety of vantage points. People are supported enough to diminish fears and make changes seem less risky. The "repeated sharing of experiences out of relationships of mutual trust is at the heart of conversational learning" (Baker et al., 2002, p. 4). They uncover together aspects of issues and situations not seen before. Participants consider them in a new light by gaining more information and broader understanding. When minds open to novel insights and perspectives, people are often able to imagine alternatives previously unrealized. They gain new insights by learning more about their complex surroundings and take away new perceptions from shared conversations and stories. Collaboratively they begin to *see* more.

Given the complexity of organizational life and global interdependencies, the new conversations must include the voices of diverse stakeholders. The real challenge is how to create an environment that fosters new kinds of conversation that involve the kind of listening that influences how the participants see the world and that changes behavior. In other words, people must really hear and learn from each other.

SHIFTING LANDSCAPES

To illustrate this approach, imagine a hypothetical example among diverse stakeholders in a situation familiar to you. Organizational stakeholders are people or groups of independent agents who have shared interests and yet represent differing kinds of expertise and constituencies. A corporation's stakeholders, for instance, include the employees, managers, customers, suppliers, board members, regulators, and community—all of whom have a shared interest in the corporation's well-being and success. Yet their priorities may be intensely different, ranging from maximizing financial gain short-term, preservation of the organization long-term, commitment to the original organizational mission, concern for quality, emphasis on the well-being of employees, passion for adapting to external demands, or dedication to making a societal contribution. Whether you imagine a proposed commercial land development project, an entrepreneurial business venture, a community development project, or a multinational corporation moving into a new arena, each has diverse stakeholders. Complex interactions, partnerships, collaborations, intrigues, and coalition building among multiple stakeholders play out their overlapping, but often incongruent, interests in complex undertakings.

In ensuing developments and controversies, as if the conflicting pressures are not enough, the process is always changing and continually in motion as time passes. At any specific point in the process, some accounts that individuals and groups give to describe the events may sound irrational and unrecognizable compared to each other, while others resonate. Over time, however, at different stages of a conflict, descriptions and stories change as the conflict progresses. These differences are a good example of what Patricia Shaw describes as "... complexity [that] is created by the fact that all the agents are responding to one another's signals all the time in an iterative, non-linear dynamic" (2002, p. 66). These iterative processes become convoluted and unpredictable as pressures from opposing points of view mount. As people get mired in opposing positions, alienations and hostilities build, for example. As people discover common goals, coalitions form.

At the interpersonal level, endless conversations take place, and relationships are negotiated and renegotiated, contributing even further to the complexity. Shaw offers an astute description of how this kind of complexity gets played out in conversations over time:

> From within the conduct of the conversation, what seems solid would be melting at the edges, while what seems shapeless would be gaining form, at the same time, not to create a single unified landscape for all, but a shifting topology of partial orderings in which we recreate our situation as both recognizable and potentially novel at the same time. (2002, p . 68)

As people influence and are influenced by others, the solid edges of their highly polarized positions can begin to melt. Alternatives, unimagined early in the dispute, emerge. These alternatives develop as conversations take place and give form over time to what was shapeless before. If people can talk without hostility and pressure to act quickly and can begin to understand each other better, the positions that they take may soften and bleed into each other a bit, almost as if the topology of the landscape is shifting. The movement at times can seem painfully slow, while at other times it feels more like an avalanche. Rarely is a *single unified landscape* created where everyone agrees on how to proceed with a project. Over time, though, decisions and plans can emerge out of earlier conversations that are both recognizable and novel at the same time. When these creative alternatives emerge, people are working together in the *zone of complexity at the edge of chaos.*

When people are able to work effectively in complex environments, their self-organizing and emergent behaviors grow out of their local interactions (Nonaka, 1994). Because the behaviors originate at the local, interpersonal level, "what is learned is in part unique to those involved because it is based on previous accumulated learning that is partly tacit" (Rycroft & Kash, 1999, p. 11). By bringing together diverse people with extensive local, tacit knowledge, managers and leaders can open environments rich with creative potential. Conversational learning environments focus on uncovering this kind of local accumulated learning in ways that catalyze new knowledge creation and innovation. Conversational learning environments kindle emergent behaviors.

EMERGENCE THEORY AND EMERGENT BEHAVIORS

Self-organizing behaviors are at the core of adaptation. Self-organizing groups grow out of the pressures for change and innovation in the natural and the social world. When people have ready access to multidirectional feedback from which they can learn, groups are more likely to adapt and be *emergent*. In emergence, "complex systems generate new properties [that] may be structures that form and interact in new ways or manifest new behaviors" (Rycroft & Kash, 1999, p. 260). Emergent behaviors are not random. They have a focus and an enhancing effect. Johnson (2001) describes this dynamic as channeling creative energy "toward specific forms for it to blossom into something like intelligence" (p. 119).

To understand how to encourage emergent behaviors, it is necessary to delve more deeply into what they are. Johnson (2001) says that

> Emergent complexity without adaptation is like the intricate crystals formed by a snowflake: it's a beautiful pattern, but it has no function. The forms of emergent behavior [of interest here] show the distinctive quality of *growing smarter over time*, and of responding to the specific and changing needs of their environment. (p. 20, emphasis added)

In other words, though it is complex, the snowflake is not capable of adapting, learning, or growing smarter. A major question facing organizations and society is how to encourage adaptation, learning, and smarter behaviors. How can people keep growing smarter over time? The process of encouraging emergence is a prime example of working at the edge of chaos. Rather than trying to identify causal links, the challenge is in creating conditions that encourage and support complex adaptive and emergent behaviors. One way is by paying attention to how, when, and whether people are talking to each other, and to whom they are talking, because talking is a primary medium through which people work. Intentionally creating conditions is necessary. A conversational learning approach focuses on the role of micro-level communication to encourage learning, feedback, adaptation, and knowledge creation.

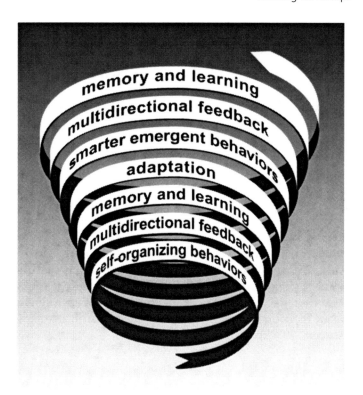

Figure 7.3 The spiral of creating the conditions.

To illustrate, Figure 7.3 shows the overlapping processes of the necessary conditions. Emergent behavior over time actually operates as upwardly spiraling cycles beginning with self-organizing behaviors.

Because feedback can provoke new ideas in unimagined directions, in feedback-rich environments these recurring patterns are even more unpredictable. Multidirectional feedback that includes bottom-up feedback is a form of tapping local, tacit knowledge that can create positively reinforcing cycles of increasing creativity. These possibilities for adapting, changing, and learning are dynamic processes that continuously unfold and evolve.

The work of Rycroft and Kash offers insight into what enables highly innovative organizations working with complex technologies to be cauldrons of continuous learning and innovation:

Central to the notion of emergence is the fact that complex networks are not always created either as a function of selection by environmental forces or conscious choices by network members. *Complex network organizations are continually emerging*... innovative organizations... are always in the process of becoming rather than ever reaching equilibrium. (Rycroft & Kash, 1999, pp. 66–67)

These emerging environments are analogous to the transitional space at the edge of chaos.

The environment does not produce an immediate result (Beeson & Davis, 2000; Johnson, 2001; Rycroft & Kash, 1999). Flexibility, reflection, and a tolerance for ambiguity, though, encourage these cycles of emergent behavior. Emergent behaviors support and extend generative change throughout groups, organizations, and communities (Beeson & Davis, 2000).

With these changes comes a challenge to walk the fine line between allowing the spontaneity for people to self-organize and yet provide enough structure so they can avoid slipping into chaos or reverting to excessive order. By offering sufficient structure to channel behaviors, continuous learning and smarter explorations can drive emergence. It is essential to provide project-wide or "'organization-wide' enabling conditions that promote a more favorable climate for effective knowledge creation" (Nonaka, 1994, p. 27). Even though "...ideas are formed in minds of individuals, interaction between individuals typically plays a critical role in developing these ideas" (Nonaka, 1994, p. 15).

Understanding more about the conditions that encourage collaborative creation of new knowledge and innovation fosters the development of such favorable climates. With conscious intentions, receptive and inviting environments can be created to support emergent behaviors. Communication and decision-making that is multidirectional and flexible rather than marked by hierarchy and rigid control are preferable. Environments that encourage and support spontaneous interactions, relationship building, multidirectional feedback, risk taking, and organizational learning provide settings for self-organizing entities to ripen and flourish. "A learning organization is skilled at developing, accumulating, and transferring knowledge, as well as modifying its behavior and structure to reflect new knowledge and insights. *Self-organization is learning in practice, and synthetic technological innovation is an organizational learning process*" (Rycroft & Kash, 1999, p. 62). All kinds of complex organizational, community, and interorganizational projects can use these approaches.

CONCLUSIONS

This chapter explores the role of differences as resources for knowledge creation and innovation in complex environments. The focus is on conversation as the primary medium for work and facilitating self-organizing and emergent behavior in transitional spaces at the edge of chaos. Often strong differences among people make it difficult for them to stay in transitional spaces long enough to reap the benefits. If differences seem too threatening, people retreat into a more orderly, more comfortable, and seemingly more predictable environments. Alternatively, if the differences are not modulated, they can get out of control, and organizations slip into a state of chaos. By creating organizational contexts that support constructive work with differences, diverse kinds of knowledge become more potent sources of creativity and innovation.

REFERENCES

Argyris, C. (1997). *On organizational learning.* Hoboken, NJ: Wiley-Blackwell.

Baker, A. C., Jensen, P. J., & Kolb, D. A. (2005). Conversation as experiential learning. *Management Learning: The Journal for Managerial and Organizational Learning, 36*(4), 411–427.

Baker, A. C., Jensen, P. J., & Kolb, D. A. (2002). *Conversational learning: An experiential approach to knowledge creation.* Westport, CT: Quorum Books.

Beeson, I. & Davis, C. (2000). Emergence and accomplishment in organizational change. *Journal of Organizational Change Management, 13*(2), 178–189.

Brown, J. S. & Duguid, P. (2000). *The social life of information.* Cambridge, MA: Harvard Business Press.

Capra, F. (1991). *The Tao of physics.* Boston: Shambhala Publications.

Capra, F. (1982). *The turning point: Science, society, and the rising culture.* New York: Bantam.

Davis, B. H. & Brewer, J. P. (1997). *Electronic discourse: Linguistic individuals in virtual space.* Albany, NY: SUNY Press.

Eisenhardt, K.M., Kahwajy, J. L., & Bourgeois, L. J., III. (1997). Conflict and strategic choice: How top management teams disagree. *California Management Review, 39*(2), 42–62.

Isaacs, W. (1999). *Dialogue: The art of thinking together.* New York: Broadway Business.

Johnson, S. (2001). *Emergence: The connected lives of ants, brains, cities, and software.* New York: Scribner.

Kauffman, S. (1995). *At home in the universe: The search for the laws of self-organization and complexity.* New York: Oxford University Press.

Nonaka, I. (1994). A dynamic theory of organizational knowledge creation. *Organization Science, 5*(1), 14–37.

Richter, I. (1998). Individual and organizational learning at the executive level: Towards a research agenda. *Management Learning, 29,* 29–316.

Rycroft, R. W. & Kash, D. E. (1999). *The complexity challenge: Technological innovation for the 21st century.* London: Pinter.

Shaw, P. (2002). *Changing conversations in organizations: A complexity approach to change.* New York: Routledge.

Tymon, W. G & Stumpf, S. A. (2003). "Social capital in the success of knowledge workers. *Career Development International, 8*(1), 12–20.

Waldrop, M. (1992). *Complexity: The emerging science at the edge of order and chaos.* New York: Simon & Schuster.

Wenger, E. (1998). *Communities of practice: Learning, meaning, and identity.* Cambridge, UK: Cambridge University Press.

Wikstrom, S., Mitroff, I., & Normann, R. (1994). *Knowledge and value: A new perspective on corporate transformation.* New York: Routledge.

CHAPTER 8

THE LOCAL-TO-GLOBAL-TO-LOCAL MOVEMENT OF KNOWLEDGE

Larry Browning, Judy Shetler, and Thierry Boudes

AN INTRODUCTION TO KM EVOLUTION

The fallout from the current information explosion that is threatening to bury many organizations brings to mind the volatile clutter stored in the legendary closet of old-time American radio character Fibber McGee. The unsorted contents of his closet became less accessible with each new addition that was crammed in, and searching for any item would inevitably trigger an avalanche of other stuff. Fibber's solutions—keep the door really tightly closed, get more shelves—were not helpful. He and his closet desperately needed some discipline.

Organizations facing a similar problem with an overload of information have turned to the discipline of Knowledge Management (KM) for help. An initial goal for KM was to achieve a systematic organizational practice, enabling the collection, storage, and delivery of the right bit of information, to the right person, at the right time, neatly extracting each precise bit of information out of the megabytes of data always threatening to become a paralyzing avalanche. If this operation was successful, the desired informa-

Complexity and Knowledge Management, pages 123–139
Copyright © 2010 by Information Age Publishing
123

tion could be manipulated purposefully, moving information from the level of individual possession to drive knowledge-driven fitness, adaptability, and enhanced performance at the organizational level. Such a focused trajectory fits neatly with so-called ballistic models of organizational management, designed for linear, on-target delivery of knowledge, with predictable results. "Best practices" were often chosen for this kind of transmission, from one successful operation to another, or to a wider arena, where success was planned.

Technology was seen as the tool for this disciplinary transformation, with smart, powerful computers capable of collecting, storing, retrieving, and moving large amounts of information rapidly. The early promise of KM has not been realized, however, and there is growing acknowledgement that its goal was based on a limited vision of knowledge, grounded on the assumption that knowledge is a pre-existing and limited resource, to be hoarded and mechanically manipulated at will (McElroy, 2003). While this may sometimes appear to be the case, such a view leaves out the crucial element: the human knower. The poet Yeats once asked, "How can we know the dancer from the dance?," reminding us of the limitations of reifying observation.

Cilliers describes this problem, saying that talking of a knowledge industry or of knowledge management can create the impression "that knowledge is something that 'exists,' that can be put on a disk or a website." He suggests that "the term knowledge should be reserved for information that is situated historically and contextually by a knowing subject. Knowledge is that which has meaning, it is the result of a process of interpretation" (2002, p.80).

To extend the implications of Cilliers' comment, excluding the knowing subject entails having no accounting for the actual dynamics of knowledge, in particular leaving out: (a) how humans create and communicate new knowledge; (b) how the creation, integration, and implementation of knowledge is related to individual and group learning; and (c) how humanly enacted knowledge affects the organization and its environment in nonlinear and unpredictable ways. After all, in the Garden of Eden, even the richly tempting bites of the fruit of the Tree of Knowledge only changed everything after human interaction and sharing.

The new sciences of complexity (see, e.g., Anderson, 1999; Lewin, 1992; Stacey, 2001; Waldrop, 1992), applied to organizations, now offer an approach to understanding knowledge as an ongoing process, and how it evolves in organizations organically. First, complex systems science (CSS) shows how knowledge emerges from aggregated information through value-laden human interaction, how this knowledge becomes embodied in organizational adaptability, how embodied knowledge generates the self-organization of more global degrees of system change, and how the enactment of knowledge triggers unpredictable and irreversible consequences that, among other things, come back full circle to affect all subsequent interaction. The mechanisms driving these progressively powerful potentials of human knowing can be graphically depicted, using the operational model of complexity science, the complex adaptive system (CAS) as a model of the organization. The CAS model is described in more detail below.

Because of the unfulfilled expectations for early KM, and the development of a more systemically dynamic view of knowledge, the earlier, data-driven KM approach is now often being referred to as first-generation KM, and the latter, more organic approach as second-generation KM (McElroy, 2003). (In this chapter, we will use the notation of KM_1 and KM_2 to distinguish between these two generations.)

DIFFERENT ASSUMPTIONS AND CONSEQUENCES

The KM_1 assumption that knowledge is a preexistent resource is still very useful within its limits, but mostly for operating technological tools and strategies for manipulating data and information, rather than for dealing with knowledge as human knowing. Stacey comments, "Systems, databases, recorded and written artifacts are usually thought of as stores of knowledge. From the complex responsive process perspective, they are simply records that can only become knowledge when people use them as tools in their processes of gesturing and responding to each other" (Stacey, 2001, p. 37). Thus the metaphorical closet is being seen as an informational resource, organized through the use of KM_1, while the CAS model of organization, using KM_2, provides for more insightful practices of knowledge creation, development, and management. The implications of this model for KM_2 practice are described in more detail below.

In particular, this chapter will look at how KM_2, rather than prescribing a well-designed "best" path for the transfer of knowledge from the local to the global level, can explore some simple patterns underlying the complex interactions that transform micro-level individual knowing into macro-level organizational knowledge, moving from local to global application. This dynamic transformation emerges as observable, ongoing system change in the organization (functioning as a complex adaptive system) and is also noticed as alteration in the organizational environment.

KNOWLEDGE CHALLENGES

KM_2 takes a new view of the basic challenges of knowledge management issues. The original, rather linear, procedural goal of KM_1 (getting the right information to right person, at the right time) is replaced by open-ended multilevel progressions and expansions typical of a complex adaptive system. A CAS is difficult to define, particularly since there are many kinds of CASs, from weather systems to living organisms, each with a unique system history, although their multifarious manifestations emerge from some common, simple rules of interaction and self-organizing processes.

For this reason, a CAS is as much a process as an entity, and a descriptive list of its functions is required to grasp CAS character (Dooley, 1996). A basic description of a CAS includes these concepts: A CAS has many autonomous parts, often referred to as agents; the agents can learn in response to local external changes, are attracted to others with similar responses, and self-organize into self-maintaining subsystems, with internal feedback loops; these responses then become embodied adaptations, governing the system's response to its environment. Attraction and connectivity among agents allow greater aggregation of these embodied adaptations, from which emerges a more globally enhanced state of optimization of function for the CAS. Because of this ongoing adaptation, Lucas says, "Such systems (CASs) are well placed to explore new niches, to search their fitness landscape, changing their composition to fit the changing patterns they encounter" (2006, p. 4). He sees this encounter as an adaptation that "internalizes environmental information, the system generates a model of the world outside, a distributed set of rules corresponding to the interesting or valuable aspects of their context" (Lucas, 2006, p. 4).

Thus, using the CAS model approach to KM_2 not only allows a much more dynamic conception of knowledge, but also invites the convergence of KM_2 with elements of organizational learning (Argyris & Schön, 1996; Senge, 1990; McElroy, 2003), since the CAS model provides an account of new knowledge creation and innovation, rather than mere transfer (Carlisle & McMillan, 2006). KM_2 also explains how a dynamic knowledge process drives the development of organizational adaptation and enhanced fit with the environment in terms of increasing complexity, moving from local agent interaction to global organizational performance (McElroy, 2003).

Conditions and requirements for using KM_2 differ from hierarchical management strategies. KM_2 depends upon freedom of interaction among agents with diverse views, including the allowance of spontaneous subsystem formation for innovation implementation. Also crucially necessary is a high degree of connectivity among parts, with feedback loops among all levels, vertically and horizontally, to allow interaction among the various subsystems from which organizational learning in the form of ongoing adaptation emerges. Support for the development and implementation of new knowledge, in the form of resources, is also necessary. If there is not strategic alignment between official organizational policies, communication, or even with unofficial practices in regard to freedom of interaction, high connectivity, and resource support, then the exponential expansion of knowledge and its progression toward a global state will be thwarted.

LOOKING AT KM USE

With this understanding, we will look at how organizational knowledge, unless stymied, moves naturally from the individual to the global level. Even when not consciously used in a KM_2 manner, complexifying processes can occur. These may include spontaneous self-organization of information toward emergent, meaningful order—that is, knowledge creation (McElroy, 2003)—with resultant increasing returns from application of new knowledge—that is, knowledge expansion (Arthur, 1995). Wherever there is human interaction, unless thwarted by top-down control attempts, this can occur. Examples of such regulating constraints might include withholding management-level information from lower-level agents whose interactions could potentially generate novel knowledge of increasing value. Other self-defeating management attempts could include limiting opportunities for connectivity among agents, or between unofficial subsystems and the potentially larger systems they could form through aggregation, and so on. Such control measures might be intended to maintain organizational stability but could actually hinder group learning and organizational adaptation.

Examples below of four kinds of movement from local to global demonstrate some differences between KM_1 and KM_2 approaches and how they operate in different contexts. The examples bring out the difference between a KM_1 approach that attempts to transfer items of knowledge from one level to another, and a KM_2 approach with an evolutionary, adaptive progression from local to global. Four types of movement of knowledge from local to global will be looked at below, with a brief example of each. The four types are: intentional, accidental, organizational, and full cycle, discussed in that order.

INTENTIONAL MOVEMENT

Intentional movement, or the purposeful attempted "transfer" of knowledge from local to global levels, resembles the approach taken by first-generation knowledge management, or KM_1. When knowledge is perceived as a pre-existent resource, then local knowledge, whether in the form of words, software, or images, typically has a special and intricate meaning that is best understood within a particular context. If the idea is to move this knowledge intact, the quality of situational uniqueness increases the difficulty of transferring it to some larger, grander application (Asheim &

Isaksen, 2002). Adding to the difficulty is the perceived need to codify and standardize the existent knowledge in order for it to be understood in the same way in all places (Maskell & Malmberg, 1999).

Situational uniqueness arises from the fact that every complex system has developed with sensitivity to initial conditions that are never quite reproducible. Recognized as complex adaptation or not, any organization has to some extent embodied its learning and adaptations to its surrounding conditions in its own distinctive organizational knowledge. To attempt to extrapolate that knowledge onto another system with different initial conditions is very unlikely to create a good fit. Transfer attempts can result in the vast accumulation or sedimentation of useless, obsolete, or even misleading information (Fibber's closet again!), rather than producing exponential progression toward a global state of humanly meaningful knowledge, through iterations of progressively aggregated local interaction. Codification accompanies this natural progression, since interaction requires and develops mutual understandings that are carried along with knowledge creation.

Intentional Transfer at Wal-Mart

An example of attempted intentional transfer is the costly difficulty that the hugely successful U.S. firm of Wal-Mart is experiencing in trying to establish operations in Germany, transferring its preexisting knowledge of how to expand successful business operations to a more nearly global arena. Wal-Mart has expanded from a small hardware store established in 1962 in Bentonville, AK, to multiple international chains, becoming the largest retailer in the world, and the second largest corporation in the world by 2006 (Wal-Mart, 2006).

Although the firm has often been severely criticized for its policies and business practices, including its deleterious impact on the local economies of many of the towns where it operates, Wal-Mart obviously has possessed effective organizational knowledge of how to go from small to large, and how to expand successfully into somewhat diverse markets, including Mexico and Canada (Wal-Mart, 2006). Perhaps previous successes created overconfidence in the universal applicability of these methods, since they have not worked successfully in Germany (Money.cnn, 2006). While Wal-Mart's difficulties may be seen as cultural; however, culture is one of the containers for the embodied knowledge of an organization (McElroy, 2003).

The New York *Times* reports, "After nearly a decade of trying (in Germany), Wal-Mart never cracked the country—failing to become the all-in-one shopping destination for Germans that it is for so many millions of Americans. Wal-Mart's problems are not limited to Germany." The article says,

"The retail giant has struggled in countries like South Korea and Japan as it discovered that its formula for success...did not translate to markets with their own discount chains and shoppers with different habits" (Landler & Barbaro, 2006). Apparently Wal-Mart management has been investing in a serious, intentional effort, without success in this instance at least, to transfer knowledge to a larger arena: knowledge that has proven effective in a previous context. Intentional knowledge management, grounded as it is in KM_1 assumptions, can fall just as short of expectations as KM_1 in general has.

Wal-Mart is reportedly negotiating to sell its assets in Germany (Wal-Mart, 2006), relinquishing its presence there, but continuing to expand in other parts of the world. Perhaps learning from its unsuccessful experience in Germany, the firm is taking a very different approach in China, even reportedly participating in the development of grass-roots development of employee unions, something it has famously resisted in the U.S. (White, 2006). Since unionization was not part of Wal-Mart's original policy, this move may represent a move toward a more adaptive type of knowledge movement, that is, from an obviously intentional attempt at knowledge transfer to one that is a more natural outgrowth of local interaction. The type of movement described below as accidental represents this progression.

ACCIDENTAL MOVEMENT

The second type of movement of knowledge from local to global can be categorized as accidental. It often appears accidental since it is unplanned, and not the result of top-down control, aimed at a predetermined goal, and often has unpredictable, nonlinear (i.e., disproportionate) results. With a KM_2 understanding of CAS processes, the accidental suddenly appears natural, even inevitable in hindsight, although the global consequences of iterative interaction, in a system with a high degree of freedom and sufficient connectivity, can yield surprisingly innovative and far-reaching results.

Accidental Movement: 3M's Post-It Notes
The mild adhesive on Post-It notes was discovered accidentally as a by-product of a project that had set out to accomplish its opposite—an adhesive that had incredibly strong "sticking" power (Fry, 1987). But rather than being disappointed with the weak adhesive, Dr. Spenser Silver, the accidental inventor, took his new product to others in the 3M company with the hopes of generating support for his discovery. His continued pursuit of the idea was not treated as an effort to make up for lack of achievement, because the 3M culture had always encouraged the testing of new ideas, even those with no strategically designed purpose. If a product emerged that had no obvious initial audience, it was usual to ask, "Can anyone use this?" During this intra-firm shopping around of the weakly adhering substance, Art Fry, also

at 3M, came to understand the characteristics of the new material as well. At this point, an off-duty experience stimulated the convergence of materials and potential product.

The now-famous story goes like this: Art used to sing in the choir in the Presbyterian Church where he would mark songs in the order of their performance with little scraps of paper that invariably fell out, causing him to lose his place. One day, as Art's mind drifted during the sermon, he remembered the odd adhesive that wasn't very sticky. The next day at work he ordered a sample of it and tried coating just the edge of little pieces of paper, putting no stickum on the rest of the paper, similar to the Post-It we now know.

As communication and sharing began to occur, by sending samples back and forth to his boss, Art grew aware that his intention to invent a book-marker had taken an unpredictable turn. Instead of a small bookmark, he was creating a communication device, with potentially large and unforeseen possibilities to exploit that would require expanded interaction with many other agents, and even changes in organizational structures and behavior (new tasks, communication networks, resource allocations, team formations, etc.).

The implications of the movement from accident of the unwanted mildly sticky material, to Art's insight in the choir, to 3M's openness and willingness to exploit odd ideas, and finally to the widely popular product known as the Post-It note, exemplify a nonlinear development story. From the individual inventor's original idea, expanding network connections of diverse interaction were generated, exponentially building on each other's aggregated accomplishments, eventually emerging as a success story out of all proportion to its small beginning.

Looking back at the beginning of process, a few additional specialists had to be recruited to solve some technical problems before an identifiably successful product could be claimed. For example, rather than staying at the top of the paper the adhesive tended to drift down the note. Also, the blend of the adhesive had to be perfected so that it did not tear old and weak paper surfaces—like old book pages—when the notes were applied. These difficulties were seen as "good" problems, since their solution contributed to a unique product, meaning that potential competitors would have difficulties knocking off a version of the product.

The small network of agents involved in successful technical solutions then widened to connect to internal product innovators: 3M executives and their secretaries. Each greater level of success surfaced issues connected to a wider network; for example, the secretaries "could not get enough" of the sticky little notes, and kept using them up. Finally, there were also unfamiliar difficulties with market tests for the product. As the project went from internal success to interaction with the external environment, formal marketing surveys struggled with pricing the innovative product. After all, these were just scraps of paper with a little adhesive on them, and building a demand for them took many adaptive iterations before the product reached enough critical mass in the market to take off as the widely distributed item that most of us can not do without, the Post-It note.

At 3M, a high degree of freedom of thought and initiative, combined with support for the necessary connectivity required for fruitful interaction, allowed knowledge to move freely from minutely local (one inventor's inspiration) to the hugely global (a ubiquitous product in large demand). The 3M culture acted as a container for this organizational knowledge process, allowing for evolutionary innovation while maintaining organizational identity. Organizational identity also plays a role in the next category of the passage of knowledge from local to global, that of organizational movement.

ORGANIZATIONAL KNOWLEDGE MOVEMENT

The third type of movement discussed here is categorized as organizational; that is, the interaction is among and between organizations, themselves acting as agents, and supported by the formal structures and policies of each organization—for example, business-to-business communication. Within any complex adaptive system, agents with similar interests are attracted to each other and form subsystems that are attracted to others, and so on, forming greater and more complex organizational structures. Each level of organization contains the nested previous ones, so that interaction at the inter-organizational level is both simplified in focus and rich in layers of embodied adaptation and knowledge. What might emerge from this richly informed, high-level interaction can be unforeseen, with surprising and far-reaching (more nearly global) consequences.

Stewart and Cohen give a name to the ongoing coevolution of change that can emerge when two or more systems engage in ongoing interaction, calling it "complicity." They describe how complicity "arises when two or more complex systems interact in a kind of mutual feedback that changes them both, leading to behaviour that is not present in either system on its own" (Stewart & Cohen, 1997, p. 63).[1]

A variation on complicity between organizations can be seen in the self-organization, or coalescence, of communities of practice. People with shared interests in some subject, challenge, or problems, find each other in order to collaborate long-term to share their ideas, to find problem solutions, and/or to develop innovations. These communities aggregate across structural lines within or between organizations, attracted by their common concerns. They come under the area of full-cycle movement since they carry out high-level interaction, not only among their own members, but, by representation, among their originating systems, generating and sharing knowledge that reflects back on the groups from which the collaborating agents come.

Organizational Knowledge Movement Example: SEMATECH

An interesting example of organizational movement, or complicity, comes from our earlier analysis of U.S. semiconductor manufacturing firms, in which chip manufacturers collaborated at SEMATECH to set a single, global standard for suppliers to meet in developing their manufacturing equipment for chip makers (Browning & Beyer, 1998; Browning & Shetler, 2000). Previously, each semiconductor maker had set secret, unique standards for chip-making equipment, a costly practice that prevented any potentially fertile information exchange or interaction among firms.

SEMATECH was the first U.S. semiconductor manufacturing consortium; its members had previously been fierce, uncommunicative rivals. Driven by the threat of nearly overwhelming Japanese competition, these chipmakers desperately formed a consortium to cope with the manufacturing challenges of their industry. With assignees from member firms working at a single location together, SEMATECH became a strong attractor: enabling, safely containing, and focusing previously impossible communicative interaction among member firms, in which common production problems could be brought to the surface and shared for the first time. From this interaction, the desirability of, and the support for, implementation of a single standard for equipment suppliers emerged. No matter how crying the need, this development could not have been realized without industry-wide collaboration. The unprecedented single standard for suppliers was not even a part of the originally stated goal for SEMATECH, but it became a powerful example of new knowledge creation and expansion through communicative interaction at the interorganizational level (Browning & Shetler, 2000).

The single standard for equipment not only provided a more efficient purchasing mechanism, but also structurally changed the previously cut-throat, low-bid organizational practices of semiconductor manufacturers in dealing with their equipment and material suppliers. These changes led to others, such as interorganizational partnering, a real innovation in the microelectronics industry at that time. "Things are complicit when their interactions change them, so that soon they have become different things altogether—and *still* they continue to interact, and change, and interact again, and change again…" (Stewart & Cohen, 1997, p. 63).

Another unforeseen organizational effect of the interaction at SEMAT-ECH was the resultant networking among assignees after they returned to their member companies. A cross-fertilization of ideas and knowledge sharing across the semiconductor industry resulted, an unprecedented development among firms previously secretive and forbidden by crippling anti-trust regulation, only relaxed in order to form the consortium in the face of competitive extinction.

New behavior at the interorganizational level comes from the knowledge embodied, not only in a single system, but in the interactional relationship between and among systems, emerging as a kind of meta-knowledge, or knowledge environment. This knowledge environment is described by Stewart and Cohen as "extelligence" (1997, p. 243), or the cultural counterpart to intelligence. Extelligence has enormous adaptive consequences, as it can be drawn upon by many agents simultaneously, and has a reflexive influence on all subsequent iterations of interaction and change, as seen in the next category of knowledge movement.

FULL-CYCLE MOVEMENT

The fourth category of movement, the full cycle, tends to have a recursive flow of embodied organizational adaptations, not only local to global, but back to influence local behavior again. This two-way flow draws on emergent extelligence, and comprises reciprocal influences both forward and backward, among adaptive changes among all the interaction levels that have contributed to their production.

The full cycle movement also connects KM_2 back to KM_1, showing the mutual dependence of these two kinds of knowledge management, a connection that has obvious importance to managers already familiar with KM_1 who have become interested in also developing KM_2 practice in their organizations. They may be wondering, if new knowledge is generated from bottom-up interaction, and emerges spontaneously at increasingly higher levels, will managers be rendered superfluous by this natural progression? What is the appropriate role for management in this process? How can KM_2 be implemented effectively?

Looking first at the natural recursive flow of organizational knowledge, we have seen that new knowledge, as it is embodied in the organization, spontaneously generates system adaptations, consisting of emergent (i.e., unpredicted and unplanned) changes. These will include behavioral changes (e.g., new, multi-level communication loops among units), as well as structural changes (e.g., new teams or subsystems), policy changes (e.g., new rules for agent interaction), and so on.

Without the willing facilitation of managers, the emergence of such adaptations may be blocked. Support for the creation of new knowledge crucially includes allowing opportunities for a high degree of connectivity, with necessary feedback loops between and among organizational levels, and maintaining ethical constraints combined with official and actual freedom to pursue new ideas. The essential opportunities (sanctions and resources) that provide favorable initial conditions at the local level where the generative bottom-up interaction originates can only be enabled and ensured by supportive, non-controlling managerial direction.

One of the key resources at a manager's disposal is the information that can be supplied by effective KM_1 practice. This is where delivering the right information to the right person at the right time makes its contribution to the process of creating meaningful knowledge through human interaction. The power over organizational knowledge that this gives to managers is considerable; if a manager attempts to constrain the process of knowledge creation and movement by controlling the flow of information (e.g., by designating only "the right person" for its delivery) or by limiting the kinds of data made available, the evolutionary process will be thwarted. Restrictive control of the knowledge processes can also occur through recruiting only agents with prescribed views, rather than those with the diversity of mindsets capable of generating creative interaction. Although knowledge emerges from agent interaction, it can all too easily be deflected back by managerial "ceilings" of many kinds, rather than being reflected out into wider ripples of expanding system adaptation and embodied knowledge. Managers of KM_2 have a worthy, challenging, and essential role to play.

FULL CYCLE MOVEMENT: THE HULA DANCE

A colorful example of the recursive nature of organizational knowledge, as contained and expressed in culture, comes from the history of the hula dance of Hawai'i. The hula dance originally was a performance art form combining aesthetic choreography and the epic poetry of chants. Although hula took various forms, sometimes presenting worshipful tributes to Hawaiian gods, or native oral history and worldview, or lively and passionate entertainment, it was always danced with a sense of spirituality. Local schools on each of the Hawaiian islands, known as *hula halau*, under the direction of a master called *kumu hula*, screened applicants for the rigorous and lengthy physical, mental, and spiritual training needed for the high calling of hula performance. With no written Hawaiian language, hula was a major means for educating generations of Hawaiians in the mythic ideology that undergirded the meaning and continuity of the culture, and was an important repository of social and cultural knowledge in old Hawai'i (Seiden, 1999).

When Calvinist missionaries arrived in the 1820s, they presided over the dismantling of much of Hawaiian culture, including the hula that they perceived to be pagan and lascivious. Worship of the old gods was officially banned. Hawai'i continued to be a monarchy, although the ostensibly sovereign government operated under heavy missionary influence. In 1883, young King Kalakaua, realizing that local history and knowledge were disappearing with the hula, invited many of the *hula halaus* that were still existing more or less secretly to perform chants and dances of their ancestors at his coronation at the royal Iolani Palace in Honolulu, in a colorful, theatrical extravaganza. This upset the Christian church authorities, who condemned the show. Nevertheless, new instruments and costume materials had been quietly introduced by immigrants to the islands by then, and following this official performance, the hula enjoyed a brief heyday of revitalization before the monarchy was overthrown in 1893, and the sovereign Hawaiian islands were annexed to the United States in 1898 (Niesse, 2006).

Without top-down support, the hula then went into a period of decline in the 20th century, becoming a debased parody of its original use as a vehicle for cultural knowledge. It was commercially exploited in response to global tourist appetites for the exotic. In the 1970s, however, just as it looked as though the ancient historical and spiritual significance of the hula would disappear entirely, a spontaneous revival of Hawaiian culture, epitomized by the hula, emerged, stimulated by the context of the burgeoning U.S. Civil Rights movement. Young Hawaiians, looking to renew pride in their ethnic artistic heritage, searched out the few remaining elders, known as *kupunas,* who remembered the old ways and wisdom. A major vehicle for this cultural knowledge was the hula, in its original role.

There are now numerous *hula halaus* in the Hawaiian islands, training young generations of devoted dancers. Rather than trying to preserve the hula as a perfectly preserved and mummified specimen, the *halaus* do research into the ancient ways in order to give new life to ancient wisdom. Although the hula connects Hawaiians to the knowledge of their past, new forms and expression are emerging as well, seen in the annual Merrie Monarch Festival performances on the Big Island of Hawaii, named to commemorate the aforementioned King Kalakaua (Merrie Monarch Festival, 2009).

The simultaneous fragility and resilience of knowledge, as contained in culture, are epitomized by the history of the hula's near disappearance under strict control, its brief resurgence with official enablement, its consequent debasement in a context of disrespectful appropriation, and its eventual resurgence in conditions of respectful facilitation. This brief history illustrates the productive, recursive interplay between a managerial role that sustains existing knowledge while facilitating the emergence of new organizational knowledge. Containers of knowledge, such as cultural forms and expression, can be forces supporting system continuity, as well as sources for innovation when provided with opportunity and resources by insightful management.

CONCLUSION

The implications for practice of knowledge management based on a CAS model raise interesting operational distinctions between the practices of KM_1 and KM_2. In particular, there is the issue of the appropriate role for a manager of organizational knowledge. In the first-generation approach, or KM_1, as preexistent knowledge is reified and manipulated, a manager's role consists mainly in organizing and managing supplies and fluxes of knowledge, including such control functions as making evaluations about what is the right knowledge (e.g., the details about a "best practice") and decisions about who should receive such information. This role is highly compatible with classical approaches of management in the sense of Taylor or Fayol. To manage knowledge in this way equates to managing databases as scarce resources, allocating their contents, and supervising the imposition of their preexistent solutions onto new problems, with expectations of predictable outcomes.

This managerial role changes drastically in second-generation knowledge management, or KM_2. In effect, knowledge is no longer more envisaged as a preexistent thing to be controlled, but as a dynamic relation, requiring support. Accordingly, a manager's mission consists of creating contexts favorable for creating new relations. In a study of repairers of photocopiers of Xerox, Orr (1996) shows how unprompted communities of practice allow the circulation of local knowledge among repairers. The author also shows that managers may take an ambiguous position in relation to these communities. On the one hand, they often look at such exchanges with a jaundiced eye because they judge the time thus spent as nonproductive. On the other hand, managers realize that these emergent communities contribute to effective performance in the daily activity of their reporting teams. Thus managers may grudgingly tolerate rather than encourage this formation of productive spontaneous community.

In the practice of KM_2, a manager's role resembles that of a facilitator. To fulfill this role, some managerial distance is necessary. Once a favorable context consisting of enabling conditions has been created by management, only light direction is indicated, allowing for self-organization among agents, attraction among subsystems, and aggregation into groups of subsystems, so that generative interaction can occur. This facilitative approach is contrary to the classical picture of the manager who plans, organizes, and controls, because KM_2 does not function as a linear, or ballistic, type of process—that is, one that is targeted at a designated outcome in the management of knowledge.

Additionally, reporting within the framework of KM2 is not easy, because the relation between means and results is not linear. In KM_1, which reifies knowledge, it is possible to count accesses, consulting, and so forth, and so to put means and uses in visible contact. In KM_2 this relation is not direct, and the investment in knowledge management might be viewed as unproductive. Surely, as the case of 3M cited above shows, once a success has been obtained, it becomes much easier to justify the relevance of KM_2. Nevertheless, to initiate the changes necessary for the practice of KM_2 necessitates personal courage along with distance—two simultaneous demands that are difficult for a manager to juggle successfully.

To return to theoretical implications, it is clear that the phenomena of complexity science, including spontaneous self-organization, emergence, and adaptation, which underlie the second generation of knowledge management make it possible to view and manage knowledge as a dynamical process. The creation and expansion of knowledge arise naturally from interactions at the level of individual agents and, wisely supported, can lead to global environmental adaptations and on to their recursive consequences. Research and discovery into the relatively young sciences of complexity are continuing, and their ongoing developments will no doubt contribute further to the informed practice of second-generation knowledge management in organizations functioning as complex adaptive systems.

NOTE

1. Although spelled the same, this use of the term "complicity" does not carry the common pejorative connotation of shared culpability, but rather indicates high-level mutually constructive involvement among or between systems.

REFERENCES

Anderson, P. (1999). Complexity theory and organization science. *Organization Science, 10*(3), 216–232.

Argyris, C. & Schön, D. (1996). *Organizational learning II: Theory, method and practice,* Reading, MA: Addison Wesley.

Arthur, W. B. (1995). Positive feedbacks in the economy. In T. Kuran, (Ed.), *Increasing returns and path dependence in the economy* (pp. 1–32). Ann Arbor: University of. Michigan Press.

Asheim, B. T. & Isaksen, A. (2002). Regional innovation systems: The integration of local "sticky" and global "ubiquitous" knowledge. *Journal of Technology Transfer,* *27,* 77–86.

Browning, L. D., & Beyer, J. M. (1998). The structuring of shared voluntary standards in the U.S. semiconductor industry: Communicating to reach agreement. *Communication Monographs, , 64,*1–25.

Browning, L. D., & Shetler, J. C. (2000). *Sematech: Saving the U.S. semiconductor industry.* College Station, TX: Texas A & M University Press.

Carlisle, Y., & McMillan, E. (2006). Innovation in organizations from a complex adaptive systems perspective. *Emergence: Complexity & Organization. Special Issue: Complexity & Innovation 8*(1), 2–9.

Cilliers, P. (2002). Why we cannot know complex things completely. *Emergence,* *4*(1/2), 77–84.

Dooley, K. (1996). A nominal definition of complex adaptive systems. *The Chaos Network, 8*(1), 2–3. (http://www.eas.asu.edu/~kdooley/papers/casdef.PDF)

Fry, A. (1987). The Post-It Note: An intrapreneurial success. *SAM Advanced Management Journal, 52*(3), 4–9.

Landler, M., & Barbaro, M. (2006, August 2). Wal-Mart finds that its formula doesn't fit every culture. *New York Times* [online]. Retrieved August 2, 2006 from http://www.nytimes.com/2006/08/02/business/worldbusiness/02walmart.html?th&emc=th

Lewin, R. (1992). *Complexity: Life at the edge of chaos.* New York: Collier Books.

Lucas, C. (2006). Complex adaptive systems—Webs of delight. Retrieved May 10, 2006 from http://www.calresco.org/lucas/cas.htm

Maskell, P. & Malmberg, A. (1999). Localised learning and industrial competitiveness. *Cambridge Journal of Economics, 23*(2), 167–186.

McElroy, M. W. (2003). *The new knowledge management: Complexity, learning, and sustainable innovation.* Oxford, UK: Butterworth-Heinemann.

Merrie Monarch Festival. (2009). Retrieved October 14, 2009 from http://www.merriemonarchfestival.org/about_king_kalakaua.html

Niesse, M. (2006). Sovereignty group attempts to claim Kaho'olawe. Retrieved August 11, 2006 from http://hawaiialoha.tribe.net/thread/10a39acc-88f0-4cf2-9c99-361c4e170ab9

Money. CNN. (2006). Wal-Mart announces sale of German business. Retrieved August 12, 2006 from http://money.cnn.com/services/tickerheadlines/prn/200607280237PR_NEWS_USPR_NYF025.htm

Niesse, M. (2006). Sovereignty group attempts to claim Kaho'olawe. Retrieved August 11, 2006 from http://hawaiialoha.tribe.net/thread/10a39acc-88f0-4cf2-9c99-361c4e170ab9

Senge, P. M. (1990). *The fifth discipline: The art and practice of the learning organization.* New York: Random House.

Seiden, A. (1999). *The art of hula.* Hong Kong: Island Heritage Publishing.

Stacey, R. D. (2001). *Complex responsive processes in organizations: Learning and knowledge creation.* London: Routledge.

Stewart, I. & Cohen, J. (1997). *Figments of reality: The evolution of the curious mind.* New York: Cambridge University Press.

Waldrop, M. M. (1992). *Complexity: The emerging science at the edge of order and chaos.* New York: Simon and Schuster.

Wal-Mart. (2006). Fact Sheets: International Operations. Retrieved September 26, 2006 from http://www.walmartfacts.com/FactSheets/8252006_International_Operations.pdf

White, B. (2006). Wal-Mart wants to talk, says Chinese union group. Retrieved August 12, 2006 from http://wmt.bloggingstocks.com/2006/08/09/wal-mart-wants-to-talk-says-chinese-union-group/

CHAPTER 9

SOCIETAL LEGAL FABRIC FOR ENGENDERING "ORDER OUT OF CHAOS"

Systemic Knowledge Modeling of the Courts in Singapore

Check Teck Foo

INTRODUCTION

Earlier, the author had, in his presentation on *Towards a Taxonomy of Judicial Thinking* (Foo, 2001) at a conference held in Chicago before an audience including U.S. judges, argued for a novel perspective of a court as a thinking organization.[1] Given the fact that courts deal with resolving uncertainties in the law, the thinking naturally has to be judicial in nature. This author then took on the example of Lord Denning, a famous English judge, for the purpose of modeling his process of judicial thinking. Hitherto, the roles of courts, whether in Eastern or Western cultures, had been viewed primarily as government-funded, independent institutions for the production of justice. From an economics perspective, the assumption is that the public is desirous of such a good as "justice." Yet as will be argued here,

Complexity and Knowledge Management, pages 141–152

courts ought to be also explored in their roles as knowledge-creating organizations (Nonaka, 1991).

By their very creations, they are what C.W. Choo (1998) had already conceptualized as knowing organizations. These are organizations involved in the modes of sense making, knowledge creating as well as in rational processes of decision making (Choo, 1998). Indeed, the courts are institutions established by the relevant governmental authorities to be *all* knowing—provided that the case is within their jurisdiction. Courts are the very last resort for people and organizations to resolve any differences in their opinions on legal knowledge—concerning what is right or wrong in one's interpretation of the law as applicable to any particular situation, the judges within the courts are the final arbiters.

Here, we expand on this by presenting an alternative conceptualization of the courts: a systemic view of the courts (see discussion later) as organizations that weave patterns of "social fabric" as a web or nesting of the legal rules. These webs of rules, though differing in their exact contents, are similarly woven across many otherwise different cultures and societies. Such a fabric, however, is essential for ensuring an orderly—or at least as it is seen on the surface—functioning of any modern society. Yet within these societies there exist, inherently, complexity—a complexity generated through the multitudes of interactions.

The intriguingly popular theme, at least at the turn of the century, is of our societies becoming increasingly "out of control" (Kelly, 1994), in the sense that as a society becomes ever more complex, our organization evolves to be more akin to the biological in nature. If so, this logically suggests one interesting insight: The stronger presence of courts in any society is in itself a reflection of evolution—one towards being even more "biological." Thus an omnipresence of order inducing institutions such as the courts is precisely to facilitate societal transformation—a transformation towards "out of control" (as intended by Kelly) and becoming an even more complex adaptive society. This makes it even more necessary that we explore the roles of the courts to complete our picture of a complex, adaptive society.

How do courts ensure order emerges out of chaos? They do so primarily by their resolving of legal uncertainties. In the very process of providing certainty, the judges acting in parallel are simultaneously generating new legal insights and knowledge. The process is incremental and on a case-by-case basis. For this reason, we are exploring here the processes in adjudications by the judges. This is something yet to be undertaken. Classical concepts of knowledge creation (for example, Polanyi) are rarely if indeed ever applied to the courts. Yet there can be no denial that there are new *legal* knowledge creations through deep, reflective thinking by the judges.

For this reason, after our systemic modeling of courts as complex adaptive systems, we turn to explain our knowledge-based, expressive-implicit matrix.

We intend to map the conceptual matrix onto the processes of the court. Our goal is to use this as a modeling tool to gain insights into the thinking processes of the judges—in particular, how judges generate new legal insights or knowledge. Five recent cases are selected that emphasize the knowledge creating processes and that our courts ought to be explored, borrowing from Choo, as "knowing organizations." Seeing courts from such perspectives may engender new insights or even a different paradigm, for example, possibly on how courts may then be reorganized so that the courts may better perform their societal roles of engendering order out of chaos and ensuring order in their pursuit ultimately of justice. The role of the courts is made even more cogent by the seemingly growing prevalence of chaos.

Finally we conclude by arguing that there is a Tao underlying the processes in generating of knowledge. Additionally we attempt to rationalize the roots of ancient Chinese legal philosophy evolving from deeply held (more than 5,000 years) beliefs in inevitability of change[2]. For our human society being part of nature, change is inherent within any society even one that may appear outwardly to be orderly. Wihelm[3] argued in his introduction to translating the book *I Ching* ("The Book of Changes") from Chinese into German, that it is "...unquestionably one of the most important books in the world's literature..." (p. xiv).

We now turn to discuss our systemic, dynamic modeling of courts' roles in generating new legal knowledge.

COURT AS COMPLEX ADAPTIVE SYSTEM

How can we picture the court as being integral to an evolving, dynamic, highly interactive society that is Singapore? We envision the court as being nested as an organic part of the very fabric of society. An institution that regularly and systematically draws, using the language of complexity science, "order from chaos"—in plain English, how the rules of law ought to be applied in a given set of facts. Now rules, when applied by the courts to cases, constitutes for the legal fraternity or community of practitioners *new* legal knowledge. Why? There is no real necessity to go to the courts when there is absolute certainty on the law. It is only when there is uncertainty to the law that parties have to opt to go to the courts.

In our conceptualization here, we are attempting to simply follow up on McElroy (2000). This is seen in our approach to the conceptual modeling of the roles: law firms and other rules-enforcing entities may be seen as "detectors" as well as "effectors" in offering advice to their clients. Lawyers may detect an uncertainty—potentially chaotic if left unresolved in a given situation—and they may then advise clients to seek a court's decision. Why? As we said earlier, to bring "order out of chaos." Indeed another equally attractive metaphor from complexity science is "attractors".[4] That is, the judges in the courts in presiding over cases are generating "attractors": principles, rules, legal concepts, ratio *decidendi* that bind people together. One powerful attractor that binds people together is the concept of justice: seeking just rules. Courts are institutional manifestations of such attractors.

In so doing the courts *also* and necessarily bring forth new legal knowledge. It may be an emerging, new legal interpretation by the courts that may impact businesses and corporations. Thus those firms operating within the relevant legal domain or environment must then to adapt to such an emergence. Prior to the emergence of such a new legal rule clarifying what ought to apply in a particular situation, there is in the language of complexity science, a state of chaos. Clearly, when there is an unsettled chaos, a lot more energy (in Chinese, "*chi*") may be expended by organizations—acting on advice of their lawyers—to take precautionary actions so as protect themselves in their interactions inside the legal environment. So far, very few if any academics had sought to relate the creation of new legal knowledge in the context of complexity science. For this reason, it may be useful to paint an even more vivid legal picture.

Take the case of lawyers performing their deeply ancient, traditional functions (as is the case in English legal system dating from 13th century). They advise their clients on the basis of given set of facts, their legal rights. To be effective, lawyers have to refer to a substantial body of legal knowledge—knowledge that may be said to have had emerged through the accumulative applications by the courts of laws (whether statutory or common law) to cases. The interpretations of given rules to specific cases become binding upon legal entities operating in the same legal domain. Organizations in their intensive interactions (as depicted by the sporadic spread of lines) have to pay attention to any new, emerging court decisions, especially if these newly made legal decisions have significant impacts on the activities or business of the organizations. Decisions come from the minds of the judges functioning as a court: one operating like a complex, adaptive system in providing order for the environment (see Figure 9.1).

It is surprising, however, that so far no one has explored how judges are actually creating new legal knowledge as part of the processes of the courts. We do this by grounding our approach in what may now be considered as classical concepts in the knowledge creation field.

EXPRESSIVE–IMPLICIT MATRIX

In knowledge literature, Polanyi's (1966) major contribution lies in emphasizing the tacit dimension of knowledge. Consistent with such an approach,

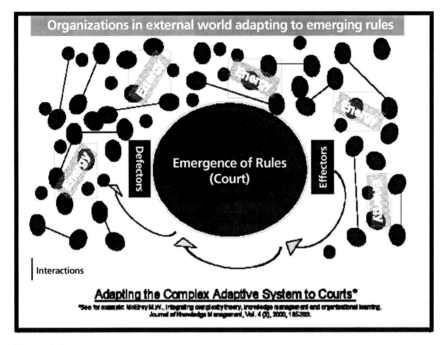

Figure 9.1

we propose here a dividing of legal knowledge into two dimensions: what remains implicit (corresponding to tacit) and the expressive. Taking this as the basis, Nonaka and Takeuchi (1995) then drew the dynamics of Japanese innovation in a circular path flowing from *explicit*, combination, *explicit*, internationalization, *tacit*, socialization, *tacit*, externalization and back again to *explicit*. The clear divide, however, is in knowledge being both explicit and tacit. We adapt that approach in our conceptual modeling.

This is reflected in Figure 9.2. We first divide the *x* and *y* axes into halves of explicit and tacit. Thus there are two quadrants that are either explicit or implicit, while another two (bold arrows) are implicit–explicit or explicit–implicit. As will be explained later, such a mapping is especially useful with regard to legal knowledge. For the creation of legal knowledge lies in rendering what is implicit in a given situation into expressive rules or decisions backed by a rationale.

Of the four quadrants however, it is the interchangeability of expressive–implicit or implicit–expressive (reflected in two quadrants) that is, in our opinion, at the core of the process in creating new legal knowledge.

To enable us to utilize the model effectively, we need to transpose only the horizontal axis from expressive–implicit into implicit–explicit. In so doing we immediately get what we term as the "next generation" figure (Figure 9.3), one that we can then map directly upon the processes of thinking of judges as clearly expressed in their public judgments.

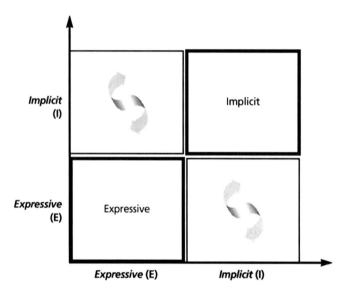

Figure 9.2 Framing of legal knowledge from within a EI matrix.

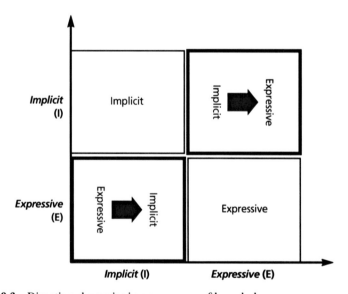

Figure 9.3 Direction dynamics in emergence of knowledge.

The lower left quadrant reflects the first dynamic of the thinking processes—that is, in the rendering of what is all "expressive" into "implicit." In the upper right quadrant is pictured the second dynamic, namely rendering the "implicit" back again into the "expressive."

Next we explain how this conceptual model may be applied to a sample of recent court cases. The goal is to illustrate how the model may yield insights into the legal thinking and decision making processes without having to investigate the specific details of the cases and that these processes may be related back to models on new knowledge creation.

MODELING KNOWLEDGE EMERGENCE

How can we model this process of knowledge emergence with the social fabric as embedded in our system of courts? Here we explore the methodology for modeling the process using the concepts discussed earlier. To do this we need samples of court cases and as such a quick review is made of recent cases.

For this overview, we select five cases. We try in each of these cases to model the entire process of reported court decision making from the perspective of knowledge emergence (the "aha"). To do so, we had to review the specific the judgments of the courts.

The detailed references to the case reports are provided as footnotes in the specific conceptual model in the Figures. Our main purpose here is to illustrate by way of actual examples our conceptual methodology for generating a generic model of knowledge emergence that underlies the processes of the courts. The cases are selected for diversity of their contexts, but they are recent cases with reports are available on the internet. Each case is now briefly mentioned.

SM v Schenker is a case concerning a lease of a warehouse in the logistics industry. In the *Advantest Corporate Office* case the central issue of contention is one of identity, whether a certain legal entity is indeed a party to a manufacturing agreement. In the *Koon Seng Construction* case, what had to be resolved by the court was whether there was a binding agreement in relation to the supply of steel bars. And in the *Chor Pee* case involving the court process of a petition, the matter at the heart of dispute is the question of legal fees. Finally we look at the more procedurally and legally more complex *Dextra* case, which involves a prior court order and amended defenses related to the subject of patents. Analyzing of each of these court cases led to a map-modeling of legally grounded, knowledge creation sequences as follows:

SM v Schenker Case

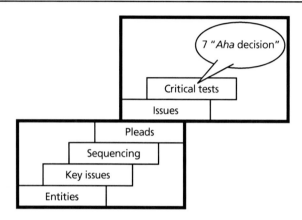

Case mapping of legal knowledge discovery in court's emergence of rules*

* *SM Integrated Transware Pte Ltd v Schenker Singapore (Pte) Ltd* [2005] SGHC 58

The Advantest Corporate Office Case

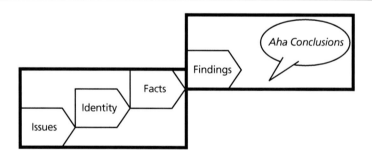

Case map of legal knowledge discovery in court's emergence of rules*

* *Advantest Corporate Office (Singapore) Pte Ltd and Another v SL Link Co Ltd and Another* [2005] SGHC 75

Koon Seng Construction Case

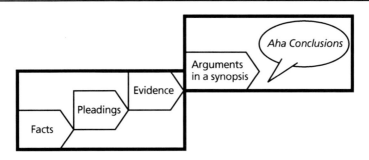

Case map of legal knowledge discovery in court's emergence of rules*

* *Koon Seng Construction Pte Ltd v Siem Seng Hing and Co (Pte) Ltd [2005] SGHC 8*

Chor Pee Case

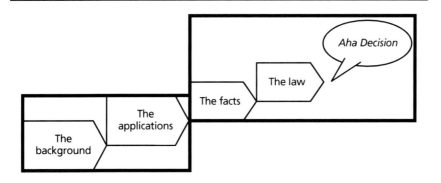

Case map of legal knowledge discovery in court's emergence of rules*

* *Chor Pee and Partners v Wee Soon Kim Anthony [2005] SGHC 101*

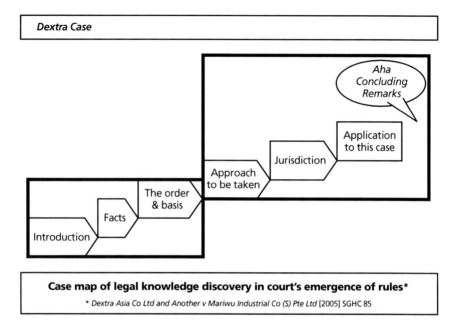

Dextra Case

Case map of legal knowledge discovery in court's emergence of rules*

* Dextra Asia Co Ltd and Another v Mariwu Industrial Co (S) Pte Ltd [2005] SGHC 85

As shown above, the processes of the courts in their judicial decision making are conceptually incongruent with creating of new knowledge. Clearly the roles of the courts in creating order out of chaos, while directionally opposite from order to chaos (Holland, 1998), should be of interest to complexity theorists. This is consistent with scholars who argue for a systems approach to the law (LoPucki, 1997), and it is timely to go even further by relating judicial decisions as part of the process of new knowledge creation. New insights are likely from taking a cross-disciplinary approach.

What is even more interesting, however, is to see this basic model of legal knowledge creation, the expressive–implicit dimensions in the context of a very ancient, possibly 5,000-year-old Tai-Chi symbolization from Chinese civilization.

TAO OF KNOWLEDGE

Simply put, creativity is a state of human mind, and by its nature, it implies dynamism. To create is to begin anew, to foster the growth of something new out of what already exists, the old. So if you look at the symbol of Tai-Chi as represented in Figure 9.4, you can see only two colors: white and black. Interestingly, in legal circles it is often standard advice by a lawyer to a client on having reached an agreement: "Put it in black and white"—that is, to nail an agreement into enforceability by expressing these intentions

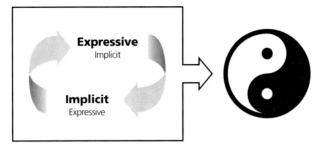

Figure 9.4   The Tao of generating knowledge.

in a signed, properly stamped contract. From the perspective of complexity language, it renders the uncertainty ("chaos" is a bit too strong a word) into certainty.

In the context of Tai Chi symbol, the colors of black and white have very different connotations. They depict exactly the opposite. Taoists in ancient China, having observed nature, found the world is always changing, however subtle the changes. They depict this creative change by using the highly abstract circular symbol, contrasting the black with the white. Moreover, in the black there is always the presence of a smaller circle of the white. Correspondingly, in the white there is a circular dot of black. The symbol is never static, it is always evolving—just like the courts, always having to make new judicial decisions.

As time flows, black grows, however slowly, even imperceptibly, within the white, but certainly there comes a time when white is transformed into black. Simultaneously, the white dot grows and so black turns into white. The symbol shown is therefore a snapshot at a given moment in time. It is also circular, like the moon, embedding the concept of transformational, dynamic change. Here we try to draw a parallel with our earlier model: the explicit (black) and the implicit (white, being a blank page). Due to space limitations, we can only highlight the possible relevance of a deeper, more ancient Chinese model on creative, transformational change, one that will become more significant as China propels her way into the global economy. Thus the reason for our subtitling this chapter: Tao of transmuting cases into knowledge.

NOTES

1. For the PowerPoint presentation on the internet, visit http://a2j.kentlaw. edu/presentations/jdss2001/schedule.html; the Justice Web Collaboratory, Chicago-Kent College of Law, Illinois Institute of Technology, Chicago, USA. See http://www.lawgazette.com.sg/2002-2/Feb02-feature.htm for his article,

The Mind of Lord Denning, where he argued for the perspective of "The Court as a Thinking Organization."

2. See in particular Richard Wihelm's translations of *I Ching,* the Book of Changes and visit this website: http://www.iging.com/intro/introduc.htm for the English version of his work.
3. He translated the book into German, working with a Taoist sage, Lao Nai-hsuan. On his return to Germany, he became a Professor of Chinese Studies at the University of Frankfurt and in 1925 founded the China Institute.
4. "The concept of attractor reminds us that there are organizing principles at work in all systems. Values, goals, theories, leadership in groups: all can be considered as attractors bringing people together." Battram (1998, p. 148).

REFERENCES

Battram, A. (1998). *Navigating complexity.* London: The Industrial Society.

Choo, W. C. (1998). *The knowing organization.* New York: Oxford University Press.

Foo, C. T. (2001, May). Towards a taxonomy of judicial thinking. *Conference on Judicial Decision Support Systems,* Chicago. http://a2j.kentlaw.edu/presentations/jdss2001/schedule.html

Holland, J. H. (1998). *Emergence: From chaos to order.* Reading, MA: Helix Books.

Kelly, K. (1994). *Out of control: The new biology of machines, social systems and the economic world.* Reading, MA: Addison Wesley.

LoPucki, L. (1997). The systems approach to law. *Cornell Law Review, 82*(3), 479–522.

McElroy, M.W. (2000). Integrating complexity theory, knowledge management and organizational learning. *Journal of Knowledge Management, 4*(3), 195–203.

Nonaka, I. (1991, November/December). The knowledge creating company. *Harvard Business Review, 69,* 96–104.

Nonaka, I. & Takeuchi, H.(1995). *The knowledge creating company.* Oxford, UK: Oxford University Press.

Polanyi, M. (1966). *The tacit dimension.* London: Routledge & Kegan Paul.

Wilhelm R. (German translator) (1967). *I Ching or the Book of Changes.* Princeton: Princeton University Press.

CHAPTER 10

PARTICIPATION AND COMPLEXITY IN COLLABORATIVE KNOWLEDGE GENERATION

Teams as Social-Intellectual Environments

Michael Beyerlein, Ph.D. and Jeffery Lin

INTRODUCTION

We live in an ocean of possibilities. Every day dozens of opportunities to create and innovate pass us by because we cannot see them, we fail to recognize their value, or we can't identify the resources for acting on them. For example, each time we are in the presence of another person but fail to engage in creative conversation, possibilities of cross-fertilization are lost. Each time we feel frustrated because of inadequate tools, frameworks, or support, we have an opportunity to invent new ways of working, but usually merely vent our emotions. An environment where more possibilities are recognized, considered, and acted on is challenging to construct. Some

Complexity and Knowledge Management, pages 153–173

of our attempts to construct such organizations have resulted in stifling systems that inhibit possibility thinking and innovation, such as the command and control structure of traditional bureaucracy. However, in recent years, a number of organizational experiments have resulted in promising new designs that seem to enable ability to innovate—that is, ability to generate new ideas and put them into practice. The evolving understanding of knowledge, knowledge work, and the knowledge worker has helped in creating new and enabling organizational designs. The organizations represent social-intellectual systems (we hyphenate the two terms to emphasize the interdependence of the intellectual system and the social system) based on networks of relationships, shared goals and understanding, and sets of routines for operating in ways that produce collaboration, learning, and creativity. Effective social-intellectual systems have been defined in a variety of ways including:

- Bundles of tangible assets—traditional categories of information for the "bean counters"
- A system of identifiable routines or activity sets
- Systems for information processing and symbol manipulation
- Systems of interpretation and sense-making
- Communities of knowledge

This sample of definitions can be read to represent a historical trend from a tangible emphasis to an intangible emphasis in the way we view organizations. This shift in framework represents a growing sophistication and creates new opportunities for how to organize and manage. In this chapter, we will assume an organization has both a formal and an informal structure for supporting the processes for learning, creating, collaborating, and decision making that enable it to adapt to environmental challenges.

The nature of collaborative knowledge generation and the multifaceted character of the problems and challenges faced in complex professional work demand a team approach within and across organizations. The intellectual assets that such work requires are rarely the property of a single individual, and integrating the required knowledge into a co-generated solution is only possible in a special social-intellectual environment governed by shared values, trust, and norms of reciprocity (Fukuyama, 1997; Woolcock, 1998).

The group of members evolves into a team by co-generating a shared framework and processes for their interaction and their work. This evolution is not automatic. Katzenbach (1999), author of such books as *The Wisdom of Teams* (Katzenbach & Smith, 1993), said that he had only seen three "real teams" in his 30 years of consulting. Real teams have achieved the highest level of development and thereby the highest level of performance. The members build a social network through conversation that enables ideas, information, and energy to flow back and forth effectively. Each member brings a set of initial schemata to the group that may evolve through learning, so understanding of the work goals and skill at facilitating the team's process improve over time. The construction of the network takes work, and persistence and is facilitated or inhibited by the surrounding work environment. The goal is to create a network that allows open sharing, creative synthesis, and consensus decision making. The network achieves a dynamic stability or homeodynamics or dynamic equilibrium (Goldberger, Rigney, & West., 1990), but it is a fragile structure. Small changes can have small, medium, or large impacts on the social-intellectual system the team creates (Bak, 1996) that follow a power law, so that the larger the change, the less frequently it occurs—with a frequency $1/x$ where x is the size of the change. There seems to be a quality like critical mass or readiness that must be created, perhaps through the accumulation of small changes, for the large changes to ripple through the system. For example, trust within the network of relationships in the team may be built by an accumulation of positive interactions and worn away by negative ones, but a single intense event, such as failure to keep a commitment or violation of a confidence, may greatly amplify the deterioration process.

KNOWLEDGE

Let's begin at the end and work backward. The end is a set of desirable outcomes that include intelligent decisions and their implementation, increase in tangible and intangible capital, increased capability for addressing challenges and opportunities in the future, competitive advantage, and market share. These outcomes depend on a system of processes that develop and share knowledge, utilizing it for new ideas and insights, and coordinating the tangible and intangible resources of the organization. The challenge is that competitors are working on their processes, too, with just as much intelligence and motivation. The flow of knowledge through the organization is the key. Knowledge management has been used as a term to describe how that flow is managed, although organizational learning, business intelligence, and organizational development also describe that flow— from other perspectives. This is not a simple situation. The challenge for organizations trying to manage and leverage explicit and tacit knowledge resources to achieve competitive advantage is substantial.

"The map is not the territory" (Korzybski, 1955, p. 747). Our knowledge is not complex enough to accurately represent the world in which we live. The world is more multifaceted, subtle, complicated, complex, and dynamic than our individual or collective intellectual maps can capture. Change in the 21st century is coming faster and producing more complexity than ever before. A system cannot comprehend another system that is more complex than itself (Seel, 1999). This implies that we need to develop more complex social-intellectual systems in order to understand the world around us well enough to function intelligently in it. No current systems seem adequate for comprehending the complex, large-scale systems that are developing globally, such as economic, political, and environmental systems; hence, our decisions and solutions seem inadequate and, at best, suboptimize— benefiting subsystems at the expense of the larger system. To build social-intellectual systems capable of addressing the challenges of large, complex systems, we need to deliberately, systematically, and systemically utilize the principles of collaboration that rest on the premise "all of us are smarter than any of us."

Here we carefully distinguish between the terms "information" and "knowledge." Information is the result of processing, manipulating, and organizing data in a way that enables the person using the information to develop knowledge of the events or objects the data represents (Novak & Gowin, 1984). Novak and Gowin created a visual hierarchy to show the levels of processing progressing from objects and events to data to information to knowledge to wisdom. Each level of processing created a higher level order among the concepts. Concept mapping provided a detailed, visual, pattern-based representation of the concepts. Trochim (1985) described concept maps as an analogy for the way knowledge grows—increasing levels of differentiation, integration, and abstractness. Low-level abstractness or minimal levels in the concept map represent a handicap referred to as "stimulus-bound," which is characteristic of both the novice and the psychologically handicapped. It provides minimal options in a response repertoire and so a pattern of behaviors develops that is reactive instead of proactive, habitual instead of creative. Learning adds to understanding, producing a more complex map, and so a better representation of the world and more options for dealing with its challenges are possible.

The value of information is unrealized until it is processed to become knowledge. Processing makes information useful and meaningful. The problem is that it also reduces the possibilities. Processing imposes structure, assumptions, and values that extract limited meanings from the data. Habits of processing become a point of view that provides the knower with a limited view of reality. However, each member of a group has a differing view and so can contribute to a shared map to make it more representative of reality—more valid. Sharing depends on the qualities of the social environment—it does not occur unless trust typifies the relationships between members.

Noise is that part of the incoming data that we cannot make sense of. Communication researchers claim that 90% of meaning is derived from the perception of nonverbal behaviors. If we are untrained in observation of group processes, we are likely to miss much of the behavioral data that teammates transmit and hence have an impoverished ability to develop understanding of what is going on or which inputs have value for the joint solution to the team's work. A lively feedback process can offset this reduction in nonverbal communication. If one member restates the utterance of another in his/her own words, the original speaker can check to see if the intended meaning got across and, if necessary, restate it again and again in various ways until there is a sense of successful communication. Feedback achieves what skill or facilitation might have achieved but in a rather haphazard way. Reading the words on this page is a limited way of acquiring the meaning the authors intend. No feedback is available during the reading. Conversation provides a natural environment for using feedback to create clarity in shared understanding. Conversation is where the work gets done (Mohrman & Tenkasi, 1997; Hansen, Nohria, & Tierney, 1999; Hardy, Lawrence, & Grant, 2005) and where the learning occurs (Brown, Collins, & Duguid, 1989; Knowles, 1990). Conversation represents a complex process of interaction among members that has nonlinear qualities.

Complexity of knowledge comes mainly from knowers and their networks instead of knowledge itself (Davenport, De Long, & Beers, 1998). For that reason, participation and collaboration are essential in complexifying knowledge, that is, improving the accuracy of its representation of the complexity of the world.

KNOWING

Knowledge is personal (Hansen, Nohria, & Tierney, 1999). The rich store of cognitive content and structure the individual brings to the interpretation of information provides a context that generates meaning. Information without the personal framework is meaningless and merely has potential value. The inputs to the team's conversation include information from a number of sources and knowledge from the members. Creative knowledge generation in such areas of work as research, new product development, and consulting emerges with the most potential when the members represent multiple functions and disciplines. Each member brings unique knowledge and perspective to the work. For example, in a four member team, the cognitive structure of the electrical engineer differs from that of the chemical engineer, the director of manufacturing, and the marketing representative. Sharing of knowledge is only possible if this diverse membership builds a social-intellectual platform together—a local culture of collaboration and common understanding. The platform emerges through a self-organizing process that generates a set of rules for interaction that is shared and recursive (Drazin & Sandelands, 1992) and operates without the control of a formal leader or controller (Anderson, 1999). This is a critical issue, because the team or project leader acting as a controller can interfere with the self-regulation and learning in the emergent network (Weick, 1979) and so limit the level of creativity the team can achieve. Some anecdotal evidence has been published suggesting that program managers may need to be more controlling, but at a high level, allowing the project teams that report to them to function with some autonomy.

The formal leaders need to develop appreciation of the emergent quality of the work and knowledge of the group dynamics, so intervention is not interruption. Maxims of management from the 20th century are dangerous guides in these situations. For example, "you can't manage what you don't measure" is a popular maxim that seduces leaders into imposing measurement processes on the team that capture only static and superficial information. The measurement process and the use of the measurement results in management decision making distracts the team from its work and its self-organizing activities, at best, and smothers both processes, at worst. Sitkin, Sutcliffe, and Schroeder (1994) developed the term "total quality learning" in contrast to "total quality management" in order to demonstrate that the controlling processes of the latter stifle the learning that is essential in knowledge work.

The social-intellectual system created by the team is a dissipative structure (Prigogine & Stengers, 1984) maintained far from equilibrium by injecting energy continuously. Controlling behaviors from the formal supervisor interrupt the flow of essential energy. "Knowledge is a resource locked in the human mind—creating and sharing it are intangible activities that can neither be supervised nor forced out of people—they only come voluntarily" (Ehin, 2000, p. 10).

A formal social system is defined by the organization in the set of roles and expectations that founders and managers chose as their best estimate of the structure that will enable the processes for achieving the organization's goals. The choice is made within the limited alternatives they can access in their planning. The emergent social system evolves to overlay the formal system. The emergence of a network of relationships occurs in response to the limitations of the formal structures that interfere with effectively getting the work done. The interference leads to an activity by the team called a "work around" where the team invents informal methods of getting the work done in spite of obstacles (e.g., Olson, 2004). One well known example of informal structure and its contribution to effectiveness is represented by the behavior of the character Radar in the television series Mash. Radar established an informal network that enabled him to work around the formidable barriers of the army bureaucracy to obtain supplies much more quickly than formal application would allow. The emergence of relationship-based supply chains such as the one established by the German manufacturer Bose deliberately capitalizes on some of the same principles to speed flow of materials in the supply chain (Ghenniwa, Dang, Huhns, & Shen, 2005).

The intellectual system also has both a formal and an informal component. The formal intellectual system includes explicit definition of policies and procedures—again representing the best guess the managers can make about what it will take to achieve business goals. The informal intellectual system emerges through conversation in all its forms, including face-to-face talk, teleconferences, emails, wikis, blogs, reading and correspondence, and so on—particularly those that occur "at the water cooler," which means spontaneously. The intellectual system provides a means for the flow of information and ideas. People who are excited about a new idea may experience the system as hindering rather than promoting flow. The story of the development of the Post-It note at 3M illustrates working around a hindrance, where Art Fry, the inventor, had to resort to indirect means of getting management attention for the new product (Brand, 1998).

Social-intellectual systems deteriorate when investment of energy drops (Adler & Kwon, 2002). Relationships deteriorate when ignored or subjected to erosive behaviors that reduce the openness of the system to inputs. The input of energy in any form involves work. In a complex adaptive system the work leads to the emergence of structure and stability (Goldstein, 1999). However, there is a critical distinction between work that generates incremental or evolutionary change in the structure and work that generates breakthrough or revolutionary change. An understanding of the latter is especially important in the paradigm shifts that lead to revolutionary new products. New sources of energy include addition of new members to the emerging network that represents teammates, suppliers, customers, consultants, and so on (Anderson, 1999). However, loss of current members can de-energize the team.

Social-intellectual systems within the organization depend on willingness of members to invest energy in them. Ulrich's (1998) formula for intellectual capital as modified by Burr and Girardi (2002) demonstrates the key role of willingness:

$$intellectual\ capital = competency \times commitment \times control$$

Commitment represents the willingness to invest by contributing energy, attention, ideas, and other resources to the conversation. When commitment or any of the terms in the equation drops to zero, no new intellectual capital is generated. Withdrawal behaviors, such as absenteeism from meetings, turnover of members, or information hording, indicate that commitment is approaching zero for the member(s). The literature on job design, job satisfaction, and commitment provides a wealth of ideas for creating environments that reduce withdrawal behaviors. That literature tends to focus on individual behavior instead of team behavior and omits discussion of the role of complexity in the dynamics of motivation, but it does provide some tips on establishing an environment that enables creative knowledge generation.

Some organizations deliberately rotate team members from one team to another to increase the opportunity for learning and cross-fertilization. This tactic seems to increase the investment of energy in the teams. However, it disrupts the social system that underlies the intellectual system—it ignores the hyphen in the term social-intellectual. In the classic literature on team development, each team experiencing a change in membership is likely to slip back from an advanced stage to engage in forming activities and spend time and attention on re-establishing an emergent structure that allows for free flow of ideas. The rotation of members represents an artificially imposed turbulence in the team's environment that increases the energy requirements for sustaining the structure that has been built through a history of interactions among members. Turbulence is a concept often applied to the conditions of the extra-organizational environment. However, here it applies to the environment of any level system within the organization as well (McKinley & Scherer, 2000). For example, one internal organization development consultant said of his division at a major oil company, "We re-organize every six months, whether we need it or not." Management decisions of this type fail to understand the subtle and delicate nature of the emergent systems (McKelvey, 1999) and the time and energy it takes to nurture them to the point of high performance levels (Anderson, 1999). Leaders should state the goal and then remove hurdles, especially themselves. The project goal is the attractor for the team that limits its problem-solving space (McKelvey, 1999), setting constraints that engender creativity.

Complex structure grows from a chain of simple interactions. In their simplest form, the interactions within a team occur when members chose to open up and share and close off to reflect (King, 1997). Opening and closing represent behavior at the team level as well. Admission of a new member depends on openness at both the individual and team levels. Integrating a new member into the team forces adjustments to the network and the rules that guide its processes.

The emergence of complex structure depends on many interactions between the members. Teams that are geographically distributed have fewer opportunities for interaction than those that meet face-to-face. Hence, the emergence of complex structure that enables the highest levels of creativity may be impossible to achieve. The ties in the system are delicate. They depend on continuous injection of energy to sustain the pattern of interactions, particularly when interactions move from the superficial level of routine (what transactional analysts describe as games, routines, and rituals) to the transparent and genuine level (Berne, 1964). This highest of levels depends on trust, which can be operationalized as the willingness to be vulnerable; to rely on another's intent, expertise, and dependability; and to be trustworthy—making this quality of relationship reciprocal. Lewicki, Tomlinson, and Gillespie (2006) argue that trust develops in stages from the calculation of benefits, to calculus-based, knowledge-based, and identification-based. The probability of open sharing at a level that allows emergence of revolutionary intellectual structure drops rapidly toward zero as loss of trust closes the channels through which shared knowledge flows.

Knowledge has been described as explicit or tacit, declarative or procedural, objective or situational. Here we will label explicit and declarative knowledge as information. It is linear, captured in objective ways such as writing, and easily shared. It has value when an individual or group accesses it and processes it cognitively and socially. In other words, it becomes useful when it is converted to knowledge. With historical roots in the field of information technology, knowledge management was founded on a definition of knowledge that equated it with the explicit and declarative. Recent work has begun to recognize the limitation of that perspective and shift toward an emphasis on the personal and tacit—a shift that requires a major transformation in perspective and process (e.g., Malhotra, 2000).

Complexity breaks down when we, as subjects, intervene (Bateson, 1972; Gherardi, 2000; Schein, 1999). Complexity science can be seen as a process-focused scientific discipline that deals with systems undergoing changes resulting from exchanging energy and information recursively over time. The basic attributes of complexity include energy/information, dimensionality and interdependency, change, temporality, and process (Dooley & Van de Ven, 1999). When complexity breaks down, the holistic nature of the phenomenon is lost, so knowledge is incomplete and the decisions based on it are inadequate.

Dooley and Van de Ven (1999) proposed approaches that can be used to harness complexity: control and cooperation. Control tends to reduce complexity while cooperation absorbs it. Control reduces the sense of uncertainty and its accompanying anxiety, so commitment to action becomes easier. Boundaries, rules, and institutionalization are three forms of control. Boundaries determine the rate of energy/information exchange, by acting as a filter which can be fully permeable, partly permeable, or impermeable. Rules also decrease complexity. A set of rules cannot account for the whole system, which is comprised of "countless, local, nonlinear, non-algorithmic, dynamic interactions" (Cilliers, 2000, p. 46). Institutionalization reduces dimensionality. By establishing hierarchies or departments, organizations not only create boundaries between levels and functions, but also decrease the number of dimensions, thus decreasing the opportunity for complexity in knowing to emerge. In contrast, collaboration tends to increase interdependency and thus makes the creation of intellectual complexity more tenable.

In the organization, knowledge is also characterized with the attributes of complexity (Coakes, 2004). First, knowledge is structured information that can transfer across boundaries. Second, knowledge varies in content and form. Third, knowledge is related to other knowledge, and thus can be combined, grouped, or merged. Fourth, the pace of knowledge updating has increased with the use of the internet. Fifth, knowledge is ever changing, due to changes in knowers and in contexts. Sixth, knowledge is processual—the verb form is more appropriate—knowing. The last attribute contrasts sharply with a more traditional account of knowledge, which sees knowledge as objects with a stable existence that can be recorded, transferred, and learned. According to Davenport, De Long, and Beers (1997), "Knowledge can be defined as information that has been combined with experience, context, interpretation, and reflection" (p.1). The process of combining is essential. The meaning that emerges from the interaction of knower and information depends on the knower's perspective.

LEARNING

We will define learning as the process of acquiring skill (knowing how) or knowledge (understanding) from experience or reflection that results in: (a) linking new pieces of information to existing cognitive structure, (b) adding new links between existing parts of the structure to create a more dense network, and (c) altering the structure, such as a shift in perspective, so processing of new and existing knowledge produces new ways of seeing. Learning results in enhanced skill and rule sets, resulting in a richer repertoire of behavioral responses to environmental opportunities and challenges and new meanings for experience. Competent, professional judgment only occurs within the context of significant learning. This definition applies at both the intra-individual and inter-individual levels. It is intended to describe learning for the individual, the team, and the organization. Piaget describes learning for the individual as a process of accommodation and assimilation (Flavel, 1967). Hargrave and Van de Ven (2006) describe institutional change resulting from collective action with similar terms.

Through learning, members of the team co-evolve with one another (Anderson, 1999). Although each member functions as a free agent adapting to changes in his/her environment for better fit and rewards over time (Holland, 1995), team members also adapt to each other's behavior and cooperate in a collective adaptation to the team environment (Anderson,

1999). This creates a dynamic process with cumulative effects because of the feedback from interaction that is represented by the power law (Kauffman 1993; Levinthal, 1997; Morel & Ramaujam, 1999).

Changes in conversation, decision making, and action continually evolve for the team, unless routines emerge where the feedback loop locks in a specific behavioral pattern. Routines provide both efficiency and ineffectiveness. Learning represents changes in a system that lead to task efficiency (March & Simon, 1958). However, important learning involves co-creation of meaning—making sense of assignments, events, and problems within the context of the team. Routines can make the creation of meaning more efficient, for example routinely practicing the principles of effective meeting management, but can also interfere when the rigidity of routine stifles dialog (Weick & Westley, 1996). For example, the time keeper in a meeting can interrupt an important dialog by saying, "Time's up." The interruption derails what might have been a productive exchange among members. The intervention becomes an interruption. More subtly, rigidity in thinking can stifle creativity. Groupthink (Janus, 1972) represents premature closure on a discussion because the social dynamics of the team bias the majority of members toward a single interpretation of the situation and discourage dissenting voices from keeping the discussion alive; monochromatic thinking displaces the rainbow of options that emerge from diversity of input. Groupthink imposes an order on the dynamic process that short circuits the feedback process necessary for working at the edge of chaos where learning occurs (Weick & Westley, 1996). Manz and Neck (1995) propose "teamthink" as a term representing the conditions where the discussion remains open and welcoming of inputs from all the diverse voices in the room.

Learners participate in communities of practitioners (also called communities of practice, learning communities, or communities of purpose). New members joining the community work to develop mastery of knowledge and skill that moves them toward full participation in its sociocultural practices. "Legitimate peripheral participation" provides a way to speak about the relations between newcomers and old-timers, and about activities, identities, artifacts, and communities of knowledge and practice (Wenger, 1998). A person's intention to learn is engaged and the meaning of learning is configured through the process of becoming a full participant in a sociocultural practice (Lave & Wenger, 1991).

In an organizational context, the member picks up insider knowledge in focusing on meaningful problems by informal and social means (Brown & Duguid, 1991). This process represents socialization and is a key part of becoming a member of a community of practice or network of learning (Powell, Koput, & Smith-Doerr, 1996). The social side of the social-intellectual system is essential to learning and thereby to knowledge management. Recognizing the social-intellectual system as a complex adaptive system makes it easier to nurture it, so greater value results from its processes.

Active learning is a process, not a product. A constructivist theory of learning requires the development of learning environments that involve collaboration, autonomy of learning, critical reflection, and authentic interactions with the real world (Barr & Tagg, 1995; Leifer, 1999; McCombs, in press). Components of active learning are learner self-responsibility, intentional learning strategies, problem-solving strategies, change of role to teacher as facilitator, anchored instruction, authentic assessment strategies designed to realistically evaluate real life skills, and cooperative learning (Bostock, 1997).

Situational cognition theory (Brown, Collins, & Duguid, 1989) espouses that learning is context-dependent and that knowledge is situated in the activity and context of the event. "Within a culture, ideas are exchanged and modified and belief systems developed and appropriated through conversation and narratives" (Brown, Collins, & Duguid, 1989, p. 40). This statement suggests that knowledge management for complex systems becomes learning management through creating social-intellectual environments with positive processes.

No learning occurs without feedback; that is, no lasting change in overt or covert behavior is generated until information is processed by the individual that indicates that goals will not be achieved without adjustments in processes. In a team, every response from every member can be considered potential feedback and is often interpreted and utilized that way by members or facilitators skilled in use of group process tools. In that sense, many member behaviors can provide feedback that significantly enhance or inhibit the social-intellectual process. Borrowing from the African Ubuntu philosophy, "I am who I am because of who we all are" (Mangaliso, 2001).

Davis (2001) describes both the learning system and its members—the learners—as self-organizing, emergent, self-transforming, disequilibriated, nested, scale independent, and recursively elaborative. When we treat learning systems as merely complicated, as public education seems to do in its quest for classroom control and achievement test scores, we squelch the dynamic processes that engender learning processes.

LEVERAGING EXPERTISE THROUGH SOCIAL-INTELLECTUAL ENVIRONMENTS

Levels of expertise may be differentiated by this distinction between complicated and complex, with the higher levels comprehending the truly complex: novice, beginner, competent, proficient, expert, master, world-class (Dreyfus & Dreyfus, 1986; Wiig, 1994). Perfect, flawless, brilliant, and simple only come from complete knowing; graceful execution is a consequence of absolute understanding (Heigh, 2006). To fully know, you have to have looked, studied, analyzed and described the depth and edge of your art. When does learning fail to occur for the members of the team? There are a number of conditions where opportunities to learn are missed, ignored, or denied. Some failures result from group process problems, such as conditions that lead to low levels of trust. Other failures result from the centrality of the belief that would be subjected to change. More central beliefs are more resistant to change (Rokeach, 1968). For example, the fundamental assumptions that differentiate a team member whose cognitive framework resembles that of a positivist would be resistant to a shift toward assumptions of the pragmatist.

Fukuyama has analyzed the link between trust, social capital, and national economic success. He defined social capital as "the ability of people to work together for common purposes in groups and organizations" (Fukuyama, 1995, p. 10). He further expanded the definition of social capital "as the existence of a certain set of informal values or norms shared among members of a group that permit cooperation among them" (Fukuyama, 1999, p. 16). Woolcock (1998) has referred to social capital as "the information, trust, and norms of reciprocity inhering in one's social networks" (p. 153). Nahapiet and Ghoshal (1998) have further elaborated the concept and defined it as "the sum of the actual and potential resources embedded within, available through, and derived from the network of relationships possessed by an individual or social unit" (p. 243).

For the each member, the team is the primary social-intellectual environment at work. Membership in the team implies interaction with the other members, which leads to a mutual influence process that shapes the team environment to achieve the goals of the individual, the team, and the organization.

Life is messy. Most NPD problems are messy, at least at the fuzzy front-end. That messiness occurs at the edge of chaos where order and chaos interface. Too much order reduces messiness but then stifles emergence. Conversation has qualities that enable it to produce messy, shared thought experiments. The team can develop into a social-intellectual ecosystem.

Participation and reification are two necessary conditions for learning to take place (Wenger, 1998). Participation denotes mutual engagement of subjects whose intentions are examined by each other, either directly or indirectly. Reification is an abstraction of experience, which has a "thing-like" existence but is subject to various translations. Knowledge is traditionally treated as reification rather than participation. As a result, knowledge is seen as an object that can be manipulated, and subjects that bear it are consistently ignored. By taking participation into account, the understanding of the complexity of knowledge can be greatly improved. Participation can take place directly between two subjects or indirectly through the medium of reifications. Direct participation is interactive and creates the opportunity to harness complexity, while indirect participation can be biased toward one's perceptions.

The most common way to manage complexity of knowledge is to establish boundaries around a specific area and limit knowledge access to certain people, reduce complexity of knowledge to a set of rules, or institutionalize the way knowledge is distributed and used. Managing knowledge through controls reduces complexity. Participation among knowers, on the contrary, increases interdependency among facets of knowledge without reducing the dimensions, thus absorbing complexity instead of reducing it. As an important concept in complexity science, the attractor dictates who will have access to what knowledge, or what kind of knowledge is dominant in the organization. It can either reduce or absorb complexity. For example, organizational climate, acting as an attractor, could either support controlling hierarchies or participative cooperation.

Individuals, groups, and organizations have different approaches to dealing with complexity of knowledge. To understand a piece of work, an individual needs to participate and explore the intention behind the work. It should be noted that the work, as reification of ideas, is subject to various interpretations. Since meaning is context-specific, people differing in socialization experience, personality, and attitudes can differ in how they perceive the work. We each possess some unique knowledge and organize it differently. We learn new knowledge and integrate it into what we have known. Prior knowledge becomes context for new knowledge and so determines its meaning. We tend to organize facets of knowledge according to their relatedness, similarities, and other characteristics, reducing complexity by control. The learning is tentative until tested. The confirmation of the new learning through test results leads to a power function where the new learning changes the overall cognitive context for the next new learning. Like Heraclites stepping into a different river each time, the social-intellectual space is modified with each new learning experience so that it continually changes—for the individual and for the team—by increasing interdependency between ideas. Creative ideas often come from such changes.

The structure that channels the team's process to produce team-like effectiveness can be created three ways: it can be imposed from the outside, accidentally evolve internally, or be formally co-created internally. Anecdotal evidence suggests that the latter is the most effective method—it most quickly moves the team toward the high-performing state. For example, shared values evolve gradually over time through a large number of conversations as people find evidence for similarity in what they value, or influence each other to shift values. However, the exercises involved in a process like team chartering accelerate the process of discovering shared values and hence move the group toward a team level pattern of interaction where we define "team" as a sustainable high-quality process of interaction resulting from structure, agreements, skills, and intentions. Does this dull the edge of chaos and limit creative thinking?

Dynamical systems do not reach a fixed-point or cyclical equilibrium (Anderson, 1999; Dooley & Van de Ven, 1999). The dynamics of a team involve three levels of interaction: intra-individual, inter-individual, and inter-team. Feedback loops proliferate within each of these levels as well as between them. The salient topic in the literature on teams is the inter-individual—interactions between team members. These have been described in a variety of ways in identifying processes of interaction that promote or inhibit team effectiveness (here we define team effectiveness as ability to achieve team goals over both the short and long term). Many of the tools used by consultants and facilitators for teams focus on developing intra-team processes but ignore the inter-team level.

The management of teams designed for creative knowledge generation is often summarized as: tell them the goal and then get out of the way. This is particularly important for team activities that have their own self-regulation, form, and self-correcting tendencies (Weick, 1979). Although it sounds simplistic, the only formal constraint on the knowledge work team should be the definition of the goal handed down from upper management.

The foci of team activity include effort invested in task and goal accomplishment, social and emotional maintenance of relationships among members, and learning and change that will increase the team's ability to address future assignments and challenges (Hackman, 1987). Purser and Pasmore (1992) describe the process of a knowledge-generating team as "building the boat while going downstream." We would add that the stream has significant white water to navigate. Their point is that the process of problem solving must be invented as the problem is being solved. Pacanowsky (1995) describes this as solving wicked problems—those that are difficult to define, involve multiple stakeholders, have ambiguous or conflicting criteria of success, and so on. Where is the stability in such a downstream voyage? Stability is both functional and dysfunctional for the team. A common analogy is the river flowing within its banks—the banks form the stable structure. However, there is structure within the river itself, such as standing waves—a dynamic stability. Functional stability is achieved by establishing routines wherever they can add efficiency in use of resources without reducing effectiveness in creative problem solving (McDermott, 1999). The line between efficiency and effectiveness is critical. Effectiveness depends on protecting a problem-solving space where collaboration enables leveraging of individual member knowledge in co-creation of joint solutions to team problems.

CREATING CONDITIONS FOR GENERATING NEW KNOWLEDGE

In complex systems, inputs change into outputs in a nonlinear way because their components interact with one another via a web of feedback loops. When two or more individuals meet and begin to get acquainted, complexity increases. This occurs gradually because of the difficulty of grasping the others' intentions and assumptions. Misunderstanding can occur easily. One way misunderstanding occurs is when one individual overpowers the counterpart by imposing one's own perspective on the knowledge the other tries to share. This can reduce complexity greatly. Another way is to say "let's just solve this problem and we can discuss that later"—postponing discussion of the underlying assumptions. Errors occur when people avoid discussing the undiscussables (Argyris, 1998). By setting up arbitrary boundaries, rules, or structures, consensus can be easier to reach. An alternative way is to engage in dialogue. Both parties need to explore their basic assumptions. With the help of the other party, one's basic assumptions can be shared and examined. As a result, interdependency increases, and knowing is enhanced as the social-intellectual system becomes more complex and so more able to validly map the realities of the members' situation. A variety of aids to discussion have been developed to assist the process of revealing assumptions, such as Five Whys, Ladder of Inference, and the Left-Hand Column (Senge, Kleiner, Roberts, Ross, & Smith, 1994).

In an organization, knowledge sharing becomes more difficult, not only because institutionalization creates boundaries, but also because organizational climate and culture form attractors that acknowledge some kinds of knowledge while ignoring others. The purpose of institutionalization is to reduce variance and risk and increase predictability, while one of the functions of culture is to ensure internal integration. It should be noted that culture is an emergent phenomenon that feeds back to impact the processes. A culture of knowledge sharing could actually improve knowledge management. Institutionalization also represents a linear approach to knowledge, which means that only causal or correlated relationships are considered. Cooperation (e.g., cross-functional teams) takes nonlinearity into account by bridging different areas of knowledge.

CONCLUSION

In this chapter, we have argued that knowledge management practices may fail to account for the complexity of the social processes of creativity and learning. Knowledge is not what we see, but what we understand, because it is only valid in certain circumstances or under certain assumptions. Like light taking on both wave and particle forms (Greene, 2004), knowledge can be viewed as having both a processual and a concrete form, which contrast understanding with information. The former view drives a different set of decisions for creating work environments that enhance creative knowledge generation because of the essential social dimension. Without considering participation explicitly, people tend to make errors by trimming down the dimensions of the problem space instead of absorbing complexity through increasing interdependency. This means that knowledge management should take participation into account and rely on it more than on control. The goal is to create the social-intellectual ecosystem that nurtures the emergence of new ideas through the emergence of new network ties and to complexify—mirror the complexity of the environment with the complexity of the thought world and protect it from the merely complicated perspectives that attempt to manage through control. Organization design is a discipline that tries to match the complexity of an organization's structure with the complexity of its environment and technology (Galbraith 1982). This principle can inform knowledge management decisions.

Complexity theory provides a promising framework for examining the behavior of effective teams as environments for creating new knowledge. Prior frameworks have been too simplistic and static to capture the dynamic, complex, and subtle evolution of teams to maturity. The social-intellectual system has to be created through intentional design decisions, formal interventions, and emergence of complex structure over time. The team represents the banks of the river through which the knowledge flows and which protects the process of collaborative knowledge generation in the team, so higher quality insights can be synergized.

REFERENCES

Adler, P. S., & Kwon, S. W. (2002). Social capital: Prospects for a new concept. *Academy of Management Review, 27*(1) 17–40.

Anderson, P. (1999). Complexity theory and organization science. *Organization Science, 10*(3), 216–232.

Argyris, C. (1998). Empowerment: The emperor's new clothes. *Harvard Business Review, 76*(3), 98–105.

Bak, P. (1996). *How nature works: The science of self-organized criticaitly.* New York: Copernicus.

Barr, R. B., & Tagg, J. (1995). From teaching to learning: New paradigm for undergraduate education. *Change, 26*(November/December), 13–25.

Bateson, G. (1972). *Steps toward an ecology of mind.* New York: Ballantine Books.

Berne, E. (1964). *Games people play.* New York: Ballantine.

Bostock, S. J. (Ed.). (1997). *Designing Web-based instruction for active learning* (Vol. 1). Englewood Cliffs, NJ: Educational Technology Publications.

Brand, A. (1998). Knowledge management and innovation at 3M. *Journal of Knowledge Management, 2,* 17–22.

Brown, J. S., Collins, A., & Duguid, P. (1989). Situated cognition and the culture of learning. *Educational Researcher, 18*(1), 32–42.

Brown, J. S., & Duguid, P. (1991). Organizational learning and communities-of-practice: Toward a unified view of working, learning, and innovation. *Organizational Science, 2*(1), 40–56.

Burr, R., & Girardi, A. (2002). Intellectual capital: More than the interaction of competence x commitment. *Australian Journal of Management, 27,* 77–87.

Cilliers, P. (2000). Rules and complex systems. *Emergence, 2,* 40–50.

Coakes, E. (2004). Knowledge management: A primer. *Communications of the Association for Information Systems, 14,* 406–489. (http://web.njit.edu/~bieber/CIS677F04/coakes-cais2004.pdf)

Davenport, T. H., De Long, D. W., & Beers, M. C. (1998). Successful knowledge management projects. *Sloan Management Review, 39*(2), 43–58.

Davis, B. (2001). Complexity research and teacher education. Retrieved January 1, 2007 from http://teach.educ.ubc.ca/faculty_resources/create/aug30.ppt 2001.

Dooley, K. J., & Van de Ven, A. H. (1999). Explaining complex organizational dynamics. *Organization Science, 10,* 358–372.

Drazin, R., & Sandelands, L. (1992). Autogenesis: A perspective on the process of organizing. *Organizational Science, 3,* 230–249.

Dreyfus, H. L., & Dreyfus, S. E. (1986). *Mind over machine: The power of human intuition and expertise in the era of the computer.* New York: The Free Press.

Ehin, C. (2000). *Unleashing intellectual capital.* Woburn MA: Butterworth Heinemann

Flavell, J. (1967). *The developmental psychology of Jean Piaget.* New York: D. Van Nostrand Company.

Fukuyama, F. (1995). *Trust: Social virtues and the creation of prosperity.* NY: Free Press.

Fukuyama, F. (1997). *The end of order.* London: Centre for Post-collectivist Studies.

Fukuyama, F. (1999). *The great disruption: Human nature and the reconstitution of social order.* New York: Free Press.

Galbraith, J. R. (1982). *Designing complex organizations.* Reading, MA: Addison-Wesley.

Ghenniwa, H., Dang, J., Huhns, M., & Shen, W. (2005). eMarketplace model: An architecture for collaborative supply chain management and integration. *Data and Knowledge Engineering, 52,* 33–59.

Gherardi, S. (2000). Practice-based theorizing on learning and knowing in organizations. *Organization, 7,* 211–223.

Goldberger, A. L.,. Rigney, D. R., &. West, B. J. (1990). Chaos and fractals in human physiology. *Scientific American, 262*(2), 42–49.

Goldstein, J. (1999). Emergence as a construct: History and issues. *Emergence, 1,* 49–72.

Greene, B. (2004). *The fabric of the cosmos: Space, time, and the texture of reality.* New York: Alfred A. Knopf.

Hackman, R. (1987). The design of work teams. In J. Lorsch (Ed.), *Handbook of Organizational Behavior* (pp. 190–222). Englewood Cliffs, NJ: Prentice-Hall.

Hansen, M.T., Nohria, N. & Tierney, T. (1999). What's your strategy for managing knowledge? *Harvard Business Review, 77*(2), 106–116.

Hardy, C., Lawrence, T. B., & Grant, D. (2005). Discourse and collaboration: The role of conversations and collective identity. *Academy of Management Review, 30*, 58–77

Hargrave, T., & Van de Ven, A. H. (2006). A collective action model of institutional change. *Academy of Management Review, 31*, 864–888.

Heigh, J. (2006, January 16). Sift experiment…evolved. Retrieved December 22, 2006 from http://www.siftstar.com/blog/2006/01/16/sift-idea/

Holland, J. H. (1995). *Hidden order: How adaptation builds complexity.* Reading, MA: Addison-Wesley.

Janis, I. (1972). *Victims of groupthink.* Boston: Houghton-Mifflin.

Katzenbach, J. R. (1999). *Keynote address.* Presented at the 10th Annual International Conference on Work Teams, Dallas, TX

Katzenbach, J. R., & Smith, D. K. (1993). *The wisdom of teams: Creating the high-performance organization.* Cambridge, MA: Harvard Business School Press.

Kauffman, S. A. (1993). *The origins of order: Self organization and selection In evolution.* New York: Oxford University Press.

King, D. J. (1997). *A structural approach to four theories of group development.* Unpublished PhD dissertation, University of North Texas, Denton, TX.

Knowles, M. (1990). *The Adult learner: A neglected species.* Houston, TX: Gulf Publishing Company.

Korzybski, A. (1955). *Science and sanity.* Fort Worth, TX: Institute of General Semantics.

Lave, J., & Wenger, E. (1991). *Situated learning: Legitimate peripheral participation.* New York: Cambridge University Press.

Leifer, L. (1999). *Engineering education unbounded.* Presentation 13 July 1999. Retrieved December 15, 2006 from http://sll.stanford.edu/pubs/presindex.html

Levinthal, D. A. (1997). Adaptation on rugged landscapes. *Management Science, 43*, 934–950.

Lewicki, R. J., Tomlinson, E. C., & Gillespie, E. C. (2006). Models of interpersonal trust development: Theoretical approaches, empirical evidence, and future directions. *Journal of Management, 32*, 991–1022.

Malhotra, Y. (2000). From information management to knowledge management: Beyond the "hi-tech hidebound" systems. In K. Srikantaiah & M.E.D. Koenig (Eds.), *Knowledge management for the information professional* (pp. 37–61). Medford, NJ: Information Today Inc.

Mangaliso, M. P. (2001). Building competitive advantage from Ubuntu: Management lessons from South Africa. *Academy of Management Executive, 15*(3), 16–22.

Manz, C. C. & Neck, C. P. (1995). Teamthink: Beyond the groupthink syndrome in self-managing work teams. *Journal of Managerial Psychology, 10*, 7–15.

March, J. G., & Simon, H. A. (1958). *Organizations.* New York: John Wiley.

McCombs, B. L. (in press). The learner-centered psychological principles: A framework for balancing a focus on academic achievement with a focus on social and emotional learning needs. In J. E. Zins, R. P. Weissberg, M. C. Wang, & H. J. Walberg (Eds.), *Building school success on social and emotional learning.* Philadelphia, PA: Temple University.

McDermott, R. (1999). Learning across teams: The role of communities of practice in team organizations. *Knowledge Management Review, 32*–26.

McKelvey, B. (1999). Avoiding complexity catastrophe in co-evolutionary pockets: Strategies for rugged landscapes. *Organizational. Science, 10*, 294–321.

McKinley, W., & Scherer, A. G. (2000). Some unanticipated consequences of organizational restructuring. *Academy of Management Review, 25*, 735–752.

Mohrman, S. A., & Tenkasi, R. (1997, April). *Patterns of cross-functional work: Behaviors and benefits.* Paper presented at the University of North Texas Symposium on Work Teams, Dallas, Texas.

Morel, B., & Ramanujam, R. (1999). Through the looking glass of complexity: The dynamics of organizations as adaptive and evolving systems. *Organizational Science, 10*, 278–293.

Nahapiet, J., & Ghoshal, S. (1998). Social capital, intellectual capital, and the Organizational Advantage. *The Academy of Management Review, 23*, 242–266.

Novak, J., & Gowin, B. (1984). *Learning how to learn.* Cambridge: Cambridge University Press.

Olson, J. (2004). Co-development: Collaborating across boundaries on joint strike fighter. In M. Beyerlein, D. Johnson, & S. Beyerlein, S. (Eds.), *Advances in Interdisciplinary Studies of Work Teams Vol. 10: Complex Collaboration.* Oxford: Elsevier/JAI Imprint.

Pacanowsky, M. (1995). Team tools for wicked problems. *Organizational Dynamics, 23*(3), 36–52.

Powell, W. W., Koput, K. W., & Smith-Doerr, L. (1996). Interorganizational collaboration and the locus of innovation. *Administrative Science Quarterly, 41*, 116–145.

Prigogine, I., & Stengers, I. (1984). *Order out of chaos: Man's new dialog with nature.* New York: Bantam Books.

Purser, R. E., & Pasmore, W. A. (1992). Organizing for learning. *Research in Organizational Change and Development, 6*, 37–114.

Rokeach, M. (1968). *Beliefs, attitudes and values.* San Francisco: Jossey-Bass.

Schein, E. H. (1999). *Process consultation revisited: Building the helping relationship.* Reading, MA: Addison-Wesley.

Seel, R. (1999). Complexity and OD: An introduction. Retrieved December 10, 2006 from www.new-paradigm.co.uk/complex-od.htm

Senge, P. M., Kleiner, A., Roberts, C., Ross, R. B., & Smith, B. J. (1994). *The fifth discipline fieldbook.* New York: Doubleday/Currency.

Sitkin, S. B., Sutcliffe, K. M., & Schroeder, R. G. (1994). Distinguishing control from learning in total quality management: A contingency perspective. *The Academy of Management Review, 19*, 537–564.

Trochim, W. (1985). Pattern matching, validity, and conceptualization in program evaluation. *Evaluation Review, 9*, 575–604.

Ulrich, D. (1998). Profiling organizational competitiveness: Cultivating capabilities. *Human Resource Planning, 16*(3),1–17.

Weick, K. E. (1979). *The social psychology of organizing.* Reading, MA: Addison-Wesley.

Weick, K. E., & Westley, F. (1996). Organizational learning: Affirming an oxymoron. In S. R. Clegg, C. Hardy & W. R. Nord (Eds.), *Handbook of organization studies* (pp. 440–458). London: Sage.

Wenger, E. (1998). *Communities of practice: Learning, meaning, and identity.* New York: Cambridge University Press.

Wiig, K. M. (1994). *Knowledge management: The central focus for intelligent-acting organizations.* Arlington TX: Schema Press.

Woolcock, M. (1998). Social capital and economic development: Toward a theoretical synthesis and policy framework. *Theory and Society, 27,* 151–208.

CHAPTER 11

A TALE OF TWO ORGANIZATIONS

Susan Burgess Miller

This is the story of two different organizations presented in case study format. The first organization's culture is engineer-based, tightly coupled, and strictly hierarchical, based upon the industrial revolution model (Schwandt & Szabla, 2007). The second's culture, loosely coupled, valuing emergence and the power of variety is based upon complexity science. Both organizations happen to be the U.S. National Aeronautics and Space Administration.

CULTURE, LEADERSHIP AND KNOWLEDGE MANAGEMENT: 1958–2003

Media reports (Alston, 2003; Gold & Vartabedian, 2003) suggested and the CAIB Report (National Aeronautics and Space Administration, 2003a) asserted that intransigence of the NASA culture contributed to the loss of the Columbia as well as the loss of the Challenger in 1986. This study informed those allegations by extending the analysis of mishap causes back throughout the lifespan of the Agency instead of limiting the analysis to the two Space Shuttle mishaps only. As such it was a meta-analysis of the analyses

Complexity and Knowledge Management, pages 175–197
Copyright © 2010 by Information Age Publishing
175

that were conducted by the official Mishap Investigation Boards appointed by NASA to determine the causes of Type A mishaps.

DISCUSSION OF MAJOR FINDINGS

Finding 1—NASA's Organizational Memory of Type A Mission-Related Mishaps is Greatly Distributed and Not Easily Retrievable

This study was designed to guard against sampling weaknesses by using the entire census of Type A Mishap Board Reports to avoid biased selectivity. NASA policy requires that these reports be sent to central repositories upon acceptance and retained permanently. I anticipated that it might indeed be difficult to retrieve all the reports from archival storage, but that the reports ultimately could be obtained because NASA policy required them to be kept so the Agency could learn from it past mishaps. The difficulty encountered in simply compiling a list of the Type A mishaps was most surprising inasmuch as NASA considers safety as the first of its core values.

NASA's mission success starts with safety. A commitment to safety permeates everything we do. We are committed to protecting the safety and health of the general public, pilots and astronauts, the NASA workforce, and our high-value assets on and off the ground. (National Aeronautics and Space Administration, 2003b)

This stated core value threads throughout the policy and procedural guidance within the Agency. The guidance on mishap investigation specifically states, "The objective of mishap and close call investigations is to improve safety by identifying what happened, where it happened, when it happened, why it happened, and what should be done to prevent recurrence and reduce the number and severity of mishaps" (National Aeronautics and Space Administration, 2004b, Chapter 1.1).

Why then wasn't there an existing listing of mishaps, especially the Type A mishaps that involve either the loss of life or the loss of high-value assets? What forces could have been at work within the organization that would discount the importance of mishaps within NASA?

What mishaps? NASA doesn't make mistakes. Developing and maintaining a listing of mishaps would constantly be a reminder of events NASA can't believe are real. The self-image of NASA as engineering perfection is so strong that it is inconceivable that NASA could be wrong. This self-image, NASA's identity, derives from the organizational culture that relies upon the role of science and engineering as a protective shield to assure perfection (Vaughan, 1996) and is a strong component of sensemaking (Weick, 1995). As Schwartz (1987) offered,

> The organization ideal is an image of perfection. It is, so to speak, an idea of God. God does not make mistakes. Having adopted the idea of NASA as the organization ideal, it follows that the individual will believe that, if NASA has made a decision, that decision will be correct. (p. 62)

An organizational culture that is built on past successes can make continued success seem more probable, continuing the aura of infallibility (Starbuck & Milliken, 1988). NASA's culture is built upon the very real basis of beating the communists to the moon during the Cold War. NASA brought the prize home to the United States. NASA did become God-like as Schwartz (1987) mused; not only God but also Savior from the Red Threat. An organizational identity and collective self-esteem that was forged within the competitive environment of the Cold War was built to last (Collins & Porras, 1994). Collins and Porras's research showed that visionary organizations almost religiously preserve their core ideology, changing it seldom, if ever. From this adherence to a fundamental set of beliefs or a deeply held sense of self-identity comes the discipline and drive that enable organizations to succeed in changing and volatile environments. But perhaps such zealotry can have a dark side also.

Brown and Starkey (2000) argue that the organizational self identity is protected by ego defenses that exert dysfunctional influence, particularly when organizational learning and change are desirable. These influences can include denial, rationalization, idealization, fantasy, and symbolization.

Denial

Denial has two dimensions. One, the refusal to admit the truth or reality, is more internally focused. Organizations may deny events or situations to themselves, defending the status quo. The second dimension, the assertion that an allegation is false, is more externally focused and involves defending the organization against external threats. Internal denial can be far more insidious than defending against outside threats (Laughlin, 1979). Internal denial requires not just getting the "party line" straight for outside consumption but requires modification of the organization's memory of what really happened. Weick (1995) stresses the importance of such retrospective sensemaking in organizations, pointing out that information and how it is interpreted is critical to safety.

NASA's workforce prides itself on its "can do" attitude. Budgets cut? No problem; work-arounds are developed, testing reduced and the projects can still be completed. Workforce spread too thin, 25 hours of overtime each week no longer surprising? No problem, we have the most capable workforce in the world, in effect super men and women who never get tired and so don't make mistakes. Support waning from the American public and political sectors? They just don't understand. After all, we are NASA.

Rationalization

NASA's workforce is among the most intellectual and educated in the nation. The collective intelligence has produced remarkable feats of engineering. This same collective intelligence is also capable of justifying otherwise unacceptable actions to the point that they become not only acceptable but normal. Vaughn called this the slippery slope of normalizing deviance (1996) while Gummer (1998) argued that NASA's culture has become bureaupathological, focusing on process and paperwork, and rationalizing deviant results away.

NASA has built its reputation and identity on engineering reality. NASA uses algorithms and testing to prove that the systems work. NASA creates and documents very elaborate processes for everything from how to design and implement a program to how to fill out forms. The external world benchmarks this documentation, believes that NASA actually follows the processes, and wants to be like NASA. What is not visible outside the organization is how often these documented processes are abandoned for time saving, cost saving, or just because (Snook, 2000). If the process or test produces the expected results, all is fine. If unexpected results are produced, the process or test can be simply disregarded. Rationalization permits this incongruence to be accepted as normal.

Idealization

Over time, the strong culture of an organization may passionately narrow its focus on a few dominant goals so absolutely that any negative aspects of these goals can be eliminated from the schema of organizational identity. Such strong cultures can make work meaningful to organizational members and generate personal enthusiasm within the organizational members. A recent culture climate survey of NASA (BST, 2004) shows that there is a strong sense of dedication and commitment to the technical work of the Agency. However, this single-mindedness can result in the establishment of impossible standards for organizational behavior and ultimately groupthink (Moorhead, Ference, & Neck, 1991). The overwhelming dominance of a single occupation such as engineering creates a monolithic culture, in which all members of influence embrace the same limited set of values and strategies. Models of the ideal social context, that of the bounded set of values and strategies, are reinforced. In so doing, "they truncate their understanding of the wider context in which they operate, and surrender their future to the way the context evolves" (Morgan, 1986, p. 242). Remembering that the ideal world within an engineering culture such as NASA is one of "elegant machines and processes working in perfect precision and harmony" (Schein, 1996, p. 14), it is understandable that mishaps would be considered singular aberrances, not worthy of remembering.

Fantasy

NASA's mission has always been making science fantasy real. From its beginning, it has been asked to transform unrealistic or improbable ideas into everyday reality for the United States, and it has succeeded. However, when NASA remembers its "glory days," it does not include memories of accidents or mishaps. Even mishaps that resulted in the loss of research test pilots or astronauts are remembered as positive achievements in the name of science and exploration. Buildings, streets, schools and awards are named after the fallen heroes, solidifying the fantasy of success, and crying out for emulation. Keeping a comprehensive and thus extensive listing of mishaps would interfere with maintaining the fantasy.

Symbolization

Laughlin (1979) offers that symbolization is the process "through which an external object becomes the disguised outward representation for another internal and hidden object, idea, person, or complex" (p. 414). This symbolization can be seen in the coveted Flight Readiness Review (FRR) process prior to major NASA missions. This process is conducted to verify that each aeronautical or space flight mission is scientifically and engineering-wise ready to fly. Within the NASA culture, "the loss of individual autonomy is replaced by the all-power autonomy of science. Science, not the individual, becomes responsible for decision making" (Feldman, 2000, p. 486). The Columbia Accident Investigation Board has called this "engineering by PowerPoint" (National Aeronautics and Space Administration, 2003a). Processes such as the FRR and other engineering-based reviews such as the Preliminary Design Review, Critical Design Review, and Operational Readiness Review become the symbolization for the mishaps that have occurred before. Similarly, the Mishap Investigation and Reporting Process has become symbolic for actually modifying NASA's organizational practices. What are valued are the investigation process and the creation of the report including the Corrective Action Plan, not the information and knowledge that the mishap reports contain. All these processes were designed to prevent future mishaps, and NASA's engineering processes always work as designed, so there is no point in keeping a listing of old mishaps.

The power of the ego defenses described above can explain why NASA did not have a complete listing of Type A mishaps prior to this study. Although all the requisite information did exist in separate documents, files and locations, it was inconsistent with NASA's self-image, that is, the NASA identity, to expend resources compiling a formal inventory of what NASA didn't want to know anyway.

Finding 2—NASA Has Lost 31% of Its Organizational Memory of Type A Mishaps

Of the 161 Type A mishaps identified during the data collection process, reports on 112 mishaps were retrievable. This represents a loss, perhaps permanent, of a significant portion of NASA's organizational memory that is no longer available to help the organization avoid similar future mishaps as was envisioned when the guidance on mishap investigation was developed. As Daft and Weick (1984) posit,

> Organizations are interpretation systems scanning the data in their environments, giving the data meaning via sensemaking and taking action as a result of the new information garnered. Some organizations limit scanning to reports and documents that in the past were important to the organization but to which the organization has become inured. (p. 298)

According to DeLong and Fahey (2000a), the organization's culture has a profound effect on what information is deemed important and worth saving.

Culture, Particularly Subcultures, Shapes Assumptions About What Knowledge Is Worth Managing

As discussed above, the NASA culture has a hard time accepting that mishaps happen. The identity defenses described—denial, rationalization, idealization, fantasy, and symbolization—enable the organization to shake off the mishap and return to normal activities. While the mishap investigation and reporting process has strong symbolic relevance, the information produced by the investigation has little value, so the reports are not valued as worth managing.

This study was designed to use a complete census of Type A mission-related mishap reports from 1958 through 2002 to avoid biased selectivity. The first requirement therefore was a listing of all Type A mishaps. The cognizant policy office at NASA Headquarters was contacted for a listing of the complete census of Type A mishaps. Headquarters program officials were able to provide a listing of mishaps that they believed constituted the complete census of Type A mishaps. This listing contained approximately 65 mission-related Type A mishaps, but the mishap reports on these 65 were not available in the Headquarters files. A Headquarters program official offered access to two drawers of microfiche files from a file cabinet in his office. He remarked that he had kept them for years but that no one ever used them and he was glad that they might be of value to this study. In addition to several mishap reports from the early 1970s that were not available in the official Headquarters files, the fiche contained images of numerous handwritten telephone logs used to record mishaps reported by NASA centers that documented additional mishaps that should have Investigation Board Reports. The Headquarters Library and History office collections and local files at NASA Centers were searched for mishap reports, as was the Center for Aerospace Information (CASI) database.

The organizations responsible for retention and storage of the mishap reports varied by center, but the records custodians were available and responsive in all but the one situation. At one center, the mishap reports had been scanned into electronic format and were provided electronically. At other centers the reports were in readily accessible file cabinets in the general office environment, sometimes chronologically ordered, sometimes not. At two centers the files had been retired to file storage in warehouse buildings with unconditioned air. At another center, the files had been retired to a National Archives and Records Service (NARS) repository hundreds of miles away and had to be retrieved and shipped.

The common thread in the data collection process at the NASA centers was the challenge in identifying the location and content of the files. In most cases, numerous contacts had to be made before the correct staff member with knowledge of the reports and their location was reached.

There appeared to be no reward, and no penalty, for assuring that the reports were archived in accordance with procedural guidance. There was no evidence that the reports were ever accessed after they were completed and the corrective action plan approved, either at the Agency level or locally at NASA Centers. The subcultures within subordinate organizations determined the priority that individuals accorded to mishap reports and the lessons-learned they contained.

Such modification of organizational procedures may have its foundation in local managerial efforts to increase immediate organizational effectiveness. "Organizational forgetting" (Martin de Holan & Phillips, in press; Martin de Holan, Phillips, & Lawrence, 2004) and "practical drift" (Snook, 2000) are developing explanations of such situations in which scarce resources are deployed differently than documented guidance requires in order to adapt to emerging local operational conditions.

Culture Mediates the Relationships Between Individual and Organizational Knowledge

The recent report on NASA culture indicates that employees do not feel valued by the organization (BST, 2004). Perceived Organizational Support was registered as one of the lowest scales across the agency. This can indicate a lack of commitment and loyalty to the organization itself. This lack can materially affect the knowledge flow from individuals to the higher organization levels.

One of the greatest challenges in this study was identifying the location of the mishap reports. In most cases, numerous contacts had to be made before the correct staff member with knowledge of the reports location was reached. Once identified, the records custodians were responsive with one noted exception. At that center the staff member stated that he would die before turning the five mishaps reports requested from that center over to anyone. He added that he would not release them even if, "Headquarters ordered him to." He did not confirm or deny which, if any, of the five reports sought were at the Center.

The records custodians with the most accessible files had each been with NASA for over 30 years, both having begun their careers in administrative support positions rather than in engineering fields. They expressed pride in their tenure with NASA and evidenced pride in maintaining the reports in accordance with the policy guidance. One custodian had actually supported several of the Mishap Investigation Boards and participated in the typing of the reports. Each had maintained detailed files on the content of retired records, which aided greatly in locating the specific files in warehouse environments. Other points of contact had joined NASA far more recently and had no information concerning any mishap reports prior to their service periods. Such variability in responses supports the premise of the role that individuals, and occupational subcultures, do play in the flow of information within the organization.

Culture Determines How Effective an Organization Will Be in Creating, Sharing, and Applying Knowledge

Norms and practices that discourage open communication between organizational levels undermine effective knowledge sharing (Baskin, 2005). The BST culture survey (2004) reported that the Upward Communication scale was one of the lowest in percentile terms of all items surveyed. The Upward Communication items measure perceptions about the quality and quantity of information employees believe they are encouraged to share with levels above them.

Culture can be particularly powerful when dealing with mistakes and mishaps (De Long & Fahey, 2000). If mistakes are ignored, explained away, or punished by the organization, individuals will intuit that the mishap information is not valued, and little effort will be made to maintain or communicate the information. If norms and practices reflect that the mishap reports are valued by the organization, much individual effort will be directed toward the maintenance and communication of the information. With the lack of emphasis NASA has placed on the mishaps themselves, it is not surprising the lack of emphasis individuals placed on assuring that the mishap reports and the lessons they contain are accessible.

Culture Shapes How New Organizational Knowledge Is Created,
Legitimated and Distributed

If senior managers strongly encourage and support "constructive con-frontation" and challenges to existing assumptions and beliefs that shaped the organization's earlier successes, employees will be more likely to par-ticipate in the process of new knowledge creation (De Long & Fahey, 2000, p. 124). Likewise, if senior managers perpetuate the impression that the raising of issues is not welcome as found in the recent culture survey (BST, 2004, p. 3), employees will not participate authentically in the knowledge creation and distribution process necessary to assure that mishap reports are openly available.

Because the NASA culture did not place value on the mishap reports and the information they contain, many employees in the organization did not spend valuable time and resources toward maintaining these archives. Some records custodians with long personal histories of involvement with the reports faithfully maintained the records necessary to access these files, but their organizations did not value their efforts as mainstream activities. On the other side of the spectrum, one employee was able to refuse access to the reports in spite of organization support for their release. Such be-haviors evidence that the role of the individual in the knowledge manage-ment activities critical to an active organizational memory should not be underestimated.

Most importantly, what NASA's culture does, its enacted values, is far more important than its espoused values concerning mishap reports. Al-though the espoused purpose for conducting mishap investigations and reporting the findings is "to improve safety by identifying what happened, where it happened, when it happened, why it happened, and what should be done to prevent recurrence and reduce the number and severity of mis-haps" (National Aeronautics and Space Administration, 2004a), little em-phasis has been placed on discerning the lessons from the reports once the investigations were completed.

In an eerily similar revelation, it was recently announced that the original high-quality video of the Apollo 11 moon landing is missing. Only tapings of television re-broadcasts can be found. Another case study can explore the causes of this loss.

Finding 3—The Patterns of Causes of Type A Mission-Related Mishaps Have not Changed Greatly Over NASA's History

Mishap investigation reports, whether they are used to assess damage, to establish responsibility or liability, or for other purposes, all contain a causal determination of why the accident happened (Urian, 2000). The mishap investigation community of practice, particularly within the engineering agencies of the Federal government, has evolved a taxonomy of standard cause codes (Department of Energy, 1992) to assist in the determination of the causes of mishaps. As with other communities, such standards become part of the practices of the community. De Long and Fahey (2000) state that "practices are the most visible symbols of a culture" (p. 115), and "cultures, and particularly subcultures, heavily influence what is perceived as useful, important or valid knowledge in an organization" (p. 116). While the evolution of the mishap investigation subculture is beyond the scope of this study, the cause code taxonomy can be viewed as the result of that evolution inasmuch as culture defines and shapes what the community defines as relevant (De Long & Fahey, 2000). The role of culture in mishap investigation is also supported by numerous authors. Urian (2000) found that organizational culture is brought to bear on the investigation of mishaps. He concluded that "self-regulation is the reluctance to discuss or give weight to issues which, even though they may be been contributing factors to an accident, are considered taboo by the investigation team members" (Urian, 2000, p. 256). Rasmussen (1990) argued that in mishap investigations there is a tendency to find and report that which the investigators expected to find at the outset of the investigation. Similarly, Gilpin (2005) and Richardson, Tait, Roos, and Lissack (2005) addressed how organizational paradigm can impact both investigations and learning in environments of complex project management.

It is possible that the similarity in mishap causes over the decades is an artifact of the mishap investigation subculture of the engineering culture (Schein, 1996). However, this subculture's standards would have developed within the larger context of the dominant organizational engineering culture as a result of the social activity of sensemaking (Weick, 1995). Such social activity takes place within the cultural system, the system of patterned and ordered symbols. This includes language and other forms of communication. Saussure (1990) posed that language itself develops or evolves both diachronically (usage over extended periods of time) and synchronically (usage at particular points in time). Thus the cause code standards can be considered the product of diachronic development of the language of mishaps and individual mishap reports as the product of synchronic development of the language of mishaps. Parsons (1951), referring to this as the cultural tradition, argued that elementary communication is not possible without "some degree of conformity to the 'conventions' of the symbolic system" (p. 11). Individual actors in different situations interpret these symbols through individual sensemaking, so each may react somewhat differently to the same set of stimuli.

For the work of an organization or group such as a Mishap Investigation Board to be effectively conducted, it is important that there be a stability in the symbol system—"a stability which must extend between individuals and over time, [and] could probably not be maintained unless it functioned in a communication process in the interaction of a plurality of actors" (Parsons, 1951, p. 11). Denison (1996) agreed with the social evolution of the relationship between symbols and sensemaking in his discussion of the evolution of social process over time. "The simultaneous creation of meaning and social structure, the evolution of interaction patterns into systems of normative control, and the close connection between the symbolic and material world can be well understood through the culture perspective" (Dennison, 1996, p.12).

The strong normative control aspects of an engineering culture such as NASA's are well known (Kunda, 1992). With a workforce of 58% scientists and engineers, NASA's engineering culture is preoccupied with designing people out of the systems rather than acknowledging the effect of human in the systems (Schein, 1996). It is understandable, then, that the taxonomy of cause codes is based upon the design and material aspects of the engineering processes, and it is thus not surprising that the constant pattern (46%) that all Type A mishaps over four decades are attributed to part or system failures.

Engineers tend to design safety into parts and systems, minimizing the human interaction required for successful operations. "The ideal world is one of elegant machines and processes working in perfect precision and harmony without human intervention" (Schein, 1996, p. 14). The engineering culture would hold, then, if a mishap wasn't caused by a part or system failure, it must have been caused by individual human intervention. Hence the taxonomy contains significant codes related to individual human failure such as violating procedures, training deficiencies, or other human errors, and 32% of Type A mishaps were attributed to Structuring processes.

Acknowledging that the members of the mishap investigation boards are predominantly engineers (National Aeronautics and Space Administration, 2004a), it is not surprising that board members would look for, and subsequently find, engineering-related causes such as material, part, or design issues instead of organizational issues such as culture. Supporting the predominant engineering culture, the cause code taxonomy—the product of the mishap investigation subculture of an engineering culture—does not include sensemaking functions or processes. The engineering culture prefers linear, quantitative reasoning that brackets out the "messy" parts of organizational dynamics such as culture, values, and basic assumptions (Schein, 1996).

Because culture plays a strong but latent role in organizations, it can be difficult to discern directly. One of the strongest characteristics of culture is that organizational actors may not be aware of it during day-to day operations. This very latency itself may account for the lack of mishap cause codes related to the sensemaking interchange medium, and the result is that few mishaps are attributed to functions such as culture within this memory and meaning subsystem.

The Influence of Sensemaking on New Information

The cybernetic hierarchy (Schwandt & Marquardt, 2000) theorizes that *sensemaking* exerts the highest control within the organizational learning system, striving to maintain the status quo. On the other hand, *new information* provides the highest source of energy, striving to encourage organizational learning and adaptation to the ever-changing environment. The influence of sensemaking on new information in the interpretation of cues can be likened to a clash of Titans. In this study, sensemaking appears to have dominated the struggle and overwhelmed the input of new information, resulting in little adaptation or change in the patterns of the causes of mishaps.

The result of this supremacy and constancy of sensemaking in the creation of organization memory was the preservation of the existing NASA culture, including organizational roles, expectations, and, most importantly, its organizational identity (Dutton & Dukerich, 1991). An organizational identity establishes legitimacy of an organization's choices and behaviors, reduces ambiguity from environmental cues, and helps members select plausible interpretations of that environment (Choo, 2001). This is consistent with earlier findings that an organization controls its interaction with its environment in order to engender its own maintenance or self-production (Morgan, 1986; Sablo, 1997; Weick, 1979), thereby sustaining a sense of organizational identity.

Plausible Rather than Accurate

Plausible explanation of mishaps provide "a good story" (Weick, 1995, p. 61) that explains the mishap in a way that is credible, coherent, reasonable, and most importantly, socially acceptable. In order to report plausible root causes, the mishap investigation boards must identify causes that fit with the organization's past experience, are believable to themselves and others, and can be supported based upon the organizational memory. However, it is important to remember that plausible does not always mean accurate.

Sensemaking is not about truth and getting it right. Instead, it is about continued redrafting of an emerging story so that it becomes more comprehensive, incorporates more of the observed data, and is more resilient in the face of criticism. People may get better stories, but they'll never get

THE story... and what is plausible for one group, such as managers, often proves implausible for another group, such as employees (Weick, Sutcliffe, & Obstfeld, 2005).

It is important to remember that this study was not a forensic re-investigation of why each mishap happened, but a study of what the official Mishap Boards concluded caused the accidents and how these conclusions have changed over time. The results of the study, showing a lack of change in the causes of mishaps, tend to support the assertions of leadership and therefore culture intransigence. Certainly the strength of the NASA culture and the dominant sensemaking it produces in the leadership cadre was evident during each aspect of this study. This research further informed the initiatives within the Agency to identify and correct underlying organizational leadership and knowledge management issues that may be impeding optimal learning and performance within NASA.

The leadership authenticated by the hierarchical formal organization chart is reflective of a rational system (Scott, 2003) rather than an complex adaptive system (Marion, 1999). The closed rational system, typified by Taylor's (1993) work on scientific management, stresses rules-based normative control, with the rules cascading down the formal hierarchy via the formal leadership. Even the open rational system theory (March & Simon, 1958) is rule-limited as typified by the concept of bounded rationality, positing that reductionist techniques must be applied to limit the information to be considered in order to conduct normal work, much less critical events such as mishap investigations. In both of these models of organizations, leadership is vested solely in the incumbents with positional power, those represented on the hierarchical organization chart (Marion & Uhl-Bien, 2007). When organizational members, particularly those with positional power, regard the organization more as a complex adaptive system, as a network of equal systems, leadership can emerge from anywhere in the system, increasing the adaptive capacity of the entire network (Griffin, 2002). Authenticating the possibility of emergent leadership would require a system-wide adaptation of organizational culture to enact such a deep structure change (Romanelli & Tushman, 1994)orkingStiff in the dominant sensemaking.

It would require the existing strong cybernetic hierarchy to participate in the development of a system-wide congruence of vision and missions. It would require also that those in positional power trust to reciprocate the trust currently expected from other members of the system. Enacting emergent leadership (Hazy, Goldstein, & Lichtenstein, 2007a) as a participative process within a complex system rather than as functions of normative control will require change in both theory and practice that will embrace the "edge of chaos" (Horn, 2005).

Such change calls for a new field of theory; one that includes both the fields of technical systems/project management and organizational leadership. Currently the fields are separated in mainstream academia and in practice. The languages of the two fields are also separate, with the result that theorists and practitioners talk past each other. Talking louder to each other will not produce better results. We must develop common language, theories, and models that are inclusive rather than exclusive. The survival of both fields and the organizations they represent depend on such adaptation in the existing fast-paced global economy. Such emerging fields as Complex Systems Leadership Theory (Hazy, Goldstein, & Lichtenstein, 2007b) demonstrate movement in this direction.

Theoretical contributions of this study include support for the nonlinear view of organizations as complex adaptive systems (Hazy et al., 2007a)—that is, as systems of systems each influenced by the other. Viewing organizational processes such as leadership as emergent rather than normative expands the field of our understanding of both technical management studies, and human and organization studies. The existing disparity and Cartesian distinctions between the professions of project management/systems engineering and organizational cognition/behavior do not honor either. Changes in the sensemaking of both will better able adaptation.

NEW BUSINESS MODEL: 2003-PRESENT

On a more hopeful note, the following case study describes an intentional experiment in organizational leadership and development based upon complexity science. The experiment was undertaken in the remote Mojave high desert California community of the Antelope Valley. It was underwritten by NASA as one method to assure the availability of the workforce needed in the 21st century. NASA realized that current programs and procedures were not going to produce the robust workforce necessary to regain U.S. pre-eminence in the science and technology fields. Too many foreign-born PhDs were returning to their home countries and taking the knowledge with them. Official studies continuously alerted society to the issues this knowledge gap was presenting (Government Accountability Office, 2005; Hart-Rudman Commission, 2001; Voinovich, 2000; Walker, 2002).

With this clarion call for action, the tenets of complexity were embraced to design a new complex adaptive system that would be aligned with the Information Revolution (Toffler, 1980, 1990) rather than the Industrial Revolution . Some of the most basic tenets of complexity—self-organizing networks, co-evolution, emergence, and differences in initial conditions (Anderson, 1999)—were intentionally operationalized in this experiment to determine the viability of such an entity.

The Environment

The High Desert, an hour north of Los Angeles, is the home of Edwards Air Force Base, NASA Dryden Flight Research Center, the Department of Defense Plant 42, Mojave Test area, China Lake, and the fast-growing cities of Palmdale and Lancaster. Also known as Aerospace Valley, the area has the highest concentration of employee aerospace engineers in the nation. Even with this ready demand for talent, the educational resources were severely constrained. The one two-year college is Antelope Valley College. With the exception of a private religious college, there were no 4-year universities at all, much less one that produced engineering graduates.

In 2003 the City of Palmdale, NASA Dryden Flight Research Center, and the California Space Grant formed an alliance to form the Aerospace Education, Research, and Operations (AERO) Institute. The AERO Institute was formed specifically to leverage NASA's 15 years of investment in the Space Grant program, which has resulted in a network of more than 500 universities, colleges and community colleges in the 52 Space Grant Consortia throughout the United States. Congress established the National Space Grant College and Fellowship Program (Space Grant) with Title II of the National Aeronautics and Space Administration Authorization Act of 1988. The City of Palmdale joined the AERO Institute to support the aerospace industry in the development of future workforce.

The Initial Conditions

The official charter of the organization documents the objectives of the new business model.

> A consortium to produce the next generation aerospace technical workforce within the aerospace community. Federal, state and local governments, industry, and academia partner to ensure that research, educational, and operations programs enable and maintain a viable aerospace workforce for the 21st century.
>
> The AERO Institute:
>
> ▪ Provides comprehensive technical, undergraduate and graduate education in aerospace science, engineering, and technical skills through participating colleges and universities by using both local facilities as well as exploiting innovative distance-learning concepts

- Conducts leading edge aerospace research and operations, and develops revolutionary new technologies by creating innovative, collaborative, synergistic partnerships among NASA DFRC, other Federal agencies, academia, local and state governments, and industry
- Incubates, stimulates, and commercializes new intellectual property
- Promotes aerospace science and engineering, provides public outreach, and stimulates public awareness and support in aerospace research and technology development.

The principal objectives of the Institute are to:

1. Leverage the assets of NASA DFRC, other governmental entities, Academia and industry for the public purposes of creating new knowledge and a better-educated workforce
2. Create a strategic partnership to conduct leading edge research, operations, education, and training necessary to maintain US technical pre-eminence.
3. Leverage the intellectual capital of the academic community to fulfill aerospace workforce needs.

Understanding the critical roles that artifacts and language play in establishing an organization's culture (Marion & Uhl-Bien, 2007), a logo and mythos were created to reinforce the importance of the organization as a network as opposed to a hierarchy. This will be critical to affirm the philosophy as the founding members leave the organization.

The AERO Institute is a consortium to produce the next generation aerospace technical workforce within the aerospace community. Federal, state and local governments, industry, and academia partner to ensure that research, educational, and operations programs enable and maintain a viable aerospace workforce for the United States for the 21st century. It was created on a philosophical foundation of collaboration vs. competition and inclusion vs. exclusion.

The design of the logo symbolizes the philosophy and guiding values of the AERO Institute. The trefoil is made of titanium, a metal used in many aerospace fabrications because of the strength of its alloys. It represents the three connected domains of Academia, Government and Industry as equal partners. The trefoil shape is reminiscent also of the outline of a lifting body aerospace vehicle. The outer ring documents the three domains that participate in the Institute. The star field, reminding that the focus of the AERO Institute is space-related depicts the constellation Aquila, the eagle. The eagle represents the United States. The logo itself can be rotated 360° and maintain legibility reflecting the network model vs. a hierarchical model of its organization.

The text displays the proper name of the Institute and spells-out the meaning of the acronym, AERO. It is the Garamond font.

The Emergence

The AERO Institute is currently conducting aerospace education and research projects with NASA centers, universities, and schools throughout the nation. Active programs include Georgia Technical Institute, Virginia Polytechnic Institute and State University, Massachusetts Institute of Technology, Purdue University, California State University–San Bernardino, Emery-Riddle Aeronautical University, Prairie View A&M, University of California–Los Angeles, California Polytechnic University at Pomona, and DeVry University, among others.

The AERO Institute is able to draw on these resources via network the 52 National Space Grant Consortia providing access to community college, college and university level training, re-training, and university level education for NASA and contractor personnel. These colleges and universities also provide a ready source of highly qualified students to integrate into student-mentor and intern positions providing the workforce with new technicians, engineers, scientists, and administrators.

The AERO Institute is also able to quickly and effectively work with the national science community, providing a ready resource of highly skilled science expertise, potential customers, and innovation. A physical presence in California's High Desert provides access to Dryden and Edwards

Air Force Base capabilities including chase aircraft and Plant 42 Aerospace Contractors and the innovative Mojave based commercial space pioneers. The entire Antelope Valley is rich with aerospace technical talent and industrial base, minimizing the need for additional infrastructure investment. A physical presence in Southern California provides easy access to the government-restricted air space at Edwards Air Force Base, China Lake, and the Pacific Test Range. A physical presence in the Southwestern United States provides access to the growing space, remotely operated aircraft, and Earth science industry throughout, benefiting national research and providing technology transfer and joint sponsored research program opportunities. With the recent certification as the nation's first inland space port and Scaled Composites' successful suborbital space flight, Mojave has secured its position at the forefront of the next generation of aerospace technology and development. Mojave is then poised for the transition to Uninhabited Aerial Vehicles.

In addition to the participation by NASA Dryden, the AERO Institute's City of Palmdale partnership provides program and administrative support through the dedication of 20,000 square feet of furnished Class A office facilities, underwriting of facility costs, marketing materials and support, office signage, lab development costs and support, and exterior facility maintenance. In addition, the City of Palmdale provides additional economic development and workforce development support through the South County Workforce Center and agreements with the prime aerospace contractors within the Antelope Valley. The Lockheed Martin Corporation's branch in Palmdale has recently joined the AERO Institute as a partner in the development and operation of a state-of-the-art nanotechnology lLaboratory supporting basic and applied research with university partners.

The AERO Institute is, both in reality and perception, an inclusive partnership organization. Participation is never constrained by exclusive or "not to compete" restrictions on its strategic partners. All who share the greater vision for success in the 21st century are welcome. This philosophy has resulted in a greater access to resources (McKelvey & Lichtenstein, 2007) than would have been possible under a traditional business model.

The Findings

The continued success of the AERO Institute proves that such an organization can be created and can function effectively. Some of the challenges and barriers to the success of such a new business model based upon complexity science follow:

1. The language of complexity (Conner & Napolitano, 2005) perplexes those not familiar with its tenets.

   In an organization that is based upon network and complex systems theory rather than bureaucratic hierarchy, even titles can be a challenge. Without a hierarchy, words such as chief, senior, lead and director have little relevance. Yet titles such as "keeper of the flame" or "systems integrator" still raise eyebrows. However, each occasion brows are raised provides an opportunity to proselytize for complexity science in organizations and business arenas.

2. Existing financial, procurement, and legal systems and vehicles are established upon a very linear hierarchical bureaucratic philosophy.

   System innovations to enable emergent collaborations and encourage partnerships are required to solve the complex problems that continue to inhibit the development of a robust technical workforce and other societal challenges. Such innovations would encourage agreements where both funding and in-kind contributions between and among industry, academia, and government are required. Until there is widespread systemic change, though, forms of legal incorporation or financing will still require a slate of officers to conform to existing templates and limit open collaboration.

3. Systemic changes to pre-service teacher's collegiate curricula are required to ensure that all classroom teachers at all grade levels have a comprehensive understanding of topical science and mathematical concepts and operations.

   Existing curricula do not contain sufficient immersion into these fields to assure competency in the classrooms. This enables math and science-phobic teachers, particularly in the K-6 grades, to pass along these phobias into their students, producing a death spiral for STEM literacy in our education systems. While remedial workshops for in-service teachers may mitigate existing deficiencies, only a system approach can hope to reverse the decline. The inertia exerted by the academic and governmental bureaucracies to maintain the existing control system quickly overwhelms ad hoc efforts at reform.

CONCLUSIONS

By all external measures, NASA's experiment has been successful. A thriving organization exists and is recognized by local, state, and national organizations, communities, and media. Its programmatic results have authenticated that it is possible to establish an organization based upon complexity theory rather than hierarchical control.

What cannot be measured by traditional means is the enormous amount of energy (Allen, Boulton, Strathern, & Baldwin, 2005) that has been imported into the system by the founding participants to achieve this outcome. The gravity exerted by the existing governmental business constructs such as legal, procurement, and financial has tugged at the fabric of the nascent organization. These existing powers were created to maintain the status quo in the industrial revolution model, and therefore, they grate against anything that does not conform to the old model. Each step in this experiment has required extensive efforts to protect the founding tenets of collaboration and inclusion.

NASA's identity is a state-of-the art, cutting-edge research and development entity. The observed reality is that NASA is subject to the same ponderous bureaucracy that shackled the Federal Emergency Management Agency (FEMA) as it tried to respond to 2005's Hurricane Katrina. Until the existing legal regulations and processes concerning finance and procurement change significantly, no federally related organization can be more responsive to its ever-changing environment. As Kuhn (1996) noted, sometimes we have to wait for the old guard to fade away before new ideas can take hold.

REFERENCES

Allen, P. M., Boulton, J., Strathern, M., & Baldwin, J. (2005). The implications of complexity for business process and strategy. In K. A. Richardson (Ed.), *Managing organizational complexity*. Greenwich, CT: Information Age.

Alston, G. (2003, Feb. 9). Shuttle diplomacy: Even now, the future of NASA looks bright. *The Daily News of Los Angeles,* pp. Viewpoint 1, 4.

Anderson, P. (1999). Complexity theory and organization science. *Organization Science, 10*(3), 216–232.

Baskin, K. (2005). Storytelling and the complex epistemology of organizations. In K. A. Richardson (Ed.), *Managing organizational complexity*. Greenwich, CT: Information Age.

Brown, A. D., & Starkey, K. (2000). Organizational identity and learning: A psychodynamic perspective. *Academy of Management Review, 25*(1), 102–120.

BST. (2004). *Assessment and plan for organizational culture change at NASA* (contractor report).

Choo, C. W. (2001). The knowing organization as learning organization. *Education & Training, 43*(4/5), 197–205.

Collins, J. C., & Porras, J. I. (1994). *Built to last: Successful habits of visionary companies* (1st ed.). New York: HarperBusiness.

Conner, P. E., & Napolitano, C. S. (2005). Machines or gardens or both? In K. A. Richardson (Ed.), *Managing organizational complexity*. Greenwich, CT: Information Age.

Daft, R. L., & Weick, K. E. (1984). Toward a model of organizations as interpretation systems. *Academy of Management Review, 9*(2), 284–295.

De Long, D. W., & Fahey, L. (2000). Diagnosing cultural barriers to knowledge management. *Academy of Management Executive, 14*(4), 113–127.

Denison, D. R. (1996). What's the difference between organizational culture and organizational climate? A native's point of view on a decade of paradigm wars. *Academy of Management Review, 21*(3), 1–36.

Department of Energy. (1992). DOE-NE-STD-1004-92: Root cause analysis guidance document. Washington DC.

Dutton, J. E., & Dukerich, J. M. (1991). Keeping an eye on the mirror: Image and identity in organizational adaptation. *Academy of Management Journal, 34*(3), 517–554.

Feldman, S. P. (2000). Micro matters: The aesthetics of power in NASA's Flight Readiness Review. *The Journal of Applied Behavioral Science, 36*(4), 474–490.

Gilpin, D. R. (2005). A complexity-based scrutiny of learning from organizational crisis. In K. A. Richardson (Ed.), *Managing organizational complexity*. Greenwich, CT: Information Age.

Gold, S., & Vartabedian, R. (2003, March 2). Challenges facing shuttle disaster inquiry include culture at NASA. *Los Angeles Times*, p. A32.

Government Accountability Office. (2005). Report to the Chairman, Committee on Rules, House of Representatives, Higher education: Federal science, technology, engineering, and mathematics programs and related trends.

Griffin, D. (2002). *The emergence of leadership: Linking self-organization and ethics*. London: Routledge.

Gummer, B. (1998). Decision making under conditions of risk, ambiguity, and uncertainty: Recent perspectives. *Administration in Social Work, 22*(2), 75–93.

Hart-Rudman Commission. (2001). Road Map for National Security: Imperative for Change, The Phase III Report of the U.S. Commission on National Security/21st Century.

Hazy, J. K., Goldstein, J. A., & Lichtenstein, B. B. (2007a). Complex systems leadership theory: An introduction. In J. K. Hazy & J. A. Goldstein & B. B. Lichtenstein (Eds.), *Complexity systems leadership theory* (Vol. 1, pp. 1–16). Mansfield, MA: ISCE Publishing.

Hazy, J. K., Goldstein, J. A., & Lichtenstein, B. B. (Eds.). (2007b). *Complex systems leadership theory: New perspectives from complexity science on social and organizational effectiveness* (Vol. 1). Mansfield, MA: ISCE Publishing.

Horn, J. K. (2005). Parameters for sustained orderly growth in learning organizations. In K. A. Richardson (Ed.), *Managing organizational complexity*. Greenwich, CT: Information Age.

Kuhn, T. S. (1996). *The structure of scientific revolutions* (3rd ed.). Chicago: The University of Chicago Press. (Original work published 1962)

Kunda, G. (1992). *Engineering culture: Control and commitment in a high-tech corporation*. Philiadelphia: Temple University Press.

Laughlin, H. P. (1979). *The ego and its defenses*. New York: Jason Aronson.

March, J. G., & Simon, H. A. (1958). *Organizations*. New York: John Wiley & Sons.

Marion, R. (1999). *The edge of organization: Chaos and complexity theories of formal social systems*. Thousand Oaks, CA: Sage Publications.

Marion, R., & Uhl-Bien, M. (2007). Paradigmatic influence and leadership: The perspectives of complexity theory and bureaucracy theory. In J. K. Hazy & J. A. Goldstein & B. B. Lichtenstein (Eds.), *Complexity systems leadership theory*. Mansfield, MA: ISCE Publishing.

Martin de Holan, P., & Phillips, N. (in press). Remembrance of things past? The dynamics of organizational forgetting. *Management Science*.

Martin de Holan, P., Phillips, N., & Lawrence, T. B. (2004). Managing organizational forgetting. *MITSloan Management Review, 45*(2), 45–51.

McKelvey, B., & Lichtenstein, B. B. (2007). Leadership in the four stages of emergence. In J. K. Hazy & J. A. Goldstein & B. B. Lichtenstein (Eds.), *Complexity systems leadership theory*. Mansfield, MA: ISCE Publishing.

Morgan, G. (1986). *Images of organizations*. Beverly Hills, CA: Sage.

Moorhead, G., Ference, R. J., & Neck, C. P. (1991). Group decision fiascoes continue: Space shuttle Challenger and a revised groupthink framework [Abstract]. *Human Relations, 44*(6), 539–551.

National Aeronautics and Space Administration. (2003a). Columbia Accident Investigation Board Report (p. 248). Washington DC.

National Aeronautics and Space Administration. (2003b). Strategic Plan(Vol. NP-2003-01-298-HQ).

National Aeronautics and Space Administration. (2004a, February 11). *NPG 8621.1A: NASA procedures and guidelines for mishap reporting, investigating, and recordkeeping*. Available: http://nodis3.gsfc.nasa.gov/displayAll.cfm?Internal_ID=N_PR_8621_001A_&page_name=ALL [2004, August 31].

National Aeronautics and Space Administration. (2004b). NPG 8621.1A: NASA procedures and guidelines for mishap reporting, investigating, and recordkeeping. Washington DC.

Parsons, T. (1951). *The social system*. New York: The Free Press.

Rasmussen, J. (1990). Human error and the problem of causality in analysis of accidents. In D. E. Broadbent & A. Baddeley & J. T. Reason (Eds.), *Human factors in hazardous situations* (pp. 449–460). Oxford: Clarendon Press.

Richardson, K. A., Tait, A., Roos, J., & Lissack, M. R. (2005). The coherent management of complex projects and the potential roles of group decision support systems. In K. A. Richardson (Ed.), *Managing organizational complexity*. Greenwich, CT: Information Age.

Romanelli, E., & Tushman, M. L. (1994). Organizational transformation as punctuated equilibrium: An empirical test. *Academy of Management Journal, 37*(5), 1141–1166.

Sablo, T. A. (1997). Autopiesis and organizational culture: A case study [Abstract]. *Dissertation Abstracts International, 58*(05), 1800A. (University Microfilms No. AAT97-31501)

de Saussure, F. (1990). *Course in general linguistics* (R. Harris, Trans.). Chicago: Open Court.

Schein, E. H. (1996). Three cultures of management: The key to organizational learning. *Sloan Management Review, 38*(1), 9–20.

Schwandt, D. R., & Marquardt, M. J. (2000). *Organizational learning: From world-class theories to global best practices*. Boca Raton, FL: St. Lucie Press.

Schwandt, D. R., & Szabla, D. B. (2007). Systems and leadership: Coevolution or mutual evolution towards complexity? In J. K. Hazy & J. A. Goldstein & B. B. Lichtenstein (Eds.), *Complexity leadership systems theory.* Mansfield, MA: ISCE Publishing.

Schwartz, H. S. (1987). On the psychodynamics of organizational disaster: The case of the Space Shuttle Challenger. *Columbia Journal of World Business, 22,* 59–67.

Scott, W. R. (2003). *Organizations: Rational, natural, and open systems* (5th ed.). Upper Saddle River, NJ: Prentice-Hall. (Original work published 1981)

Snook, S. A. (2000). *Friendly fire: The accidental shootdown of U.S. Black Hawks over northern Iraq.* Princeton, NJ: Princeton University Press.

Starbuck, W. H., & Milliken, F. J. (1988). Challenger: Fine-tuning the odds until something breaks [Abstract]. *The Journal of Management Studies, 25*(4), 319–341.

Taylor, F. W. (1993). *The principles of scientific management; and shop management.* London: Routledge/Thoemmes Press.

Toffler, A. (1980). *The third wave* (1st ed.). New York: Morrow.

Toffler, A. (1990). *Powershift* [sound recording]. New York: Bantam Audio.

Urian, R. K. (2000). Sensemaking and knowledge creation: How organizations learn through industrial accident team investigations. *Dissertation Abstracts International, 61*(05), 2479B. (University Microfilms No. AAT99-73089)

Vaughan, D. (1996). *The Challenger launch decision: Risky technology, culture, and deviance at NASA.* Chicago: The University of Chicago Press.

Voinovich, G. V. (2000). Report to the President: The Crisis in Human Capital -: Subcommittee on Oversight of Government Management, Restructuring, and the District of Columbia Committee on Governmental Affairs.

Walker, R. S. (2002). Final Report of the Commission on the Future of the United States Aerospace Industry.

Weick, K. E. (1979). *The social psychology of organizing.* New York: McGraw-Hill, Inc.

Weick, K. E. (1995). *Sensemaking in organizations* (Vol. 231). Thousand Oaks, CA: Sage Publications.

Weick, K. E., Sutcliffe, K. M., & Obstfeld, D. (2005). Organizing and the process of sensemaking. *Organizational Science, 16*(4), 409–421.

SECTION 3

TOOLS FOR CREATING, MAINTAINING, AND USING KNOWLEDGE

CHAPTER 12

METAPHORS FROM NATURE FOR KNOWLEDGE WORK IN A COMPLEX WORLD

Alice MacGillivray

This chapter explores the potential for metaphors from the natural world to supplant the Industrial Age suite of metaphors, *when there is a need to focus on learning in, and for, complex, knowledge-rich environments.*

A SPONTANEOUS CONVERGENCE

A strange thing happened in the 1990s. Several individuals, myself included, were working with the human and social aspects of knowledge management when we somehow encountered literature about complexity thinking. This literature was an attractor—exposing practitioners to new information and diversity of thought—linking one community with another in a compelling and ultimately satisfying way. It was valuable to converse with like-minded strangers who had arrived at that juncture before me, and who joined us later.

I should step back and describe what I mean by knowledge management. I say describe, rather than define, because I believe its nature and

Complexity and Knowledge Management, pages 201–216
Copyright © 2010 by Information Age Publishing

purpose depend on context. This is one of the reasons one can find so many definitions and debates about the essence of the field. Knowledge management involves the creation of new knowledge and the sharing of existing knowledge across boundaries. I agree with Tom Davenport, Larry Prusak, Verna Allee, and many others that *knowledge is richer, more human, and more social than information or data.* Aspects of data management, information management and the Information Era are rooted in Industrial Era thinking. Working with knowledge is complex. At a high level, I like Dave Snowden's descriptor of knowledge management as "establishing common context" (personal communication) because it gives a sense of a space with potential, yet does not prescribe steps, components, or techniques. At a more detailed level, the practitioner makes critical choices about appropriate frameworks, practices, and tools to address needs and issues such as impending retirements, communication barriers, unnecessary redundancies, or the need for innovation. These choices happen at many levels, from strategic through operational. For example, Mallach and Agger-Gupta developed a strategic framework with four modes, each of which has different approaches to information networks, communication strategies, and organizational requirements and which vary in complexity. They point out that "transitions between modes require shifts in organizational culture, strategy, and operations as well as technologies. Inaccurate assessment of the organizational impact of these shifts, often resulting from applying strategies that were successful in earlier intermodal transitions, results in unexpected costs and failures" (Mallach & Agger-Gupta, 1998, p. 249). The term knowledge management is problematic. Based on trends from internet searches, it is increasingly described as an oxymoron because it is impossible to *manage* something as personal, social, and contextual as knowledge. Though the *term* may not survive, the *work* will become more urgent as we deal with complex, global problems viewed by stakeholders through varied cultural and epistemological lenses.

If the nature of our work is changing, we need to review, reflect on, and adapt the ways in which we facilitate learning. Knowledge management and complexity literatures have not yet put much emphasis on the reform of workplace training and learning. Learning in knowledge-rich, complex environments happens in more emergent and informal ways than in most funded training and education programs. As a Canadian study of new approaches to lifelong learning indicates:

> Adults in Canada now spend an average of 15 hours per week on informal learning. In light of this finding, if the crews of our big education and training ships do not increasingly look out for the massive, detectable icebergs of informal learning, many of their programs may sink into Titanic irrelevancy. (Livingstone, 2000)

Managers spend considerable time, effort and funds on standardized training programs for employees. Although trainers admit that the transfer of knowledge to actual work is difficult in complex environments, few organizations make time to explore complexity-oriented learning strategies, practices, or technologies. I use *technology* broadly, to describe the practical application of knowledge, as Karl Wiig has done in his exploration of knowledge management as a technology, discipline, philosophy, and movement (Wiig, 2002).

When we train people for relatively routine old-economy work, behavioral psychology and machine metaphors are useful. They can help us to optimize safety, quality, and efficiency. In this realm, we can polish, codify, and upgrade training in predictable ways. It makes sense to store knowledge (I actually prefer the term *information* here because the act of storage separates content from most of the human and contextual aspects of knowledge) in repositories, manuals, and standard operating procedures. It makes sense for definitive experts to upgrade training materials for complicated tasks such as medical equipment repair, ATM programming, and cardiopulmonary resuscitation. Curriculum designers generally assume that the knowledge and skills will be needed at some time in the future.

Different paradigms, metaphors, and learning environments deserve exploration for new-economy work, where knowledge is more of a flow than a thing. Learning often takes place just-in-time, and may be intimately intertwined with the work as it unfolds in distinctive contexts. Boundaries between being and becoming, generating and sharing knowledge, and learning and doing are blurred. The public sector includes many examples of this new economy work. For example, Mintzberg describes park managers as "sitting between all this [stakeholder groups with very different, deeply-held values] ... monitored closely by the press looking for good stories, the politicians wishing to accommodate their supporters...and the public servants in the national capital intent on avoiding scandal" (1997, p. 135). Exploration of new organizational and related learning paradigms is also important for the socioeconomic health of Western firms, as they outsource routine tasks. Metaphors are an important part of this exploration, because they can have a powerful influence—positive or negative (Czarniawska, 2004)—on creativity, the development and use of language, symbolic understanding, formation of theories, and research approaches (Morgan, 1980), which cascade into all aspects of organizations: even processes as seemingly objective as accounting (Poletti, 2004). They may help people organize conceptual knowledge and new information—and there is evidence from psychological studies that use of similar metaphor-based schemas may aid in recognition responses and help readers to connect and retain concepts (Allbritton, McKoon, & Gerrig,1995). In her unpublished conference paper entitled Chaos Theory, Metaphor Processing and Complexity, Rita Weinberg (2005) writes: "From chaos theory perspective, meta-phors reflect two parallel systems, each stable in their own right. Mapping across destabilizes each system, leading to entropy and an emergent self organizing system. This re-organization produces new insight consciously or unconsciously. Metaphoric meaning produces different perceptions, re-framing or a solution to a problem." Metaphors can be particularly valuable in this early phase of applying complexity thinking to organizations because a metaphor that resonates with the reader increases his or her interest, and "when metaphorical content attracts and interests the listener, it motivates the listener to engage in effortful and systematic processing of literal mes-sage arguments" (Ottati, Rhoads, & Graesser, 1999, p. 695).

CONTEXT: A CRITICAL CONSIDERATION

In designing a learning intervention, it is important to think about context: Is the work environment old or new economy; predictable or unpredict-able; complicated or complex? Metaphor clearly has a role in unpredict-able, complex environments. On paper, it sounds easy to categorize work as old or new economy. In the old economy, products and basic services are valued; in the new economy, the focus is on people, knowledge, relation-ships, and interaction (Lissack, personal communication). Old economy work is more routine and predictable than new economy work. In practice, there are grey zones. For example, consider Peter Drucker's saying that management is about doing things right and leadership about doing the right things. Learning to *do the right things* does not lend itself to standard operating procedures with training evaluations showing that participants can lead 19 times out of 20 with no errors. And yet promotional materials for leadership development imply there is a great deal of certainty about the competencies and techniques required, many of which can be devel-oped through pre-designed training packages. The question isn't as simple as *is leadership old or new economy work?* A more helpful question is *what is the nature of this work for which leadership is needed, and how can we develop appropri-ate styles of leadership?* The use of resources and techniques suited to the old economy may be wasted on the new economy, or vice versa. Tom Stewart writes: "People who make decisions for a living are coming to realize that in complex or chaotic situations—a battlefield, a trading floor, or today's brutally competitive business environment—intuition usually beats rational analysis" (Stewart & Einhart, 2002). Another valuable question is: "where are the intersections of old and new economy work in our organization?" as those are places where leaders may be able to enable learning (Lissack, 2002, p. 8).

PERSPECTIVES FROM INSIDE COMPLEX SYSTEMS

Even if we take one metaphor from nature: the metaphor of boundaries/ edges/ecotones, which are zones of species richness where ecosystems connect, we see that researchers from many fields, including anthropology, community psychology, health care, architecture, and education are beginning to adopt the metaphor in their thinking (MacGillivray, 2006). For example, Nancy Turner and her colleagues were familiar with ecotones in nature before they set out to explore cultural boundaries. They have proposed that "indigenous peoples whose living territories traverse ecological edges have a correspondingly increased access to economically important resources and therefore have a greater capacity for flexibility" (Turner, Davidson-Hunt, & O'Flaherty, 2003, p. 440).

I led an action research project to help a large park organization set priorities during a phase of rapid expansion. In that initiative, we found that an organic, opportunistic approach based on a risk management framework helped managers work with contexts from beyond their normal roles and boundaries was well-received and had good results. To set defensible priorities, they were essentially working with ecological principles. In other words, the management process and their work contexts were metaphors for each other. Greenhalgh and colleagues noted that "organisations that promote and support the development and execution of boundary-spanning roles are more likely to become aware of, and assimilate, innovations quickly" (Greenhalgh et al., 2004, p. 19). However, much of this research looks in on systems from the outside. How do people working *in* complex, knowledge-rich environments understand their work in relation to metaphors from nature? The following are two examples from Canada and the United States, which show how individuals make sense of learning in complex environments.

A Federal Network of Counterterrorism Communities

I recently explored the experience of working in a complex knowledge-rich environment with thirteen public servants in a Canadian "network of communities, working to prevent and mitigate terrorism impacts" (government-produced CD). This network is overseen by the Chemical, Biological, Radiological, and Nuclear (CBRN) Research and Technology Initiative (CRTI). These voluntary communities, which are sometimes referred to as *communities of practice*, focus on knowledge sharing and innovation, and are quite different than traditional government departments. Members usually refer to their groups as *clusters*, rather than communities, so I will use the term cluster in the remainder of this description. Cluster members work in various organizations in a range of responsible positions and participate in the cluster voluntarily. Almost all consider themselves scientists; many are nationally and internationally respected authorities in their fields. Some work on the front line; others focus on behind-the-scenes work.

Metaphors from nature can help people reflect on whether work is complex or not, whether it is important to think about it as complex, and/or whether to behave as if it were complex. In one question, I presented participants with a graphic (see Figure 12.1) and asked two questions: How would they characterize the work of their cluster now? and Where would they like to see it in the future? They represented these perspectives with two marks within the Figure 12.1 triangle. For the purposes of this chapter I am ignoring the *y* axis, which focuses on how well they thought they were functioning.

Many of my knowledge management colleagues have worked with these metaphors for years, but they seemed new to the persons I interviewed, which was refreshing. Often, they began by asking what I meant by a *healthy ecosystem*, and—less frequently—what I meant by a *well-oiled machine*. I would respond by encouraging them to tell me what the concepts meant to them in relation to their work. This was awkward for individuals without ecology backgrounds, but they made sense of the question in ways that helped them talk about their cluster work. In relation to the ecosystem metaphor, Penny (all names are pseudonyms) began by saying "I'm assuming that this has to do with—well—sort of balance. You have a group of experts in varying fields, all focused on one issue, and you give and take."

Many of the descriptions of *healthy ecosystem* were coherent with complexity thinking.

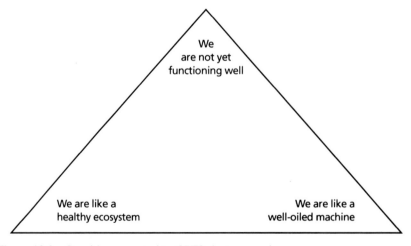

Figure 12.1 Graphic presented to CRTI cluster members.

I guess if you're saying healthy ecosystem you're talking about synergy between—*true* synergy between—the clusters. An ecosystem reacts to changes in
circumstances in environment, and if the environment changes—as threats
emerge or they back off—you really want to be towards [the ecosystem end].
But CRTI has evolved; they've listened to first responders and they evolved.
It's enhancing first responders' capabilities to respond more and more. And
maybe your healthy ecosystem analogy is more in truth than the well-oiled
machine, which is designed for a certain thing, and then just runs and runs.
It doesn't react to pressures as well as an ecosystem does. (Barry)

There are all sorts of levels of ecosystem, all of which are necessary to sustain
it. And we have that in the cluster: individuals who are quite keen on working
with food; chemicals and food; individuals with chemicals in air and water;
individuals who are very keen on chemical warfare agents anywhere; and so
on , and so forth...and this all fits together. (Gord)

A well-oiled machine is like . . . you throw in something and Bup! Well, you get
a piece at the end of the chain. This is more like an organic system, where
there are always pros and cons, and things don't always show up as expected,
but it bounces back. (David)

David also spoke about coherence between the nature of his cluster's
work and the nature of an ecosystem. For him, the ecosystem was not just
a metaphor for communication; it was guidance for practice. He emphasized that his cluster's focus is strategic, that they are not focused on developing "widgets," and therefore they should aspire to become like a healthy
ecosystem.

It was interesting to note where participants positioned their clusters
now, and in a more idealized future. Of thirteen people who responded to
this question, one (omitted from the data below) would not make marks
on the page, but described how the group was not yet functioning well, and
how there would be benefits in having some work machine-like and some
ecosystem-like. Although some of the other 12 participants spoke to different contexts, they generalized their responses and made a single mark for
present and another one for future. The average locations for these on the
x-axis are shown in Figure 12.2.

Five participants thought their community should become slightly or considerably more ecosystem-like, and three thought theirs should be slightly
more machine-like. Where others were happy with the current state, that
state was *never* to the right of the mid point in the Figure 12.2 graphic.

Metaphors shape or enable the way readers or listeners make sense situations, learn from others, and communicate the distinctive nature of the
cluster work. Consider a term used by Barry, one of the CRTI research
participants. The content he described was from hard science and first-
responder work. Yet when he spoke about successes in this complex, interorganizational, interdisciplinary and international environment, he used

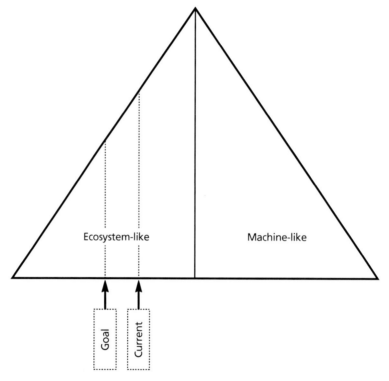

Figure 12.2 Perceived current and ideal nature of the clusters ($n = 12$).

the verb *blossom*. Barry was excited by new links being made between scientists and users of their knowledge, and talked about how effectiveness was compromised when those groups had operated more autonomously. He said, "*That* is what has blossomed in [our] cluster." I was surprised to hear this metaphor from the man who sat across from me, and was intrigued by the layers of meaning it revealed. A blossom or flower is a plant's announcement to pollinators that there is something of value worth visiting. Pollinators receive benefits: nectar and pollen. The process of pollination can increase the yield of the individual plant and can result in cross-pollination with unpredictable and sometimes valuable results. The metaphor involves motion, sharing, uncertainty, and potential, and it reflected the kinds of local to international networking, learning, and synergies that Barry described. Mechanical metaphors cannot capture the connections, innovations, and progress happening within and across these clusters nearly as well as his metaphor of blossoms.

Martin and Stan used metaphors to explain the challenges of training front-line responders to unlearn aspects of the machine-like standard-operating-procedure thinking they had developed for more routine work such as catching a thief. They both acknowledged they were in unfamiliar territory as they embark on the cultural change of encouraging front-line workers' learning to facilitate diverse counter-terrorism experts, as well as command, control, and enforce laws.

Royal Roads University and CPsquare (www.cpsquare.org)

John D. Smith and I (MacGillivray & Smith, 2004) studied the design of an international, emergent e-learning opportunity, which was an unusual collaboration between a university and a not-for-profit organization with deep expertise in course content. In this Royal Roads University graduate course about communities of practice (CoP), participants could take a seven-week virtual field trip to the international CPsquare Foundations Workshop, in which many elements of community of practice work are embedded. Elements of the course are described in a recent paper (MacGillivray, 2008).

At the time, I was the graduate course designer, instructor, and program director; John was a core member of CPsquare and a workshop facilitator. We found that the kind of learning we were enabling had not yet entered the mainstream, with some notable exceptions at institutions including Fielding Institute, Cambridge University, Pepperdine University, and University of California at Berkeley. Riel and Polin contrasted traditional education and communities of practice as follows: "Traditional classrooms, weighted down by the burden of a prescribed curriculum...and with compulsory attendance, lack the defining characteristics of a community. Collaborative learning might be employed for a specific lesson, as an instructional strategy. However, for most of the time, the traditional classroom is a thinly contextualized, unfocused collection of tasks that does not support a community of learners" (Riel & Polin, 2004, p. 22). In "Coping with Complexity: Educating for Capability," Fraser and Greenhalgh (2001) note that educational efforts focus on competence (such as measurable changes in knowledge) rather than on building capability through use of non-linear methods. They describe capability as the "extent to which individuals can adapt to change, generate new knowledge, and continue to improve their performance" (2001, p. 799), a definition that goes beyond common descriptors of competence. Perhaps universities suffer from what Richard Bernstein (1983, pp. 16–25) described as "the Cartesian anxiety"—the paralyzing fear that if we do not have absolute certainty, we have no knowledge at all. As a solution, Seely Brown and Duguid (2000, p. 8) suggest: "the way forward is paradoxically to look not ahead, but to look around."

Course participants were all professionals well into their careers. They found the collaboratively designed and facilitated course to be distinctive and valuable. Through course surveys, we observed participants' initial discomfort with the openness and flexibility of the design, but they adjusted. Course ratings were consistently excellent. "It is the best learning experience that I have had in my academic life (two undergraduate, one graduate, one certificate degree)," wrote one participant. "Bravo Alice and the team who put this together. It has been so stimulating that I know I will continue learning in this area far after the course is completed." Every course participant stated that the CoP-like experience of the workshop was a valuable complement to the theoretical aspects of course.

We often spoke about the deliberately "under-designed" nature of the learning experience, which left room for emergence, and the development of capabilities needed in rapidly changing environments. We were able to do this because assessment was based on high-level learning outcomes, such as self-knowledge, critical thinking, and helping others to learn, rather than on retention of facts. Because the learning environment was more ecosystem-like than machine-like, we found genetic and ecological metaphors were useful. In an Association for the Advancement of Computing in Education (AACE) conference paper, we used three metaphors from nature: hybrid vigor, mutualism and the selfish gene as frames for our sensemaking. I have adapted the hybrid vigor section of that paper below.

Hybrid Vigor—Beware of the Drive for Efficiency

Hybrid vigor refers to the improved strength, health, or yield that sometimes occurs with crossbred plants and animals. Rutgers geneticists have discovered what may be the science behind hybrid vigor through analyses of maize genomes. "If you have two members of a gene family but expressing themselves in two different tissues," explains Hugo Dooner, "then a crossbred plant could contain both of the genes and may therefore be better off" (Blumberg, 2002, p. 1).This may be particularly true under stressful environmental conditions. So, the benefits of crossbreeding come from diversity and redundancy (a negative concept in business), especially in conditions of stress.

In nature, hybridization happens at the edges of ecosystems, and innovation often occurs at the edges of organizations. John Seely Brown (2004) comments that "most of the really interesting stuff within an organisation is happening on the edge . . . If you're on the edge of an organisation you are constantly trying to make sense of what's going on. It struck me that sense making and knowledge sharing were two sides of the same coin."

By blurring boundaries between a university course and a workshop offered by John Smith, Etienne Wenger and Bronwyn Stuckey of CPsquare, we brought different strengths to this relationship and to the course design.

Some participants discovered opportunities to collaborate across boundaries (levels of government, national boundaries or organizational divisions) in their project work. One graduate student wrote: "I am now definitely aware of the difference between learning about a CoP and learning in a CoP....I always think of academics as learning about something, and in some ways that is a lot easier than learning in something—for me it requires more self-confidence to do the latter." This participant has experienced the hybrid vigor of "learning about" and "learning in"—a powerful combination.

As designers, we talked about elements of the metaphor including redundancy, diversity, and vigor. As we integrated the course with a self-contained online workshop, we encountered redundancies and left several intact. For example, the informal self-assessment that forms naturally around a workshop project or a community-wide inquiry was left to coexist with the self-, peer- and instructor-assessments that were essential components of the university education. We also found that the power of our joint networks to identify and recruit guest speakers was greater than what either CPsquare or Royal Roads University could command separately.

Hybrid vigor became a valuable metaphor for exploring the organizational collaborations that online learning enables. Just as the genetic diversity of two blended populations can increase the vigor of a species, we propose that diversity and synergies resulting from organizational collaborations such as ours can enrich learning environments and increase the adaptability of our educational offerings. Individuals wanting to develop formal or informal learning opportunities should consider whether a potential partnership could improve strength, quality or yield through diversity of content, contexts and connections, and a healthy degree of redundancy.

In the Royal Roads course/workshop combination, participants were interested in using metaphors to make sense of their learning, though they sometimes struggled with the elements of the metaphor on which to focus. No one took them so literally as to be prescriptive; their comments fit with Michael Lissack's suggestion that "complexity science provides models for thinking from which conclusions for management can be made" (Lissack & Rivkin, 2002, p. 272).

CATALYZING CHANGE

If organizations focusing on knowledge generation, sharing, and use want to break out of old training paradigms, there needs to be a powerful catalyst for change. Mark Michaels draws on his own work and that of Jeff Goldstein in describing a new complexity-oriented model of change. Goldstein says that people don't resist change per se; they are held to an "attractor" or "constellation of habits" and that a new attractor is needed for change. Michaels (2000) suggests that a three-phase process may be needed: this single-point attractor and associated stability as a starting point; increased diversity, information, and complexification pushing the group towards the edge of chaos; and the emergence of improvements through positive or reinforcing feedback happening in various parts of that diversified environment. This is very unlike the visioning—alignment building—outlier-alienation model with which we are all familiar. It is more like the process of natural selection in nature, where variations become advantageous in an evolving environment.

Can metaphors help to catalyze change? Jim Suchan researched correlations between metaphors used by professional communicators to describe their work, their stylistic choices, and impacts of their styles. He concluded that "communications researchers have not understood the complex web of organizational factors that influence writers' perceptions...and rhetorical choices" (Suchan, 1995, p. 26), and that root metaphors are significant influences, deserving of more attention. If one were to unearth and pull apart an organization's root metaphors, it would likely increase diversity, information, and complexification, and push people in the direction of chaos. Sometimes root metaphors are explicit and well-understood: "Walt Disney Enterprises is very self-conscious of its 'other worldly, happiest place on earth' metaphor" (Suchan, 1995, p. 13), and it permeates all aspects of learning and operations. Often employees have an intuitive grasp of root metaphors, but the implications of these metaphors are not apparent until they are unearthed to the point where people can reflect on their associated values and taboos. Diversity could emerge from this reflection and provide conditions for rapid change.

ARE METAPHORS ENOUGH?

One of the debates in complexity science is around whether the *science* itself can be used in the study of humans and knowledge management, or whether it is metaphorical. There are tensions amongst the natural science brand of rigor, the implicit inaccuracies of metaphor, and practitioners' desires to communicate provocatively. For example, Lichtenstein wrote that business authors sometimes misrepresent science. He illustrated this with Margaret Wheatley's comparisons of Schrodinger's experimental system box with boxes in organizational charts, concluding that "the link between science and reality has all but vanished" (Fitzgerald, Lichtenstein, & Black, 1999, p.85). Tom Petzinger (2002) adds other perspectives when he tells a story of theorist Ralph Stacey's response to this issue:

> I am sick and tired of hearing people asking, Is it just a metaphor? My inclination is to counter by saying, Is it just more science? Metaphor precedes sci-

ence. Complexity is a metaphor; it is a science. It is both at once, and depending on what the application is, one may be preceding or following the other. (Petzinger, 2002, p. 245)

Richardson (2001) has described perspectives in this debate as falling into three overlapping categories. *Neo-reductionism* advocates of this school believe the science can be applied, or will be of value in the future when it better incorporates the nuances of human free will, and use tools such as bottom-up agent-based modelling in their search for principles. Richardson describes this school as "strongly allied to the quest for a theory of everything (TOE) in physics, i.e., an acontextual explanation for the existence of everything. This community seeks to uncover the general principles of complex systems, likened to the fundamental field equations of physics" (Richardson, 2001, p. 182). At the other extreme is a perspective Richardson calls *soft complexity*. Metaphor plays a strong role in this school, for reasons ranging from a lack of understanding of the hard science, to an understanding coupled with the belief that the science cannot be transferred from one discipline or field (such as biology) to another (such as human and organizational development). Proponents use complexity as a lens for new ways of understanding and working. He finds both extremes simplistic and not particularly valuable. He describes a third category, based on thoughtful choices of tools and perspectives (drawn from complexity and other fields) and horizontal and vertical pluralism, in which one examines a diverse array of worldviews (Richardson, 2006). To build on the value of metaphor, collaborative work amongst complexity science and organizational science researchers can explore critical, practical approaches to *complexity thinking.*

CONCLUSIONS

This chapter explores the potential for metaphors from nature—including edges, ecotones, ecosystems, pollination, and hybrid vigor—to help organizations work and learn effectively in complex, knowledge-rich environments.

Workplace training is often designed with an emphasis on fact, logic, and the assumption of predictable work environments. In describing similar patterns in economics, Best and Humphries explore fact, logic, metaphor, and story, forming a rhetorical tetrad of approaches to argument. They claim that many economists "deny the power of metaphor and story to make sense of the complexities of economic reality" (Best & Humphries, 2003, p. 52). Richardson writes that "As all explanations must be by their very nature metaphorical, then we must treat them as such rather than implicitly assuming that our explanations are homological with the object they claim to describe... Though Truth might not ever be obtained in an absolute sense, our words, concepts and theories can point towards the Truth without ever fully expressing it" (2001, p. 236).

Metaphors stimulate interest, insights, and action and help us to understand context. Metaphors from nature can bring us back to our roots, where a recognition of interrelationships can help us to create a more humane and sustainable environment. Moreover, the interconnections implicit in metaphors from the natural world facilitate thinking about sustainability in a strategic light, with economic, social, and ecological elements. Metaphors from nature can help us to understand knowledge as a flow, and the value of trust and respect needed to build a web of interconnected entities. For situations in which there are many interactions, feedback loops, unpredictable events and emergence, this paints a very different picture of a learning landscape. In this new landscape, knowledge and expertise flow among members of a network as needed, rather than being dispensed by experts—acontextually—just in case a need arises.

I have brought diverse voices from several disciplines to this ecosystem-like narrative, and their differences highlight the fact that use of metaphors from nature is not without challenge. In our societies and organizations, we have little tolerance of ambiguity and paradox. In our urbanized world, we are losing contact with our natural environments. And we must acknowledge that too much emphasis on metaphor sells complexity thinking short. In order to lead the changes needed to make workplace learning more effective, we need to model what we promote, and constantly learn from each other across the boundaries of unexpectedly related disciplines: organizational development, learning theory, ecology, and complexity science. Then, perhaps, we can enable effective learning, using fact, logic, story, and metaphor.

ACKNOWLEDGEMENTS

I would like to thank the federal government of Canada, specifically the Chemical, Biological, Radiological, and Nuclear (CBRN) Research and Technology Initiative (CRTI), as well as Fielding Graduate University, for supporting aspects of this research.

REFERENCES

Allbritton, D. W., McKoon, G., & Gerrig, R. J. (1995). Metaphor-based schemas and text representations: Making connections through conceptual metaphors. *Journal of Experimental Psychology: Learning, Memory and Cognition, 21*, 612–625.

Bernstein, R. J. (1983). *Beyond objectivism and relativism: Science, hermeneutics and praxis*. Philadelphia: University of Pennsylvania Press.

Best, M. H. & Humphries, J. (2003). Edith Penrose: A feminist economist? *Feminist Economics, 9*, 47–73.

Blumberg, J. (2002, June 11). Rutgers geneticists discover probable causes of hybrid plant vigor. *Eurekalert*. Retrieved September 21, 2009 from http://www.eurekalert.org/pub_releases/2002-06/rtsu-rgd061102.php

Czarniawska, B. (2004). Metaphors as enemies of organizing, or the advantages of a flat discourse. *International Journal of the Sociology of Language*, 45–65.

Fitzgerald, D., Lichtenstein, B. M. B., & Black, J. A. (1999). Leadership and the new science: A simpler way (book review). *Emergence, 1*, 78–89.

Fraser, S. W. & Greenhalgh, T. (2001). Coping with complexity: Educating for capability. *British Medical Journal, 323*, 799–803.

Greenhalgh, T., Robert, G., Bate, P., Kyriakidou, O., Macfarlane, F., & Peacock, R. (2004). *How to spread good ideas: A systematic review of the literature on diffusion, dissemination and sustainability of innovations in health service delivery and organisation*. London: National Co-ordinating Centre for NHS Service Delivery and Organisation R & D (NCCSDO).

Lissack, M. (2002). Complexity, management, coherence, and understanding. In M. Lissack & J. Rivkin (Eds.), *The interaction of complexity and management* (pp. 4–12). Westport, CT: Quorum Books.

Lissack, M. & Rivkin, J. (2002). *The interaction of complexity and management*. Westport, CT: Quorum Books.

Livingstone, D. W. (2000). Exploring the icebergs of adult learning: Findings of the first Canadian survey of informal learning practices. *NALL Working Papers: Ontario Institute for Studies in Education*.

MacGillivray, A. (2006). Learning at the edge, Part 1: Transdisciplinary conceptions of boundaries. *Emergence: Complexity & Organization, 8*(3), 92–104.

MacGillivray, A. (2008). Learning at the Edge (Part 2): Scholar-practitioner Reflections on Boundaries. *Emergence: Complexity & Organization, 10*(2), 129–132.

MacGillivray, A. & Smith, J. D. (2004). Genetic diversity as inspiration for instructional design. *AACE E-Learn* Washington DC.

Mallach, E., & D. (Agger-Gupta) Eastman (1998). Four modes of organizational network usage: An information management framework for organizational assessment and choice management. Proceedings of the International IRMA (Information Resources Management Association) Conference in Boston, MA, May 1998, pp. 249–256.

Michaels, M. (2002). A practitioner's perspective. In M. Lissack and J. Rivkin (Eds.), *The interaction of complexity and management* (pp. 173–181). Westport, CT: Quorum.

Mintzberg, H. (1997). Managing on the edges. *International Journal of Public Sector Management, 10*, 131–153.

Morgan, G. (1980, December). Paradigms, metaphors, and puzzle solving in organization theory. *Administrative Science Quarterly, 25*, 605–622.

Ottati, V., Rhoads, S. & Graesser, A. C. (1999). The effect of metaphor on processing style in a persuasion task: A motivational resonance model. *Journal of Personality and Social Psychology, 77*, 688–697.

Petzinger, J. (2002). Reality and complexity. In M. Lissack & J. Rivkin (Eds.), *The Interaction of Complexity and Management* (pp. 241–246). Westport: Quorum.

Poletti, E. J. (2004, February). The gold in the heads of scientists: Metaphor and public sector reform. *Financial Accountability and Management, 20,* 19–38.

Richardson, K. A. (2006). Complexity systems thinking and its implications for policy analysis. In G. Morcol (Ed.), *The handbook of decision making* (pp. 189–221). Boca Raton FL: CRC Press.

Richardson, K. A. and Cilliers, P. (2001). What is complexity science? A view from different directions. *Emergence, 3,* 5–22.

Riel, M. & Polin, L. (2004). Models of community learning and online learning in communities. In S. A. Barab, S. A. Kling, & J. H. Gray (Eds.), *Designing for virtual communities of learning* (pp. 16–50). Cambridge: Cambridge University Press.

Seely Brown, J. (2004). "Keynote interview: John Seeley Brown, Xerox."

Seely Brown, J. & Duguid, P. (2000). *The social life of information.* Boston: Harvard Business School Press.

Stewart, T. A. & Einhart, N. (2002). How to think with your gut in a fluid, competitive environment, the best decisions come from intuition. A fascinating body of research is beginning to explain why. *Business 2.0.* Available at: http://money.cnn.com/magazines/business2/business2_archive/2002/11/01/331634/index.htm.

Suchan, J. (1995). The influence of organizational metaphors on writers' communication roles and stylistic choices. *The Journal of Business Communication, 32,* 7–29.

Turner, N. J., Davidson-Hunt, I. J. & O'Flaherty, M. (2003, September). Living on the edge: Ecological and cultural edges as sources of diversity for social–ecological resilience. *Human Ecology, 31,* 439–461.

Weinberg, R. (2005). *Chaos theory, metaphor processing and complexity.* Paper presented at the 2005 Society for Chaos Theory in Psychology & Life Sciences Conference, Denver Colorado.

Wiig, K. (2002). "Knowledge management has many facets," Knowledge Research Institute. Available at: www.krii.com/downloads/Four_KM_Facets.pdf

CHAPTER 13

SYNPLEX

Making Decisions in Complex, Multi-Stakeholder Situations

William H. Rodger

There is no greater impediment to the advancement of knowledge than the ambiguity of words.

—Thomas Reid, Scottish philosopher
'Essays on the Intellectual Powers of Man' (1785)

INTRODUCTION

This chapter will provide an overview of one approach to turning the ideas that have emerged from research on complexity in the last 20 years into an effective situation analysis and decision support tool. Named Synplex, it is intended to improve the quality and speed of decision making for organizations faced with complex, high value, multi-stakeholder issues. The tool is a combination of a facilitated group process and a language-based software tool that captures and helps structure verbal and written information used by participants in the process.

Complexity and Knowledge Management, pages 217–235

We will attempt to clarify organization needs for management decision support tools that deal with complexity and identify where Synplex fits with other tools.

What we are trying to do is to improve the effectiveness and efficiency of agents in a system as they interact, adapt, and co-evolve in ways that produce the desired outcomes. Synplex provides a methodology and a framework within which creative interaction and emergence can occur and pragmatic action steps can be captured that are optimized to produce the desired outcomes. Authors such as Taptiklis (2005) have stated that "managerialism is intrinsically inimical to complexity" (p. 2). I intend to show that management of complex issues is not an oxymoron.

ORGANIZATION NEEDS

There is a spectrum of needs in organizations when one considers the time frame for change. Changing the social, technical, and cultural conditions in an organization takes considerable time but in many cases is needed if the organization is to break away from destructive patterns of behavior (e.g., see Mitleton-Kelly, 2003). The organization has to want to change in some significant way and has to commit to an extended program of work similar in some ways to the large-scale organizational development programs of past decades.

At the other end of the time frame spectrum of needs in today's global business environment, complex issues arise that need resolution in time frames shorter than those required for an overhaul of the whole organization. Synplex quickly exposes the patterns of influence connecting the set of key factors controlling the complex issue of immediate concern and starts new conversations around these factors. It enables both immediate actions to be taken to ameliorate the current situation (e.g., changing the conditions under which people do their day-to-day work, processes/methods, information flows, etc.) and have these integrated with longer term activities to address fundamental social, technical, and cultural factors.

The challenge for organizations attempting to manage complex issues is to design an approach such that the right conditions are created to support the emergence of the new knowledge and understanding needed to resolve the particular issue/challenge/problem facing the organization. Included in this is the consideration of how to move people beyond their current modes of thinking in order to foster creativity and innovation.

In trying to make step function changes and deal with the social, technical, and business factors pertinent to their environment, the leadership of organizations today face a global environment that can dictate both the direction and nature of the change required so that senior managers do not have total control over the change agenda. Karl Weik (2006, p. 2) has written about the movement that needs to occur for leaders to come to grips with this increasingly complex environment. His description of the movement from superficial simplicity through confused complexity to a state of profound simplicity corresponds largely to what happens in the Synplex process. His state of profound simplicity, which he describes as "seasoned simplicities, simplicities that have been tested by mentally simulating their consequences," is akin to the state that participants in the Synplex process arrive at having constructed the Influence Map that is the result of their analysis of their particular complex issue.

Warren Weaver (1948, pp. 536–538), in his paper "Complexity and Science," talked about "problems in disorganized complexity" and "problems of organized complexity." The key attribute of the latter, as Weaver explained it, is that "they are all problems which involve dealing simultaneously with a *sizable number of factors which are interrelated into an organic whole.*" The point he was making is that there are a large but not infinite number of factors that are pertinent to a specific situation. The key to unlocking complex problems and challenges is identifying in a comprehensive way the factors which are truly pertinent to the situation/issue and then surfacing the patterns of how these factors operate and influence each other. Recognizing these patterns of influence relationships is needed to develop a set of actions that can change and reshape the situation to move to a new (and better) position. From experimentation with groups over the last 17 years we have found that when we ask teams of between 20 and 30 people to think of any and all issues or factors that might in some way have a bearing on the situation we are focused on, they come up with a maximum size of list that is between 200 and 300 items in length, including redundancies. A typical list with redundant items removed is in the range of 150 to 200 items.

A key problem for decision makers in most complex situations is that the set of key relevant factors and the influence relationships between them is hidden from view, leaving individual and group decision makers wrestling to make sense of the symptoms or outcomes of this interplay of the various factors. Decision making based on these recognizable outcomes or symptoms does not result in high-quality decisions. Nor is the application of the limited resources available in most organizations attempting to manage these symptoms an efficient or effective use of resources. Synplex is aimed at making it possible for people in a wide range of different environments to expose and understand the pattern of relationships that connect the factors that are pertinent to their particular situation. When people have developed the necessary understanding of their "organized complexity," the tool then supports the exploration of what can be done in practical terms to shape the desired outcome with an optimal use of the resources available.

WHERE DOES SYNPLEX FIT IN THE MANAGEMENT TOOL SPECTRUM?

The tool itself is essentially a methodology supported by software for capturing and structuring language-based information. It has particular features and attributes that have proven to be effective in helping people as they try to develop a deeper, shared understanding of the patterns of influence at work in their specific situation. To help the reader locate where this tool might fit within the spectrum of tools being developed that utilize complexity concepts, I would place it as being designed to deal with social complexity and supporting Stacey's ideas around complex responsive processes of relating (Stacey, Griffin, & Shaw, 2000). The planning phase of the methodology identifies the diversity required to develop a new understanding of the issue, which is an essential first step for decision making.

In designing the team we try not to be confused by the titles and positions occupied by individuals. The focus is on individuals and the content information, position in internal networks, and stakeholder interests they represent. As Stacey et al. have pointed out, "Humans accomplish sophisticated cooperative, joint action through their capacity for communicating with each other in the medium of symbols, particularly those that constitute language" (2000, p. 187). The Synplex tool is intended to facilitate such sophisticated cooperative, joint action, but a prerequisite for this to happen is to bring together the right group of people. Making do with whoever happens to be available will not produce a high-quality output.

In the landscape of management as put forward by Dave Snowden and Peter Stanbridge (2004; see Figure 13.1), our domain of interest is social complexity—that is, unordered ontology, heuristic-based epistemology.

Our use of computer technology, while necessary to support the exposure of the connectivity and influence relationships between factors pertinent to the specific situation, is subservient to the human dynamics framework established to facilitate the interactions of individuals using language and

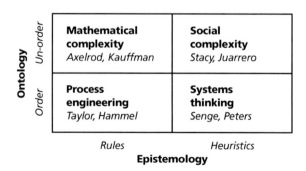

Figure 13.1   The landscape of management.

the development (negotiation) of shared meaning. This latter point related to the negotiation of meaning is at the heart of the methodology, and its application tries to address the problem referred to in the quotation at the beginning of this chapter. Wenger (1998) develops the idea of negotiation of meaning in detail in his writing on Communities of Practice. While there are existing communities of practice with their own networks in organizations, Synplex in its typical application normally creates new groupings and networks among people who would not normally interact directly in their day to day activities.

A description of the methodology and the supporting software technology and a case example of an application will be given.

YOU CAN'T GET THERE FROM HERE

There are a variety of possible futures ahead of us, any one of which depends on the confluence of a large number of factors coming together in a particular way. However, given the traditions of scientific management and the largely reductionist approach to problem solving and decision making, managers have been left poorly provided for in terms of tools and techniques that can help them see and begin to understand the *patterns of influence* at work in their environment. Understanding the web of influence connecting the different factors that shape their situation is a first step in opening up the possibility of changing both the significance of an individual factor and also the influence relationships with other factors, hence changing the set of future possibilities.

The title of this section is meant to convey the idea that to get to the future that we aspire to, we have to set about changing the web of influence that predetermines the set of future possibilities. And we need to understand that there is no "silver bullet" that is the ultimate solution for any situation. Successful change requires a coordinated approach to several key factors to produce the desired outcome.

This is not to say that one can't learn something from other organizations (e.g., looking for relevant "best practice") or that careful process and systems design, people development, and organization design do not have a key part to play in being able to reach our desired future state. They do. But on its own, the traditional scientific approach to management is inadequate to develop the more holistic understanding we need to develop for our increasingly complex environment. In fact the management education legacy of Taylor (1919/1998) and his successors, with their assumption of order, stability, and control as being what we should continually strive for, unfortunately places people mentally in the wrong starting position and makes it difficult for them to accept ideas of adaptability, the embracing of change and experimentation, and the need to harness the knowledge and wisdom at all levels of an organization in planning and organizing for change.

ACCESSING THE KNOWLEDGE THAT EXISTS WITHIN THE ORGANIZATION

One can observe the functioning of an organization and people carrying out specific tasks and delivering particular outcomes, but in turning to the documented knowledge captured in the organization database (and process descriptions), one discovers a gap between what one can observe in terms of knowledge being applied and the knowledge that is captured by the organization. The gap is largely comprised of the tacit knowledge people have acquired based on their experience.

I will make the statement at this point that many organizations operate successfully *in spite of* the systems, tools, and processes (usually designed by "experts") that have been inserted into the organization. Human beings are wonderfully complex, adaptive organisms that, when faced with the limitations inherent in the organization and the processes they are told to follow, can innovate and create ways of actually delivering what they understand is the desired output. I have listened as a facilitator to dialogue in multiple group workshops where the senior executives were adamant that things operated in a particular way, and lower levels of management and non-management people in the group tried to explain that in reality that was not how things operated. In one case it took two days of listening to multiple anecdotes and stories before a CEO came to accept that his view of the world was at odds with reality. This type of situation fits Boje's (1995) concept of organizations as "Tamara," where people live in different rooms of the same house and perceive the world in different ways. Storytelling is an integral and powerful part of the discourse in the group workshops and helps to tackle the key challenge in organizations of how to utilize their whole knowledge base (explicit and tacit) in a way that can expose how different factors in their environment relate to each other.

An obstacle to accessing the total knowledge base is stratification or participation based on status as the main criterion. Using the familiar pyramid structure of most organizations, one needs to access knowledge at all the vertical levels of the structure. However, a common approach taken to making decisions on high-value, complex issues is to create a "task force" and keep its membership as small as possible and confine it to key managers in the belief that the smaller the numbers of people involved, the faster will be the decision making. This approach works against the inclusion of the necessary diversity of knowledge, experience, and perspectives.

Also central to this approach is an implicit belief that there is one "right" decision for the organization. It is also the case that while people in this situation often use powerful numerical analysis tools to examine various scenarios and perform risk assessments, the methods used to make sense of critical non-numeric (i.e., language-based) information are simplistic and have inherent weaknesses that are often not visible and understood by the users. Synplex fills a gap in an organization's ability to utilize and make sense of critical non-numeric information, hence providing a more complete picture of performance.

APPLYING COMPLEXITY CONCEPTS
TO MANAGEMENT TOOL DESIGN

When we look at what the various streams of research into complexity and complex adaptive systems have produced, we see several ideas that provide the basis for an enhanced approach to management.

The idea of organizations being a "network of networks," with people being the nodes in the network, is not in itself a fundamentally new concept. People in the organizational development domain and social scientists have observed and studied this for years (Krackhardt & Hanson, 1993). There has been a recent resurgence of interest in organizational/social network analysis as more powerful software tools have become available. However, Stuart Kauffman (1995) added new understanding of how these networks can operate in an optimal way with his work on connectivity and information flow across networks. The key concept of sparsely connected networks that exhibit internal order with relatively simple information-processing rules at the nodes of the network suggested the possibility of designing teams of manageable size that would have the requisite diversity to tackle truly complex issues. Not only do you not have to directly connect everyone in the organization with everyone else for day-to-day operations, but you don't have to involve everyone in problem solving and decision making. However, you do need to be able to access the total knowledge base of the organization.

As people attempt to capture more of the knowledge existing within an organization, we need to be careful that the knowledge is not filtered, summarized, and synthesized in a way that destroys the knowledge itself and turns it in to something else that we mistakenly consider to be real knowledge. Dave Snowden (2000) has looked at the issues of knowledge capture in formal and informal communities. Approaches based on surveys and the interpretation by someone doing an analysis of what they thought the contributor meant can distort the original meaning to the point where the actual knowledge is lost. A key aspect of the Synplex methodology is to capture and keep the ideas and information provided by participants in their original language and work during the group sessions to bring the meaning behind the words to the surface so that participants come to understand and share the same meaning. The tool has the capability to capture additional words and explanations in addition to the original statements that can help to fully capture the meaning for others in the organisation who were not present in the workshops.

The idea of dynamic fitness landscapes and an adaptive walk in pursuit of a better position on the landscape relate to the set of possible futures unfolding in front of us. The analogy I would use for fitness landscapes is a sailing one. Anyone who has sailed a small boat knows that the course the boat follows is dependent on a number of factors that are interacting dynamically in real time. In sailing a course in a competition (and in business we are in a constant state of competition) we intuitively—using all that we know and understand—adjust the controls at our command (tiller, sail position, etc.) to steer the optimal course. But we know and understand that whether we can actually get around the buoy as close as possible or whether we end up several yards off and lose several seconds and possibly the race depends on shifts in the wind and currents (external factors) as well as our personal ability and experience as a helmsman (an understanding of the interplay of different factors). Similarly with fitness landscapes, our ability to navigate across a surface changing beneath our feet depends both on the external factors that we can recognize but can't control and the understanding within the organization of how to respond effectively. It hardly needs saying that an organization with limited understanding and rigid processes will not respond to change in an effective way.

The sailing analogy is also useful for understanding the distinction between scientific management's search for the "correct" solution and the more adaptive approach linked to complexity concepts. The helmsman is conscious that he has to adapt quickly to even small changes in conditions that will affect his course and that ahead of him there are a set of possible courses he might be forced to sail depending on conditions. Every one of these will require its own adjustments, but there is a subset of the total number of possible courses that will leave him in a "winning" position. There is no thought that there is only one course, so the mental approach is different.

On the subject of emergence related to management/decision making tools, the question of whether it occurs or not is answered by the outcomes produced. Are the outcomes both unexpected *and* do the outcomes enable effective, practical change? So the tool has to, by design, set up the conditions that make emergence possible without having any prior knowledge of the shape/structure/content of the answer. In fact, even the original question and issue that were framed to provide an initial starting point for a situation analysis can become irrelevant given what emerges from the group conversations. One cannot plan for emergence in the scientific management sense, but thoughtful consideration of the starting conditions and having some simple rules for framing conversations and supporting them in an ongoing way makes emergent results possible; that is, emergence is process-dependent.

SYNPLEX—METHODOLOGY OVERVIEW

The methodology has three steps. Each of these steps and the overall structure has emerged from continuous experimentation and 'tinkering' over a period of sixteen years. The genesis of the idea which evolved into the current methodology and its integration of group process and language based software technology started in 1989. It was based on Warfield's (1994) work in the 1970s and 1980s, which took a systems engineering approach to complexity and is laid out in his book originally published in 1990.

However, our own implementation of his approach experienced a serendipitous event at an early stage, which started the process of change and experimentation. This event occurred at the start of one of our first applications with a client. It became apparent on day one that the structure of the process as described by Warfield would not work in the particular circumstances we encountered. Basically we were faced with a group whose members did not want to be there (most of them had been told to attend) and did not believe they would be listened to if they tried to say what was on their minds. So some immediate group process reengineering was needed to get past the block. We completely changed the focus of the opening conversation (and hence what we were doing in the process) and within a short time had an explosion of energy and engagement by all participants. With the engagement of all the participants, we could move forward with the other steps of the process. The learning for us was that the *type* of conversation that can be productive at a particular time is context-dependent.

This understanding helped to shape our approach to subsequent experimentation. The basic question became "What are the types of conversation that need to happen and in what sequence to achieve the desired end point?" The understanding of the importance of dialogue, different types of conversations and what they make possible under particular conditions has been laid out by a number of writers over many years. Drucker (1986) points to the questions that are asked in innovative companies to start certain types of conversation. David Bohm (1996) treats dialogue as a multi-faceted group process that is central to innovation—for example, "I'm suggesting that there is the possibility for transformation of the nature of consciousness, both individually and collectively, and that whether this can be solved culturally and socially depends on dialogue." It is this transformation in awareness and thinking that we strive for by the way we stimulate dialogue within the framework of the methodology, starting with an exploratory conversation around a common point of interest (the "issue" as we refer to it). The sequence of steps in the methodology provides a framework to link several different types of conversation in order that the group can move from an analysis/discovery phase to a forward-looking solution design phase. The actual outcome of the sequence of conversations has two principal components. The first is a new understanding of the issue in terms of the patterns of influence relationships that link factors that are significant in the context of the issue (using Weaver's concept of "ordered complexity"). The second component is a set of actions to effect change in both individual factors and in their relationships.

Steps in the Process

There are three main steps in the process. They are (1) a planning meeting with the individual in the client organization who "owns" the issue ("owns" = has the responsibility and authority to resolve), (2) a group analysis phase whose purpose is to enable people to explore what is known about the situation and all the factors that are possibly pertinent to it, and (3) a design phase where people create and explore different ways of changing the current situation and moving in the direction they have decided they wish to go. The steps are shown in Figure 13.2 and are labeled Planning, Influence Mapping and Solution Design.

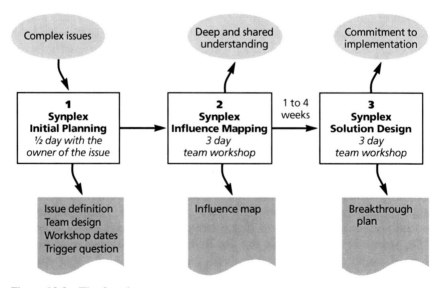

Figure 13.2 The Synplex process.

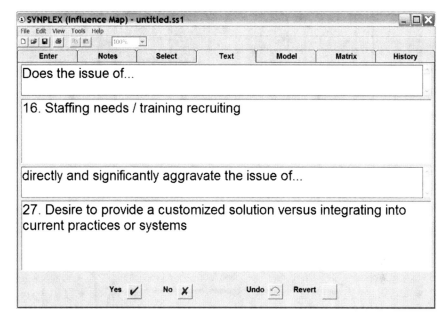

Figure 13.3 Synplex screen for Influence Map.

The software tool used to capture the language based information and present it in pair-wise comparison format has been developed by Complexity Solutions and its evolution driven by the results of process experimentation and client feedback.

The principal screen projected for the group members and used for factor analysis is shown in Figure 13.3.

For an influence analysis, a relationship statement is set up as shown in Figure 13.3, and pairs of factors chosen by the group are reviewed using the relationship. The relationship statement chosen for an analysis is dependent on the type of relationship being explored, which in turn depends on the context for the work. On completion of group conversations around a particular pairing, the group decides (based on a majority view) if the answer to the relationship question is yes or no, and this decision is captured by the software. Another pairing is presented, and the conversations take place around the new pairing.

The individual decisions determine linkages between factors, and the software builds the map of these influence connections. An example of part of such an influence map is presented in Figure 13.4. The map has been laid out such that the general flow of influence between factors is from left to right across the map. However, the text boxes with the thick, black outlines contain more than one factor. These are examples of situations where several factors are mutually interacting (a normal occurrence in the real world).

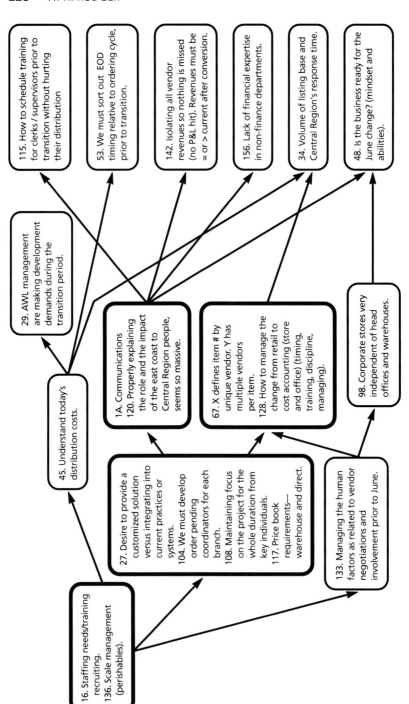

Figure 13.4 Part of an influence map.

At each stage of the development of the map, it is reviewed by the group, challenged by anyone who has a concern, and iterated as the group feels necessary. This process of mapping, review, and iteration is called interpretive structural modelling (ISM), and is explained by Warfield (1994).

A completed map has the key drivers of a particular situation towards the left-hand side of the map. The factors towards the right-hand side are more symptoms or end effects created, maintained, and driven by the key drivers on the left. Hence, the group comes to understand that the flow of influence necessitates attention to the factors on the left if they are to modify the outcomes. In most organizations people readily recognize the problems they have identified in their operations and overall company performance as part of the set of factors on the right. What they have not been able to see clearly is the fundamental nature of the set of factors on the left. Now that they understand these for what they are and their influence on other factors, there is a significant shift in mental outlook by participants. As I alluded to earlier, this shift in perspective opens up paths for action that were previously closed to the organization.

Once the influence map has been completed, the next stage in the process is to carefully think about where the organization needs to move to (definition of desirable end points) in order to eliminate/change key driving factors on the left of the map. This is done as part of a collaborative group effort, since in virtually all cases the group will come up with end-point definitions that are better than any that the senior executives produce on their own. It also creates group ownership of the defined end points.

Using these end points, the remainder of the process is to work to explore possible sets of actions that could achieve all the end points and create a coherent set that takes into account the reality of practical restrictions on various options (e.g., finite amounts of money, people resources, time limits, etc.). While this part of the process is similar to project planning, we have found, by experimenting, ways in which to support creativity in the action plan development—for example, building intellectual "bias" into subgroup work to foster diversity of approach to achieving the same goal. Most subgroup work in organizations is designed within an "efficiency" paradigm. Our approach is based on an "effectiveness" paradigm. The goal is not to get the work done as fast as possible by having separate groups work in parallel on different tasks. The goal is to come up with a coherent plan of action that will produce the best possible outcomes for the organization.

Results

The Synplex tool has been applied to a wide range of issues in government, different industries, and company cultures in North America and

Europe. Issues range from strategic business planning to critical problem resolution, mergers and acquisitions, supply chain restructuring, procurement, and social services operations planning. Client perspectives have a common theme, and that is that Synplex does produce effective change in organizations wrestling with complex, difficult issues. The surprise for clients is what they discover along the way things that need changing that were not on their list at the outset. The ongoing benefit from the process is the shift in mindset that occurs and the opening up of new perspectives and understanding of their business plus the new social connections created within the organization that help to improve communications and productivity.

CASE STUDY

The Context/Environment

The context for this application was an organization having to change to meet a range of new business and technical requirements and deal with a number of challenges in its operating environment. The focus of the work was a concept for organizational change and determining whether the concept was capable of being implemented in a practical way that would meet all the needs of the business.

The nature of the business was a government military procurement and supply organization serving the needs of all three forces (air, land, and sea). The changing business and technical requirements were driven by the changes in the operating requirements of the three forces as well as the need for more rapid and cost-effective deployment of advanced technology platforms. These advanced technology systems were developed and manufactured by suppliers.

The desired change in the organization was set in the larger context of constrained military expenditures (as percentage of GDP) and pressure for cost reductions in the short term.

Design of Intervention

The planning meeting with the "owner" of the issue provided the facilitators with an understanding of the background and history of the current situation and allowed them to discuss and agree with the client on the specific focus for the work and the desired outcome. The team of people who needed to participate was designed, including both key stakeholders and individuals with content knowledge covering all the key areas pertinent to the business.

With agreement on the focus and scope, a trigger question was designed to focus participants thinking within the agreed frame of reference around the issue and elicit preliminary thoughts that people had as they began to focus on the challenge they faced. The trigger question in this case was: Given that the new business model will require new structures to allow it to work effectively and efficiently, what are the issues, challenges, problems, and opportunities in optimizing the organization to deliver the required output to customers at best value?

Workshop Preparation

Prior to coming together for the first of the group workshops, participants were provided with the trigger question and some guidelines for providing input. Using the trigger question as a stimulus, they captured their thoughts and sent them to the facilitators. The individual statements were input to the Synplex software and also printed out in a format suitable for viewing on the walls of the meeting facility.

Workshop 1

Many of the workshop participants were managers of different lines of business and responsible for a variety of advanced technology platforms. It rapidly became apparent that the great majority of the participants were opposed to the reorganization being proposed. They viewed it as complicating their lives and putting at risk their ability to deliver against their business objectives. The hostility was overt and extremely vocal. Certain words and terminology were challenged every time they were spoken.

Since decision making had been vested in the participants, it was possible to discuss and agree on the fundamental goal of the exercise—that is, determining what needed to be changed (and how) in order to meet new and changing customer requirements in an environment of increasing financial pressures. Terminology that was like a red flag to a bull was dropped, and clear language was substituted that still allowed the issues to be dealt with. The group could now begin to consider the content information generated in response to the trigger question.

A set of 170 factors was identified. To begin an analysis of these, the group was asked to choose an initial subset of those they considered to be key factors. This was done by individual choice, not a group decision to avoid group-think and to allow a diversity of views to be represented.

The chosen subset was selected in the Synplex software tool and pairings of factors were presented to the group for discussion and determination of whether one factor had a significant influence on another. Using a pair-wise comparison keeps the group discourse focused and avoids the cognitive overload caused by the finite capacity of short-term memory, which is used for analysis and decision making. Keeping the discourse to consideration of only two factors at a time also heads off the efforts of individuals with differing agendas to obfuscate or derail the conversations as they try to steer the group towards their particular agenda. Individuals in the group have to share information and/or a particular perspective relative to the two factors being considered to support their view on whether an influence relationship exists or not. The group members decide if the information/ evidence offered does support the view being put forward.

The rules for speaking are simple (e.g., only one person speaks at a time and everyone else is actively listening), together with rules for ensuring senior people don't dominate the discussion. The verbal interaction is comprised of people sharing factual information, verbalizing thoughts that have just occurred to them as they listened to others, people relating anecdotes and stories that illustrate a point, and asking questions of individuals or the group to extract more information that they need to complete a mental picture of possible relationships between factors. It cannot be emphasized enough that this fundamental activity takes time and is essential to the development of new insights by members of the group.

After discussion and listening to any member who wishes to speak, the group made a decision based on all the information and different perspectives articulated by individuals as to whether there was a significant influence linkage between the pair of factors. This was done for both directions of pairing (i.e., A on B and B on A). The software tool recorded the decisions and presented another factor pairing for discussion. Decisions were made based on a strong majority view. Discussion of a pairing was continued until enough information had been shared for this majority view to emerge.

This fundamental process continued until the selected set had been fully analyzed and an influence map produced. The participants reviewed the results of their discussions and were able to question the positions of individual factors and also the linkages (or lack of linkages) between factors. Any challenge was dealt with by removing the factor involved and then reintroducing it and reopening the discussion as the factor was presented to the group in various pairings with other factors. The new influence map produced by this iteration of the analysis was again reviewed by the group. Only when the group reached a consensus that the map did indeed represent the influence relationships, for which there was reasonable evidence in the real world, did the group proceed to add a new subset of factors (chosen by the same individual choice methodology) and extend the analysis.

As the analysis output developed, the group continually reviewed both the factors incorporated in the analysis and the remaining factors displayed on the wall. The latter were from time to time augmented as new thinking and changing perspectives of participants produced new thoughts about factors that might be significant. At a certain point determined by the group (not the facilitators), it was agreed that out of all the factors produced by the "brainstorming" activities of the participants, the key factors were incorporated in the analysis. What was left on the wall were in many cases details or fragments of factors already incorporated into the analysis or else were judged to be not of sufficient relevance to be included. The analysis was then terminated. Typically the influence map work is ended by the group when anywhere from 25 to 40 factors are included in the analysis. In this situation the group included 34 factors.

The total influence map was reviewed to determine what the key patterns of relationships were and understand the key drivers/leverage points that were essential to achieving the optimized organization. The old saw about a picture being worth a thousand words really comes in to its own in this situation. To be able to see the web of relationships and the flow of influence resulting in a recognizable set of organizational outcomes (problems and difficulties) helps people develop a deep understanding of the key drivers of performance of the whole organization.

Once the review was complete and people understood the significance of the relationships between the different factors, they moved on to the next task of carefully defining the end points they needed to reach for the key leverage factors in order to make the organization capable of delivering the results needed by their customers. This was done as a group exercise to obtain the highest quality definition of the end points/objectives. The form of the statement is usually about how things would be if the transformation were successful. Typically groups define a set of 10 to 15 key end states that taken as an integrated set provide the capability required. This group defined eight end states that covered sixteen key factors.

At this point the workshop ended. In the couple of weeks before the second workshop, people had time to reflect on what they had come to understand about the organization. They were also able to gather information about aspects of their operations that they had not previously considered important.

Workshop 2

The activities in this workshop were focused on developing an optimal plan of action to move the organization to its new set of capabilities. Work began with a review of the objectives identified at the conclusion of work-shop one.

The group was then divided into three subgroups. This was done tak-ing into account the background and position of each member of the group. The subgroups formed in this way had the greatest amount of differ-ence from each other that it was possible to create given the original design of the group. The task they were given (all subgroups had the same task) was to create for each objective the set of actions that they believed were op-timal to achieve the end point. The outputs of this task provided different sets of actions for each objective with some overlap across subgroups. The group was then able to look at a range of thinking around how to achieve each objective and develop a consensus based on what they considered to be the best ideas.

Normally the remaining tasks are to sequence and put time estimates on the sets of actions and check the final outcome against a set of "must-meet" criteria that the group had identified earlier as necessary criteria for the plan to be accepted by the organisation. However, in this case the group took over the process at the end of day two of the second workshop. They were so excited about what they could now see as the pathway to success that they completed the work themselves.

So from outright hostility on day one ("we don't want to go there," "it is the wrong thing to do," and similar comments), the group developed their own understanding of why this was the right path to pursue and took over complete ownership. Not only was the new organization design implement-ed very successfully, but the key learning and new thinking that emerged was used to move the whole organization into alignment with customers' needs while reducing costs. A key long-term benefit was people in the or-ganization recognizing that there was an approach to understanding very complex issues that could utilize knowledge and experience in the organi-zation to produce solutions instead of relying on outside consultants, and also that by following a few simple rules the quality of internal conversa-tions could be dramatically improved.

REFERENCES

Bohm, D. (1996). *On dialogue* (L. Nichol, Ed.). London: Routledge.

Boje, D. M. (1995). Stories of the storytelling organization: A postmodern analysis of Disney as "Tamara-land." *Academy of Management Journal, 38*(4), 997–1035, (http://cbae.nmsu.edu/~dboje/papers/DisneyTamaraland.html)

Drucker, P. F. (1986). *The frontiers of management: Where tomorrow's decisions are being shaped today.* New York: Truman.

Kauffman, S. (1995). *At home in the universe: The search for the laws of self-organization and complexity.* New York: Oxford University Press.

Krackhardt, D & Hanson, J. R. (1993). Informal networks: The company behind the chart. *Harvard Business Review, 71*(4), 104–114.

Mitleton-Kelly, E. (2003). Complexity research—Approaches and methods: The LSE complexity group integrated methodology. In A.Keskinen, M. Aaltonen, & E. Mitleton-Kelly (Eds.), *Organisational Complexity. Scientific Papers 1/2003* (pp. 1–12). Helsinki: TUTU Publications, Finland Futures Research Centre.

Snowden, D. (2000). The social ecology of knowledge management. In C. Despres & D. Chauvel (Eds.), *Knowledge horizons: The present and promise of knowledge management* (pp. 237–265). Oxford, UK: Butterworth-Heinemann.

Snowden, D. & Stanbridge, P. (2004). The landscape of management: Creating the context for understanding social complexity. *E:CO, 6*(1/2), 140–148.

Stacey, R. D., Griffin, D. & Shaw, P. (2000). *Complexity and management: Fad or radical challenge to systems thinking?* New York: Routledge.

Taptiklis, T. (2005). After Managerialism. *E:CO, 7*(3/4), 2–14.

Taylor, F. W. (1998). The principles of scientific management. Mineola, NY: Dover. (Original work published 1919)

Warfield, J. N. (1994). *A science of generic design: Managing complexity through systems design* (2nd ed.). Ames, IA: Iowa State University Press.

Weaver, W. (1948). Science and complexity. *American Scientist, 36*, 536.

Weick, K. E. (2006). Leadership when events don't play by the rules. Center for Positive Organizational Scholarship, Stephen M. Ross School of Business, University of Michigan.

Wenger, E. (1998). *Communities of practice: Learning, meaning and identity.* Cambridge: Cambridge University Press.

CHAPTER 14

"GETTING THERE IS NOT A VERY NEAT CIRCLE OR PROCESS"

An Illustrative View of Complexity within a Knowledge Management Learning Community

Rosemary C. Reilly and Madeleine Mcbrearty

Knowledge management [KM] refers to any managed process leading to the effective creation, acquisition, access, or transfer of valid knowledge (Blackman & Henderson, 2005). KM is a framework that includes systems, procedures, and cultures, in and through which individuals and communities create and validate knowledge. It is a means to capture and share existing individual knowledge and to collectivize it in order to create distributed knowledge that impacts the existing organizational knowledge base. KM includes practices for optimizing access to knowledge for individuals and teams operating within a given system, relevant actionable advice, imported knowledge and experiences from outside the system, and support for sus-

Complexity and Knowledge Management, pages 237–265
Copyright © 2010 by Information Age Publishing

tainable innovation and distributed problem-solving (Gorelick & Tantawy-Monsou, 2005; Desouza & Hensgen, 2005). However, there is a shift in emphasis within the KM field; methods and processes that promote innovative knowledge creation are replacing strategies that only stress dissemination (McElroy, 2000), resulting in second-generation KM.

LEARNING COMMUNITIES AS KM SYSTEMS

Within KM systems, knowledge is focused on: (1) capturing and cherishing what is known, (2) developing organic relationships, (3) capitalizing on the effectiveness of the knowledge about system processes, (4) maximizing the usefulness of knowledge about solutions or problem-solving routines (Earl, 2001), and (5) the production of new procedural knowledge as workplaces experience continual change (McElroy, 2000). Therefore, KM is conceived as an organic process whereby knowledge transferred creates new experts, or new practice knowledge is created in response to changing work conditions. These notions are in line with the concept of communities of practice or learning communities [LCs].[1] LCs and second-generation KM systems value cognition as the means for generating knowledge, and they both approach learning from a socially shared perspective. In this context, cognition is seen as an adaptation of the individual's consciousness to social and cultural interactions. It involves the learner as an active agent in dynamic relation with other active agents. KM systems and LCs are not bound by the limitations of any one person's cognitive capacity or experience. They are comprised of individuals in relationship actively molding and influencing each other's knowledge and reasoning processes. Therefore active agents build epistemology on the basis of what they tell and are told by others (Resnick, 1991). Given their correspondence, we combine KM systems and LCs as KM learning communities within which knowledge unfolds in the meanings, relations, and skillful executions of praxis (Wenger & Snyder, 2000). Here, cognition is seen as co-emergent with environment, individuals, and activity (Fenwick, 2004).

Generally, workplace KM learning communities attempt to generate three kinds of knowledge: (1) "knowing-why" (knowledge about the kind of work they do), (2) "knowing-how" (formal and tacit knowledge, skills, and expertise to perform the work), and (3) "knowing-whom" (knowledge about working relationships within and beyond the workplace) (Arthur, Defillippi, & Lindsay, 2004). When generating shared or distributed knowledge, KM learning communities engage people's intrinsic motivation (*knowing-why*) to develop and implement a shared vision and purpose. They incorporate people's skills and ways of interacting (*knowing-how*) into a shared repertoire of practice. As well, they draw on their members' social investments (*knowing-whom*) in each other to create patterns of mutual engagement. As conditions in the marketplace change, workplace KM learning communities also engage in the process of revising, refreshing, modifying, and innovating knowledge and practice in these three areas.

ASSESSING KM LEARNING COMMUNITY EFFECTIVENESS

When considering the effectiveness of KM learning communities, there is often a tension between exploring their two major dimensions: the technical, which emphasizes measurement with a linear focus on outcomes, and the social, which focuses on individual and group learning processes as the foundation of organizational KM (Easterby-Smith & Araujo, 1999). Currently, the most common assessment approach relies on the concept of "KM performance" to describe the improvement between an enterprise's current capabilities and those improved by KM (Tseng, 2008). Within traditional assessment methodology, performance indicators are generally costs, product quality, profit levels, and customer satisfaction (Germain, Dröge, & Christensen, 2001). However, using a complexity perspective, the focus of assessments can be shifted to relationships, patterns, processes, and context.

KM LEARNING COMMUNITIES AND COMPLEXITY THEORY

Complexity theory is a set of concepts that describe and model complex nonlinear dynamics and integrate biological, cognitive and social dimensions (Capra, 2005). Complexity theory illuminates learning in dynamic, complex, and unstable systems. KM learning communities can be envisioned as complex adaptive systems [CAS] (Holland, 1996) that respond and adjust to changing and evolving knowledge environments. Knowledge in KM learning communities is created and embedded in the relationships between members (Fenwick, 2004). Interactions within relationships shape cognitive processes that result in system-wide, distributed, continuous learning and problem-solving (Desouza & Hensgen, 2005). This shared cognition fashions the unpredictable emergent evolution of KM learning communities that in turn shape their members (Capra, 2002). This interactive effect results in the co-emergence of knower and environment in a co-evolutionary pattern. In this way, learning is the activity, which continually embodies the KM learning community's pattern of organization, serving to function as the means for its recurrent invention, exploration, and co-evolutionary adaptation (Capra, 2002).

Within these communities, learning is *the* generative mechanism for the increasing and decreasing complexity of social systems as they co-evolve within their milieu (Espejo, 2003). Within KM learning communities, there is a blurring of boundaries with distributed knowledge rippling through internal subsystems and networks, both within and across individuals and teams (Arthur et al., 2004), and into other systems in which individuals are members. KM learning communities evolve historically. Past history and experience are added on and therefore potentially shape future trajectory. As well, throughout KM learning communities, there is an allowance of diversity that includes differences in learning styles, epistemological stances (Hofer & Pintrich, 1997), and subjective knowledge. This acceptance of difference results in the emergence of knowledge from multisubjectivity[2] and is seen as the source of innovation (McElroy, 2000). Multisubjectivity also facilitates the flow of distributed knowledge across the system (Arthur et al., 2004).

Since KM learning communities are self-organizing systems that have the capability for adaptation, the ability and motivation to learn live within the existing subsystems and networks of members. These learning capacities result in the ability of nodes within the system, in the form of formal teams or informal subgroups, to rapidly come together, separate, and reform in different permutations according to need, while maintaining long-term relationships with other community members throughout the rest of the system (Arthur et al., 2004). Therefore, distributed knowledge and continuous problem-solving, produced by the dynamic processes of interacting autonomous agents, become unanticipated emergent phenomena that are non-deterministic and nonlinear in nature. Emergence plays an essential role in the evolution of KM learning communities, which is why they demonstrate a great deal of unpredictability.

Learning is activated and linked to the disequilibrium experienced in the community (Fenwick, 2004). When KM learning communities approach the far-from-equilibrium state, they are subject to spontaneous, dramatic reorganizations. These points of instability, or bifurcation points, allow the community to branch off into an entirely new state where new forms of order may emerge (Capra, 2005). Systems capable of this kind of reorganization are dissipative structures. These types of structures illustrate the close interplay between structure on the one hand and flow and change on the other. In KM learning communities, this may herald new configurations, procedures, or culture shifts to meet the requirements of effective knowledge production. Emergence is integral to the dynamics of dissipative structures, affording them the potential to evolve (Capra, 2002). Change, consequently, is understood as the self-reorganization resulting from the interconnectivity among community members, subsystems, and the environment. Connectivity amplifies nonlinearity through multiple densely connected overlapping feedback loops that link and let go and link again within the nodes and networks (Agar, 1999). The cultivation of diverse viewpoints and experimentation with alternative structures also facilitates the process of change and knowledge production.

Within complexity theory, cognition is *the* organizing, life-giving activity for the KM learning community since it creates self-generation and self-perpetuation as a living network. Interactions between members and with the environment are cognitive social interactions, inextricably interconnecting community life and cognition (Maturana & Varela, 1987). KM learning communities, therefore, represent the integration of the theories of complex adaptive systems (Stevenson & Hamilton, 2001), organizational learning (Argyris, 1993; Senge, 1990), and knowledge management (Blackman & Henderson, 2005). The following case study will illustrate this synthesis.

METHODOLOGY AND METHODS

This case study (Stake, 1994) used a complexity perspective to illuminate the unique trajectory of a KM learning community and the nonlinear dynamics associated with a reiterative self-assessment process. We focused our inquiry on gleaning the lived experience (Kvale, 1996) of members of a KM learning community in order to reveal its complexity. Members were recruited as representatives of the community, as complex adaptive subsystems within the community, and as individual CAS (Stevenson & Hamilton, 2001).

Context

This KM learning community is embedded in a two-year masters program entitled Human Systems Intervention [HSI], which is designed to provide expertise for work as organizational leaders and consultants facilitating change processes within human systems. HSI cohorts consist of approximately 20 to 25 members, who are given the opportunity to shape a learning community into an effective second-generation KM system designed to maximize the benefits of experiential inquiry. In order to facilitate the meaningfulness and usefulness of the LC, members work in teams of various configurations on knowledge projects. This learning methodology allows for the integration of theory, values, and skills in practical application. Knowledge extends to understanding and intervening effectively in social processes, the capacity to shape an environment, and the impact of transformative processes on environments and self.

Participants

Participants in the inquiry were members of an HSI KM learning community. Four individuals were interviewed, two women and two men, ranging in age from 24 to 56 years: George, HB, Margaret, and Rachel.[3] Aside from their full-time involvement in this professional education program, three of the four participants were employed as inside or independent consultants in either public or private organizations.

Data Collection and Transformation

Data were collected through interviews at two points in time: the end of year one and again at the end of year two. All interviews lasted from 60–90 minutes. Using a semi-structured guide, the interview attempted to elicit stories reflective of participants' consciousness and perceptions (Vygotsky, 1987). The interview focused on: (1) participants' experiences of the community and its self-assessment, (2) the impact of their experiences on themselves as learners and as members of a KM learning community, (3) processes that influenced the interactions within the community and its ability to manage knowledge, and (4) insights into the functioning of the complex community as a KM system. All interviews were taped. As well, a co-author maintained observational, theoretical, and personal notes (Richardson, 1994) from her interactions within the KM learning community, in order to track processes and critical events, hunches or hypotheses, and observation statements about the workings of the community. Audiotapes were transcribed and rendered into text for analysis. A conceptual display (Miles & Huberman, 1994) was created illustrating the fundamental concepts, processes, and their relationships.

ILLUMINATED PATTERNS OF THE HSI KM
LEARNING COMMUNITY

M: So, how does a LC work?
Margaret: Painfully (laughter). I think at the beginning...

Cilliers (1998) suggests that it is not possible to tell a single, exclusive story about something that is complex; however, the following is a blending of the stories and dynamics that emerged from the interviews and the field notes. Models reduce complexity in order to achieve a level of understanding (Cilliers, 2004). Though the authors admit something is lost from this

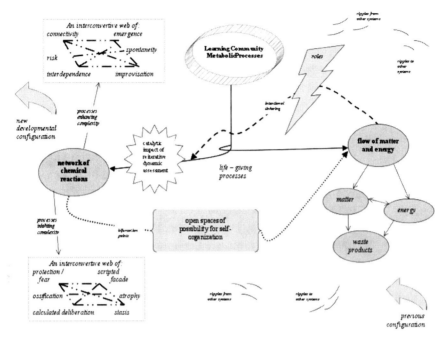

Figure 14.1 A KM learning community as a living evolving complex system

representation, Figure 14.1 characterizes a graphic slice of the interplay of the workings of a complex KM learning community.

KM Learning Community Metabolic Processes

Whole systems are characterized by flows of energy and materials between and among component parts (Linds, 2006). Metabolism is the essence of life; it is that which enables a living organism to continually generate, repair, and perpetuate itself. Therefore, we chose this metaphor as the foundation for the examination of the life of the KM learning community. Metabolism includes the continuous flow of matter, the continuous flow of energy, the elimination of waste products, and a network of chemical reactions that transforms the matter into energy (Capra, 2005; Maturana & Varela, 1987).

Continuous Flow of Matter: Knowledge Creation
Since knowledge is the central organizing principle of this KM learning community, knowledge creation was the primary matter for the system. This included: declarative knowledge (knowing-why); procedural knowl-

edge (knowing-how); tacit cultural knowledge (knowing-whom); subjective knowledge (linking personal experience to theory); and emancipatory knowledge (Habermas, 1971) (critical reflections of taken-for-granted assumptions). Knowledge was created within the context of members' relationships; it prompted the community to adapt and evolve in dynamic and complex ways.

> **HB:** Well, it's messy sometimes . . . a LC works in an inadvertent
> way. It's tentative at first, it becomes more proficient about
> sharing information, more proficient around different
> learnings, a common topic . . . we become more open and
> more trusting in terms of receiving feedback, in terms of giv-
> ing feedback . . . it's not at a steady pace. . . . Where we might
> start off around a topic, we become interested in the process
> of learning and how it could be applied to the topic.

In addition, members' knowledge gained from previous experiences flowed into the KM learning community and was shared throughout the system, forming the basis of future individual and community learning.

> **HB:** One of the areas I've been able to help some people out is
> in terms of theory and models . . . a lot of the stuff with non-
> profit, that they may not have worked with before. . . . So, I'm
> able to share different types of valid information . . . like how
> volunteer boards are set up, how non-profit boards are set up,
> different types of community development approaches. . . .

Feedback loops created additional knowledge and contributed to the learning community effectively functioning as a KM system. Members experimented with and tested relevant skills in their relationships within the cohort. Knowledge of self and one's impact on others was developed through critical reflection and additional feedback from peers. This additional knowledge enhanced the ability to develop organic relationships in community.

> **Rachel:** . . . The cohort has really allowed me the space in which to
> try out these new behaviors. . . . I'd learn something, or I'd
> be reading, or I'd be working on my project, and then we'd
> suddenly be working together and I would be able to try out
> these new things . . . for me the cohort was the space in which
> to be the way I really wanted to be.

Continuous Flow of Energy: Collective Conversation

Energy is a means for maintaining order in the face of challenge and it is the power to create order in the face of inertia (Bradley & Pribram, 1996). Energy also involves the mobilization of the potential for activity and the directing of activity towards collective ends. Diversity was a strong source of energy for this KM learning community.

> **Rachel:** I have an image. It's . . . attributed to a sense of flow. It's kind of this energy and timelessness . . . Now, that doesn't always happen to sustain itself. But, I think that there's a sense of flow and energy when we're working together. And the thing is that the diversity is an asset . . . bringing ideas that you wouldn't have thought of; being in that diversity . . . learning from others. I think it's really based on an energy level. When I've worked with a group of people, and it's working really well, there's a sense of . . . time has stopped, but we're moving. . . . It's kind of that optimal experience.

In the KM learning community, potential energy also became engaged and released within social interactions. These energizing effects were evident when the members worked on the task of knowledge creation and when they tapped into the community's emotional life (e.g., feelings associated with constructive conflict, closeness, and growing competency). The most common processes that generated and revealed the community's energy included public reflection (Raelin, 2000), which promoted the creation of order, and collective dialogue (Bohm, 1996), which allowed the community to become a dissipative structure. Interaction became even more influential when it took the form of collective dialogue of braided language and emotion (Espejo, 2003).

> **George:** Whenever we stopped and engaged in dialogue, we grew as a group. Relationships improved, task effectiveness was enhanced.

Therefore, the primary cultural tool for facilitating interactions and knowledge creation in this KM learning community was language: speaking, listening, and meaning-making. Conversation was how the social collective achieved and maintained patterns of organization and how it distributed and managed knowledge. Information about the collective's internal organization was gathered, processed, and distributed through the collective as a *whole*.

> **Margaret:** It's an environment where... we learn from each other... and we listen enough to learn from each other. It also has an emotional component. I was talking about a safe environment, but also a pleasure to be with people.... If it's only emotional, it can bring you everywhere, and rational... it sometimes just keeps you on one track. So, having both of them and listening to both of them was an interesting way of being.

Within this community, the cognitive content, the emotional material, and the linguistic aspects of social interaction shaped, and were shaped by, socially shared cognition, revitalizing the individual and the KM learning community.

> **George:** I don't know if I've cleared anything away as much as rediscovered what I already knew... kind of reinvigorated my intellectual side and reinvigorated my emotional side.

Additional sources of energy, which instigated reorganization of the KM learning community, were conflict and tension, individual and collective values and goals, and power dynamics.

> **George:** I think a shared value was the desire to contribute to productive, effective organizations regardless of how. I think another shared value was to value each other's contributions, whatever they were... egalitarianism... the value of each person, the opinions, thoughts, feelings, and their contributions...

In particular, values acted as moderators for interpersonal and community relationships. They operated as tacit rules for governing the cognitive and social interactions (Reilly, 2005). The values most often cited as those that promoted KM realization were respect, risk-taking, openness, perspective-taking, and presence.

> **Rachel:** ... There was this deep respect for differences in the cohort... it just allowed for differences and commonalities to exist in the same person.
>
> **Margaret:** ... Risk taking... trying to name what's going on. And if it's not perfectly mentioned, at least we tried to name it. The will of every member, or most members, to be part of the process. I think that's key. A generosity, also... that's one thing I'm struck by my community... generosity towards

each other. Somebody said, "Showing up," and I also think
that's part of the will of being there. . . .

HB: There was . . . openness. In that I don't think there were
any sacred cows or taboo subjects. Really, whether or not
we would do something about it is a different subject. But,
I think it's pretty open in terms of sharing observations,
knowledge, and that sort of thing. And I think it's positive
energy.

Finally, energy was also generated from the raw power associated with the
construction of new dimensions of identity (agency, voice, and confidence).

Rachel: I think that if you're in your Buddha nature, if I can refer to
Buddhism, where there's this belief that you are this perfect
entity . . . as we're going through life, we're trying to remove
the layers to get to that entity. I feel in a way that's kind of
what's happened to me. I've always been this person, this
Rachel, yet there's been always layers and obstacles to that
person, but I've always sensed it and maybe through my two
years, double layers have dissolved and I'm kind of reaching
more the essence of myself.

Waste Products: Eliminating Outmoded Patterns

Waste products were formulated as patterns that had been subjected to
or targeted for change. They included outmoded ways of thinking and being, resistance to change, and old, ineffective habits. Discarding these waste
products was seen as an important part of the work of the KM learning
community.

Margaret: I know now the difference between when I'm in a drama
queen period in my life making a big fuss over nothing . . .
I'm starting to clear that away . . . That's something that
stopped being fun. I didn't gain anything from that except
self-destruction.

Discarding outmoded patterns formed a space for more adaptive ways to
take root.

George: . . . By nature I've never been the type of person that thought
about asking for help . . . I've always felt like I'll figure it
out . . . I can do this. I can manage this. And, one thing I
learned from my affiliations with the cohort is that it's not
only smart to ask for help, it helps both people when you

ask for help. So, I've become much more comfortable with saying I really don't understand this or I really have no clue what's going on but I'm gonna net with some people and figure it out. And, that's something I've taken to doing at work as well, and I found it to be pretty effective.

Networks of Chemical Reactions: Transformational Webs of Relationships

Networks are the basic patterns of organization in living systems. They are functional in enacting nonmaterial, nonlinear patterns of relationships between various processes. A key characteristic of human CAS is that living networks are self-generating and form the basis of more systemic social interaction. They continually create, and recreate, themselves by transforming or replacing components. They undergo recurrent structural changes while preserving their web-like pattern of organization (Capra, 1996). Within this KM learning community, networks took three forms. One was engaging with the community as a collective.

> **M:** Are there some interactions... in your cohort that helped you go through the change that you went through?
> **Margaret:** I would say that it's more the cohort as a cohort; in many ways, every individual did help me but it is more the group as a group.

As well, members formed formal teams in order to carry out set tasks or projects as part of the knowledge management focus of the LC. The pattern of organization within these networks both reproduced the patterns of the larger community and infused patterns into the KM learning community.

> **George:** Although we were separated into subgroups, I believe that the process that each group went through mirrored the effect of the big group.
> **Rachel:** I definitely noticed that people had dyadic relationships and I think openness was created a lot of times in pairs. And, I'm wondering whether that rippled into the LC...

Finally, more loosely formed nodes based on perceived need, affinity, and benefits to the KM task were formed.

> **George:** ... One of the informal groups that formed was a handful of us who come from out-of-town, so we would be there for the weekend, and usually go out and have dinner and a drink or something together. And those types of sessions where you

> just get together informally and talk about the day's work
> and what you were working on, that type of thing...

These three kinds of relationship patterns created a dense web of reciprocal relations, both cognitive and affective, interconnecting all members.
These networks and nodes generated knowledge as unanticipated, emergent phenomena, and embodied this complex adaptive system's patterns
of organization.

Relational Patterns that Inhibit or Enhance Complexity

Though the metabolic dimensions were always present, they did not necessarily result in relational patterns that enhanced complexity. Some emotions and dynamics (fear, avoidance of conflict, and emotional or relational
distancing) created patterns that blocked the efficient conversion of potential energy to kinetic energy in the service of knowledge production. These
configurations led to states of ossification, stasis, and predictability of the
KM learning community. Other emotions (commitment and a willingness
to engage in conflict) created a patterning that enhanced the conversion of
potential energy into distributed knowing.

Patterns Inhibiting Complexity

In this KM learning community, social interaction did not always produce growth. Instead, the community sometimes displayed processes that
reflected the state of the system as moving towards rigidity. In turn, these
processes resulted in social interactions that emphasized protection from
fear, which resulted in system atrophy.

> **M:** Say more about messy.
> **HB:** Not being open, not being able to deal with conflicts....It
> starts off tentative, and then as we get more knowledge, and
> knowledge of each other, more trust, we start getting to the
> areas where people aren't being heard, people are with-
> drawn, and we start to get more into the issues....I think
> the messy part is when we don't deal with that, because it
> ends up derailing.

Fear resulted in missed opportunities for learning and was a fundamental dynamic that promoted calculated deliberation and facades. This then
reduced the spontaneity, honesty, and effectiveness of the feedback loops
within the relationships and the networks.

> **Rachel:** I think people, myself, were fearful, and . . . I think that's
> what hindered . . . the sensation of fear and what fear en-
> tails. . . .
> **HB:** I guess the issue of being open about what was missing in
> the group. About what didn't feel completely authentic in
> the relationships between individuals . . . why we weren't de-
> claring ourselves, why we weren't willing to be in conflictual
> relationships . . .

An inability to effectively work through conflict was the most often-cited dynamic that lead to a decrease in the system's generativity and adaptability.

> **M:** So, would you say conflict was avoided?
> **George:** . . . For most of the first year, yes. Unless someone was able
> to put some structure around it . . . it was avoided. So rather
> than just dialogue, we'd make three different lists and find
> out which one people want the most . . . that type of thing.
> **M:** And then what would happen with the diverging opinions?
> **George:** They just get cast off. . . . It was just, "Let's just find out which
> one we think will work and go with that." And a lot of time
> what we'd do is just go round and round in circles until
> people got tired of it. And all they'd want to do is end it and
> go home for the night. It would get solved through default.

As well, being involved in faux-intellectual discussions as a substitute for engaging with salient issues (i.e., relational distancing) allowed the KM learning community to distance itself from the here-and-now, and this promoted
scripted facades.

> **Margaret:** The last community session . . . instead of talking about gen-
> der in the group, we started to talk gender at work . . . and
> it's only after that one member of the cohort said, "We never
> cleared that thing out. We never talked about gender." And I
> think that was part of the struggle, gender, and not wanting
> to talk about it.

Patterns Enhancing Complexity

These patterns refer to interactional processes that promoted complexity
and self-organization: risk taking, improvisation, emergence, spontaneity, and
interdependence. These characteristics, unlike those previously discussed, allowed the members of the KM learning community to seize and capitalize on
opportunities for learning. Thus, knowledge production became inextricably
linked to life within the community (Maturana & Varela, 1987).

Rachel: . . . There was a task that we needed to see fulfilled as far as presenting our year to the cohort, and because of all that we learned up to that point, we were really finally applying what we were learning . . . And we were creative, and spontaneous, and people let go. . . . I let go of certain fears, and whatever expectations, and if didn't work out . . . I just had confidence that it was going to. The LC was functioning itself, on its own with our interdependent energy; it became effective on its own.

Authentic emotional engagement emerging during times of spontaneous improvised dialogue became the way in which community members built relational and systemic connectivity. This connectivity enhanced the system's ability to reorganize itself in times of perturbation in such a way as to further augment the connectivity within the nodes and networks. The most often-cited example of a process that promoted complexity was the use of collective reflection and dialogue as a means to engage with conflict.

M: Tell me about a specific time when you thought the LC was most effective?

George: . . . We self-organized a discussion dealing with our effectiveness as a group.

M: What was happening at that time?

George: This came as a result of a conflict around values, vis-à-vis the role of a consultant. We had quite a blow up . . . and decided to do something about it. . . .

In the face of patterns that supported predictability and atrophy, risk-taking played a key role in dismantling the ossifying configurations.

M: What are some of the things that helped the LC develop?

HB: Individuals who took risks, started to disclose concerns that they had with the way the community was working . . .

Nonlinear Dynamics

Interactions in complex systems are characterized by nonlinear dynamics (Cilliers, 1998). Nonlinearity refers to the principle that the whole is not necessarily equal to the sum of its parts. Dissipative nonlinear dynamic systems are capable of exhibiting self-organization and chaos, illustrating the close interplay of structure and flow/change. As well, nonlinearity is a process in which a relatively small change can lead to significantly different system states (Human-Vogel & Brown, 2005). Since small changes are amplified as they feed back on each other, this produces complex patterns of unanticipated consequences that make it impossible to predict long-term behavior (Linds, 2006).

> **George:** I am not so sure that there is formula as to how it works. Each group will evolve according to its reason for being. I do believe that a learning community must evolve of its own accord; it cannot be mandated or established according to a predetermined plan.

In this KM learning community, nonlinear dynamics were promoted in various ways: historical patterns, intentional tinkering into structural and relational configurations, the adoption of facilitative roles, and the creation of open spaces of possibilities. This allowed the community to reconfigure itself and permitted the KM learning community to operate on the edge of chaos. Furthermore, nonlinear dynamics extended beyond the boundaries of the KM learning community and rippled out into other CASs.

Historical Patterns

Complex systems have a history. They not only evolve through time, but their past is co-responsible for present behavior (Cilliers, 1998). Patterns of human interaction produce further patterns of interaction (Stacey & Griffin, 2005). History can also include practices incorporated into the KM learning community's patterns of relating, embodied knowledge within the networks and nodes (Espejo, 2003), and a series of the system's structural changes (Maturana, 1987). This KM learning community evolved historically in that its past, both its history and prior experience, was added onto its patterns of relating; this shaped the community's possible trajectories.

> **HB:** Everything that we've done has been cumulative. So, we wouldn't have gone there if there wouldn't have been frustration over feeling heard, or frustration over perceptions of how much influence or how much power we had. The trigger to that particular expression of dissent was the outcome of everything else that we'd gone through. But that particular statement... precipitated where we went with it. And what we've done since...

The subsequent evolution of the community depended upon the critical choices its members made around which pattern to reorganize the KM learning community (Mitleton-Kelly, 2003).

Intentional Tinkering

Interventions by members of the community demonstrated the intentional performance of an action designed to perturb, influence, or shape the community. Those interactions that were performed with the intention of furthering knowledge production and learning resulted in opening up spaces of possibility (Fenwick, 2004). The KM learning community displayed the properties of a dissipative structure, in that it was an open system capable of operating far from equilibrium. As well, it was capable of self-reorganizing to higher levels of order. Intentional tinkering served to activate the fluctuating states of chaos and order within the system.

> **Margaret:** We know where we wanted to go ... But, how to get there is a very big challenge for us because we're inventing as we go along. We don't have models; we just know that we want a certain way.

In particular, the community used the structural process of self-assessment of its patterns and effectiveness as an opportunity to exercise intentional tinkering.

> **Rachel:** I believe what helped was that each individual had to decide that they were there, and present, and wanted to be part of the community. For whatever reason ... some people were very there and present and willing to make it happen.

As will be discussed later, dynamic self-assessment provided an historical structure that would activate chaos and promote higher levels of organization.

Roles

Certain facilitative roles (Fenwick, 2004) fulfilled by members of the community tended to promote intentional tinkering. The most common roles observed were: the noisemaker, the interpreter, the mapmaker, and the facilitator. The *noisemaker* either observed disturbances or planned them. He or she would amplify these perturbations by highlighting contradictions and silences or by encouraging members to experiment with different paths to see where they might lead.

> **Rachel:** Lots of time people would say that I sometimes made them upset and angry but they would go back to it later and felt that I was not right, but that it was kind of an interesting thing to do and as a result they realized that it would just push them into a learning curve sometimes.

This role created opportunities for the KM learning community to experience disequilibrium. Depending upon the structural choices of the community, disequilibrium could produce open spaces of possibility resulting in new knowledge and more effective levels of organization.

The *interpreter* assisted individuals to name what was unfolding around and inside of them. Frequently this took the form of observing and naming in the moment dynamics and patterns that promoted ossification and stasis, thus strangling emerging possibilities.

> **Margaret:** Somebody else in the group took the leadership at that point, saying, "Whoa, we're swirling. Let's stop doing that."

The interpreter helped the KM learning community to transform outmoded patterns of behavior and eliminate them as waste products.

The *mapmaker* traced and created meaningful cognitive and social interactions within the community and the networks. He or she would help members make communal sense of the patterns emerging among the complex networks. In essence, this role functioned like a historian, highlighting patterns of effective relating, webs of embodied knowledge, and useful structures. As well, this role could amplify generative disturbances by drawing attention to the possibilities these create, and help divert patterns that may create undesirable conditions, unsafe spaces, or power inequities (Fenwick, 2004).

> **HB:** I've been able to help out there . . . basically to ask perhaps some uncomfortable questions. Start a thought process. . . .
> **M:** You got good feedback about that?
> **HB:** Yes.

The *facilitator* helped the community navigate through disequilibrium it experienced. He or she helped the KM learning community members to forestall the impulse to predict, contain, and control social interactions and to remain more flexible and adaptable, in order to work through disequilibrium creatively.

> **Margaret:** There's one who has the power of wisdom. Every time he talks people . . . things change when he speaks because it's so appropriate and so wise and so calming. . . .

This role allowed the community to experiment with different patterns of relating and to be courageous and inventive in its experimentation.

The community saw these roles as fundamental to the process of becoming an effective KM learning community. However, it was not just the role itself that encouraged complexity. An important element was the way in which the role was enacted. The values that functioned as sources of energy for the social interactions informed the enactment of the role. Especially salient was the value of presence, that crisp awareness of one's current process and a willingness to be met and known. Presence was the subjective measure of an individual's emotional sense that he or she was a part of an environment.

> **George:** My role was like that of anyone in the group... be open, listen, respond...

Bifurcation: Open Spaces of Possibility

Bifurcation in a complex system occurs when a system destabilizes temporarily and subsequently evolves to a higher form of self-organization. Bifurcations are necessary since systems would be unable to self-organize without them (Human-Vogel & Brown, 2005); in addition, bifurcations become the birthplace of emergent nondeterministic possibilities.

> **Rachel:** I think it really comes down to the community making that time available for itself... creating that space for things to happen.

Intentional tinkering became the initiator of bifurcated openings. Sustained collective dialogue held open spaces for the coherent movement of explicit and tacit knowledge (Stevenson & Hamilton, 2001). These open spaces were times of reflective self-examination and conversation. They created opportunities for experimentation with alternate structures or relational patterns and allowed future possibilities to emerge (Espejo, 2003).

> **M:** Tell me about a specific time...
>
> **George:** Easy, when we had to self-organize into groups [for a project]. A melee ensued. This represented a confluence of issues: values, task vs. process, inter-group relationships... a whole stew of conflict-laden issues. It was cathartic, though, in that it triggered a good dialogue about the issues at hand.... It was a necessary event....

Knowing evolved through the creation and recreation of the KM learning community as a result of the choices offered by the open spaces of possibility. A key factor in the creation and selection of these choices were the individual CAS within the KM learning community.

Rachel: I've opened up myself more. I feel more grounded, so I think the first thing that changed is the relationship I have with myself which ultimately has changed the relationship I have with others... how I moderate my impact on others, and how I can now have a sense of how others are impacting me and then I can really kind of sense how I'd like to respond or not respond.

Ripple Effects

Knowledge cannot be contained in any one dimension of a system, for knowledge is forever spilling into other systems (Fenwick, 2004). In this KM learning community, this rippling was apparent; the perturbations experienced in the community extended to other CAS outside its boundaries, accentuating their blurred nature.

George: The first thing that comes to mind is who I've become is someone who's interested in continuing to become the best that he can be.

M: And that's different from before?

George: Well it's different in that I was, before, being somewhat complacent. I'd achieve a certain position at work and... I didn't have the same aspirations that I do now, and my aspirations are not necessarily focused on my job. They're about how do I contribute more to the world around me.

The greater the interdependence of the members of the community, the wider the disturbance of the perturbation is felt. Knowledge generated in the KM learning community became available to and shared with other CASs, spreading tendrils of distributed cognition throughout the systems (Mitleton-Kelly, 2003).

HB: If as a result of my being in the LC I acquire new skills, and new ways of behaving, then people I come into contact with also have the benefits of those. So there're benefits for the people that I interact with, benefits for the people that other members of the community interact with... and something that I've observed at work... being more aware of different learning styles, communication styles has resulted in a greater level of comprehension around what we are trying to accomplish at work with projects that I lead; it has also led to exploring different phases of organizing around tasks.

DYNAMIC ASSESSMENT

Dynamic assessment has two underlying assumptions: (1) Human learners are open systems and (2) The purpose of assessment is capacity development (Elliott, 2000; Greenberg, 2000; Lidz, 1997). It presupposes that substantive changes can occur if feedback is provided across an array of increasingly complex tasks (Swanson & Lussier, 2001). This standpoint makes dynamic assessment compatible with a complexity perspective. Dynamic assessment allows for multiple opportunities to demonstrate competence in several contexts across network cultures and it can facilitate the novice-expert transition (Jenson, 2000).

Within this context, reiterative dynamic self-assessment focused on the learning community as an effective KM system. It examined knowledge acquisition as a reciprocal co-implicating process at the system level, an approach that privileged community knowledge. Since dynamic self-assessment was ongoing and recursive in this KM learning community, it reproduced the dynamics of workplace learning. It allowed individuals the opportunity to shape the community to their self-identified objectives; in turn, it made space for the community to shape effective KM practices.

Community Self-Assessment

The HSI cohort was introduced to the activity of self-assessment early in year 1. Community members were presented with various models of assessment, including the framework of dynamic assessment. The KM learning community was then offered the challenge of performing ongoing dynamic self-assessments of its progress and potential. The community undertook the task to map out its path of evolution, to identify what it needed to become a more effective KM learning community, and to implement interventions and actions that would enhance its development. The cohort used the Five Disciplines (Senge, Roberts, Ross, Smith, & Kleiner, 1994) as criteria for self-assessment: shared vision, personal mastery, team learning, systems thinking, and mental models. These five dimensional criteria were deemed essential elements of systems that can truly learn and create knowledge (Senge, 1990). They were considered comparable to dimensions for assessing the development of organizations (Patton, 1999). The KM learning community continually defined and redefined what these dimensions meant in terms of its own unique context.

Catalytic Impact of Assessment

A living organism is an open system whose overall structure is maintained in spite of ongoing flow and changes of components (Capra, 2005). Reiterative dynamic assessment became the structural means for this KM learning community to hover at the edge of chaos. However, creating chaos was not about creating unpredictable situations in which members were challenged beyond their means (Human-Vogel & Brown, 2005); it was about creating open spaces of possibilities and bifurcation points. During the times of self-assessment, intentional tinkering became purposeful. Self-assessment was a way for the community to exchange energy, matter, and information with its environment. As well, it allowed the KM learning community to become a dissipative structure providing opportunities for self-reorganization.

> **George:** The figural event for me was the weekend that we spent with R and G. . . .
> **M:** What was happening at that time?
> **George:** We talked about leadership, gender, age groups . . . it was a big event and spawned much after class interaction.

Being a dissipative structure pushed the KM learning community into a state far from equilibrium; it permitted the creation of new emergent structures, patterns, and mental models. The assessment–dissolving–reorganization cycle illustrated the close interplay between order and chaos. The farther from equilibrium the LC was, the greater the complexity and the higher the degree of nonlinearity (Capra, 2005).

> **Rachel:** . . . What made it into a working LC? I think it was bringing it back to community. It was when we planned an intervention. We saw something that was happening and were like, "Oh my god, what the hell is happening?" And we would put it out there . . . an intervention in that community that would stop people in their tracks, and ask them to look at something in that time.

When two systems coincide, the perturbations of one system ripple into the other. Change occurs through disturbances amplified through the multiple, densely connected, overlapping feedback loops within and among the nodes and the networks of the CASs.

> **Rachel:** I will say that because what's happening in my LC now, I feel is somehow benefiting my work environment . . . How do I make that link? I have noted that different communities are

responding differently 'cause I'm different because of what's happening. . . .

As this KM learning community approached a state far from equilibrium, the waves of disequilibrium washed over both the KM learning community itself and the individual CASs. The resulting reorganization spawned a unity of action and identities that could not have been achieved independently by either (Fenwick, 2004). Knowledge existed in the interstices of this complex ecology.

> **Rachel:** I'm wondering whether it's around wholeness. . . . So maybe output exists in the process . . . it's like a higher sense of being. . . . It's actually having those questions that you didn't have before . . . simultaneity, where once you ask the question things change.

Dissipative structures do not necessarily effectively contain and transmute energy. If unconstrained, an excessive dissipation of energy could result in disorganization (Bradley & Pribram, 1996). Using the five disciplines as the criteria for the process of dynamic self-assessment focused this KM learning community's attention and created a loose guide to organize the concerted action during self-reorganization.

> **George:** Assessment was a participatory process where . . . we co-created a shared description or understanding of a moment in time. It was mutual, and equal.

These five criteria acted as constraints bounding the dissipation of energy and channeled that energy into high levels of order.

> **George:** If learning is construed as knowledge and behavioral change over time, then the community existed to support this activity. This included a public declaration of one's intent, supported by feedback. The community learned about itself through shared assessment and feedback.

In the KM learning community, reiterative dynamic self-assessment created explicit and intentional opportunities for the appearance of emergent properties generating synergy (Montuari & Purser, 1999). This was primarily achieved through language as feedback loops, to create, maintain, and transform conventions and structures by which the KM learning community constituted its life (Barrett, 1999). Moment-to-moment interactions happened through conversations in shared interactive spaces or structural networked contexts. Multisubjectivity was a key dimension that distinguished the dialogue and allowed dynamic self-assessment of the system to function as a feedback loop.

Reiterative dynamic self-assessment shaped an ambiguous problem space, which created and contained the disequilibrium needed for self-organization. Environments only trigger structural changes; they do not specify or direct them (Capra, 2002). Structural changes were directed by the tinkering prompted by the self-assessment resulting in nonlinear patterns of organization. "The most important aspect of information is whether its influence on behavior enhances the ability of the system using it to adapt. And this ability…is most likely to be enhanced if the information itself actually corresponds to the reality of the system's environment" (Firestone & McElroy, 2005, p. 197). Reiterative dynamic self-assessment provided such correspondence by selecting those processes that fit the environmental constraints in which the KM learning community lived and functioned. The space between monitoring and evaluating was the point at which matches and mismatches were identified, and subjected to intentional tinkering.

CONCLUSION

There is a general but ingrained assumption that all learning is a deliberate activity and can, therefore, be planned and achieved. In reality, learning is also spontaneous, unsystematic, and unintentional (Huysman, 1999). Examination of this case illustrates that unexpected, powerful knowledge was created, not just by specifying knowledge targets, but also by creating emergence. The KM learning community underwent recurrent structural changes, prompted by reiterative dynamic self-assessment, public reflection, and dialogue while preserving its web-like pattern of organization. The components of the network continually produced and transformed one another by self-renewal and the creation of new structures and connections. These components altered the future behavior of the community itself and of its individual members. By providing spaces of emergent possibilities, KM learning communities can tap into improvised, spontaneous knowledge opportunities.

Additionally, achievement curves in self-organizing KM systems do not increase over time. Rather they are characterized by phase transitions (Stadler, Vetter, Haynes, & Kruse, 1996): linear increasing (cognition is optimized and structures are transferred into performance), stagnation (learning plateaus), and significant sudden improvements (critical fluctuations caused by structural destabilization and re-assembly into a higher state of order). This progression suggests that it is important in KM learning communities to allow members, nodes, and networks to find their own self-organized rhythm. This also includes the explicit permission to make mistakes, since these may produce an unexpected nonlinear result with significant ripples.

To survive and thrive, a KM learning community needs to explore its spaces of possibilities and generate variety in terms of knowledge, solutions, and relational patterns. The search for a single and optimum strategy is neither possible nor desirable. Any strategy can be optimum only under certain conditions for limited periods of time. When those conditions change, the strategy may no longer be optimal (Mitleton-Kelly, 2003). Feedback processes can produce complex patterns of reactions, where one aspect of feedback has a compounding influence on the next iteration. Within this KM learning community the feedback structures of reiterative self-assessment, public reflection, and dialogue, allowed entity and medium to merge: members of the community were both inside the community as constituents, and outside the community as observers and input formulators, providing feedback on its "adequate conduct" (Maturana, 1987). This process allowed KM learning community members to both plan and learn in a co-implicating dynamic. In essence, encouraging a LC to reiteratively self-assess unites creator and creation.

Reiterative dynamic self-assessment allowed the KM learning community to engage in a collective and explicit community building–destroying–rebuilding process, moving from pseudo-community through chaos into real community, hovering in the creation space at the edge of chaos (Stevenson & Hamilton, 2001). As individuals engage in dialogue with the world and with each other through behavior, relationships, and conversations, they continually create spaces of possibility, the metaxic in-between (Linds, 2006). This in-between is not empty but alive with energy and opportunity for (re)creation.

> **HB:** . . . Every time we get together . . . every time we have a conversation . . . every time we work with other people, and help them work on something they want to work on and support their learning and ability to feel free to express themselves, the community gets stronger and stronger. Every interaction, one day at a time . . . So, was it bad, yeah; is it better, yeah; will it get better yet, yeah . . . it's just ongoing.

NOTES

1. Though the authors acknowledge that these two types of communities can differ significantly, within this chapter, these terms are used interchangeably.

2. This is the collectively created and shared understanding constructed by community members who are working on a KM task with multiple and differential levels of understanding and expertise. Multisubjectivity is an important component of self-regulation and self-organization.
3. All participants are identified by pseudonyms.

ACKNOWLEDGMENT

This research was supported through a grant from the Faculty Research Development Program of Concordia University, Montreal, Quebec, Canada.

REFERENCES

Agar, M. (1999). Complexity theory: An exploration and overview based on John Holland's work. *Field Methods, 11*(2), 99–120.

Argyris, C. (1993). *Knowledge for action.* Hoboken, NJ: Jossey-Bass.

Arthur, M., Defillippi, R. & Lindsay, V. (2004). Careers, communities, and complexity theory. In P. Andriani & G. Passiante (Eds.), *Complexity theory and the management of networks* (pp. 155–162). Singapore: World Scientific Publishing Company.

Barrett, F. (1999). Knowledge creating as dialogic accomplishment: A constructivist perspective. In A. Montuari & R. Purser (Eds.), *Social creativity: Vol. 1* (pp. 133–151). Cresskill, NJ: Hampton Press.

Blackman, D. & Henderson, S. (2005). Know ways in knowledge management. *The Learning Organization, 12*(2), 152–168.

Bohm, D. (1996). *On dialogue* (L. Nichol, Ed.). London: Routledge.

Bradley, R. & Pribram, K. (1996). Self-organization and the social collective. In K. Pribram & J. King (Eds.), *Learning as self-organization* (pp. 479–506). Mahwah, NJ: Lawrence Erlbaum Associates.

Capra, F. (1996). *The web of life: A new scientific understanding of living systems.* New York: Anchor.

Capra, F. (2002). *The hidden connections: Integrating the biological, cognitive, and social dimensions of life into a science of sustainability.* New York: Doubleday.

Capra, F. (2005, October). Complexity and life. *Theory, Culture, and Society, 22,* 33–44.

Cilliers, P. (1998). *Complexity and postmodernism: Understanding complex systems.* London: Routledge.

Cilliers, P. (2004). A framework for understanding complex systems. In P. Andriani & G. Passiante (Eds.), *Complexity theory and the management of networks* (pp. 23–27). Singapore: World Scientific.

Desouza, K. & Hensgen, T. (2005). *Managing information in complex organizations: Semiotics and signals, complexity and chaos.* Armonk, NY: M.E. Sharpe.

Earl, M. (2001). Knowledge management strategies: Toward a taxonomy. *Journal of Management Information Systems, 18,* 215–233.

Easterby-Smith, M. & Araujo, L. (1999). Organizational learning: Current debates and opportunities. In M. Easterby-Smith, L. Araujo & J. Burgoyne (Eds.), *Organizational learning and the learning organization* (pp. 1–21). London: Sage.

Elliott, J. (2000). Dynamic assessments in educational contexts: Purpose and promise. In C. Lidz & J. Elliott (Eds.), *Dynamic assessment: Prevailing models and applications* (pp. 713–740). Greenwich, CT: JAI Press.

Espejo, R. (2003). Social systems and the embodiment of organisational learning. In E. Mitleton-Kelly (Ed.), *Complex systems and evolutionary perspectives on organisations: The application of complexity theory to organizations* (pp. 53–69). Oxford: Pergamon.

Fenwick, T. (2004). Learning in complexity: Work and knowledge in enterprise cultures. In P. Kell, S. Shore, & M. Singh (Eds.), *Adult education @21st century* (pp. 253–267). New York: Peter Lang Publishing.

Firestone, J. & McElroy, M. (2005). Doing knowledge management. *The Learning Organization, 12*(2), 189–212.

Germain, R., Dröge, C. & Christensen, W. (2001, July). The mediating role of operations knowledge in the relationship of context with performance. *Journal of Operations Management, 19*, 453–469.

Gorelick, C. & Tantawy-Monsou, B. (2005). For performance through learning, knowledge management is the critical practice. *The Learning Organization, 12*(2), 125–139.

Greenberg, K. (2000). Inside professional practice: A collaborative systems orientation to linking dynamic assessment and intervention. In C. Lidz & J. Elliott (Eds.), *Dynamic assessment: Prevailing models and applications* (pp.489–519). Greenwich, CT: JAI Press.

Habermas, J. (1971). *Knowledge and human interests.* (J. Shapiro, Trans.). Boston: Beacon Press.

Hofer, B. & Pintrich, P. (1997). The development of epistemological theories: Beliefs about knowledge and knowing and their relation to learning. *Review of Educational Research, 67*, 88–140.

Holland, J. (1996). *Hidden order: How adaptation builds complexity.* New York: Basic Books.

Human-Vogel, S. & Brown, C. (2005). Creating a complex learning environment for the mediation of knowledge construction in diverse educational settings. *South African Journal of Education, 25*(4), 229–238.

Huysman, M. (1999). Balancing biases: A critical review of the literature on organizational learning. In M. Easterby-Smith, L. Araujo & J. Burgoyne (Eds.), *Organizational learning and the learning organization* (pp. 59–74). London: Sage.

Jenson, M. (2000). The mind ladder model: Using dynamic assessment to help students learn to assemble and use knowledge. In C. Lidz & J. Elliott (Eds.), *Dynamic assessment: Prevailing models and applications* (pp.187–227). Greenwich, CT: JAI Press.

Kvale, S. (1996). *InterViews: An introduction to qualitative research interviewing.* Thousand Oaks, CA: Sage.

Lidz, C. (1997). Dynamic assessment approaches. In D. Flanagan, J. Genshaft & P. Harrison (Eds.), *Contemporary intellectual assessment: Theories, tests, and issues* (pp. 281–296). New York: Guilford Press.

Linds, W. (2006). Metaxis: Dancing (in) the in-between. In J. Cohen-Cruz & M. Schutzman (Eds.), *A Boal companion: Dialogue on theatre and cultural politics* (pp. 114–124). London: Routledge.

Maturana, H. (1987). Everything is said by an observer. In W. Thompson (Ed.), *Gaia: A way of knowing* (pp. 65–82). Hudson, NY: Lindisfarne Press.

Maturana, H. & Varela, F. (1987). *The tree of knowledge.* Boston: Shambhala.

McElroy, M. (2000). Integrating complexity theory, knowledge management and organizational learning. *Journal of Knowledge Management, 4*(3), 195–203.

Miles, M. & Huberman, M. (1994). *An expanded sourcebook: Qualitative data analysis* (2nd ed.). Thousand Oaks, CA: Sage.

Mitleton-Kelly, E. (2003). Ten principles of complexity and enabling infrastructures. In E. Mitleton-Kelly (Ed.), *Complex systems and evolutionary perspectives on organisations: The application of complexity theory to organisations* (pp. 23–50). Oxford: Pergamon.

Montuari, A. & Purser, R. (1999). Social creativity: Introduction. In A. Montuari & R. Purser (Eds.), *Social creativity: Vol. 1* (pp. 1–45). Cresskill, NJ: Hampton Press.

Patton, M. (1999). Organizational development and evaluation. *The Canadian Journal of Program Evaluation, 14*, 93–113.

Raelin, J. (2000). *Work-based learning: The new frontier of management development.* Reading, MA: Addison-Wesley.

Reilly, R. C. (2005). *The synergistic confluence of social creativity, values and the development of shared expertise,* Unpublished doctoral dissertation, McGill University, Montreal.

Resnick, L. (1991). Shared cognition: Thinking as social practice. In L. Resnick, J. Levine & S. Teasley (Eds.), *Perspectives on socially shared cognition* (pp. 1–20). Washington, DC: American Psychological Association.

Richardson, L. (1994). Writing: A method of inquiry. In N. Denzin & Y. Lincoln (Eds.), *Handbook of qualitative research* (pp. 516–529). Thousand Oaks, CA: Sage.

Senge, P. (1990). *The fifth discipline: The art and practice of the learning organization.* New York: Doubleday Business.

Senge, P., Roberts, C., Ross, R., Smith, B. & Kleiner, A. (1994). *The fifth discipline fieldbook: Strategies and tools for building a learning organization.* New York: Doubleday Business.

Stacey, R. & Griffin, D. (2005). Introduction: Researching organizations from a complexity perspective. In R. Stacey & D. Griffin (Eds.), *A complexity perspective on researching organizations: Taking experience seriously* (pp. 1–12). London: Routledge.

Stadler, M., Vetter, G., Haynes, J. & Kruse, P. (1996). Nonlinear phenomena in learning processes. In K. Pribram & J. King (Eds.), *Learning as self-organization* (pp. 157–169). Mahwah, NJ: Lawrence Erlbaum Associates.

Stevenson, B. & Hamilton, M. (2001). How does complexity inform community, How does community inform complexity? *Emergence, 3*(2), 57–77.

Stake, R. (1994). Case studies. In N. Denzin & Y. Lincoln (Eds.), *Handbook of qualitative research* (pp. 236–247). Thousand Oaks, CA: Sage.

Swanson, H. L. & Lussier, C. (2001). A selective synthesis of the experimental literature on dynamic assessment. *Review of Educational Research, 71*, 321–363.

Tseng, S-M. (2008, January). Knowledge management system performance measure index. *Expert Systems with Applications, 34,* 734–745.

Vygotsky, L. (1987). *Thought and language.* (A. Kozulin, Ed.). Cambridge, MA: MIT Press.

Wenger, E. & Snyder, W. (2000, January–February). Communities of practice: The organizational frontier. *Harvard Business Review,* 139–145.

CHAPTER 15

SYSTEM DYNAMICS SUPPORTING COMPLEXITY MANAGEMENT

Case Studies from a Small Economy within an Economic Integration Environment

Stanislava Mildeova

INTRODUCTION

Complexity is still an open question in theory and managerial practice. Since the transitional economic system is the main focus of interest, this topic is analyzed from the viewpoint of the current turbulent economic situation in post-communist countries, of which the Czech Republic is one.

The Czech Republic is one of the new member states of the EU, and is one of the strongest ones in the new member states group. This seems to be very important, reflecting the deep changes connected with the membership of the CR in the EU, and the functioning of the internal market as a new challenging environment for the economy (Mildeova & Nemcova, 2005):

Complexity and Knowledge Management, pages 267–283
Copyright © 2010 by Information Age Publishing
All rights of reproduction in any form reserved.

- Globalization brings with it a large increase of interactions
- The number of unstable and disturbing effects in the competitive environment rises
- Time urgency gets into the foreground
- randomness and uncertainty increase
- The risk of wrong decision-making threatens more than ever before
- The complexity of the decision-making problem grows
- Regularity and predictability decrease

It is important that the Czech economy is a very small, open economy and so it is inter-related in a very complex manner to surrounding economies. Concerning import and export it is typical that modern ITC contributes to a significant acceleration in the flow of information. In this current highly complex business environment, there are less constants or predictable states. The product life cycles change in such a way that we can problematically predict them based on their past form. Also, the future structure and nature of the competition can be estimated only with extreme difficulties and sufficient probability. In the context of this changing environment, the decision-makers require efficient support, such as a tool which allows us to work up through specific problems in systems with height complexity. The growing complexity necessitates the application of modern approaches, including systems theories as well, in order to understand behavior in complicated situations (Cancer, 2006). It is useful to provide some kind of system detachment and information on how System Dynamics helps in solving complex problems, mainly with respect to the gathering of new knowledge.

System Dynamics (SD) is a methodology (the servomechanic thread) with foundations already laid down by J.W. Forrester in the early sixties (Forrester, 1961). However, in the Czech Republic it is a relatively young, newly developing field (Mildeova & Vojtko, 2005). It is a discipline that aids our better understanding of surrounding systems. Model building and simulation are at the core of SD. It is especially useful for analyzing systems with a high amount of detail and dynamic complexity, such as any complex social systems. An organization is a typical example of a complex social system.

This chapter builds on empiric research,[1] where all Czech companies were approached in 2005–2006, and on a survey[2] from 2006–2007 within companies already using SD models, and first of all on the briefings with system consultants implementing SD models in the country.

SYSTEM DYNAMICS CASE STUDIES

Model Building in Profit Making Companies

The management of organizations is not only a theory, but also a way of thinking (Senge, 1990), and first and foremost a practice, the aim of which is to assist companies in further development or survival. For this purpose a number of SD models were created and applied in major Czech businesses. Dynamics methodology is used here as a discipline, which can help in solving concrete problem situations, and is able to work through specific problems in a system with dynamics complexity. We sort them according to the branches (in NACE EU codes), in which they work:

D .0.00—Manufacturing:
- A major Czech automotive supplier, created an enormous five-dimensional model of logistics and finance, which simulates the space usage depending on the variability of production.
- The largest Czech producer of white goods with large export activities was using a SD model to solve the problem of dynamic cash flow and simulation of the production process. Part of the model was also the modeling of foreign market sales.
- One company, a traditional producer of inorganic chemical products that are mostly for export, is currently training employees for the model of the production process.
- The creation of the production model was also needed for a distillery's production of brand liqueurs. The model allows a simulation of real production conditions, and test reactions for a "virtual" production process.
- For one of the world's major producers of machine tools, a dynamic company model of the whole company's operation with the purpose of evaluating the company strategy, was the first step in the preparation for the implementation of the dynamic Balanced Scorecard.

I .64.20—Telecommunications
- This was a behavioral model of the telecommunication market, for a forerunning telecommunication company, a model of all company operations and a model for the support of strategic planning—for billing, product pricing, and the verification of the profitability of customer "packages."

- In order to evaluate employees, and in the approach towards customer satisfaction, the application of a SD model in a mobile network provider was used. Currently the company is also testing dynamic models of its shops.

M .0.00—Education

- For supporting the business strategy and finding critical limits of growth for a language school to predict cash flow, SD methodologies were used. The dynamic model simulates cash flow under given parameters, and changes this prediction based on changes in the business environment parameters.

G .0.00—Wholesale and retail trade; repair of motor vehicles, motorcycles and personal and household goods

- Modeling the distribution chain was implemented for the development strategy of a Slovak company (the Slovak Republic was connected with the Czech Republic until 1993). A model with approximately 2000 components was developed (as a sub delivery for IBM) for the need of evaluating the cash flow, project return, personnel needs, and verification of further financing.

J .0.00—Financial intermediation

- SD principles were used to create a model of price trends of rents. The rent of housing units has been a big socioeconomic and political issue in the Czech Republic for a long time, and a new law concerning one-sided rent increase should bring clearer understanding.

K .74.00–Other business activities

- A knowledge-based company built a dynamic model including the learning organization concept.

The first firms to implement SD models were a producer of vegetable oils and toilet soaps, a telecommunications firm, and a producer of plastics and construction chemistry supplies. SD principles were further used in a food-solutions company, in a Czech brewery, in a petrochemical company, and in a producer of metal parts.

Model Building in Non-Profit Making Companies

This chapter focuses primarily on profit-making companies' corporate systems; it will be useful to list briefly some successful applications of SD models in non-profit organizations, such as public administration, the army, and the government. Highly complex problems found in business practice (Sterman, 2000) were also solved here—for example, looking for an optimal strategy, support for communication between stakeholders, personnel planning, the possibility of testing impacts of variable scenarios, or principles of sustainability, where holism comes up. Namely:

- Due to the complex nature of strategies in Czech regions, city management must develop systems thinking and "dynamic intuition." In a dynamic model the perspectives of Balanced Scorecard are applied. Learning is based on a strategic map, in which we find topics such as "coping with community scheduling," "maintenance of a favorable environment in the city council," and so on. Cities and eligible regions at the same time will learn how to measure unaffected, so-called soft factors (satisfaction, quality, etc.). The other purpose of this model is to test communication policy; the City Hall faces problems in communication and explaining some of its long-range goals (Kostron, Susta, & Lakomy, 2005).
- To support personnel decisions within the Czech Army, the Defense Department of the Czech Republic uses SD models of the labor market and personnel mobility to solve the problem of divided management between human and financial resources.
- A SD model was also created for NATO for the evaluation of inner and outer security risks.
- The model of the French economy with the link to carbon dioxide emissions was successfully tested in Czech conditions. In this way it is possible in specific dimensions to estimate the consequences of contemporary development in the area of ecology and to identify the consequences of different policies with the aim of preserving the situation towards sustainable development (Yamaguchi, 1997).

MANAGEMENT (BY COMPLEXITY)

Perspective Learning

The new international environment, and the related complexity and turbulence of the business environment, necessitates changes in managerial thinking (Richardson, 2005a). Managers' perceptions of how their organization operates are frequently drawn from fuzzy outputs of the empirically perceived processes inside the organization. Information presented to top managers—very often in the form of reports—is of an abstract nature; it is aggregated, averaged, and edited (Ulicna & Kacin, 2003). Therefore, during this process the really dynamic information is lost and the decision-making is conducted as if the organization had few dynamics, as if it worked linearly with a low level of internal dependencies (Seeley, 2003).

From survey evaluations it is clear that some managers in Czech managerial practice have a problem moving from the prevailing paradigm of thought that is based on the simple causality of observed processes, towards the system approach paradigm based on the principle of relating every cause to its impact and to every other cause with a feedback loop. If they are able to shift the approach from a simple causality to loop causality, from mutually independent factors to mutually dependent ones, the organizations could see the world as a lasting, mutually dependent self-supporting dynamic process. Managers can gain deep insight when observing a simulation that clearly shows the interdependencies (Mildeova, 2006). This can also change their ideas about how to improve the co-operation between "resources" (functional departments) and the subjects participating in supply chains. This is aided by the virtual form of learning in two loops, without being consciously recognized. It is interesting that on the basis of simulations, a change in understanding the connections and dependencies was shown at an operational level as well.

The premises of SD today leave their functionalistic beginnings, tied to epistemology, and move toward phenomenology to approaches close to interpretative and learning paradigms. Case studies from Czech practice prove that the SD concept moved from the hard end of the managerial disciplines to a much softer paradigm, and try to synthesize positivist tradition and interpretivist tradition. (Only two companies use purely deterministic models, where they are directly based on production technology.)

All required changes mentioned are not possible to implement without people and their development. The implementation of the model puts higher demands on the qualifications of these people (managers, analysts, other knowledge workers). Companies understand the simpler structures of the model, but for more advanced applications they need special training. Training was, for the most part, not a problem. In the Czech business environment a demand for IT knowledge is typical.

Management Complexity

Decision-making in economic integration frameworks is a complex activity, the recognition of the impact of firms' policies is very complicated. We can see clearly, in the case of the language school, a misunderstanding of dynamic complexity at management level. The relative simplicity of doing business in that field allows it a deep knowledge of the language school management. However, the management does not accept the fact that such a relatively simple system with basic characteristics of behavior can lead to very complex structures (because of feedback structures, delays, nonlinearities, and factors of uncertainty in this business field). Feedbacks could reflect these measures. These SD tools can cope better with the complexity, allowing the transferring of complexity into simpler schemes that help managers to find the correct solution for a present situation. The schemes can show principles of adverse situations and demonstrate the symptoms of problems. They decrease perceived complexity, make the study of complex firms systems easier, and provide a key to the understanding of the systems' structures, possibilities and limitations (Figure 15.1).

One advantage of SD-based models is the ability to enable computer models to reach a higher complexity and to cover a higher amount of simultaneous calculations than mental models—even though this is sometimes questioned (Richmond, 1993). Nevertheless it is undeniable, and our experience confirms that SD-based models can be useful for a quicker understanding of the possibilities, and for how the real system could behave (Mildeova, 2003). Alternatively, it may help in verifying what could perhaps happen if something in the model changed.

It is useful because managers feel that randomness and uncertainty have increased due to system changes of complex environments, connected with both *economic transition* and economic integration, and the number of uncertain factors that could influence business is nearly endless (government regulations, decisions of key politics makers, duties, taxes, competition, new technologies and innovation, market behavior, prices of energy, etc.). According to our research, some companies were not able to realize that the model also allows you to work with uncertainty using scenarios. (Factors of randomness and uncertainty are clear in situations with obvious outside influences and where the model works with techniques—for example, white noise—pink noise in the call center model of a mobile company.)

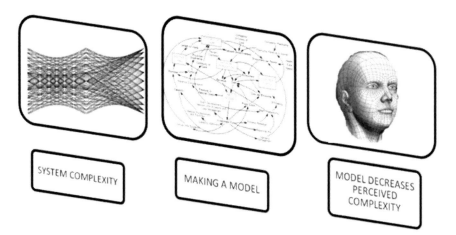

Figure 15.1 The reduction of the perceived complexity.

Management Methods

Our research shows that the majority of the firms are trying to apply some of the modern management methods; approximately only 8% of firms are using traditional management methods, follow rigid management hierarchy, or just use common sense. The main source of innovation in management is most frequently Knowledge Management and the implementation of international ISO standards. Leadership principles, Coaching and Quality Management (CQM) are not used by many companies. A trend that is becoming increasingly popular in Czech managerial practice is Process Management, the main advantage of which is quick adaptation to changing market conditions from the viewpoint of dynamic complexity.

But some managers refuse new ideas, new ways of thinking, and innovative methods of management, despite all the efforts and proclamations about implementing modern managerial trends. It seems that mental inertia still persists in managerial practice, and due to the tendency toward conservativeness, many managers lean toward a functional organizational structure even though the word "process" is very frequently used in management, and "process organization" is a marketing weapon. It is not systematic, although such an approach can sometimes work.

So-called alternative managerial concepts, such as reengineering, systems thinking, systems dynamics, soft approaches, and heuristics are used by relatively few firms. This analysis has to be related to the size of the firm (number of employees and turnover) and their market position. For example, SD is not being used by many firms (less than 2% of firms), but SD models dominate in certain industries.

Surveys show that firms using SD principles are using other innovative management methods as well. The simulation contributes to shifts in mental frameworks, which are the basis for changing procedures of process management. The simulation also contributes to the application of holistic system understanding in the development of business and decision-making. Those firms frequently combine multiple modern management styles, and consequently benefit from their synergic effects. If firms use SD, they consider this methodology as a modern management trend, and a factor for the development of a firm's knowledge management.

The question "What is the role of knowledge in the model building process, and what knowledge do simulations provide us with?" is the topic for the next section of this chapter.

KNOWLEDGE TRANSFER

The knowledge economy needs efficient support to contribute to the "building of knowledge" of the decision-makers. A lot of theoretical approaches to knowledge and knowledge management exist. Questions in the survey were put in the context of the currently prevailing understanding in the Czech Republic (Rosicky, 2006), which corresponds to theories according to Richardson (2005b). The research shows that the understanding of the term "knowledge" in Czech management practice is not clear. Similarly in firms where there are successful SD applications, the term *knowledge* is explained in different ways. Such variability corresponds to the objective nature of knowledge in the context of technologically designed knowledge applications, in comparison to the clearly subjective nature of knowledge in soft systems approaches. However, only some managers realize that a model is a synthesis of both these approaches.

In order to evaluate the role of SD models for knowledge formulation we can use the SECI model (Nonaka, 1994; Nonaka & Takeuchi, 1995; Mildeova & Klas, 2006) and follow this structure:

Socialization

The spiral of knowledge through as a continuous process of dynamic interactions between tacit and explicit knowledge starts with sharing tacit knowledge through face-to-face communication or shared experience.

Externalization

By repeatedly executing an action people gain skills, abilities, and knowledge based on this action. Such knowledge is often not documented; it is latent, and its holder is often not aware of having such knowledge. SD methodology could be used for the codification of tacit knowledge, stored as mental models or experiences in the brains of the people involved, into an explicit form expressed by the model. Czech businesses usually construct models for gaining information about the system behavior in specific conditions. The "side product" in the model creation stage was the externalization of knowledge, when knowledge changed from tacit to explicit form. All the described forms used the interview form during this rather difficult transfer process from an unexpressed to an expressed form. The consultant–modeler (the person leading the interview) needed to know the situation and internal and external environments *ex ante*.

Teamwork

Every effort was made by the system consultant (Proverbs, http://www.proverbs.cz) to use the teamwork model, where the strategy would be verified, and shared vision and team learning realized, this being the basic foundation of a learning organization. The team, depending on the purpose of the model, combines knowledge, experience, and the point of view of people from the same or different area, and the team connects knowledge, experience, and points of view with different expertise (e.g., of management, top managers, advisors, IT specialists, sales specialists, system analysis specialists, and specialists) for particular parts of the problem being solved. Management uses the model and prefers complex information; the model usually forces the departments to co-operate. Applying systemic information at management level brings the subordinates to do this as well, and teamwork (meetings, team learning, and training) comes into play. The ideal solution is a shared mental model, not only formalization of enterprise knowledge, but also visions.

Teamwork in model building contributed not only to the efficiency of SD applications, but it also contributed to confidence in the results of the models. The survey confirmed the direct correlation between the company's participation in the whole process and the validity of the model. If the model's author was the only one who understood his own system, this would not bring the expected results. The model's author, equipped with knowledge, has to be responsible for the fact that other people without such a knowledge base must understand the model (Drucker, 2003).

Czech practice showed that especially when strategy was created using the model, a multidisciplinary approach was needed. Both psychological and behavioral aspects would be included, as well as business economics, technical and technological aspects, and social aspects including group psychology and insights from cognitive psychology. Models simulating strategies contain many soft variables, including factors such as intentions, perception, and expectation.

Combination

Knowledge of system behavior was gained based on the behavior of the created dynamic model. From the SECI model you could see that in the "explicit–explicit" phase, a conflict could appear between static and dynamic enterprise models, conflict between explicit knowledge of one and the other.

Internalization

Managers greatly improve their mental models by using the knowledge from the model, and they also fulfill a communicator role for the transfer of information to employees for the purpose of influencing their work attitude and behavior. There exists insufficient communication within Czech enterprises (as a continuous bidirectional process of information exchange). Through SD models as a base of shared knowledge, better communication is possible, and the enterprise culture can be changed as well. According to a survey in Czech companies, middle-level management and the operational level use email, phone, and face-to-face meetings as key forms of communication. Meetings are the most frequent form of communication at higher management levels. The use of a model led to a change in communication policies between City Hall and the inhabitants of two major Czech cities where the SD application was implemented.

In the next phase of the SECI model, externalized knowledge is then available for other employees. They familiarize themselves with such knowledge, compare it with their existing knowledge, and include it in their own knowledge "portfolio." In this way the cycle goes on: The employees apply the gained knowledge in operational activities and will learn new things, new habits, feedback loops, non-linearities, systemic and dynamic thinking—all of which they will share. Knowledge can also initiate the creation of new knowledge, both tacit and explicit, and the whole cycle can start anew. Of course the whole knowledge transformation process is influenced by the nature of the organization and its dependency on knowledge. However, the general conclusion could be: By creating and using the SD models, the knowledge base of a company will be expanded (Figure 15.2).

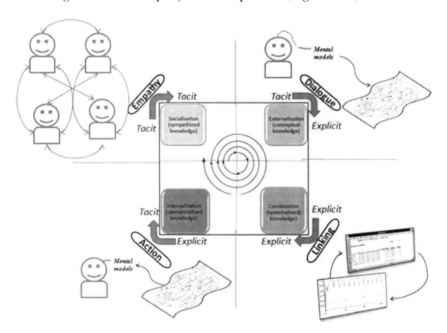

Figure 15.2 SECI model (using the SD models).

Patterns of Information Sharing

Many analyses state that the most successful implementations of externally produced technologies are those that take advantage of established patterns of information sharing in companies (Doucek, 2004). The applications of SD models described here showed that this is where the problem often lies, because these established patterns of information sharing must not only be built on, but also adapted. Not only changes in understanding the information processes are necessary. Implementations of SD applications present a solution whose presumptions are connected both to changes in the access to information and to a whole change of thinking in order to understand the system structure and resulting behavior in time.

STRENGTH AND WEAKNESS

Strength

If we want to understand business problems in a systematic manner, we must look at a system as a system of mutually connected parts. By using causal loops it is possible to describe and analyze complex feedback systems and to predict how the systems might behave. The necessity of considering feedback is ignored by many models, but the feedback between items of the system can be a basic characteristic of complex firms' systems. A similar situation is that many models do not deal with the issue of delay, even though it significantly influences the stability of the system. Connected to this is the distance of cause and effect in time and space. We can see this in the effects of globalization, which are related to the high number of relationships between the system's components, and to delays in such relationships. Such relationships can be difficult to predict and model.

SD methodology, and its instruments, helps to analyze complex systems and to find causal relationships, delays, and feedback loops, often leading to a different behavior of the system (Mildeova & Vojtko, 2006). I see that SD has a positive influence on an improvement of decision making and learning in companies, corporations, and public institutions that need to cope with dynamic complexity. The model can support other forms of communication in the organization; it can help to remove conflict between the information at the strategic decision-making level and the operative information (the latter being necessary for efficient operative decisions).

On the level of a complex social system such as a company, SD models or simulators should lead to an increase in performance. According to the survey, most employees have no idea about the company's strategy.

Thanks to the transparent cause–effect relationships, it was possible to implement a strategy in the companies with SD models and share the strategy uniformly at all organizational levels. It is obvious that the higher decision-making level, in better harmony with the operative reality, allows the organization better adaptability in terms of market competition. In the telecom company, a large number of customer packages have been found to be unprofitable only after dynamic modeling. The simulation led to a policy change. In the machine production company using the simulation, the strategy suggested by external experts was evaluated and characterized as faulty, and a new strategy was accepted. The creation and follow-up work with the model in the distribution company led to a complete reworking of company strategy in financial, supply, and human resource areas. Thanks to simulations of cash flow for supporting the business strategy, the language school was able to negotiate successfully with a bank about receiving a bridge loan.

As was shown, an important aspect supporting a SD approach is the fact of the growing number of interactions. In the case of the post-communist countries, there is not only a consequence for company behavior seeking optimal modes but also of fundamental changes in the economic and political environment as a result of the participation within the Internal Market of the EU. The impact on Czech society could be expected in the higher competitiveness of the companies in the up-and-coming EU environment, the higher resource allocation efficiency, and the consequences of various market structures, etc.

Critical Success Factors

At the same time we have to say that the applications of models touch a number of critical success factors, and one of them is people. A precedent is the chemical production company where personnel changes negatively impacted on the use of the model. Therefore, SD was clearly effective in proving negative impacts of short-term resource exploitation. Sometimes in managerial practice, SD can be difficult to accept, and the cost effectiveness of SD applications is hard to prove, which is an excuse for managers who consider it unhelpful. Related critical factors are the slow adaptation of management to change, and an inclination not to lead the ideas to their conclusion. In current managerial practice it seems that mental inertia still persists, and some managers refuse new ideas, new ways of thinking, and innovative methods of management. A similar situation to this exists in the Slovak Republic (Stricik, Nawka, Hura, & Ocvar, 2003).

Systems Movement

There are limits within the SD methodology itself as well. As with other theories and methodologies, SD has not only strengths but also weaknesses. Being aware of the limitations is necessary. Especially during the interpretation of results, firms should keep in mind the original assumptions. It has been proven that the ability to interpret the analytical solution is related to the future inability to solve the problem.

The limits of SD models, or of computer models in general, are currently well known (Sterman, 1991). The explanatory abilities of a simulation language are limited; information about examined systems' behavior was gained on the basis of a model created using expert knowledge, so there is always the risk that this knowledge was not exhaustive and may have missed some important characteristics. Almost all models contain simplifications, so their scenarios generating the changes in time and space can be understood only as instructions for possible futures; they are not predictions in the narrow scientific sense, but they are tools for exploring the effects of our actions on the future. In addition, the other question is: SD is a problem-solving oriented approach, and how can system dynamicists find a solution to something if the "problem" has not been formally defined?

Therefore, it is useful to consider complementarities and potential synergies from combining SD with the other strands of the systems movement. It is necessary to understand that the systems movement has many roots, in order to see the role of SD in the context of the evolution of the systems movement (Schwaninger, 2006). For the modeling of the unstructured complex system of today, the behavior of which exhibits dramatic dynamics with unpredictable impacts, it is necessary to use a different tool, to combine various approaches or to integrate them. Keep in mind complexity theory, which renews principles of the general systems theory (Mulej, 2005), and press unpredictability of systems. This theory could provide recommendations to management to seek the edge of chaos (Rosenhead, 1998), which is acceptable in Czech practice as well.

SUMMARY

A fundamental part of globalization is the processes of integration that interlink companies to form larger integration areas with a high level of complexity. The growing complexity of problems solved in today's world forces us to change our views of the system and requires the application of modern approaches including systems theories. The goal of this chapter was to contribute to the topic of management complexity with a discussion of a strand of the systems movement: System Dynamics. The premise of the

SD paradigm is based on the hypothesis that even if the real world exhibits a large measure of complexity, it can be recorded in a SD model. The focus of SD on modeling the problem instead of the whole system is very helpful here. It has been proven by Czech SD models, which were built to study concrete dynamics to answer questions of why some businesses grow while others stagnate or decline; which causal patterns drive displayed behavior of a corporate subjects; which strategic measures have the biggest impact on the organizational behavior of a firm; how small changes in organizational structure can produce dramatic changes in organizational behavior; what causes oscillation and amplification in supply chains; how sensitive organizational behavior is to changes in the environment; or how organizational behavior will change when properties of a firm's resources or the structure of their relationships change.

Under knowledge sharing from the described applications, it appears that simulation widens the horizons for possible variants of solutions; it is also able to point out the key areas of decision-making, to contribute to the application of holistic system understanding in the development of business, and to improve decision-making and learning in organizations that need to cope with the dynamic complexity of real-world problems. The firms are able to better recognize structures that are not evident, and to see those that are fundamental for understanding complex situations. This forms a double loop in learning, within which we edit, innovate, and change its imperfect notions dependent on changes in the surrounding environment and internal relations of the organization. But there are large differences in how the companies can use this potential. A firm with a defunct corporate culture considers the model bad and useless. This does not mean, of course, that SD principles are usable only for prospering dynamic companies with plenty of resources to experiment with alternative management methods, or only for knowledge-oriented companies in turbulent and fast-growing markets. Furthermore, companies in stable markets can solve their problems using dynamic models, it depends only on their willingness to learn. Using the model allows a reduction in the number of items for analysis and synthesis, and reduces the perceived complexity.

The success of SD models allows us to assume that System Dynamics can be used as a tool for knowledge transfer and a method for the application of complexity ideas in real organizations—not only in the Czech Republic, but generally. Keeping in mind the current limitations of System Dynamics, I consider the SD methodology an adequate method and SD models suitable tools to support "complexity thinking." Conclusions therefore lead to obvious recommendations for the implementation of System Dynamics principles for Management Complexity. This approach is not yet usual in Czech common managerial practice and requires a shift in thinking.

NOTES

1. Empiric research was managed by Rosicky, A. within project GACR No. 409025, and managed by Nemcova, I., Remtova, K., and was funded by the Institute of National Economy of Josef Hlavka.
2. The survey was managed by Mildeova, S., and granted by the grant GACR 402/05/0502.

ACKNOWLEDGEMENT

This paper is a part research supported by the grant GACR 402/07/0521.

REFERENCES

Cancer, V. (2006). Systems thinking and decision analysis in managing complexity. In A. Rosicky, S. Mildeova, & V. Subrta (Eds.), *System approaches 2006* (pp. 83–95). Prague: Oeconomica

Doucek, P. (2004). *Information systems project management.* Prague: Professional Publishing.

Drucker, P. F. (2003). *The new realities* (Rev Ed.). Edison, NJ: Transaction Publishers.

Forrester, J. W. (1961). *Industrial dynamics.* New York: Productivity Press.

Kostron, L., Susta, M., & Lakomy, L. (2005). Communicating the vision of an urban city development: A model. In J. D. Sterman, N. P. Repenning, R. S. Langer, J. I. Rowe, & J. M. Yanni (Eds.), *Proceedings of the 23rd International Conference of the System Dynamics Society* (pp. 94). Boston: System Dynamics Society.

Mildeova, S. (2003). System dynamics. *Acta Oeconomica Pragensia, 11*(8), 106–114.

Mildeova, S. (2006). Simulation for the shift of paradigm. In L. Magnani (Ed)., *Model based reasoning in science and engineering,* (pp. 67–74). London: Department of Computer Science.

Mildeova, S. & Klas, J. (2006). Spiral for knowledge creation. In A. Rosicky, S. Mildeova, & V. Subrta (Eds.), *System Approaches 2006* (pp. 213–217). Prague: Oeconomica,

Mildeova, S. & Nemcova, I. (2005). System dynamics market model with aspects of economic policy. In J. Gu & G. Chroust (Eds.), *IFSR 2005 [CD-ROM].* Kobe, Japan: JAIST Press.

Mildeova, S. & Vojtko, V. (2005). Result of first steps in application of system dynamics principles at University of Economics in Prague, Czech Republic. In J. D. Sterman, N. P. Repenning, R. S. Langer, J. I. Rowe, & J. M. Yanni (Eds.), *Proceedings of the 23rd International Conference of the System Dynamics Society* (p. 113). Boston: System Dynamics Society.

Mildeova, S. & Vojtko, V. (2006). *Selected Chapters of System Dynamics.* Bratislava: KARTPRINT.

Mulej, M. (2005, December). Complexity theory in five main systems. In K. A. Richardson (Ed.), Systems thinking and complexity science: Insights for action:

Proceedings of the 11th ANZSYS / Managing the Complex V conference (pp. 173–178). Litchfield Park, AZ: ISCE Publishing.

Nonaka, I. (1994). A dynamic theory of organizational knowledge creation. *Organizational Science, 5*(1), 14–37.

Nonaka, I. & Takeuchi, H. (1995). *The knowledge creating company: How Japanese companies create the dynamics of innovation.* Oxford: Oxford University Press.

Richardson, K. A. (2005a). "To be or not to be? That is [NOT] the question": Complexity theory and the need for critical thinking. In K. A. Richardson (Ed.), *Managing organizational complexity: Philosophy, theory, and application.* Greenwich, CT: Information Age Publishing.

Richardson, K. A. (Ed.). (2005b). *Managing organizational complexity: Philosophy, theory, and application.* Greenwich, CT: Information Age Publishing.

Richmond, B. (1993). Systems thinking: critical thinking skills for the 1990s and beyond. *System Dynamics Review 9*(2), 113–133.

Rosenhead, J. (1998). Complexity theory and management practice. Retrieved March 12, 2007 from http://www.human-nature.com/science-as-culture/rosenhead.html

Rosicky, A. (2006). Information and/or knowledge society: Cybernetics ideas changing traditional conceptions. In International Institute of Informatics and Systemic (Ed.), *EISTA '06* (pp. 300–305). Orlando, FL.

Seeley, D. (2003, October). *Cybernetics in the knowledge ecology of 21st century organizations.* Lecture in Project Scientia Interdisciplinaria, University of Economics in Prague.

Senge, P.(1990). *The fifth discipline. The art and practice of the learning organization.* New York: Random House.

Schwaninger, M. (2006). Dynamics and the evolution of the systems movement. *Systems Research and Behavioral Science. 23*, 583–594.

Sterman, J. D. (1991). A skeptic's guide to computer models. In G. O. Barney et al. (Eds.), *Managing a Nation: The Microcomputer Software Catalog* (pp. 209-229). Boulder, CO: Westview Press.

Sterman, J. D. (2000). *Business dynamics: Systems thinking and modeling for a complex world.* New York: McGraw-Hill.

Stricik, M., Nawka, P., Hura J., & Ocvar L. (2003, March). Economic analysis of current state of mental health care in Slovakia and possibility of its transformation. Theory and practice of transition towards market relations: Economic and legal, international, informational and technological, educational and legal aspects. In Uzgorod State Institute of Information Sciences, Economic and Law (Ed.), *International Scientific Conference Proceedings* (pp. 39–44).

Ulicna, S. & Kacin, R. (2003). Paradigm of statistical analysis of economic data. In S. Mildeova (Ed.), *System Approaches 2003* (pp. 187–193). Prague: Oeconomica,.

Yamaguchi, K. (1997). *Sustainable global communities in the information age: Visions from futures studies.* Santa Barbara, CA: Praeger Publishers.

CHAPTER 16

QUESTIONING CULTURAL ORTHODOXY

Policy Implications for Ireland as an Innovative Knowledge-Based Economy

Dermot Casey and Cathal M. Brugha

INTRODUCTION

A decade of phenomenal growth has seen Ireland achieve close to full employment and with incomes at European levels. The cultural orthodoxy sees fortuitous planning by development organizations, enlightened taxation policy, and educational excellence as the successful rain dance that brought economic progress (MacSharry & White, 2000). The witchdoctor's orthodoxy views Ireland as well placed to become Europe's leading knowledge economy, a stated policy goal. The cultural orthodoxy envisions the possibility of foreseeing and influencing the future. The real world, however, is wicked. It is nonlinear, a system of "punctuated equilibriums" where order persists for periods of time and is followed by rapid change (Casti, 1991; Gell-Mann, 1995; Gould, 2002; Johnson, 1996; Kauffman, 1993; Taleb, 2003). The insidious consequence of this is that the past provides a poor guide to the future.

Complexity and Knowledge Management, pages 285–316
Copyright © 2010 by Information Age Publishing

The shift to the knowledge economy is a problem of change. Change is essentially a wicked problem, with issues of interconnectedness, complicatedness, uncertainty, ambiguity, conflict, and societal constraints (Mason & Mitroff, 1981; Rittel & Webber, 1973; Roberts, 2001). Understanding change and addressing the problems of change requires tools that address complex problems. One method for exploring difficult problems is through the Priority Pointing Procedure (Brugha, 2000), rooted in Nomology. Nomology is based on abstracting existing "regularities in human behaviors that are present in almost all fields of decision making" (Brugha, 2000, p. 229). It derives from Kant's idea that our knowledge of nature conforms to the structure of the human mind (Kant, 1781/1985). The origin of Nomology was related to an attempt to resolve policy problems of transport in a conurbation (Brugha, 1974). It specifically addressed the issue of large-scale complex societal problems too difficult to solve using any mathematical or computer model.

The basic inference of Nomology is that qualitative structures are not unique to particular subjects, times, and regions. They are central to how the mind works and are the reason for similarities between languages and cultures and academic fields. Nomology does not fit into any field; it is a meta-modeling approach that suggests that the generic categorizations of human activities should be applicable to every field, including policy (Brugha, 1998a, 1998b, 1998c). Nomology is focused on understanding the nature of problems. It works on the basis that people attempt to resolve complex problems by breaking them down into less complex ones using simple questions (Brugha, 1998a), reflecting our common mental structures. These questions have the form "is the problem more of this sort, or that?" Derived from Nomology, Priority Pointing uses three such dichotomies to identify the general location of the priority problem within any system under investigation. In developing our argument we make the link between Nomology and a number of other areas. We draw the links to Stacey (2000, 2002), who has developed a theory of knowledge, which is rooted in complexity theory. Stacey starts from George Mead's idea of gesture and response in animals, where meaning arises from the complex coordination of gesture and response in social acts, a process that is the result of the emergent behavior of increasingly complex self-organizing systems. We develop this idea with examples from research and practice on knowledge and innovation (Cook & Brown, 1999; Lundvall, Johnson, Andersen, & Dalum, 2002; Mokyr, 1998, 2002), and link to the idea of a national system of innovation (Freeman, 1995; Godin, 2004; Lundvall, 1992, 2004).

We illustrate a misunderstanding at policy level of the term "knowledge" and suggest that Ireland may be less well positioned than imagined to capitalize on becoming an innovative knowledge-based economy. Questioning received orthodoxy, we show that Irish culture should put more value on scientific skills, promote a scientifically literate culture, and reform institutional and structural support systems to develop an innovative knowledge-based economy. In terms of a complex system, we illustrate how the structure of the social systems and the history of those systems determine the space and capability for future development and innovation.

COMPLEXITY, POLICY AND THE KNOWLEDGE ECONOMY: STATE POLICY AND THE IMPORTANCE OF THE KNOWLEDGE ECONOMY

State policy has played a critical, if not always a positive, role in the development of the Irish Economy. Despite visionary schemes such as rural electrification, economic development in Ireland stagnated up to the end of the 1980s (Lee, 1989; Ó'Gráda, 2002). De Valera's vision of comely maidens dancing at the crossroads yielded to the cruel reality of the emigrant boat. State initiatives were more discursive than action oriented. The Telesis report (NESC, 1982), withheld from publication for more than a year, was substantially ignored in the 1984 paper on industrial policy (Lee, 1989). More recently, the Culliton report (1991) focused on the importance of economic policy as the driver of industrial policy and of prosperity. Through a combination of State policy, location, and luck, the late 1990s saw the development of the "Celtic Tiger," and has led to a clustering of IT and Pharmaceutical companies in Ireland (O'Riain, 1997a, 1997b, 2000; Tallon & Kraemer, 1999; Plice & Kraemer, 2001; Krugman 1997).

More recently the Irish State, through the Information Society Commission (ISC, 2002), has recognized the importance of the knowledge-based economy, envisioning a move to a "knowledge-based society" as the prerequisite for future economic development. "Holding the status quo is not an option. We move forwards and embrace the conditions necessary to underpin higher value economic activity, better jobs, and new social prosperity. Or we prepare to fall into relative decline" (ISC, 2002, p. 7).

We are constantly reminded of the rise of the "knowledge economy" (Godin, 2004), with the attendant requirement for change in State, business, and society (ISC, 2002). There is no doubt that change is important, something recognized since Heraclitus commented that "the only constant is change." In the biological world, Darwin determined that "it is not the strongest of the species that survive, nor the most intelligent, but the one most responsive to change," and evolution provides a powerful metaphor for the development of society and business. Even the rate of change and renewal appears to be increasing. Drucker (1994, 1999) suggests that increasing interconnectedness and intensifying complexity will require change and renewal more frequently, alluded to by Toffler (1970) and reinforced by Gleick (1999). It is clear that the ability to learn to manage change is a *sine qua non* in today's world and that those economies that thrive will be knowledge-based "learning economies" (Johnson & Lundvall, 2001).

Driven by the growth of Information Technology and the strength of the U.S. and other economies in the 1990s, and fueled by a number policy documents on the importance of a knowledge economy (OECD, 1996a, 1996b, 1997; Stiglitz, 1998, 1999), a consensus has emerged. A number of states, including the UK (Department of Trade and Enterprise, 1998), New Zealand (MTI, 1999), and Australia (Australia, 2001), have produced reports on the importance of the knowledge economy. Ireland takes this a step further in discussing the term "knowledge society" (ISC, 2002). At a regional level the avowed aim of the European Union is to make Europe "the world's most innovative knowledge-based society" by 2010 (EU, 2000a).

We begin by asking if this is more than empty rhetoric, a debate generating more heat than light? The knowledge-based economy, under various guises, is seen as the cure for all society's ills. Decades of experience in IT tells us there "there are no silver bullets" (Brooks 1987, 1995). There is a problem inherent in the idea of the "magic bullet." As Bond (2003) points out, "Technology is frequently imagined as society's 'magic bullet', and as such will silence all opposition to its critics. However, it may prove to be a flawed solution to longer term problems" (p. 2). Life is more complex than any panglossian approach would suggest. Each era of change brings with it losers as well as winners at both micro (individual) and macro (country) levels. Why is an innovative knowledge-based economy seen as a panacea? A synonym of panacea is "magic cure," and one wonders if the focus of the knowledge economy is the modern equivalent of the alchemist's quest for the philosopher's stone. Alchemy holds a lesson for us. Newton was one of the last of the alchemists and one of the first scientists (White, 1997). By exploring the phenomenon of the knowledge-based economy, we may be able to begin the winnowing process, and find the true value in the idea.

POLICY AS A WICKED COMPLEX PROBLEM

An obsession with predicting the future is a universal human characteristic (Brown, 1991; Casti, 1991; Johnson, 1996; O'Nuallain, 2002; Pinker, 2002). From the shaman's reading entrails and the Oracle at Delphi, to astrologers preparing horoscopes, people seek to determine what the future will be. Modern attempts at long-range economic and weather forecasts have fared little better than their predecessors, due to the nonlinear nature of the phenomena (Casti, 1991). If predicting the future is difficult, influencing the future is more arduous, akin to the witchdoctor who commands rain from the heavens—if the rain comes, the witchdoctor is the cause. The past decade of phenomenal growth has seen Ireland achieve close to full employment and incomes at European levels. The cultural orthodoxy sees the fortuitous planning by development organizations, enlightened taxation policy, and educational excellence as the successful rain dance that brought economic progress (MacSharry & White, 2000). The witchdoctor's orthodoxy sees the location of high technology companies such as Intel, Microsoft and Dell as exemplifying the success of the past rituals, and views Ireland as well placed to become Europe's leading knowledge economy. The cultural orthodoxy envisions the possibility of accurately predicting the future. This ignores the wicked, nonlinear, nature of our world (Casti, 1991; Gell-Mann, 1995; Gould, 2002; Johnson, 1996; Kauffman, 1993; Taleb, 2003). The insidious consequence of believing the witchdoctor is that it builds complacency, reinforces vested interests, and dwells on the past, itself a poor guide to the future.

Unfortunately for the orthodoxy, the Irish economic miracle is due as much to exogenous factors as to endogenous ones. A complex combination of location and luck played no small part in the development of the Celtic Tiger, as Ireland's economy caught up with that of other European countries after three quarters of a century of under-performance (Krugman, 1997; Ó'Riain, 1997a, 1997b, 2000; Tallon & Kraemer, 1999; Plice & Kraemer, 2001; Ó'Gráda, 2002). One could as easily ask why the Irish economy stagnated for so many decades while other countries thrived, as ask why it grew in the 1990s (Lee, 1989; Ó'Gráda, 2002; Garvin, 2004). Tactically we may have been doing things right, but strategically were we doing the right things?

Krugman (1997) has examined the growth of Ireland from a geographic perspective, and sees a number of elements to its success. First, the development of "weightless" goods (e.g., Financial Services and Software), where peripheral location is not a serious restricting factor, makes Ireland as good a choice as any other in Europe, becoming a backshop (a location easily accessible when required) within the European Union. Second is the possibility of self-reinforcing success—the possibility that the early location of firms created a demonstration effect, which resulted in herding. Ireland appeared attractive as a location. Early firms set up and did well. Other firms chose Ireland as it delivered on the early success, creating a cascade effect. This is similar to the model developed by economist Brian Arthur (1990), where historical accidents can create a self-reinforcing mechanism that concentrates an industry geographically (Arora et al., 2000). This is similar to the idea of path dependency in complexity theory, where the process of future choices are constrained by past decisions. The fundamental problem is that the link between cause and effect is weak and not predictable.

This problem becomes more apparent in relation to policy questions raised by Amsden and Mourshed, who asked, "Why, in fact, did heavy investments in education in Korea and Taiwan initially lead to brain drain and unemployment, not spillovers in the domestic economy?" (Amsden & Mourshed, 1997, p. 356). This parallels the experience of mass exodus of the first fully educated generation of youth from Ireland in the 1980s. Amsden and Mourshed pointed to the importance of policy packages in Korea and Taiwan countries that were "designed to build long-run technological capabilities and subsidize companies so they could compete immediately abroad and at home" (Amsden & Mourshed, 1997, p. 356). The route Ireland followed in late industrialization was the converse of this approach: "industrialization by invitation" through attracting Foreign Direct Investment (FDI) in the form of Multinational Corporations (MNCs) (Trauth, 2000; Ó'Gráda, 2002).

ADDRESSING THE POLICY PROBLEM

What is required for Ireland to prosper, to develop as an innovative knowledge-based economy? This is neither an easy nor a simple question to investigate. We are looking at a national agenda for development, in a rapidly changing world. Given the difficulties, it could be compared to attempting to steer a canoe on a safe course through white water rapids, at night, in a fog. The nature of change means that the question being addressed is often only properly understood when an answer is found (Mason & Mitroff, 1981; Roberts, 2000). One of the respondents to the primary research ventured as much when commenting, "These are difficult problems to solve; there are no easy solutions and the new directions are not obvious." The Priority Pointing Procedure (Brugha, 2000) helps to identify new directions in a systemic way.

Nomology utilizes some of the concepts described by Simon (1996): "Complexity frequently takes the form of hierarchy and that hierarchic systems have some common properties independent of their specific content," and that "nature is organized in levels, and the pattern at each level is most clearly discerned by abstracting from the details of the levels far below" (p. 184). There is a larger sense in which nature appears to be fractal, an idea that patterns of behavior repeat at different levels of complexity. This has parallels across many streams of thought from Koestler (1964/1990) to Pirsig (1992, 1995) to Maturana and Varela (1992), and we see this in the complex behavior that emerges in the natural world.

The basic inference of Nomology is that qualitative structures are not unique to particular subjects, times, and regions. They are central to how the mind works and are the reason for similarities between languages and cultures and academic fields. Nomology does not fit into any field; it is a meta-modeling approach that suggests that the generic categorizations of human activities should be applicable to every field including policy (Brugha 1998a, 1998b, 1998c). Nomology is focused on understanding the nature of problems. It works on the basis that people attempt to resolve complex problems by breaking them down into less complex ones using simple questions (Brugha, 1998a), reflecting our common mental structures—our underlying shared phylogeny (Maturana & Varela, 1992). Derived from Nomology, Priority Pointing focuses on three dichotomies to identify problems within a system. The first dichotomy examines what needs to be done to resolve the problem within a system. If we are uncertain about the action to take, then we will focus on planning. If, on balance, we feel relatively clear about the direction that should be taken, we will focus on a putting a solution into effect. The second part of the dichotomy examines where the action needs to take place. The resolution to the problem is either through actions on place—for instance, in some structural element of the State, or through focusing on the people involved in the system. Finally, this dichotomy asks which way a problem should be resolved. Should we rely more on using position, an impersonal approach, or should we be focusing more on people, using a personal solution to the problem? This dichotomy is the perennial dilemma of a top-down versus a bottom-up approach to problem solving. In the section titled "Knowledge, complexity and culture: Understanding problems through Priority Pointing" below, we explore the issue of problem understanding and link it to the core concepts of knowledge and innovation, explaining how Priority Pointing can improve our understanding of complex policy problems.

ANALYZING AT THE LEVEL OF THE NATIONAL SYSTEM OF INNOVATION

In examining the problem it is important to focus our analysis at the right level of detail. In our discussion we focus on the level of the State and the State's role in innovation and development. How do countries innovate, and how do they create the systems of innovation that drive national growth? We can see this generally in historical analysis by Wright (2000) and Mokyr (2002). Wright (2000) points to the agglomeration of states in the late middle ages in Europe as the advent of technology (e.g., the printing press) created defined language boundaries across Europe as a driving force behind innovation and development: people shaping technology, then being shaped by it. The increasingly complex nation states were able materially to support the societal conditions that preceded growth. There was a new openness as the "scientific method" developed in the age of "industrial enlightenment" (Mokyr, 2002). These developments set conditions for growth and development (Mokyr, 2002). To structure this historic analysis and to understand current development, we need to use the idea of a *national system of innovation.* The concept of a national system of innovation derives from the work of Freeman (Freeman, 1995; Lundvall, 2004).

In developing the idea of a national system of innovation Lundvall et al. (2002), highlight the problematic nature of the difference between tacit and codified knowledge (Johnson & Lundvall, 2001), an issue we return to in the next section. General macroeconomic theory has focused on rational expectation and general equilibrium frameworks. This purely instrumental rationalism of traditional economics leaves no room for learning by individual human agents. *New growth theory* (Romer, 1986, 1990) stresses the importance of investment in research and education. Lundvall et al. (2002) link the role of innovation to relationships involving non-price relationships, questions of trust and the difficulties in transmitting tacit knowledge, illustrating the importance of diffusing cultural constraints for the transfer of tacit knowledge. Acemoglu and Robinson's work on the role of politics in economic performance reinforces this view (Acemoglu & Robinson, 2002). Lundvall et al. (2002) demonstrate how rationality is tied to performance and the idea of communicative rationality (Habermas, 1984)—"characterized by a shared and genuine interest in understanding new phenomena, mastering new techniques and sharing their knowledge" (Lundvall, 1996, p. 16)—is preferable to strict instrumental rationality, under which no learning would take place. This approach resolves the problem of the contradictory predictions of economic theory. This is supported by Sala-i-Martin's (2002) examination of new growth theory. Reiterating Mokyr (2002) and Acemoglu and Robinson (2002), Sala-i-Martin finds clear evidence that institutions are important for growth in that they affect the efficiency of the economy. The key argument is that it is hard to come up with better technologies within an economy if it does not have the right institutions.

The structure of the system of national innovation is critical to economic progress in that its structure guides what is produced and what competencies are developed. The question Lundvall et al. (2002) address is how does the capacity for learning one of the key elements of the communicative rationality in a knowledge economy develop? The rate of change within economies places a premium on rapid learners in the current learning economy (Lundvall & Johnson, 1994; Archibugi & Lundvall, 2001). The effectiveness of investment in Information Technology (a human-defined artifact) is linked to tacit knowledge and the understanding of social relations (Markus, 1983; Markus & Benjamin, 1997; Remenyi, White, & Sherwood-Smith, 1999; Remenyi & Sherwood-Smith 1999; Brown & Duguid, 2002).

Systems that are better able to innovate are better able to change. The emphasis is on dynamic structures, and Lundvall et al. (2002) argue for building new institutions for policy learning and co-ordination to improve national systems of innovation. The idea of a national system of innovation (Johnson & Lundvall, 2001) encompasses both the cultural context of innovation and institutional structures that affect innovation from an autopoietic perspective. Governments, policies, and institutions shape economic incentives and the rules of the market and have a first order effect on economic development (Mokyr, 2000, 2002; Acemoglu & Robinson, 2002). The importance of the system of national innovation is that its culturally embedded structure guides the development of competencies and the dynamics of production within a state.

Examined in the light of the national system of innovation, the invidious consequences of concentrating policy on Foreign Direct Investment (FDI) in Ireland over the past decade become apparent. FDI has had a distorting effect on indigenous industry. Arora, Gambardella, and Torrisi (2000) have found that Irish software companies have tended to be smaller than the international average and have a lower life expectancy to relate to the presence of multinationals. There have been few spillover effects to the local economy (Arora et al., 2000). The over-reliance on FDI was commented on as far back as the Telesis report (NESC, 1982), which "queried the Irish emphasis on foreign investment, and advocated greater commitment towards developing an indigenous industrial base" (Lee, 1989, p. 531). More recently, Ó'Gráda describes the policy of encouraging FDI as a replacement of a strategy of "export-subsidizing industrialization" replacing a strategy of "import-substituting industrialization" (Ó'Gráda, 2002).

The idea of national systems of innovation recognizes that innovation is engendered in language and dialogue as dynamic forms of interaction generate new knowledge. Knowledge is *autopoietic*, a term that means self-producing, generated at the boundary as data from outside perturbs the system. Dynamism is central to understanding knowledge and innovation. To generate knowledge requires a dynamic element. Our access to knowledge is socially mediated; culture constrains patterns of thought and of value. The more open a culture is to ideas, the more dynamic and questioning it is, and the better ecosystem it creates for generating innovation and knowledge. The more static a culture is, trying to preserve everything and resisting the dynamic element, the poorer the ecosystem. The culture, structure, beliefs, and values of a society create a national system of innovation that ideally links theory and practice, using learning based on human communication generating new innovative forms.

KNOWLEDGE, COMPLEXITY AND CULTURE: UNDERSTANDING PROBLEMS THROUGH PRIORITY POINTING

Autopoiesis, Culture and Complexity

Autopoiesis is a complexity-based theory that can be used to examine the issues of culture and the national system of innovation. Autopoiesis provides a biological analogy for understanding the development of human language and understanding (Maturana & Varela, 1980, 1992). Autopoiesis's claim is that basic principles of biology can be traced from simple cells up through animal societies to man. For instance, people use chemicals such as pheromones to communicate in a way similar to other species (Watson, 2000). At a higher level of development, mammals and especially humans use language as an autopoietic function. The key difference is that "human language confers the capacities for self-identity, self-consciousness, and reflection" (Denning, 2003, p. 19), to a degree not seen in other species, including higher primates (Deacon, 1997). Pirsig (1992, 1995) traces similar patterns of increasing complexity from inorganic life to the levels of society in a comparable, albeit not identical, mechanism to Maturana and Varela (1980, 1992).

Autopoiesis has been used to examine a number of aspects of information systems, knowledge, and social systems (Kay & Cecez-Kecmanovic, 2002; Luhmann, 1986; Mingers, 1995). Sveiby (2001) recognized the link between autopoiesis and Polanyi's (1958) concept of "personal knowledge" and uses the idea of autopoiesis as a basis for epistemology in his "knowledge based theory of the firm." Winograd and Flores (1986) used autopoiesis to consider the question of design: "how a society engenders inventions whose existence in turn alters that society" (p. 4). Using autopoiesis we can describe social activities in human terms as a "highly sophisticated process of cooperative interaction between people in the medium of symbols in order to undertake joint action" (Stacey, 2000, p. 4). This impinges directly on our understanding of innovation. Innovation is defined as "the action of innovating; the introduction of a new thing; the alteration of something established; a new practice or method" (Innovation, 1992). Innovation is essentially a creative endeavor, generating something—be it simple or profound—that did not exist previously. Koestler defines creative acts as "the combination of previously unrelated structures in such a way that you get more out of the emergent whole than you have put in" (Adams, 1996, p. 23). This is the idea of synergy as the basis for human progression described by Corning (2003).

This symbiotic combination of ideas as the basis for human innovation parallels the genomic combination that underpins the evolutionary process of speciation, the innovation of new forms in nature (Marguiles & Fester, 1991; Dennett, 1995; Marguiles & Sagan, 2002). Autopoietic interaction underpins the evolution of species (Marguiles & Fester, 1991; Marguiles & Sagan, 2002). In autopoietic terms, the structure of the systems and the history of those systems determine the space and capability for future development and innovation. In biological terms, the development of cells necessarily preceded the evolution of flora and fauna. In social terms, interaction and language, the swapping of ideas in a synergistic manner, form the basis for innovation. At the same time, cultural frames constrict what actions and innovations are possible. Foucault illustrated this problem when describing "regimes of truth" that constrain us: "it acts upon their actions: an action upon an action, on existing actions" (Foucault, 1983, p. 220). This anticipates Kuhn's analysis of how paradigms constrain normal science (Kuhn 1970), and Mokyr's description of how the openness of the industrial enlightenment, the culture of the time created systems of national innovation that led to the industrial revolution (Mokyr, 2002).

Knowledge, Contingent, Complex and Emergent

The question of *what knowledge is*, is vexatious. It is beyond the scope of this piece to provide more than a précis of this question.[1] Our view is that understanding the idea of knowledge and the nature of knowledge is best understood by understanding the paradox of knowledge. The essential paradox of knowledge is that it exists in two forms: a tacit form which cannot be processed—the idea of knowledge as flow—and an explicit form of knowledge as a thing (Snowden, 2002). Snowden (2002) and Allee (1997) both use the idea of the wave and particle theories of light to explain this paradox. Light exists both as a wave and as particles, each is important as it explains different elements of light and our understanding of light is incomplete if we take a single perspective. Snowden (2002) links to Stacey's view of knowledge when he describes the flow element of knowledge as "an ephemeral, active process of relating."

This dual nature of knowledge is reflected in the etymology of the word. Wittgenstein said, "the limits of my languages are the limits of my knowledge." The word knowledge illustrates the limits of our language and the difficulty in recognizing the dual nature of knowledge. The words "data" and "information" are nouns—words that represent things. The word "knowledge" in English has both a noun and a verb form, and "covers the ground formerly occupied by several verbs, and still answers to two verbs in other Teutonic and Romanic languages" creating

[a] difficulty in arranging its senses and uses satisfactorily.... It covers the ground of the Ger. *wissen, kennen, erkennen,* and (in part) *können,* of Fr. *con-naître* to 'know by the senses' and *savoir* to 'know by the mind'.... To know may mean either to perceive or apprehend, or it may mean to understand or comprehend... Thus a blind man, who cannot know about light in the first sense, may know about light in the second, if he studies a treatise on optics" (Knowledge, 1989)

When we talk of knowledge we are talking of a process and a thing.

Knowledge in this sense is essentially complex and autopoietic—emergent, as is language itself. Drawing on Damasio (1996), Stacey finds that "Mind is the action of the brain, rather like walking is the action of the body." Stacey concludes that "knowledge is that act of conversing and new knowledge is created when ways of talking and therefore patterns of relationship change." This view of knowledge is reflected in the embodied, emergent nature of language. Ramachandran (2003) has detailed how the mind, the body, and language may have co-evolved, indicating at the same time how the body, language, and creativity are intimately linked together. Recent work (Ramachandran & Hubbard, 2001; Ramachandran, 2003), based on an examination of people with synesthesia, leads to the theory that language was boot-strapped by a number of factors in the brain. These include the hierarchical nature of tool-making being co-opted for the hierarchical nature of language—the "pre-existing translation if you like between the visual appearance and the auditory representation" (Ramanchandran, 2003, p. 84), and the cross activation between the hand and the mouth. Ramachandran illustrated this through an example of Darwin's: "When people cut with a pair of scissors you clench and unclench your jaws unconsciously as if to echo or mimic the movements of the finger" (Ramachandran, 2003, p. 84). Language is therefore an emergent complex phenomenon. We see in this a reflection of the base cognitive structure of Nomology. Recent theories about the embodied mind support this view (Damasio, 1996; Deacon, 1997; Lakoff & Johnson, 1999; Maturana & Varela, 1992). Regularities in the mind, and the presence of human universals, are a consequence of our evolutionary descent (Deacon, 1997; Dennett, 1995). This underpinning for Nomology has been confirmed in neurobiology (Damasio, 1996) and by the presence of human universals across all cultures (Pinker, 2002; Harris, 2000) and behaviors (Ekman, 1992). It reflects the commonality of universal grammar and the role of metaphor as a core constituent of language (Lakoff & Johnson, 2003).

This raises the fundamental question of how can an economy be based on something that cannot be possessed, or can only in part be possessed. Knowledge is embodied and embedded in people, their relationships, their interactions, and their reflective actions. Knowledge is generated in language and dialog as dynamic forms of interaction generate new knowledge.

A national system of innovation is essentially an ecosystem that ideally gives rise to and supports a rich and diverse set of innovative possibilities. The more open a culture is to ideas and the more dynamic and questioning it is, the better ecosystem it creates for generating innovation and knowledge. The more static a culture is, resisting and inimical to change, the less innovation is generated. The danger is that a policy approach becomes a monoculture, favoring ideas that have worked in the past. For Ireland the over-reliance on FDI could be perceived as similar to the over-reliance on the potato as the staple food crop, a development that led to the Irish famine.

The culture, structure, beliefs, and values of a society create a national system of innovation, ideally generating links between theory and practice—learning based on human communication generating new innovative forms. These elements are reflected in the economic development of states and in the technical progress that states make. The economics of knowledge generate a nonzero-sum game with the possibility of increasing returns to an economy, returns based on human capital and the interaction of people. Learning in a knowledge-based economy creates both the capability to generate new innovation and the capacity to absorb knowledge generated elsewhere. The active participative nature of knowledge and its fundamental importance for growth force us to recognize that learning is a lifelong process. It also points to the need for educational reform to ensure that educational structures recognize and respond to the needs of students.

Our understanding of knowledge and its role in generating wealth emphasizes the importance of having the correct national structures to maximize innovation within the economy. Our understanding of knowledge illustrates that Irish dependence on mobile external intellectual property for wealth generation is a pernicious legacy of an over-reliance on Foreign Direct Investment. Fundamentally, Ireland needs the correct state policies in place to foster local innovation, a system of secondary education that produces a scientifically literate and knowledgeable society, a system of tertiary education that generates new knowledge, an industrial system that works with the educational system to produce innovative goods and services, and a system of state structures that provides the overarching framework to support innovation. The system must be dynamic enough to anticipate, pre-empt, and adapt to exogenous change yet static enough to preserve the ability to change. These are key priorities for Ireland if it is to really become an innovative knowledge based economy.

Understanding the Nature of Problems

Understanding the nature of the problem is the key to addressing the problem. Problem framing and understanding are key to problem solving.

Simon, (1996, p. 187) notes "much problem-solving effort is directed at structuring problems, and only a fraction of it in solving problems once they are structured." Halverson (2002, p. 15) describes "the problem-setting stage, where the issue is defined as a member of a certain class, as critical to understanding is the exercise of Aristotle's concept of *phronesis*. Phronesis is often translated as "'prudence,' 'practical wisdom,' or sometimes simply 'ethics.' It is an action-oriented concept, associated with doing the correct thing in a given situation, and is often characterized as wise deliberation."

The idea of framing the problem draws on a number of domains. Fundamentally we see the world as portioned into a number of problem domains. These have been variously described by a number of authors. Weinberg (2001) describes the problems as existing in three domains: *simple* problems, amenable to linear cause effect analysis; *machine simplicity*, problems with large numbers of elements that can be resolved through statistical analysis; and the set of problems he refers to as *organized complexity*, resolvable through whole systems thinking. Snowden (2002) takes this a stage further and uses four types of classification (see Figure 16.1): problems to which the solutions are known, those that are knowable though analysis, those that are chaotic and unconnected, and complex problems.

Snowden's definition mirrors that of Roberts (2000), who proposes that wicked problems are those where

> 1) There is no definitive statement of the problem; in fact, there is broad disagreement on what 'the problem' is. 2) Without a definitive statement of the problem, there can be no definitive solution. In actuality, there are competing solutions that activate a great deal of discord among stakeholders–those who have a stake in the problem and its solution. 3) The problem solving process is complex because constraints, such as resources and political ramifications, are constantly changing. 4) Constraints also change because they are generated by numerous interested parties who "come and go, change their minds, fail to communicate, or otherwise change the rules by which the problem must be solved (Conklin & Weil, 1997)

This is the definition of a policy problem such as the development of an innovative knowledge-based economy. Snowden (2002) calls his approach to addressing complex problems "multi-ontology sense making." In a similar vein, Roberts' approach requires a plurality of perspectives in framing and resolving the problem. This parallels Richardson's (2005) view of pluralism in Management Science that "to fully understand complex systems we must approach them from many directions—we must take a pluralistic stance" (p. 112).

In adopting Nomology and Priority Pointing to address the problem, we are explicitly adopting a pluralistic approach. Priority Pointing is, in Snowden's terms, developing an environmental probe to enable us to sense the priorities and to respond to them. We have developed this notion of

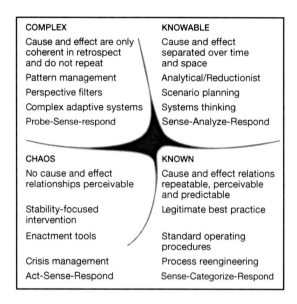

Figure 16.1

pluralism in a number of previous papers (e.g., Brugha, 2001). The essence of pluralism is reflected in how we deal with our natural dichotomies. We see dichotomies reflected in the everyday world—the conflict between tacit and explicit knowledge, left- and right-brained thinking, thought versus action. In developing a pluralistic approach, we seek to accommodate all dichotomies in a dynamic cycle of understanding. Nomology recognizes that every system involving qualitative understanding will have an inbuilt tendency to try to find balance between all the relevant dichotomies. Nomology's idea of balance parallels that of Fitzgerald and Howcroft (1998), who proposed the metaphor of 'polarity' to analyze the notion of meaning, an idea also used by Carroll (2001)—the idea being that magnets have both a north and south pole. Neither can exist without the other—remove the north pole section of a magnet, and a new magnet is created from this section with both north and south poles. "These poles exist not in isolation of each other, but by virtue of each other" (Fitzgerald & Howcroft, 1998, p. 232). A metaphor also echoed by Carroll (2001). We must learn to live with these contraries (our dialectic paradoxes or dichotomies), which generate creative tensions (Carroll, 2001).

The Priority Point Probe

Priority Pointing treats the issue under investigation as a system focusing on three dichotomies to identify problems within a system. The first dichotomy examines what needs to be done to resolve the problem within a system. If we are uncertain about the action to take, then we will focus on planning. If, on balance, we feel relatively clear about the direction that should be taken we will focus on a putting a solution into effect. The second dichotomy examines where the action needs to take place. The resolution to the problem is either through actions on place, for instance in some structural element of the State, or through focusing on the people involved in the system. The final dichotomy asks which way a problem should be resolved. Should we rely more on using position, an impersonal approach, or should we be focusing more on the person, using a personal solution to the problem? This dichotomy is the perennial dilemma of a top-down versus a bottom-up approach to problem solving.

The development of two dichotomies for each of three questions produces eight principal activities described by Brugha (1998a, 2000). This is illustrated in Figure 16.2. A healthy, balanced system will find equilibrium between doing too much and too little of each activity (Brugha, 1998b). The development of any system naturally flows through each of the eight activities beginning with uncertainty, moving to more certainty over time. Within these dichotomies, a vigorous system will alternate between people versus place (structure-orientated) approaches, and personal versus positional (non-personally-interacting) approaches to resolving a problem, establishing equilibrium along the way.

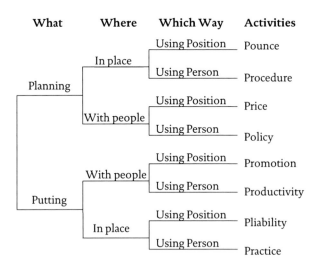

Figure 16.2

The first two dichotomies lead to the four general, termed Push, Pull, Perception, and Proposition. The third dichotomy leads to the eight principal activities—Pounce, Procedure, Price, Policy, Promotion, Productivity, Pliability, and Practice. These activities are represented in the Priority Pointing Wheel (Figure 16.3). The imagery of the wheel is important as Nomology takes a systems approach to decision making, considering the whole, not just the parts. Within Priority Pointing, the focus can move between the four quadrants and eight sectors, which operate in a cycle when solving a problem in management. Each activity is important, and there is a natural flow through the quadrants to resolve a problem, figuring out conceptual proposition of the problem, agreeing on the common perception of the solution, pulling people into alignment to ensure that the plans can be put into effect, and finally pushing the system into alignment to ensure the changes to the system are practiced. The application of the procedure is based on asking six open questions (Brugha, 2000). The questions are designed to elicit responses along existing dimensions that are believed to reside in the minds of the respondents. The six questions are broken down into two general questions and four specific questions that address the four general activities (quadrants) of the Wheel. These questions need to be "expressed in colloquial language familiar to the re-

Figure 16.3

spondent, relate specifically to that sector, and be completely open and unbiased" (Brugha, 2000).

The questions are divided into two categories: Punch and Prevention. Punch is defined as "the need to have sufficient support for some activity," and Prevention as "the need to ensure that no activity is used excessively" (Brugha, 1998b). Punch and prevention are used to indicate the flow of power within a system. A balanced system will find equilibrium between doing too much and too little of any activity. In a complex environment, this balance is a dynamic, not a static equilibrium, and is responsive to change, calling for the constant adjustment of the system. This reflects our understanding of complex nonlinear systems and is indicative of change in the modern business environment.

The two general questions are divided into a general punch and a general prevention question. The questions in the four quadrants can be either punch or prevention questions, creating the possibility of a pool of eight questions to draw from. In analyzing the four quadrants, we are examining two specific dichotomies: planning versus putting, and people versus place. These dichotomies represent the vertical and horizontal halves of the wheel, respectively. The questions need to be carefully chosen to ensure that there are both punch and prevention questions in both people and place halves of the wheel. Similarly, there should be a punch and a prevention question in both of the planning and putting halves of the wheel. Using this approach, a questionnaire comprising the six questions listed in Table 16.1 was developed.

TABLE 16.1   Survey Questions

Sector	Question
General Punch	What is needed for Ireland to become an innovative knowledge-based economy?
General Prevention	What is preventing Ireland from becoming an innovative knowledge-based economy?
Prevention Question in Proposition Sector	What is stopping us from resolving these problems?
Punch Question in Perception Sector	What should be done to increase our understanding how to become an innovative knowledge-based economy?
Prevention Question in Pull Sector	What is holding us back from working better as a society to become an innovative knowledge-based economy?
Punch question in Push Sector	Are there any structural or policy changes we can make which will help us become an innovative knowledge economy

DETERMINING IRELAND PRIORITIES

Primary Research

Primary data were gathered using a survey mechanism using six questions. The primary questions were about "what does Ireland need to do to become an innovative knowledge-based economy?" 135 questionnaires were posted to individuals within Irish-based Information and Communications Technology (ICT) companies and related organizations who have an interest in this area. Individuals were selected from Chief Executive Officer/Chief Technology Officer level from companies who are involved in industry trade and lobby organization such as The Irish Software Association, and ICT Ireland. Further questionnaires were sent to university researchers and senior members of semi-state organizations including Forfás,[2] Science Foundation Ireland, Ireland Information Society Commission, and Enterprise Ireland. A total of 39 responses were received, giving a response rate of 28.78%. To maintain the anonymity of the respondents, the single-page survey included identical stamped, addressed envelopes for returning the surveys. The option was provided for respondents to identify themselves to receive a summary of the completed research.

The replies to the primary survey point to a number of fundamental issues. There was recognition that "these are difficult problems to solve. There are no easy solutions, and the new directions are not obvious." In the current climate, there is a competition for resources—a "lack of commitment at Government level and other more critical priorities with respect to resources." Having achieved success in the 1990s, respondents saw Ireland "resting on the laurels of the 'Celtic Tiger'"; we have become too complacent to the dangers. "We are in the 'fat dumb and happy' phase of our economic/industrial development. When we wake up to the threat of east European and Chinese knowledge economies it may be too late." There is a clear "recognition that a knowledge-based economy will not come out of the current business/education/union structure we have today." The national system of innovation is flawed and inimical to innovation.

Underlying all of these issues are cultural attitudes. There is a problem of "vested interests and cultural apathy," and there is an acknowledgment that "culture takes time to change"—particularly the issue of our cultural attitudes to science and entrepreneurship. The Irish education system is not geared to science, reflecting "people's attitudes to science in general." Institutions and structures do not just shape attitudes, values, and beliefs in a vacuum; they embed and reflect existing values, beliefs, and attitudes—making change difficult. Ireland's approach to universities as places of learning, not places of commerce, results in a "mindset in universities, which does not recognize that its role is essential in creating knowledge, protecting IP and commercializing it." This combination of problems results in "inertia at all levels." Ireland does not value science and is not willing to pay for it, illustrated by the historic low levels of investment in R&D. The "government's percentage of the contribution for R&D (about 26%), is much less than in other countries. It follows that we are dependant on non-governmental investment, which while admirable, yields outcomes which are less readily altered for Ireland's strategic interests." "Our attitude as a nation that science is highbrow and not for the masses" and a "cultural bias against science particularly since the down turn" are at the core of the problem. A number of other problems are competing for attention, and people are "preoccupied with the current bread and butter issues distracted from the problems in these areas."

The issues that are holding us back are deep structural and cultural issues, not superficial ones. There is a clear incongruity between where Ireland needs to go and the current value system. There is an unwillingness to pay the price required to become an innovative knowledge-based economy. Ultimately it requires a "question of belief in what the building blocks of the future are; people must be convinced of the value of the knowledge-based economy"; without an appreciation of this there can be no real progress towards a culture of lifelong learning ("education at all levels") and entrepreneurship ("risk culture").

Identifying Ireland's priorities

Brugha (2000) suggests a three-level analysis of the results of the priority pointing procedure.

> The primary diagnostic method is to seek the greatest imbalances, e.g., push versus pull, then pliability versus productivity, and then, within pliability, punch versus prevention. The secondary diagnostic method is to accept the view of the greater number, e.g., push rather than pull, and then practice rather than pliability. Notice the conflict that can arise between the primary and secondary methods. The tertiary method is by content analysis. (p. 238)

Applying all three methods in this case leads to the same conclusion: A culture apathetic to science does not value the skills and activities needed to develop an innovative knowledge-based economy. This problem is preventing us from taking action to resolve our difficulties. There is an urgent need for a debate at a societal level to highlight this problem. Concomitant with this is the need for the State to promote the scientific and engineering skills required to develop an innovative knowledge-based economy as well as reforming the institutional and structural support systems to enable this to happen. The content analysis also throws up the issue of lack of resources to solve the problem. This ties in the areas of "price" and "practice" and shows some of the deeper issues with "pliability" in the State.

The primary data provide us with a cogent summary of the current situation of the Irish State on the route to becoming an innovative knowledge-based economy. The problem is one of awareness and of the negative perception of the value of science in society. The problem is a pernicious one, with self-reinforcing negative feedback circuits. There are problems with the education system because we do not value science. The route to resolving the problem is through promotion and pliability, essentially reforming the structures to improve the education system to create a scientifically literate culture. But because we do not value science, promoting these changes is difficult, and making the necessary changes to the existing structures is complex. The proper framework for an innovative knowledge-based economy is missing. There is poor understanding of science, little research and development, and poor linkages between university and industry—essentially a lack of communicative rationality. The structures and the policies that should enable a dynamic, vibrant, informed citizenry are missing. In its place are bureaucratic, static structures, inflexible and resistant to change. Intractable problems including changing attitudes, reforming obstinate cultures, and transforming obdurate vales have yet to be tackled. There is a lot to be done, and it must be done in a coherent, systematic way, treating the whole rather than each part of the system individually.

Supporting Research

There is significant supporting research for our conclusions. There is a general problem of education for the innovative knowledge-based economy; difficulties in research and development; problems with structures, university, industry, and technology transfer; issues of culture, values, and innovation; and difficulties caused by the role of the State and its institutions. We provide a summary of these findings here. For the full details of this research, we direct you to Casey (2003) and Casey and Brugha (2004)

The Global Information Technology Survey 2003 (WEF/Insead, 2003), which examines readiness for the knowledge-based economy of the future, ranked Ireland 24th in quality of mathematics and science education, 28th for literacy, and 37th for secondary school enrollment. One notable point was that it found there is only a 77% completion rate for secondary education, figures confirmed by the Central Statistics Office. The IMD Global Competitiveness survey examination of Ireland in relation to 29 small economies ranked Ireland 17th for scientific education (IMD, 2003). In recent EU surveys Ireland ranked last of the EU 15 in the belief in the importance of the development of new skills for career advancement (EU, 2002b, 2002c; EuroStat, 2001).

The problems with the education system are ongoing issues that were in one sense compounded by the introduction of free secondary education in 1966. As Wickham (1997) points out, "Because it simply made access to the academically oriented system easier, rather than changing the system itself, it ensured for the next thirty years Irish education would be marked by continual 'academic drift'." The education system values rote learning over vocational development and distorts the content of second level education, setting the focus of education as jumping a specific hurdle rather than as a preparation for life. The problems of the points system are linked with Lee's criticisms of the educational aspirations of the Irish professional classes and their "obsession with entry into secure professions (law and medicine) rather than science and technology" and "their lack of entrepreneurial drive" (Wickham [1997] referring to the work of Lee [1989]). The high points required for law and medicine and the ongoing decline in points for science and engineering illustrate the persistent nature of this problem.

David Guile points to similar deficiencies in the structure of education systems within the EU, systems that foster an impoverished notion of knowledge as a process of acquisition of facts (Guile, 2003). The flaw he points to is that this approach conflicts with the needs of a knowledge-based society to generate new knowledge, to innovate. Guile calls for the development of tools for intellectual exploration, criticism, and understanding among students, further emphasizing the urgency of the Taskforce recommendations.

In relative terms, the EU currently lags U.S. spending by 0.75% of GDP. In absolute terms this means that the U.S. spends 40% more on government funded R&D as a percentage of GDP than the EU. When converted into monetary terms, the difference is US$92.67 billion. The figures for Ireland indicate a miserly approach to investment in R&D. Ireland spends 1.21% of GDP on R&D using the GERD approach. Accounting for the distortion to GDP caused by transfer pricing of multinationals in Ireland (Barry, 2002) and using the lower figure of GNP, Ireland still emerges with a figure of 1.42% investment in R&D. These differences are magnified when compared to the EU target figure of 3% (Gannon, 2003).

The Irish State is required to invest an extra US$595 million per year to make up its current shortfall. In 2000, the Irish Government established Science Foundation Ireland (SFI) with the goal of establishing a world-class scientific infrastructure in Ireland. The figures above include investment by Science Foundation Ireland in R&D since, and indicate that even if SFI realizes its ambition to establish 50 world-class research groups within Ireland, Ireland will not even manage to keep pace with other countries. The Higher

Education Authority (HEA) recognizes the "the need for significant allocations for research technology and innovation will be difficult trajectory for Ireland" (HEA, 2002, p. 35). This again points toward the issues of price and promotion and the problems with pliability in the Irish innovation system.

The Irish Council for Science, Technology and Innovation's report on "Utilizing intellectual property for competitive advantage" (ICSTI, 2003) points out that there are significant problems with the commercialization of research in Ireland. Key among these is that there is no system of management of publicly funded IP, and there is a lack of professionalism in technology transfer. Underpinning this is that there is no backlog of IP waiting to be commercialized in Irish universities. The poor level of R&D at a national level in Ireland is reflected in the lack of intellectual property developed by the university system. The ICSTI report also points to cultural gaps between universities and industry.

ICSTI (2003), in similar findings, states that "ten-fold increase in resources would not bring us to the level of our principle competitor countries" (p. 14). Technology transfer does not just happen it has to be actively pursued. There are a number of models available. Harding (2002) provides examples from the German innovation system while Abramson et al. provide examples of the U.S. model. People cause spillovers and knowledge transfer. The presence of MNCs and large-scale investment in FDI in the Irish economy has resulted in some contradictory outcomes and very poor spillovers (Arora et al., 2000; Ó'Gráda, 2002). Ó'Domhnaill (2003) describes how the boundaries between disciplines and organizations cause knowledge fragmentation. Referring to research on Japan, Ó'Domhnaill (2003) points out that technology transfer between universities and firms involves transfer of tacit knowledge linked with co-location (Wen & Kobayashi, 2001; Ó'Domhnaill, 2003). This is the idea of knowledge developed above: the creation of meaning and shared understanding through the interaction of people, leading to learning and the development of innovation and new knowledge. One specific approach to accomplishing this is through the development of business incubators designed to foster economic growth. There is a lack of development of such centers in Ireland when compared to other EU countries (EU, 2002b). Notably, those countries better at transferring and diffusing knowledge have more incubators.

Summarizing the Priorities

The ominous state of R&D in Ireland further illustrates issues of how we value science and how our institutions' structures are inadequate for future growth and development. The issue of technology transfer further reinforces these issues and also illustrates the link between knowledge, innovation structure, and promotion. The detailed examination of culture points to the historical origins of the problem in the rigid cultural system and describes some steps towards changing this culture, again bound up in issues of structural change, and promotion and management of change within the structures and the value system. The final step involves reviewing the role of the State, the center where these changes must begin if Ireland is to become an innovative knowledge-based society. The combination of the primary data analysis, supported by the secondary data, has uncovered the priority for Ireland in developing as an innovative knowledge-based economy: the need to appreciate the value of science, innovation, and knowledge. The necessary steps to resolving this situation begin through active promotion of a scientific culture and the active creation of the dynamic flexible structures—literally a national system of innovation, to support, nourish, and encourage this new culture.

CONCLUSIONS

This project set out to explore the question: "What are the key priorities for Ireland to become an innovative knowledge-based economy?" In an earlier paper (Casey & Brugha, 2004), we presented some of these findings. Fundamentally the national system of innovation is flawed and inimical to innovation. There is a problem of "vested interests and cultural apathy"[3] and an acknowledgment that culture takes time to change—particularly the issue of cultural attitudes to science and entrepreneurship. The Irish education system is not geared to science, reflecting people's attitudes to science in general. The problem is one of awareness and of the negative perception of the value of science in society (price in the wheel in Figure 16.3). This is a pernicious problem, with self-reinforcing negative feedback circuits. It affects the education system because it does not adequately value science. The route to resolving the problem is through promotion of science, and pliability, essentially reforming the structures to improve the education system to create a scientifically literate culture. A further exploration of this is given in Casey & Brugha (2004).

In this chapter we have examined the policy implications for Ireland as an innovative knowledge-based economy. By highlighting the complex nature of knowledge, innovation, and social policy, we have questioned the cultural orthodoxy that sees Ireland well placed to become an innovative knowledge-based economy. Tolstoy (1911) wrote,

> It is beyond the power of the human intellect to encompass all the causes of any phenomenon. But the impulse to search into causes is inherent in man's very nature. And so the human intellect, without investigating the multiplicity

and complexity of circumstances conditioning any event, any one of which taken separately may seem to be the reason for it, snatches at the most comprehensible approximation to a cause and says: 'There is the cause.' (p. 254)

We have attempted to address this question without falling into the trap that Tolstoy has discussed. By using a number of ideas derived from various strands of complexity theory, the nature of knowledge, language and embodied cognition; by relating them to the national system of innovation and by subscribing to the importance of a plurality of perspectives, accessed through the Priority Pointing Procedure, we have begun to probe this question and to deepen our understanding of what is required to develop an innovative knowledge based economy.

Priority Pointing does not offer a detailed prescription. There is no suggestion of a magic bullet; there are no magic bullets to resolve complex problems. Priority Pointing points to where the solution is not (e.g., not more planning), rather than to where the solution is. It does not suggest the form of activity within the promotion and pliability sectors. It does provide a rich language with which to discuss the issues further, a language provided by the respondents. This overcomes the Wittgenstein problem— "the limits of my language are the limits of my thoughts"—by creating a language based on a shared context that points towards the actions to be taken. It is a very practical and useful procedure. The same study could be done in other countries or regions, and the results compared, both the emerging priorities and their language. The same procedure can be applied to any strategic question. The main difficulty is with the interpretation of the answers.

Ireland has relied and continues to rely on external support for the development of the economy. There is a perception that the way to resolve the knowledge deficits is through the spending programs such as Science Foundation Ireland. The problem is that these programs will fail without the creation of a communicative rationality that perceives the value of knowledge sharing, without the structural support to encourage such sharing and without the cultural belief in the importance of science and technology. As with any healthy system, the Irish national system of innovation needs to be capable of dynamic changes, of autopoietic second-order learning. Not being able to predict the future means we need to hedge our bets by sustaining the requisite fit with our current environment while planning for (and creating) changes in this environment. The key to future economic success is diversity, trying many things, accepting that not all of them will succeed, and maintaining a healthy doubt over our own plans and predictions. Like the witchdoctor, we are not able to control the rain. However, a healthy dynamic system of national innovation could provide us with an umbrella.

NOTES

1. For a more detailed treatment see Casey (2003) and references therein.
2. Ireland's National Policy and Advisory Board for Enterprise, Trade, Science, Technology and Innovation.
3. Quotes in this section are taken from responses to the six questions.

REFERENCES

Abramson, H. N., Encarnacao, J., Ried, P., & Schmoch, U. (Eds.) (1997). Technology Transfer Systems in the United States and Germany: Lessons and Perspectives. National Academy Press, Washington DC.

Acemoglu, J. & Robinson, D (2002). *Economic backwardness in political perspective.* Massachusetts Institute of Technology, Department of Economics Working Paper Series, Working Paper 02-13, http://papers.ssrn.com/sol3/papers.cfm?abstract_id=303188.

Adams, J. L. (1996). *Conceptual blockbusting: A guide to better ideas.* Philadelphia: Perseus Books.

Allee, V. (1997). *The knowledge evolution: Building organizational intelligence.* Newton, MA: Butterworth-Heinemann.

Amsden, A. & Mourshed, M. (1997). Scientific publications, patents and technological capabilities in late-industrializing countries. *Technology Analysis & Strategic Management, 9*(3), 343–360.

Archibugi, D. & Lundvall, B.-Å. (2001). *The globalizing learning economy.* Oxford, UK: Oxford University Press.

Arthur, B. (1990). Silicon Valley locational clusters: Do increasing returns imply monopoly? *Mathematical Social Sciences, 19*, 235–251.

Arora, A., Gambardella, A., & Torrisi., S. (2000, July). *International outsourcing and emergence of industrial clusters: The software industry in Ireland and India.* Paper prepared for the "SV and its imitators" meeting, SIEPR, Stanford University (http://siepr.stanford.edu/conferences/silicon_papers/Aagtjuly.pdf)

Australia. (2001). *Backing Australia's innovation.* Retrieved October 13, 2009 from http://pandora.nla.gov.au/pan/32884/20030307-0000/backingaus.innovation.gov.au/statement/index.htm

Barry, F. (2002). *A note on transfer pricing and the R&D intensity of Irish manufacturing.* Centre for Economic Research Working Paper Series, WP02/30, University College Dublin.

Bond, P. (2003, July). *The biology of the technology of the "magic bullet": From BPR to objects of art.* Paper presented at the Standing Conference on Organizational Symbolism (SCOS), Cambridge.

Brooks, F. P. (1987). No silver bullet: Essence and accidents of software engineering. *IEEE Computer, 20*(4), 10–19.

Brooks, F. P. (1995). *The mythical man month: Essays on software engineering.* Reading, MA: Addison-Wesley.

Brown, D. E. (1991). *Human universals.* New York: McGraw-Hill.

Brown, J. S. & Duguid, P. (2002). *The social life of information* (Rev. ed.). Boston, MA: Harvard Business School Press.

Brugha, C. (1974). *The appraisal and alleviation of transportation needs in a conurbation.* Unpublished MBA dissertation, Trinity College Dublin.

Brugha, C. (1998a). The structure of qualitative decision-making. *European Journal of Operational Research, 104*(1), 46–62.

Brugha, C. (1998b). The structure of adjustment decision-making. *European Journal of Operational Research, 104*(1), 63–76.

Brugha, C. (1998c). The structure of development decision-making. *European Journal of Operational Research, 104*(1), 77–92.

Brugha, C. (2000). An introduction to the Priority Pointing Procedure. *Journal of Multi-Criteria Decision Analysis, 9,* 227–242.

Brugha, C. (2001). A decision-science based discussion of the systems development life cycle in information systems. *Information Systems Frontiers, 3*(1), 91–105.

Carroll, C. (2001). The primacy of imagination. In T. Dromgoole, S. J. Carroll, L. Gorman & P. C. Flood (Eds.), *Managing strategic implementation* (pp. 183–195). London, UK: Blackwell Business.

Casey, D. (2003). *Exploring Ireland's priorities in becoming an innovative knowledge-based economy.* Unpublished MBA dissertation, University College Dublin.

Casey, D. & Brugha, C. (2004). Implications of knowledge economy for citizens: An empirical exploration. *Systemic Practice and Action Research, 17*(6), 557–571.

Casti, J. L. (1991). *Searching for certainty: What scientists can know about the future.* London: Abacus.

Conklin, E. J. & Weil, W. (1997). *Wicked problems: Naming the pain in organizations.* Touchstone Consulting Group White Paper (http://www.touchstone.com/tr/wp/wicked.html)

Cook, S. & Brown, J. S. (1999). Bridging epistemologies: The generative dance between organizational knowledge and organizational knowing. *Organization Science, 10*(4), 381–400.

Corning, P. A. (2003). *Nature's magic: Synergy in evolution and the fate of humankind.* Cambridge, UK: Cambridge University Press.

Culliton, J. (1995). *Ireland: Department of Industry and Commerce Report, Industrial Policy Review Group.* Department of Industry and Commerce, Dublin IDA.

Damasio, A. R. (1996). *Descartes' error: Emotion, reason, and the human brain.* London, UK: Papermac.

Deacon, T. W. (1997). *The symbolic species: The co-evolution of language and the brain.* New York: W. W. Norton.

Dennett, D. (1995). *Darwin's dangerous idea.* New York: Simon & Schuster.

Denning, P. J. (2003). The profession of IT: Accomplishment. *Communications of the ACM, 46*(7), 19–23.

Department of Trade and Enterprise. (1998). *Building the knowledge driven economy.* London, UK: DTI.

Drucker, P. (1994). The age of social transformation. *The Atlantic Monthly, 274*(5), 53–80.

Drucker, P. (1999). Knowledge worker productivity: The biggest challenge. *California Management Review, 41*(2), 79–94.

Ekman, P. (1992). Are there basic emotions? *Psychological Review, 99,* 550–553.

EU. (2000). Preparing the transition to a competitive, dynamic and knowledge-based economy: Presidency conclusions March 23 and 24, 2000, Brussels, European Union.

EU. (2002a). *Eight report from the commission on the implementation of the telecommunications regulatory package.* Retrieved September 1, 2003 from http://europa.eu.int/information_society/topics/telecoms/implementation/annual_report/8threport/finalreport/com2002_0695en01.pdf.

EU. (2002b) *2002 European innovation scoreboard: Technical paper no 4–Indicators and definitions.* European Trend Chart on Innovation. Retrieved September 1, 2003 from http://www.google.com/search?hl=en&q=Technical+paper+no.+4%3A+Indicators+and+definitions.

EU. (2002c). *Annex Table B: European Innovation Scoreboard 2002–Member States and Associate Countries.* Published in Commission staff working paper: 2002 European innovation scoreboard. Retrieved September 1, 2003 from http://trendchart.cordis.lu/Reports/Documents/SEC_2002_1349_EN.pdf.

EuroStat. (2001). "Labour force survey 2001/2000," EuroStat.

Freeman, C. (1995). The national system of innovation in historical perspective. *Cambridge Journal of Economics, 19*(1), 5–24.

Fitzgerald, B. & Howcroft, D. (1998). Towards dissolution of the IS research debate: From polarization to polarity. *Journal of Information Technology, 13*(4), 313–326.

Foucault, M. (1983). Power and truth. In H. L. Dreyfus & M. Rainbow (Eds.), *Michel Foucault: Beyond structuralism and hermeneutics* (2nd ed., pp. 184–203). Chicago: University of Chicago Press.

Gannon, F. (2003). Government rhetoric and their R&D expenditure. *EMBO Reports, 4*(2), 117–120.

Garvin, T. (2004). *Preventing the future: Why was Ireland so poor for so long?* Dublin: Gill & McMillan.

Gleick, J. (1999). *Faster: The acceleration of just about everything.* New York: Little Brown.

Gell-Mann, M. (1995). *The quark and the jaguar: Adventures in the simple and the complex.* London: Abacus.

Godin, B. (2004). The new economy: What the concept owes to the OECD. *Research Policy, 33*(5), 679–690.

Gould, S. J. (2002). *The structure of evolutionary theory.* Cambridge, MA: Belknap Press.

Guile, D (2003). From "credentialism" to the "practice of learning": Reconceptualizing learning for the knowledge economy. *Policy Futures in Education, 1*(1), 83–105.

Habermas, J. (1984). *The theory of communicative action, Vol. 1.* Boston: Beacon Press.

Halverson, R. R. (2002). *Representing phronesis: Supporting instructional leadership practice in schools.* Unpublished Ph.D. thesis, Northwestern University (http://www.soemadison.wisc.edu/edadmin/people/faculty/halverson/Halverson-DissSummary.pdf)

Harding, R. (2002). Competition and collaboration in German technology transfer. *European Management Journal, 20*(5), 470–485.

Harris, J. R. (2000). *The nurture assumption.* London, UK: Bloomsbury.

HEA. (2002). Creating and sustaining the innovation society, The Higher Education Authority, Dublin. Retrieved September 1, 2003 from http://www.hea.ie/uploads/pdf/HEA%20Innovation.pdf.

ICSTI. (2003). ICSTI Statement: Utilizing Intellectual Property for Competitive Advantage. Irish Council for Science Technology and Innovation, Dublin. Retrieved September 1, 2003 from http://www.forfas.ie/icsti/statements/030409_icsti_intellectual_prop.pdf.

IMD (2003). World competitiveness yearbook 2003, IMD. Retrieved September 1, 2003 from http://www02.imd.ch/wcc/pricing/.

Innovation, *n.* (1992).Shorter Oxford English dictionary, 9th Edition 1992, Oxford University Press.

ISC (2002). Building the knowledge society: Report to government, Dublin: Information Society Commission December. Retrieved September 1, 2003 from http://www.isc.ie/downloads/know.pdf.

Johnson, B. & Lundvall, B.-Å. (2001). *Why all this fuss about codified and tacit knowledge?* DRUID Winter Conference. Retrieved September 1, 2003 from http://www.druid.dk/conferences/winter2001/%20paper-winter/Paper/johnson%20&%20lundvall.pdf.

Johnson, G. (1996). *Fire in the mind: Science, faith, and the search for order.* New York: Vintage.

Kant, I. (2003). *Critique of pure reason* (rev. 2nd ed.). N. K. Smith (Trans.). London: Palgrave Macmillan. (Original work published 1781)

Kauffman, S. (1993). *The origins of order: Self-organization and selection in evolution.* Oxford, UK: Oxford University Press.

Kay, R. & Cecez-Kecmanovic, D. (2002, December).Toward an autopoietic perspective on information systems organization. In L. Applegate, R. Galliers & J. DeGross (Eds.), *Proceedings 23rd international conference on information systems, 15th-18th December, Barcelona, Spain* (pp. 383–390).

Knowledge. *n.* (1989). Oxford English Dictionary 1989 Edition, accessed online through Athens.

Koestler, A. (1990). *The art of creation.* London: Penguin. (Original work published in 1964)

Krugman, P. (1997). Good news from Ireland: A geographical perspective. In A. W. Gray (Ed.), *International perspectives on the Irish economy* (pp. 38–53). Dublin: Indecon Economic Consultants.

Kuhn, T. S. (1970). *The structure of scientific revolution* (2nd ed.). Chicago: University of Chicago Press.

Lakoff, G. & Johnson, M. (1999). *Philosophy in the flesh: The embodied mind and its challenge to Western thought.* New York: Basic Books.

Lakoff, G. & Johnson, M. (2003). *Metaphors we live by* (2nd ed.). Chicago: University of Chicago Press.

Lee, J. J. (1989). *Ireland, 1912-1985: Politics and society.* Cambridge, UK: Cambridge University Press.

Luhmann, N. (1986). The autopoiesis of social systems. In F. Geyer & J. van der Zouwen (Eds.), *Sociocybernetic paradoxes: Observation, control and evolution of self-steering systems* (pp. 172–192). Beverly Hills: Sage.

Lundvall, B.-Å. (1992). *National systems of innovation: Towards a theory of innovation and interactive learning.* New York: St. Martins Press.

Lundvall, B.-Å. (1996). *The social dimension of the learning economy.* DRUID working paper no. 96.1. Retrieved September 1, 2003 from http://ideas.repec.org/p/aal/abbswp/96-1.html.

Lundvall B.-Å., (2004). Introduction to "Technological infrastructure and international competitiveness" by Christopher Freeman. *Industrial and Corporate Change, 13*(3), 531–539.

Lundvall, B.-Å, & Johnson, B. (1994), The learning economy. *Journal of Industry Studies, 1*(2), 23–42.

Lundvall, B.-Å., Johnson, B., Andersen, E. S. & Dalum, B. (2002).National systems of production, innovation and competence building. *Research Policy, 31*, 213–231.

Macsharry, R., & White, P. A. (2000). *The making of the Celtic Tiger: The inside story of Ireland's boom economy.* Dublin: Mercier Press.

Margulis, L. & Fester, R. (Eds.). (1991). *Symbiosis as a source of evolutionary innovation: Speciation and morphogenesis.* Cambridge, MA: MIT Press.

Margulis, L. & Sagan, D. (2002). *Acquiring genomes: A theory of the origin of species.* New York: Basic Books.

Markus, M. L. (1983). Power, politics and MIS implementation. *Communications of the ACM, 26*, 430–444.

Markus, M. L. & Benjamin, R. I. (1997). The magic bullet theory in IT-enabled transformation. *Sloan Management Review, 38*(2), 55–68.

Mason, R. & Mitroff, I. (1981). *Challenging strategic planning assumptions.* New York: Wiley.

Maturana, H. R. & Varela, F. (1980). Autopoiesis and cognition: The realization of the living. In R. S. Cohen & M. W. Wartofsky (Eds.), *Boston studies in the philosophy of science, vol. 42.* Dordecht, Holland: D. Reidel Publishing.

Maturana, H. R. & Varela, F. (1992). The *knowledge tree: The biological roots of human understanding* (Rev. ed.). Boston: Shambala.

Mingers, J. (1995). *Self-producing systems: Implications and applications of autopoiesis.* New York: Plenum Press.

Mokyr, J. (1998). *Science, technology, and knowledge: What historians can learn from an evolutionary approach.* Working papers on Economics and evolution, #98-03, Jena, Germany: Max Planck Institute for Research into Economic Systems.

Mokyr, J. (2002). *The gifts of Athena: Historical origins of the knowledge economy.* Princeton: Princeton University Press.

MTI (1999). The knowledge economy. submission to the New Zealand Government, Ministry of Trade and Industry, Wellington.

National Economic and Social Council (NESC), (1982). *Telesis: A Review of Industrial Policy.* Dublin: NESC.

Ó'Domhnaill, C, (2003). *The Irish innovation imperative: What do we know?* MBA Dissertation, UCD Smurfit Business School.

OECD (1996a). *Measuring what people know: Human capital accounting for the knowledge economy.* Paris: OECD.

OECD (1996b). *Employment and growth in the knowledge-based economy (OECD documents).* Paris: OECD.

OECD (1997). *Industrial competitiveness in the knowledge-based economy: The new role of governments.* Paris: OECD.

Ó'Grada, C. (2002). *Is the Celtic Tiger a paper tiger?* Centre for Economic Research Working Paper, University College Dublin.

O'Nuallain, S. (2002). *Being human: The search for order.* Bristol: Intellect.

Ó Riain, S. (1997a). An offshore Silicon Valley? The emerging Irish software industry. *Competition and Change: The Journal of Global Business and Political Economy, 2,* 175–212.

Ó Riain, S. (1997b). The birth of a Celtic Tiger? *Communications of the ACM, 40*(3), 11–16.

O Riain, S. (2000). The flexible developmental state: Globalization, information technology, and the "Celtic tiger." *Politics and Society, 28*(2), 157–193.

Plice, R. K. & Kraemer, K. L. (2001). *Measuring payoffs from information-technology investments: New evidence from sector-level data on developed and developing countries.* Center for Research on Information Technology and Organizations, IT in Business, Paper 270, http://repositories.cdlib.org/crito/business/270.

Pinker, S. (2002). *The blank slate: The modern denial of human nature.* London: Penguin/Allen Lane.

Pirsig, R. (1992). *Zen and the art of motorcycle maintenance* (2nd ed.). London, UK: Black Swan.

Pirsig, R. (1995). *Lila: An enquiry into morals.* London, UK: Black Swan.

Polanyi, M. (1958). *Personal knowledge: Towards a post-critical philosophy.* Chicago: University of Chicago Press.

Ramachandran, V. S. & Hubbard, E. M. (2001). Synaesthesia: A window into perception, thought and language. *Journal of Consciousness Studies, 8*(12), 3–34.

Ramachandran, V. S. (2003). *The emerging mind: The BBC Reith Lecture 2003.* London, UK: Penguin.

Remenyi, D. & Sherwood-Smith, M. (1999). Maximize information systems value by continuous participative evaluation logistics. *Information Management, 12*(1/2), 14–31.

Remenyi, D., White, T. & Sherwood-Smith, M. (1999). Language and a post-modern management approach to information systems. *International Journal of Information Management, 19,* 17–32.

Richardson, K. (2005). Pluralism in management science. In K. A. Richardson (Ed.), *Managing Organizational Complexity: Philosophy, Theory, and Application* (pp. 109–114). Greenwich, CT: Information Age Publishing.

Rittel, H. & Webber, M. (1973). Dilemmas in a general theory of planning. *Policy Sciences, 4,* 155–169.

Roberts, N. C. (2000, March). Coping with wicked problems. Paper presented to the 3rd bi-annual research conference of the International Public Management Network, Sydney, Australia (draft available at http://www.inpuma.net/research/papers/sydney/nancyroberts.html)

Romer, P. M. (1986). Increasing returns and long-run growth. *Journal of Political Economy, 94*(5), 1002–1037.

Romer, P. M. (1990). Endogenous technological change. *Journal of Political Economy, 98*(5), 71–102.

Sala-i-Martin, X. (2002). *15 Years of Growth Economics: What Have we Learnt?* Columbia University Department of Economics Discussion Paper Series, #0102-47, http://www.columbia.edu/cu/economics/discpapr/DP0102-47.pdf.

Simon, H. (1996). *The sciences of the artificial* (3rd ed.). Cambridge, MA: MIT Press.

Snowden, D. J. (2002). Complex acts of knowing: Paradox and descriptive self awareness. *The Journal of Knowledge Management, 6*(2), 100–111.

Stacey, R. (2000). The emergence of knowledge in organizations. *Emergence, 2*(4), 23–49.

Stacey, R. (2002). *The impossibility of managing knowledge.* RSA Lectures, http://www.thersa.org.uk/acrobat/ralph_stacey270202.pdf.

Stiglitz, J. (1998). *Towards a new paradigm for development: Strategies, policies, and processes.* Prebisch Lecture at UNCTAD, http://siteresources.worldbank.org/CDF/Resources/prebisch98.pdf.

Stiglitz, J. (1999, January). Public Policy for a Knowledge Economy Remarks at the Department for Trade and Industry and Center for Economic Policy Research. London, 27th January, http://web.worldbank.org/WBSITE/EXTERNAL/NEWS/0,,contentMDK:20025143~menuPK:34474~pagePK:42770~theSitePK:4607,00.html.

Sveiby, K. E. (2001). A knowledge-based theory of the firm to guide in strategy formulation. *Journal of Intellectual Capital, 2*(4), 344–358.

Taleb, N. N. (2003). *Fooled by randomness* (2nd ed.). London: Thompson Textere.

Tallon.P & Kraemer K. L. (1999). *Information technology and economic development: Ireland's coming of age with lessons for developing countries.* Center for Research on Information Technology and Organizations, I.T. in Business Paper 136, http://repositories.cdlib.org/cgi/viewcontent.cgi?article=1075&context=crito.

Trauth, E. M. (2000). *The culture of an information economy: Influences and impacts in the Republic of Ireland.* Norwell, MA: Kluwer Academic Publishers.

Tolstoy, L. (1911). *The novels and other works of Lyof N. Tolstoï, Volume 5.* New York: Scribner.

Toffler, A. (1970). *Future shock.* New York: Random House.

Watson, L. (2000). *Jacobson's organ: And the remarkable nature of smell.* London: Penguin.

WEF/Insead (2003). *Global information technology report: Readiness for the networked world.* New York: Oxford University Press.

Weinberg , G. M. (2001). *An introduction to general systems thinking.* New York: Dorset House.

Wen, J. & Kobayashi, S. (2001). Exploring collaborative R&D network: Some new evidence in Japan. *Research Policy, 30*(8), 1309–1319.

White, M. (1997). *Isaac Newton: The last sorcerer.* London: Fourth Estate.

Wickham, J. (1997, April). *Where is Ireland in the global information society?* Paper presented at Ireland, Europe and the global information society: A conference for social scientists, Dublin (http://www.dcu.ie/communications/iegis/Jw-pap.htm)

Winograd, T. & Flores, F. R. (1986). *Understanding computers and cognition: A new foundation for design.* Norwood, NJ: Ablex.

Wright, R. (2000). *Nonzero: History, evolution and human cooperation.* London: Abacus.

CHAPTER 17

FACILITATING LEARNING AND INNOVATION IN ORGANIZATIONS USING COMPLEXITY SCIENCE PRINCIPLES

Carol Webb, Fiona Lettice, and Mark Lemon

INNOVATION: THE NEED FOR LEARNING AND COMPLEXITY SCIENCE

Rothwell (1994) proposes five generations of models of innovation: the technology push model, the market pull model, the coupling model, the integrated model, and the fifth generation—the systems integration and networking model. These models have been developed and implemented in industry, to greater and lesser degrees, over the course of the last 50 years. While the fifth-generation model seeks to incorporate a systems thinking perspective on the processes of innovation, recent recognition of the phenomenon of discontinuous (or disruptive) innovation, in addition to new literature from the complexity science domain, suggests that the fifth-generation model may be in need of further refinement.

Complexity and Knowledge Management, pages 317–334
317

Discontinuous innovation, also referred to as "disruptive innovation," "transformational innovation," or "paradigm shift innovation," is said to deliver major change and creates new value networks that eventually replace traditional mainstream markets with a new value proposition (Moore, 1995). As such, environmental conditions prevalent with this type of innovation are said to be characterized by high competency-destroying turbulence and technical and market uncertainty—in essence, creating a shake-up for previously dominant players. Such discontinuity can be brought on by a range of triggers, including, for example, the emergence of new technologies and markets, changes in a political regime or social attitudes and behavior, or the introduction of new business models such as low-cost airlines (e.g., Ryanair). Subsequent disruptive innovations require new skills, abilities, and knowledge (Tushman & Anderson, 1986). While continuous innovation could operate within mental frameworks based on clear and accepted rules of the game, discontinuous innovation means there are no clear rules, and that these emerge over time, with a high tendency toward lack of clarity and high ambiguity. While continuous innovation was suited to path-dependent strategies and refined, stable operating routines, discontinuous innovation calls for path-independent strategies based on an emergent, probe-and-learn approach, where operating patterns are emergent and "fuzzy" (Dvir, Lettice, & Thomond, 2004).

Theory has sought to address these challenges experienced in practice, and one domain offering highly relevant resources is that of complexity science. In their proposition of innovation in manufacturing as an evolutionary complex system, Rose-Anderssen, Allen, Tsinopoulos, and McCarthy (2005) demonstrated how a complex systems view could provide an overall conceptual framework for thinking about innovation and for considering how this helps to provide understanding and advice for the organization of new product development in different circumstances. At the project level, Harkema (2003) advocates the use of a complex adaptive perspective on learning within innovation projects and argued in favor of applying a complex adaptive approach to evaluate and analyze learning and innovation processes. In line with this, she suggests that a manager's perception of reality should acknowledge that reality is not static and linear, but complex, dynamic, and nonlinear, and as such unpredictable. Meanwhile, Fonseca (2002) views innovation from the perspective of complex responsive processes of relating and describes innovation in this way as a new patterning of our experiences of being together, as new meaning emerges from ordinary, everyday conversations that take place in the working environment. In this vein, Stacey (2000, 2001, 2003a, 2003b) and Stacey, Griffin, and Shaw (2000) have suggested that analogies from the complexity science domain can help us learn about, and make sense of, such experiences.

What has been missing in this regard is a set of tools to help initiate, and begin to facilitate, learning about complexity science in a way that will enable individuals in the context of innovation, or indeed any other context, to understand their work and interactions with others by means of it. While the case has been made that it is of use to apply complexity science to the domain of innovation, no means have been provided to address this issue. This chapter, however, presents a set of tools that do. The tools proposed are designed in harmony with key principles of complexity science, experiential learning, and diverse learning styles and preferences, and they aim to communicate complexity science principles effectively to different audiences.

EXPERIENTIAL LEARNING

For the purposes of this chapter, Kolb's (1973, 1979, 1984) ideas concerning experiential learning and the learning cycle are of relevance and are described here in more detail. Kolb and Fry (1975) presented their applied theory of experiential learning, which Kolb (1984) later elaborated upon, and on which research has been carried out and expanded upon into the fields of business, management, and with specific types of application made in organizational contexts (Garvin & Ramsier, 2003; Paul & Mukhopadhyay, 2004; Van Reekum, 2005). In proposing a continual process of learning, Kolb (1979) presented the learning cycle (see adapted representation of this in Figure 17.1), which is based on the notion that learning is a cyclical process which needs to contain elements of each quadrant of the cycle

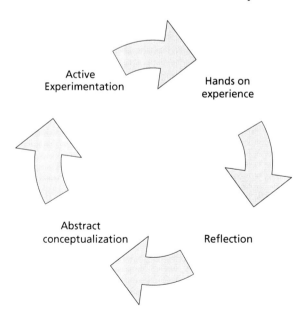

Figure 17.1

before learning is possible. This cycle is described in the following way: "Immediate concrete experience is the basis for observation and reflection. These observations are assimilated into a 'theory' from which new implications for action can be deduced. These implications, or hypotheses, then serve as guides in acting to create new experiences" (Kolb, 1973, p. 2).

Kolb's learning cycle became pivotal in many theories tying learning to organizational activities and organizational survival—for example, in terms of arguing in favor of giving employees time to reflect on what is going on, and how things could be tackled differently:

> David Kolb of MIT clearly has a good point when he stresses that learning from experience should be a cyclical process involving a period of Experience followed by a separate period of Reflection. Ideally this should be followed by a chance to put all the different pieces of the puzzle together (Conceptualizing) and possibly a reasonably risk-free opportunity to test out this new understanding through Experimentation. That should lead to further Experience, and so on. (Easterby-Smith, 1990, p. 5)

How this has been integrated in organizational practice and applications can be seen particularly in the literature pertaining to organizational learning, the learning organization, and the learning company.

ORGANIZATIONAL LEARNING, THE LEARNING ORGANIZATION, AND THE LEARNING COMPANY

Experiential learning was a major inspiration to Argyris and Schön (1978), Revans (1982), and Garrat (1987), who were early proponents of organizational learning and the learning organization, as were Senge (1990), Easterby-Smith (1990), and Pedler, Burgoyne, and Boydell (1991). Pedler et al. (1991) talked about the idea of the learning company, which they defined as "an organization that facilitates the learning of all its members and continuously transforms itself" (p. 1). The aim of this endeavor was to:

- Design and create organizations that are capable of adapting, changing, developing, and transforming themselves in response to the needs, wishes, and aspirations of people, inside and outside
- Enable companies to realize their assets without predatory takeovers
- Flex without hiring new leaders
- Avoid sudden and massive restructurings.

The choice of the term "learning company," as opposed to "learning organization" was grounded in the preference of the authors, who felt that while the word "organization" had connotations of an abstract and lifeless mechanism, the word "company," on the other hand, conveyed the idea of a group of people engaged in a joint enterprise: "In everyday terms we 'accompany' others and talk of doing things 'in company'. So we use the word 'company' for any collective endeavor and not to identify or give preference to a particular legal form or ownership pattern" (Pedler et al., 1991, p. 1). This conception of the learning company was, therefore, more heavily grounded in the importance of the people who were the members of the learning company. These people could include, for example, employees, owners, customers, suppliers, neighbors, the environment, and even competitors. In order for a company to realize itself as a learning company, Pedler et al. advocated a radical transformation in the form and character of what was already there, and said that this change could be facilitated through the deployment of the right tools—for example, through an electronic learning net (a company intranet with open access to data and the facilitation of group discussion), self and peer assessment, personal development plans, story-telling, and self-development groups. (Pedler et al. provide 101 such tools.)

The focus of such tools was sharpened when Easterby-Smith (1990) presented advice to help facilitate organizational learning, which included learning about organizational learning, promoting experimentation, and regulating awareness. Easterby-Smith advocated that people become aware of the learning process by starting with their own learning experiences—by reflecting on past experiences. The examples and the reasons why these people think they have managed to learn in the past should then become the focus of discussion. Making the link and transferring this to organizational learning was then to be done by providing illustrations from their own experiences of organizations learning or failing to learn from their mistakes, either from the present or past organizations in which people have worked. Easterby-Smith also advocated flexibility in the organizational structure and the need to introduce necessary slack into the organization so that people could have time to reflect on what was going on, and how things might be tackled differently. Easterby-Smith suggested that an obsession on the part of the organization with activity and the need to keep the product coming out at the other end was one of the biggest hindrances to organizational learning, and thus the need to refer back to Kolb's cycle of learning, which advocated steps of action, reflection, conceptualization, and experimentation (Easterby-Smith, 1990).

In this context, the use of narrative has been recognized as a facilitative learning tool that bridges reflection and performance (Ramsey, 2005). However, individuals have different learning styles, and therefore the methods and means by which they learn best will depend largely on factors relating to learning styles and preferences. In terms of individual learning styles, Boyle (2005) draws on the learning styles theory literature and describes the perceptual, physiological, sociological, psychological, environmental, and emotional ele-

AUDITORY: Those with auditory strengths learn by listening

TACTILE: You learn best when physically involved—e.g., in a meeting by note-taking

VISUAL PICTURE: You learn best by creating images in your mind's eye

KINESTHETIC: You learn best when employing your whole body—e.g., by role-playing

VISUAL TEXT: You learn best by reading the written word

VERBAL KINESTHETIC: You learn best when discussing information with others

Figure 17.2

ments and preferences of learning that differ from person to person. Perceptual elements, he explains, affect the way we learn and retain information, and this category includes six main learning styles: auditory; visual picture; visual text; tactile; kinesthetic; and, verbal (internal) kinesthetic. Boyle argues that individuals have personal preferences or strengths in at least one of these styles of learning, but that this differs from person to person. These styles and their implications for learning are represented in Figure 17.2.

Boyle's (2005) sociological elements category touches on learning styles—how we interact with others and our preferences for learning with others. These include:

- Working or learning alone
- Working or learning alone but then interacting with others after having had time to think things through
- Working in pairs
- Working in small groups or teams
- Working under the guidance of a supervisor and being critical of peers
- Preference for working with an expert—authority-oriented
- Varied preferences

The psychological elements refer to how people differ in the ways they absorb information, either in terms of being global or analytic processors, or impulsive versus reflective processors. While an *analytic processor* learns facts sequentially, with one fact following another, a *global processor* requires a big picture first and real-life application. Some, says Boyle, are combinations of the two. And, he adds, an *impulsive processor* is likely to shout out an answer before others get a chance, while a *reflective processor* needs time to think about their answer before providing one. These learning styles and preferences need, therefore, to be considered when designing and implementing any learning program and accompanying tools and methods.

The learning strategies, styles, and preferences outlined above were all taken into consideration and found to correspond with various aspects of complexity science, as suggested below.

COMPLEXITY SCIENCE

In the context of dominant schools of thought in the complexity science domain, on the one hand, Stacey (2003a, 2003b) and Griffin (2002) approach complexity science critically, and with a keen interest in the implications it brings to bear on humans, their interactions, and what emerges from them through self-organization. On the other hand, Weick's (2001) perspective is more solutions-oriented, and his interest in complexity is one that encourages flexible thinking by management in the face of impending disaster. Olson and Eoyang (2001) propose an interesting combination of the two. Their work, as with that of others (Eoyang & Berkas, 1999; Harkema, 2003; Axelrod & Cohen, 1999; Fuller & Moran, 2001; Fleming & Sorenson, 2001; Dooley, 1996; Morel & Ramanujam, 1999), is based on the direct application of complexity science-based thinking to the organizational domain—specifically, in terms of complex adaptive systems (CAS). All three views can be seen to be enhanced if put in the context of Kolb's learning cycle and related to a person's ongoing experience within the context of the organization.

The theory of complex adaptive systems (CAS) originated in the natural sciences and articulates how interacting agents in systems adapt and co-evolve over time, and who, through their interactions, produce novel and emergent order (see Figure 17.3) in creative and spontaneous ways. Latterly, academics and practitioners in the domain of organizational science have applied principles of complexity science to the way both organizations and the people in them interact and operate (Beinhocker, 1998, 2001; Horgan, 1995; Pascale, 2001; Plexus, 1998; Santosus, 1998). In this way, implications for organizational strategy, for example, correlate closely with what Mintzberg, Ahlstrand, and Lampel (1998) refer to as the "learning school," where strategy formation is acknowledged to take place as an emergent process, and the "cultural school," where strategy formation is seen as a collec-

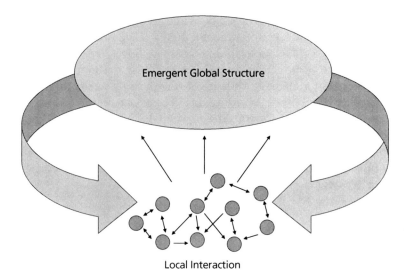

Figure 17.3

tive process. This coheres tangibly with Pedler et al.'s (1991) definition of the learning company, outlined above, and therefore suggests the potential involvement of anyone and everyone involved in the process of conducting and interacting with business.

CAS is presently the most commonly accepted view of complexity science, pervading the literature and practice, and is most likely the understanding Weick (2001)—mentioned above—has rested his theorizing upon. According to Olson and Eoyang (2001), a complex adaptive system (CAS) behaves or evolves according to three key principles:

1. Order is emergent as opposed to hierarchical
2. The system's history is irreversible
3. The system's future is often unpredictable.

The agents within the complex adaptive system are thought to behave according to simple rules in their local, and random, interactions with one another, and power is decentralized (Johnson, 2001). In line with this, Stacey describes complex adaptive systems in the following way: "A complex adaptive system consists of a large number of agents, each of which behaves according to some set of rules. These rules require the agents to adjust their behavior to that of other agents. In other words, agents interact with, and adapt to, each other" (2003a, p. 237).

In the context of learning about complexity science in general and about the potential of decentralization as a key lesson from the metaphor of the complex adaptive system in particular, Resnick (1998) advocated a mixture of observation, participation, construction, invention, and experimentation in order to develop strong intuitions and rich understanding, and he put this forward as a challenge for educators and educational developers. This resonates again with Kolb's learning cycle and also coheres with Easterby-Smith's (1990) suggestions for how to integrate employee learning based on reflections of experiences into organizational learning.

However, in addition to the view of complex adaptive systems, an alternative perspective is offered by Stacey (2001, 2003a) and Griffin (2002), who propose the theory of "complex responsive processes of relating" (CRPR) for understanding human relating. In CRPR, humans are understood to have both freedom of choice and the ability to view organizations "as if" they act as an entity in their own right, whilst not actually being an entity at all. This view follows that of Mead (1934), who worked with the idea that there is in reality no split between the individual and the social. In the context of this view, the observer experiences the dynamics of human interaction with the subject of his/her enquiry personally, as opposed to the complex adaptive system view which seems to position the observer outside the system being discussed (Stacey, 2003a; Griffin, 2002). Stacey develops his argument in favor of using complexity science principles as analogies that resonate strongly with human experience and—similarly to Kolb, Easterby-Smith, and Resnick—stresses the importance of acknowledging in this context the importance of feelings, the importance of reflection-in-action, and the importance of abstract thinking (Stacey, 2001). In tandem with this is the possibility to explore how specific complexity science ideas could be used as analogies in order to make sense of complex responsive processes of relating. Therefore, it is the personal resonance with complexity science that individuals encounter that becomes important, and, increasingly so it seems, in the business world. Lewin (1999) validates this thought:

> In our conversations with business people we saw that there was powerful resonance between their thinking about their organizations and what is known about the world of biology. This interest in applying a complexity perspective to business organizations is growing....After all, most of us work in organizations of one sort or another, and so the world of business represents the most immediate experience of complex systems on a day-to-day basis. (Lewin, 1999, p. xi)

The change management area has been one such field of application and therefore an opportunity to use narrative as a facilitative learning tool to bridge the reflection and performance (Ramsey, 2005). Smith (1999, 2003) and Smith and Saint-Onge (1996) have argued that unfreezing management mindsets, or not allowing them to set, was critical to the acceptance of new ideas in a change management process in one organization. They did this by changing individual learning through the re-structuring of roles and grounding them in principles fundamental to complexity science (e.g., autonomy). They report placing great emphasis on action learning and communities of practice as a way to generate space for dynamic knowledge conversion and emerging relationships. As such, complexity science principles inspired their implemented approach. The authors noted, however, that in spite of limited "management take-up" of "complexity and chaos," "management mindset" remained an inhibitor to the take-off regarded necessary to allow such principles to have any great and long-lasting impact. Dominant management mindsets, suggested the authors, stood in the way of potential implicit or explicit impacts on the exploration and/or adoption of these ideas. The dominant mindset preventing this was described as a "mechanistic" one. To combat this mechanistic mindset, arguing in favor of "aggressive organizational redesign, based on the emergent principles of chaos and complexity, with due regard for people-factors," Smith (2003, p. 322) recommended that the rules of organizational structure, tools and processes be re-designed to enable a radical change in the way people in organizations think and behave, the way they interact, and the environment in which they interact, therefore increasing the potential for new contexts and patterns to emerge. In doing so, however, Smith advocated a strategy whereby mention of complexity science and its principles should be avoided, and instead merely used by those whose task it is to re-design the organization in order to foster a climate where the principles of complexity science could flourish.

This chapter acknowledges a different view, though, and advocates instead that through an "awareness creation phase" grounded transparently in complexity science principles, managers and other organizational employees can be quickly and effectively introduced to complexity science and undergo a substantial move in mindset through the use of tools and methods based on Kolb's learning cycle and the other authors already mentioned. This then lays the foundation to allow individuals to learn interdependently (Stacey, 2003a) about the meaning of complexity science principles in their own organizational contexts, and goes a long way towards creating the kind of environment Smith talks about, but without the probably large incumbent expense.

THE COMPLEXITY STARTER KIT

The awareness creation phase developed was supported by a module called the "Complexity Starter Kit" (Webb, Wohlfart, Wunram, & Ziv, 2004). This included:

- A visually high-impacting six-day calendar—one day per principle
- A half-day workshop—with a game based on the metaphor of the complex adaptive system where agents follow simple rules (instructions in this case) and are also acting according to their own free will
- A follow-up web-based tool to further develop understanding, and to provide a link to the next phase and module of the process.

The purpose of this first module is threefold:

1. To introduce the terminology of six complexity principles
2. To create an experience around them to facilitate personal understanding in a group situation and from which to relate the principles to working life
3. To enable group sensemaking and knowledge development to continue after the workshop by means of interactive discussion over time with other colleagues.

The Starter Kit Calendar

The importance of time in reference to understanding human action in a theoretical way is emphasized by Stacey's theory of complex responsive processes of relating (2001, 2003a). The use of a temporal metaphor to indicate the relevance of the past, present, and future to the here and now, in reference to patterns of human action and conversation arising out of human interaction, was fundamental to the development of certain aspects of the Complexity Starter Kit. The idea of using a six-day calendar (see Figure 17.4) with accompanying water-cooler posters rested on this theoretical position, with the accompanying assumption that participants in this awareness creation phase would begin to make sense of the six complexity principles by themselves, and with other work colleagues, in terms of their own frame of reference before they got to the next stage of the Starter Kit, the Exercise Class and Game.

The visually high-impacting nature of the materials used on the calendar and posters presented in Figure 17.4 added an extra dimension of stimulation for potential participants. As was noted recently by McKenzie and James (2004), the value of the aesthetics of learning in the context of complexity should not be underestimated. This was also appreciated by participants in the implementation of these calendars and posters. Participants receive the calendar and water cooler posters seven days before the Exercise Class and Game, along with instructions to familiarize themselves with some "key complexity concepts." This provides opportunity for the experiential learn-

Figure 17.4

ing cycle to begin, starting with reflection and abstract conceptualization, in addition to a narrative building exercise encouraged through personal reflection and interaction with others. In terms of learning preferences and styles adhered to, this part of the Complexity Starter Kit is deployed so as to make use of visual text and verbal kinesthetic learning styles, in addition to leveraging the visual picture style. Regarding sociological learning preferences, this part of the Complexity Starter Kit caters to those preferring to learn alone, those preferring to learn alone and then interacting with others after having had time to think things through, and those who learn in pairs or small groups. The tool is not authority-oriented, however; it particularly avoids this because of the aspect of decentralization fundamental to the nature of complex adaptive system theory. This part of the Starter Kit is good for analytic processors who can learn the new vocabulary sequentially, as well as global processors, who are given an introduction to the "bigger picture," which is then followed by real-life application in the second part of the kit. This first part of the kit gives the reflective processor time to think about the new words before the next stage of the endeavor.

On the seventh day after receiving the calendar and posters, participants engage in the Exercise Class and Game, a half-day workshop.

The Starter Kit Exercise Class and Experience Game

This workshop is an exercise and experience by name and nature. It begins with the Experience Game, the design of which was based firmly on the metaphor of the complex adaptive system. A facilitator, as an objective observer, tells the group (from 4 to a maximum of 25 people) that they will receive a card with 4 instructions on it and that they must carry out all their instructions written on the card. Most of the cards have different and conflicting instructions, but all cards have one instruction that is the same: 'Free choice: do something that does not negate your prior instructions'. This mirrors the application of the spatial metaphor provided by the theory of complex adaptive systems to humans, i.e., the idea that system agents interact while following simple rules and out of this system-wide adaptation occurs—like ants and bees, but with the addition of free-will. The big difference here of course is that the instructions—or simple rules—are provided for those taking part in the game, whereas in real life the 'rules' are not predetermined in this way. Therefore the game is understood to mirror the idea of the complex adaptive system, and not replicate it.

As one complexity science expert said in a validation workshop session, the potential of this game to 'unhook' participants from their normal way of perceiving things is great (Webb, et al., 2004). While playing the game participants both encounter obstacles and reach compromise in attempting to carry out their instructions. After this event the group is facilitated through a sensemaking session based on the six principles:

1. Self-organization and emergence;
2. The edge of chaos;
3. Diversity;
4. History and time;
5. Unpredictability, and;
6. Pattern recognition.

All of which can be used very well to describe examples of human interaction in the experience just encountered. This conversation is easily transformed into one where the participants can use the principles to talk about their own experiences of working in their respective organizations. Full details and facilitator instructions can be found in the project book (Webb, et al., 2004).This second part of the kit builds in the extra dimensions of Kolb's learning cycle and leverages the action and experimentation which took place in the game through a facilitation of discussion, reflection and necessary abstraction and conceptualization based on their experience. This discussion is used as a basis to move to reflecting on organizational experiences and making sense of them by means of the complexity science principles. This part of the kit caters to learning styles and preferences relating to kinesthetic, tactile, verbal kinesthetic and visual picture strengths; sociological elements of preference relating to group or team work; and, psychological elements of preference corresponding with a combination of reflective and impulsive processors.

After taking part in this workshop, participants are introduced to the web-based Follow-Up Pop-Up, the third part of the Complexity Starter Kit—each stage of the Complexity Starter Kit is represented visually in Figure 17.5. To ensure continuity, the same graphics are used here as in the Starter Kit Calendar, but at this stage the six principles are expanded upon in terms of anecdotal content and explanation. In addition, thought-provoking questions are left as rhetorical prompts, or to provide the basis of online group dialogue in order to further develop knowledge on and around the six principles. The time-based interdependent learning concept was deployed here as well, the idea being in this case that participants continue to learn by taking time out over the week following the workshop to take part in subjective sensemaking in conversation with others in their work place. This third part of the kit continues to repeat iterations of Kolb's learning cycle and enables further experimentation, reflection and abstract conceptualization to take place. This part of the kit caters more for those with learning styles and preferences relating to visual text strengths, and

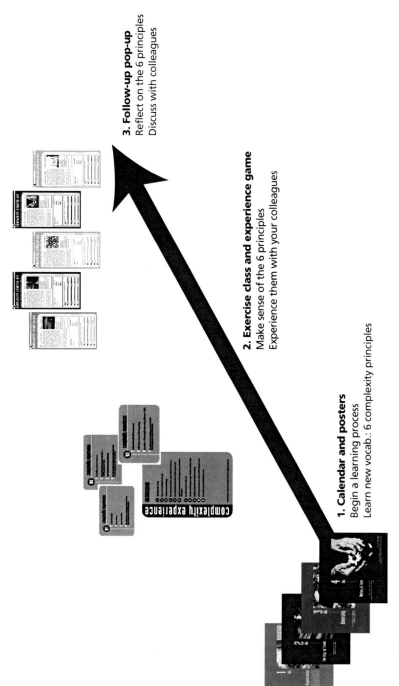

3. Follow-up pop-up
Reflect on the 6 principles
Discuss with colleagues

2. Exercise class and experience game
Make sense of the 6 principles
Experience them with your colleagues

1. Calendar and posters
Begin a learning process
Learn new vocab.: 6 complexity principles

complexity experience

Figure 17.5

a type of verbal kinesthetic facilitated by online discussion. The reflective processing encouraged also of course makes use of strengths relating to visual picture learning styles.

This chapter has focused on the Complexity Starter Kit as a means to transparently ground interventions in complexity science principles and thereby communicate them in a more easy-to-understand and user-friendly way. The Starter Kit also potentially provides the opportunity to integrate learning about and by means of complexity science principles into any pre-existing innovation strategy or organizational learning program, while considering the learning styles and preferences of the individuals taking part.

REFERENCES

Argyris, C. & Schön, D. A. (1978). *Organizational learning: A theory in action perspective.* London: Addison-Wesley.

Axelrod, R. & Cohen, M. D. (1999). *Harnessing complexity: Organizational implications of a scientific frontier.* New York: Simon & Schuster.

Beinhocker, E. D. (1998). Strategy at the edge of chaos. *McKinsey Quarterly, 1,* 109–118.

Beinhocker, E. D. (2001). Robust adaptive strategies. In B. A. Turner (Ed.), *Strategic thinking for the next economy* (pp. 131–153).San Francisco: Jossey–Bass.

Boyle, R. A. (2005). Applying learning-styles theory in the workplace: How to maximize learning-styles strengths to improve work performance in law practice. *Saint Johns Law Review, 79*(1), 97–126.

Dooley, K. (1996). A nominal definition of complex adaptive systems. *The Chaos Network, 8*(1), 2–3.

Dvir, R., Lettice F., & Thomond, P. (2004). *Are you ready to disrupt it? An illustrated guide to disruptive innovation.* Israel: Innovation Ecology.

Easterby-Smith, M. (1990). Creating a learning organization. *Personnel Review, 19*(5), 24–28.

Eoyang, G. H. & Berkas, T. H. (1999). Evaluating performance in a complex, adaptive system (CAS). In M. R. Lissack & H. P. Gunz (Eds.), *Managing complexity in organizations: A view in many directions.* London: Quorum.

Fleming, L. & Sorenson, O. (2001). Technology as a complex adaptive system: Evidence from patent data. *Research Policy, 30*(7), 1019–1039.

Fonseca, J. (2002). *Complexity and innovations in organizations.* London: Routledge, Taylor & Francis.

Fuller, T. & Moran, P. (2001). Small enterprises as complex adaptive systems: A methodological question? *Entrepreneurship and Regional Development, 13*(1), 47–63.

Garratt, R. (1987). *The learning organization: And the need for directors who think.* Aldershot, UK: Gower Publishing Company.

Garvin, M. R. & Ramsier, R. D. (2003). Experiential learning at the university level: A US case study. *Education and Training, 45*(5), 280–285.

Griffin, D. (2002). *The emergence of leadership: Linking self-organization and ethics.* London: Routledge, Taylor & Francis.

Harkema, S. (2003). A complex adaptive perspective on learning within innovation projects. *The Learning Organization, 10*(6), 340–346.

Horgan, J. (1995, June). From complexity to perplexity. *Scientific American,* June: 74–79.

Johnson, S. (2001). *Emergence: The connected lives of ants, brains, cities and software.* London: Penguin.

Kolb, D. A. (1973). *On management and the learning process.* Sloan School Working Paper 652–73, Cambridge, MA: Massachusetts Institute of Technology.

Kolb, D. A. (1979). *Organizational psychology* (3rd ed.). Englewood Cliffs, NJ: Prentice-Hall.

Kolb, D. A. (1984). *Experiential learning.* Englewood Cliffs, NJ: Prentice Hall.

Kolb, D. A. & Fry, R. (1975). Towards an applied theory of experiential learning. In C. L. Cooper (Ed.), *Theories of group processes* (pp. 33–58). Chichester, UK: John Wiley & Sons.

Lewin, R. (1999). *Complexity: Life at the edge of chaos.* Chicago: University of Chicago Press.

McKenzie, C. & James, K. (2004). Aesthetics as an aid to understanding complex systems and decision judgements in operating complex systems. *Emergence: Complexity & Organization, 6*(1-2), 32–39.

Mead, G. H. (1934). *Mind, self and society.* Chicago: Chicago University Press.

Mintzberg, H., Ahlstrand, B., & Lampel, J. (1998). *Strategy safari: The complete guide through the wilds of strategic management.* London: Prentice Hall.

Moore, G. A. (1995). *Inside the tornado: Marketing strategies from Silicon Valley's cutting edge.* New York: HarperCollins.

Morel, B. & Ramanujam, R. (1999). Through the looking glass of complexity: The dynamics of organizations as adaptive and evolving systems. *Organization Science, 10*(3), 278–293.

Olson, E. E. & Eoyang, G. H. (2001). Facilitating *organization change: Lessons from complexity science.* San Francisco, CA: Jossey-Bass.

Pascale, R. T. (2001). Surfing the edge of chaos. In M. Cusumano & C. Markides (Eds.), *Strategic thinking for the next economy* (pp. 105–129). San Francisco: Jossey-Bass.

Paul, P. & Mukhopadhyay, K. (2004). Experiential learning in international business education. *Journal of Teaching in International Business, 16*(2), 7–26.

Pedler, M., Burgoyne, J. G. & Boydell, T. (1991). *The learning company.* Columbus, OH: McGraw-Hill.

Plexus (1998). Edgeware, http://www.plexusinstitute.com/edgeware/archive/think/.

Ramsey, C. (2005). Narrative: From learning in reflection to learning in performance. *Management Learning, 36*(2), 219–236.

Resnick, M. (1998). *Turtles, termites, and traffic jams: Explorations in massively parallel microworlds* (4th ed.). Cambridge, MA: MIT Press.

Revans, R. W. (1982). "The enterprise as a learning system," in R. W. Revans (ed.), *The origins and growth of action learning,* Malabar, FL: Krieger Pub. Co., ISBN 9144990715.

Rose-Anderssen, C., Allen, P. M. Tsinopoulos, C. & McCarthy, I. (2005). Innovation in manufacturing as an evolutionary complex system. *Technovation, 25*(10), 1093–1105.

Rothwell, R. (1994). Industrial innovation: Success, strategy, trends. In M. Dodgson & R. Rothwell (Eds.), *The handbook of industrial innovation* (pp. 33–53). Northampton, MA: Edward Elgar Publishing.

Santosus, M. (1998, April 15). Simple, yet complex. *CIO Enterprise Magazine*, 63–67.

Senge, P. (1990). *The fifth discipline.* New York: Currency Doubleday.

Smith, P. A. C. (1999). The learning organization ten years on: A case study. *The Learning Organization, 6*(5), 217–224.

Smith, P. A. C. (2003). Implications of complexity and chaos theories for organizations that learn: Guest editorial. *The Learning Organization, 10*(6), 321–324.

Smith, P. A. C. & Saint-Onge, H. (1996). The evolutionary organization: Avoiding a Titanic fate. *The Learning Organization, 3*(4), 4–21.

Stacey, R. D. (2000). The emergence of knowledge in organizations. *Emergence, 2*(4), 23–39.

Stacey, R. D. (2001). *Complex responsive processes in organizations: Learning and knowledge creation.* London: Routledge.

Stacey, R. D. (2003a). *Complexity and group processes: A radically social understanding of individuals.* New York: Brunner-Routledge.

Stacey, R. D. (2003b). *Strategic management and organizational dynamics.* Harlow, UK: Pearson Education.

Stacey, R. D., Griffin, D., & Shaw, P. (2000). *Complexity and management: Fad or radical challenge to systems thinking?* London: Routledge.

Tushman, M. L. & Anderson, P. (1986). Technological discontinuities and organizational environments. *Administrative Science Quarterly, 31*, 439-465.

Van Reekum, G. (2005). Experiential learning in organizations: Applications of the Tavistock group relations approach. *Organizational and Social Dynamics, 5*(1), 147–152.

Webb, C., Wohlfart, L., Wunram, M., & Ziv, A. (Eds.) (2004). *The secrets of the six principles: A guide to robust development of organizations.* Israel: Innovation Ecology.

Weick, K. E. (2001). *Managing the unexpected: Assuring high performance in an age of complexity.* San Francisco: Jossey-Bass.

ACKNOWLEDGEMENTS

Acknowledgements of assistance go to the European Commission and the consortium of partners on the RODEO Project (www.e-rodeo.org). This paper was originally presented at the Complexity, Science and Society Conference, 11th–14th September 2005, Centre for Complexity Research, University of Liverpool, UK.

ABOUT THE CONTRIBUTORS

Peter M. Allen is head of the Complex Systems Research Centre, School of Management, Cranfield University. He worked for 20 years with the Nobel Laureate, Ilya Prigogine, in Brussels. For almost 30 years he has been working on the mathematical modeling of change and innovation in social, economic, financial and ecological systems, and the development of integrated systems models linking the physical, ecological, and socio-economic aspects of complex systems as a basis for improved decision support systems.

Ann C. Baker is an Associate Professor in the School of Public Policy at George Mason University. She has been teaching in the Masters in Organization Development and Knowledge Management since 1996 and teaches in the four other Masters degree programs and the PhD program in the School of Public Policy (SPP). She serves as an external consultant to a variety of organizations and has experience as an internal consultant as well. Dr. Baker's research interests include organizational change, knowledge creation, complexity theory as it relates to organizational dynamics, conflict and change, group dynamics, cross cultural dialogue, and virtual conversations. She is the author of numerous publications related to her research interests including her new book, *Catalytic Conversations: Organizational Communication and Innovation,* which is forthcoming in fall 2009. Her previous book, *Conversational Learning: An Experiential Approach to Knowledge Creation,* was published in 2002. In May 2006, Dr. Baker received the Don Lavoie Teaching Award from the SPP and in 2008 was a Finalist for the Teaching Excellence Award at George Mason University. Prior to joining GMU, Dr. Baker was a Kellogg Fellow, having received a three-year Leader-

Complexity and Knowledge Management, pages 335–343
Copyright © 2010 by Information Age Publishing
335

ship Development fellowship from the W.K. Kellogg Foundation for International Leaders of the Future. Before she moved to the Washington, DC area, she was the Director of the Charleston Higher Education Consortium (consortium of six universities) and the Director of Special Projects for the President of the Medical University of South Carolina.

Ken Baskin is an ISCE Fellow who is exploring the integration of recent work in complexity thinking, storytelling, anthropology and neurobiology in the study of "storied space." Among other activities in this area, he has worked with David Boje to co-edit a special issue of *Emergence: Coherence & Organization* on complexity and storytelling, and co-hosted a workshop on the topic, from which a collection of essays is forthcoming. Baskin's publications include his book, *Corporate DNA: Learning from Life* (1998) and articles in journals including *Chinese Management Studies* and *Social Evolution and History.*

Michael Beyerlein is Department Head and Professor for Organizational Leadership & Supervision at Purdue University. Formerly, he was Director of the Center for Collaborative Organizations and Professor of Industrial/Organizational (I/O) Psychology at the University of North Texas (UNT). His research interests include all aspects of work teams, organizational design and change, creativity/innovation, knowledge management and the learning organization, and science education. He has been a member of the editorial boards for *TEAM Magazine, Team Performance Management Journal*, and *Quality Management Journal* and senior editor of the Elsevier annual series *Advances in Interdisciplinary Studies of Work Teams* and the Jossey-Bass/Pfeiffer *Collaborative Work Systems* series. He has authored or edited 20 books, including *The handbook for high performance virtual teams: A toolkit for collaborating across boundaries* (in press), *Guiding the journey to collaborative work systems: A Strategic Design workbook* (2004), and *Collaborative capital* (2005).

Thierry Boudés is an associate professor of strategy and project management at ESCP Europe, a European business school with campuses in Paris, London, Berlin, Madrid, and Torino. He has been visiting scholar in 2002 at the University of Texas at Austin (McCombs School of Business) and visiting professor at HEC Montréal in 2007–2008. His research is concentrated on the narrative processes in organizations, and the narrative dimensions of strategy and project management. Managers are not only counting, they are recounting!

Larry Browning (PhD, Ohio State) is a professor of organizational communication in the Department of Communication Studies, College of Communication, University of Texas at Austin and professor at Bodø Graduate School of Business, Norway. His research areas include the role of structures in organizations as evidenced by lists and stories, information-communication technology and narratives, cooperation and competition in organizations, and grounded theory as a research strategy. In addition to over 50 articles and book chapters, he, along with his co-author, Judy Shetler, wrote: *Sematech: Saving the U.S. Semiconductor Industry.* College Station, TX: Texas A & M University Press (2000). Larry's most recent book, along with his co-authors, is: Browning, L. D., Sætre, A. S., Stephens, K., and Sørnes, J. O., *Information and communication technologies in action: Linking theory and narratives of practice,* New York: Routledge, (2008).

Cathal M. Brugha is an Associate Professor in the School of Business and Director of the UCD Centre for Business Analytics, University College Dublin, Belfield, Dublin, Ireland. Originally a mathematician, he did his PhD in combinatorial optimization and was previously General Editor of *International Transactions in Operational Research,* the official journal of the International Federation of Operational Research Societies. He is President of the Management Science Society of Ireland and a Fellow of the Marketing Institute of Ireland. His main theoretical research is in Nomology, the study of the decision processes of the mind, the structures or "covering laws" that frame people's thinking and provide commonalities between different fields and cultures. He is currently completing a book *Understanding Methodologies and Systems in Management* (Springer). Out of this work he has developed two multi-criteria research procedures, which he uses for his empirical research. Direct-Interactive Structured-Criteria (DISC) is used to facilitate choice and the Priority Pointing Procedure (PPP) is used for strategy. Website at http://mis.ucd.ie/Members/cbrugha.

Dermot Casey is a PhD student in the School of Business University College Dublin (UCD), Belfield, Dublin, Ireland, where he is also an adjunct lecturer in Management Information Systems. He works full time as a project manager and consultant in the private sector. With a B.Sc. in Computer Science and an MBA, both from UCD, he has spent the past 12 years working in systems development and project management. He is a member of the IEEE, the ACM and the AIS. His research is focused on the challenges of problem framing and understanding in systems development adopting ideas from Cognitive Science, Nomology and Complex Systems. His research interests include how sense and perception guide how we understand, decide, and act; and how our underlying cognitive commonalities can be used to improve understanding in complex situations at both organizational and societal level.

Foo Check-Teck is an award-winning researcher and scholar. He is founding Editor of *Chinese Management Studies* and sits on the Editorial Advisory Board of several international journals including *Management Decision.* He is qualified as English Barrister as well as called to the Singapore Bar as

Advocate and Solicitor. His first work on complexity science is published in recent special issue of *Emergence: Complexity & Organization*.

Mark Lemon is a social scientist with the Institute of Energy and Sustainable Development at De Montfort University. His research is focused on the complexity of the human–technical interface as it affects the built environment and the use of natural resources. Within this broad area he has a particular interest in the characteristics of integrative research and the development of trans-disciplinary skills and has published and supervised extensively in this area. Dr. Lemon has undertaken and managed cross-disciplinary qualitative research and consultancy on a range of environmental projects for European and UK research agencies and commercial organizations.

Fiona Lettice is a senior lecturer within the Norwich Business School at the University of East Anglia in the UK. The main focus of her research and teaching is in new product development and innovation management. She has received funding from the European Commission and the Engineering and Physical Science Research Council (EPSRC) for her research in discontinuous innovation, knowledge management and innovation, complexity science, and innovation in regional clusters. Prior to her academic career, Fiona worked in industry as a Project Manager within Centrica's Business Development directorate, and for a small consultancy company, where she worked predominantly with BMW/Rover Group in design and engineering projects. In her work with multi-disciplinary teams, Fiona uses graphic facilitation as a way to encourage dialogue and communication between different disciplines and organizations.

Yue Lin works as a consultant for Personnel Decisions International in Shanghai China. His undergraduate work was done in China. Then he worked in a human factors lab for three years. He completed his masters in I/O psychology at the UNT in 2005. The thesis was presented at the annual Society SIOP conference in 2006. He completed his doctorate in I/O Psychology at UNT in 2007. His dissertation entitled "Cultural implications of self–other agreement in multisource feedback: Comparing samples from U.S., China, and globally dispersed teams" will be presented at the SIOP conference in 2009. He published one book chapter in 2006 with Michael Beyerlein, "Communities of practice: A critical perspective on collaboration."

Alice MacGillivray, PhD, is proprietor of a consulting company where her work focuses on the generation and sharing of knowledge as elements of organizational development and change. Alice supported and directed the design and development of knowledge management graduate programs at Royal Roads University from 2001–2006, where she is now an associate faculty member. Previously, she worked in the fields of organizational development, ecology and sustainability in the public sector. Her research interests include distributed leadership, complexity, boundaries and learning. Alice has presented papers at several conferences including the McMaster World Congress on Intellectual Capital, the Canadian Association of Law Librarians, the Association for the Advancement of Computing in Education E-Learn Conference, the GeoTec Global Conference in Vancouver and the International Society for the Systems Sciences in Brisbane. For more information, see www.4KM.net.

Madeleine Mcbrearty PhD (candidate) is a faculty member in the Department of Applied Human Sciences at Concordia University in Montréal, Québec, Canada where she teaches principles of interpersonal communication and wellness. Madeleine also teaches in the Personal and Professional Coach Certificate program offered by the Centre for Human Relations and Community Studies at Concordia. She is an organizational change agent and executive coach who prefers to work with people in community and not-for-profit organizations. Her research and practice are focused on understanding how individuals change their behavior patterns. Madeleine's passion is to walk alongside those who want to achieve their personal life vision.

Stanislava Mildeova is currently an Associate Professor in the Department of Systems Analysis, the part of the Faculty of Informatics and Statistics at the University of Economics in Prague. She gained PhD in Planning and Management and Associate Professor degree in Informatics. Stanislava is a guarantor of specialization for "Orientation in the Information Society" and a guarantor of seven university courses. Her major professional interest is systems science, particularly System Dynamics, Decision Support Systems, informatics, and models supporting the sustainable development. Recently she has been for more than a decade a manager of a regular conference, "System Approaches," and the editor of the conference proceedings. She was responsible for the solution of a module for a PHARE project, and a research project for the Czech Science Foundation. She is a member of the Czech Society for the Systems Integration, the System Dynamics Society (and International System Dynamics Conference reviewer), and she is a member of the editorial board of the Journal on Efficiency and Responsibility in Education and Science.

Susan Burgess Miller is Founder and Principal of Complex Culture Change Consulting, LLC in Palmdale, CA. Retired from the National Aeronautics and Space Administration in 2006, she was most recently the Director, Academic Investments at NASA Dryden Flight Research Center, Edwards, CA. There she was responsible for all academic and education programs, K–20, and development of the Aerospace Education Research and Operations (AERO) Institute. The AERO Institute is a revolutionary, new business model to produce the next generation aerospace technical workforce within the aerospace community. Federal, state, and local governments; industry; and academia partner to ensure that research, educational, and operations programs enable and maintain a viable aerospace workforce for the 21st Century. Earlier in her career she worked at three NASA field Centers and at NASA HQ in a variety of management positions spanning personnel, facilities, and workforce strategies. She also was the Deputy Director, Personnel Services, Small Business Administration and the Agency Personnel Director, National Oceanic and Atmospheric Administration. During a 2-year sabbatical, she served at the County Administrator for King George County, Virginia with overall responsibility for all county services including public utilities and functions. Dr. Miller is a graduate of the College of William and Mary (BA) and George Washington University (MS and EdD). Her areas of research interest and publication include organizational culture, complexity science and high reliability organizations.

Rosemary C. Reilly, PhD, CCFE, is an associate professor in the Department of Applied Human Sciences at Concordia University in Montreal, Quebec, Canada and a faculty member in the Human Systems Intervention program. Her research areas of interest include learning communities and thought communities as complex systems; social creativity and shared expertise; organizational learning and change processes; community resilience as complex adaptation following a trauma; and collaborative processes in qualitative research. Dr. Reilly is also a member of the Centre for Human Relations and Community Studies, chairing the Centre's community collaborative research initiative.

Kurt A. Richardson is the Associate Director for the ISCE Group and is Director of ISCE Publishing, a publishing house that specializes in complexity-related publications. He has a BS (hons) in Physics (1992), MS in Astronautics and Space Engineering (1993) and a PhD in Applied Physics (1996). Kurt's current research interests include the philosophical implications of assuming that everything we observe is the result of complex underlying processes, the relationship between structure and function, analytical frameworks for intervention design, and robust methods of reducing complexity, which have resulted in the publication of over thirty journal papers and book chapters and ten books. He is the Managing/Production Editor for the international journal *Emergence: Complexity & Organization* and is on the review board for the journals *Systemic Practice and Action Research, Systems Research and Behavioral Science,* and *Tamara: Journal of Critical Postmodern Organization Science.* Kurt is the editor of the recently published *Managing Organizational Complexity: Philosophy, Theory, Practice* (Information Age Publishing, 2005) and is coeditor of the forthcoming book *Complexity and Knowledge Management: Understanding the Role of Knowledge in the Management of Social*

Networks (due August 2009). Kurt is also a qualified spacecraft systems engineer and has consulted for General Dynamics and NASA.

William H. Rodger, BA, MS, is an engineer by training and spent twenty-nine years in the telecommunications industry in the UK and North America, nineteen of them in R&D organizations. His diverse activities have included operations management, international strategic marketing, intergovernmental negotiations on non-tariff trade barriers, and international standards committees (ISO9000). In his management consulting role, he has worked for the UK, U.S., Canadian, and Japanese governments as well as a number of major corporations in the U.S., Canada, and Europe. Since 1989 he has been applying new software technology within a group process framework to enable clients to more effectively deal with complex, multi-stakeholder issues. Bill is Chairman of Complexity Solutions Limited.

Duska Rosenberg is Professor in Information and Communication Management and Director of the iCOM Research, a multi-disciplinary centre for research in information, computing and communication at Royal Holloway University of London. Her research interests include analysis and design of shared information environments, computer-mediated communication, and natural language interaction in media and virtual spaces, while her consulting activities focus on human communication, information sharing, and introducing intranets into geographically dispersed organizations. Professor Rosenberg is also a Senior Researcher at CSLI (Centre for the Study of Language and Information) Stanford University. Her recent research includes EU-funded projects with partners from construction and manufacturing industries, as well as technology-enhanced learning in higher education and life-long learning.

Jane Galloway Seiling has a degree in Business Administration, a master's in Organization Development and a PhD in social science with an emphasis in managerial psychology. Her interests in organization development, social constructionism, and consulting are based on working 20+ years inside organizations and her academic studies and explorations in the membership paradigm. She is an adjunct professor in the Department of Management at Lawrence Technological University, Southfield, Michigan, USA. She has written two books: *The Membership Organization* and a book on advocacy issues in the workplace (*The Meaning and Role of Organizational Advocacy*), and she was co-editor of *Appreciative Inquiry and Organizational Transformation* and (being written) *Leading Change and Capacity Building in Nonprofits*. She has published in *The Journal of Management and Organization, Journal of North American Society, The Journal for Quality and Participation, KTB Business Journal*, Singapore, *AI Practitioner, OD Journal*, and various trade journals. She is an associate of The Taos Institute, Cleveland, OH, and senior editor of Taos

Institute Publishing's Focus Book Series on social constructionism. Her current focus of interest is the ability of organizations to "combine capably" the information that is embedded in the minds and interests of the members, the movement of accountability inside the work of working, change and capacity building in nonprofits, and the elements of the "psychology of working" that make work meaningful to organizational members at all levels.

Judy C. Shetler, PhD is currently an alpaca rancher in the Colorado Rockies. She and her husband care for and breed a herd of 36 huacaya alpacas. The complex cultural and communication practices of highly intelligent social animals, as manifested in their group dynamics, are her current field of observation. Shetler's academic interests include self-organization and the complexity of organizational change. Her previously published or presented work includes studies of cooperation, roles of culture and discourse in negotiated order between groups, and the relationship between leadership and self-organized emergence of terroristic behavior.

Ralph Stacey is Professor of Management and Director of an innovative Master and Doctoral program in complexity, leadership and organizational change at the Business School of the University of Hertfordshire in the UK. He is a Member of the Institute of Group Analysis. He has devoted many years to addressing the theoretical foundations of how the complexity sciences are used to understand sources of stability and change in organizations. His work on complex responsive processes elucidates a view that shifts our understanding of complexity from adaptive systems to responsive processes of relating. He is the author of a number of books and articles which include *Complexity And Organizational Reality: The Need to Rethink Management After the Collapse of Investment Capitalism* (to be published by Routledge in December 2009), *Strategic Management and Organizational Dynamics* (5th edition published by Pitman in 2007), *Complexity and Group Processes: A Radically Social Understanding of the Individual* (published by Brunner-Routledge 2003), *Complex Responsive Processes in Organizations* (published by Routledge 2001), *Complexity And Management: Fad or Radical Challenge to Systems Thinking* (with Griffin & Shaw, published by Routledge in 2000), *Complexity and Creativity in Organizations* (published by Berrett-Koehler in 1996), *Managing the Unknowable* (published by Jossey-Bass in 1992), *Chaos Frontier* (published by Butterworth-Heinemann in 1991).He is a co-editor of the book series *Complexity and Emergence in Organizations* as well as the series *Complexity as the Experience of Organizing*, which includes *Experiencing Emergence in Organizations: Local Interaction and the Emergence of Global Pattern*, and *Complexity and the Experience of Managing in Public Sector Organizations* co-edited with Douglas Griffin.

Andrew Tait is currently cofounder and Chief Technology Officer of Idea Sciences, a Virginia-based software and consulting firm specializing in the creative use of technology to improve organizational decision-making. During his career he has designed commercial, off-the-shelf solutions for strategic planning, performance improvement, and conflict management. This has led to numerous consulting and training relationships with major commercial and government organizations. Prior to forming Idea Sciences, Andrew held various commercial (technology consulting), government (defense) and academic (business) positions. Andrew's research interests include: decision-making, performance improvement, electronic voting, virtual communities, conflict management, visualization, and improving understanding of complex socio-technical systems.

Carol Webb was a Senior Lecturer within the Sheffield Business School at Sheffield Hallam University, UK, until the end of August 2009. She gained her first degree, BA Ancient History & Social Anthropology, at University College London (UCL) in 2001, and then completed her doctoral thesis, entitled "An Exploration of Sense-Making & Learning with Complexity Science: A Diary-Based Study" at Cranfield University in 2005. While conducting her doctoral research Carol also worked on the EU co-sponsored RODEO project, where she took a pivotal role in the development of the RODEO Starter Kit Calendar and Experience Game, led the project evaluation and validation process, and from this jointly published "The Secrets of the Six Principles: A Guide to Robust Organizational Development." Carol also worked on a UK Engineering and Physical Science Research Council (EPSRC)-funded project to develop a complexity science taught course for research students.

Lightning Source UK Ltd.
Milton Keynes UK
UKOW030644050712

195522UK00002B/17/P